A Descriptive Catalogue of the Bension Collection of Sephardic Manuscripts and Texts

A Descriptive Catalogue of the Bension Collection of Sephardic Manuscripts and Texts

Saul I. Aranov

The University of Alberta Press

First published by
The University of Alberta Press
Edmonton, Alberta, Canada,
1979

Canadian Cataloguing in Publication Data
Bension, Ariel, 1881-1932, collector.
A descriptive catalogue of the Bension
collection of Sephardic manuscripts and texts

Includes index.
ISBN 0-88864-016-1

1. Sephardic—Manuscripts—Catalogs.
2. Manuscripts, Hebrew—Catalogs. 3. Bension,
Ariel, 1881-1932. I. Aranov, Saul I. II. University
of Alberta. Library. Special Collections Dept. III. Title.
Z6605.H4B45 016.909'04'924 C78-002013-8

Printed by Hignell Printing Ltd.,
Winnipeg, Manitoba, Canada.

The University of Alberta Press
acknowledges the interest and
support of Mr. Samuel Green and
Mr. Samuel Goldsmith of Edmonton,
without which this book would
not have been possible.

Contents

List of plates

Preface

People talk of the experience of travel as culturally enriching. Others do their travelling by reading a variety of books that transport them to the four corners of the earth and to the far reaches of outer space. When valuable books and manuscripts, heretofore unknown, begin to travel then history is made and the details of a previous age are discovered.

The acquisition of the Bension manuscripts and texts for the University of Alberta by the Harry R. Cohen Memorial Foundation was an even more exciting experience for a number of reasons. This was the first time that Hebrew manuscripts had ever been discovered in Canada. Secondly, there is a dearth of scholarly source material in the field of North African Sephardic studies to which a good portion of the collection pertains, and yet a growing number of universities in France, the United States, and Israel are establishing institutes which are specializing in the field of Sephardic studies. Thirdly, scholars in a variety of cognate fields of Jewish study will be able to draw upon the scholarly resources which are now housed in the Special Collections department of the Library of the University of Alberta. This collection will bring the University of Alberta into the orbit of select libraries and institutions of higher learning throughout the world which possess unique materials in the field of Jewish scholarship and which make these sources available for scholarly investigation. Fourthly, the collector, who was a scholar in his own right, has been rediscovered.

There is a social aspect to the significance of the Bension collection. Exhibitions of specimens in the collection have already been held in eastern and western Canada. At a recent exhibit which was held in Montreal, under the sponsorship of the Organisation Sepharade Francophone, several thousand Jews of Moroccan extraction were in attendance. The Jewish community of Morocco once numbered over a quarter-of-a-million people. The majority of these people presently make their domicile in Israel, but a sizeable number migrated to France since they are French-speaking, and it is estimated that about twenty thousand Moroccan Jews emigrated to Quebec. It is therefore quite proper that after Israel and France, Canada should possess and disseminate materials which will preserve the cultural continuity of North African Jewry for their descendants who have found refuge on Canadian shores. The acquisition and dissemination of material from the Bension collection by the University of Alberta is a major effort in this direction.

The element of uniqueness should not be sacrificed as people of diverse cultural backgrounds join together to achieve a united society. While there is a natural tendency for minorities to assimilate into the mainstream of society, sooner or later there arises a quest for one's identity which must be satisfied. An exposition of the valuable efforts that were made by outstanding Jewish scholars of the Maghreb, who have contributed to the dynamic development of communal organization in Morocco for hundreds of years, will serve as a source of pride to all who would inquire about their heritage.

A fascinating aspect of the collection is the story of how the Bension collection arrived at the Library of the University of Alberta. The collector, Ariel Bension, passed away suddenly in Paris at the age of fifty-two, in 1932. His collection came into the possession of his second wife, née Ida Siegler, who lived in Montreal where she had served as a Hebrew teacher prior to their marriage. Before Ida Bension passed away in 1952 she sold the collection to a book dealer. There is evidence that the collection contained more items than at present. Some of these works were probably sold by Ida Bension separately. At one time the collection was supposed to have contained thirty letters composed by the illustrious scientist Albert Einstein on the subject of Zionism. These were presumably sold at an earlier date. Since Ariel Bension was an important emissary for the World Zionist Organization, it is logical to deduce that he possessed correspondence of this nature.

A noted Montreal collector, Mr. Saul Muhlstock, who was an acquaintance of the late Ida Bension, subsequently acquired the collection from the book dealer to whom she sold it. In the spring of 1973, Mr. L.E.S. Gutteridge of the Library of the University of Alberta was contacted by a book dealer who was supposedly acting for Mr. Muhlstock. The latter was prepared to sell the collection to a Canadian institution of higher education. I was lecturing in the Department of Religious Studies at the University of Alberta when I was asked to assess the value of the Bension collection for scholarly research. I was surprised to find that, indeed, a treasure trove of manuscripts and texts were before me, especially since this was the first collection of Hebrew manuscripts ever to be discovered in Canada. The result of my findings are incorporated in part IV of this work.

A meeting was held in the Cameron Library Board Room, at the University of Alberta, on Monday, June 25, 1973. Among those in attendance were Messrs. Sam Goldsmith, Sam Greene and Tom Mayson, Q.C., representing the Harry R. Cohen Memorial Foundation; Messrs. L.E.S. Gutteridge and Bruce Peel, representing the Library of the University of Alberta; members of the University Committee on Scholarly Acquisitions and myself, Saul Aranov. At the conclusion of this meeting, the Harry R. Cohen Memorial Foundation of Edmonton, Alberta, had acquired the Ariel Bension Sephardic Manuscripts and Texts for the Library of the University of Alberta. This is the initial acquisition and showpiece of the Harry R. Cohen Memorial Collection at the University of Alberta.

I express my gratitude to the trustees of the Harry R. Cohen Memorial Foundation for their munificent benefaction and their interest in establishing a collection of Hebraica and Judaica at the Library of the University of Alberta. Their sponsorship will be instrumental in helping to establish Jewish scholarship in Canada on a more sound basis. Their effort is a genuine testament to the character of Harry R. Cohen, who was truly a high priest in the temple of philanthropy and culture in the general and Jewish communities of Edmonton, Alberta throughout his lifetime.

I am particularly indebted to Messrs. Sam Goldsmith and Sam Greene who have made the publication of this catalogue possible by their benevolence. I also express to them my everlasting gratitude for the many kindnesses that they showed me during the past years. I shall always cherish the support of this project by Dr. Henry Kreisel, who served as Vice-President (Academic) at the University of Alberta, at the time of purchase and who initially suggested that I should study the Bension collection.

Thanks are especially due to Mr. Bruce Peel, Librarian to the University of Alberta. His foresight in desiring to make the acquisition available for the Library at the University of Alberta will always be remembered in gratitude. I also wish to thank Mr. L.E.S. Gutteridge for his guidance in matters pertaining to the publishing of this work as well as for his efforts in making available to me works that were generally inaccessible. Mrs. Helen Cramer was devoted in her efforts to type the drafts for this volume and I appreciate her dedication.

In the course of the preparation of this catalogue my mother, Sarah M. Aranov, went to her eternal reward. It is in humility that I memorialize her for my physical being and for the sacrifices she endured while I pursued my studies. My maternal grandfather, Reverend Zisel Gedalia Goodkin, a lover of humanity, taught me to appreciate the contributions of the diverse cultures that make up the landscape of mankind. Any abilities that I possess I owe to his pedagogic powers while my imperfections are my own.

I am indebted many times over to my revered father-in-law, the scholarly Rabbi Shlomo Amor, of Tivon, Israel, for introducing me to Sephardic culture and for his many comments that went into the preparation of this volume; also for the gift of his daughter, Dina, that princess of patience, who endured until this work was brought to completion. Finally, I dedicate this volume to my children Noam, Shalhevet and Sarit Aviva and to all of their generation who are the products of Ashkenazi and Sephardi culture. Learn to cherish your origins and to fuse them into something beautiful for God and mankind.

I give thanks to the Almighty who helped me bring this work to completion.

Saul I. Aranov-Tov Elem
Edmonton, Alberta
April, 1976.

An appreciation of Ariel Bension

The collector was known as Dr. Ariel Bension. The name Ariel was derived from the original given name of the collector, Judah, and the family name Bension was derived by him from the second of the two given names of his father, R. Joshua Ṣion Halevi. The original name of the collector was Judah Levi.

Ariel Bension was born in Jerusalem in the year 1880. His father was the Rabbi and Mystic, Joshua Ṣion Halevi and his mother Mazal Toḅ, the daughter of R. Solomon Ezekiel Yahuda. R. Joshua Ṣion had migrated from Fez, Morocco to the Holy Land while he was yet a youngster. His ancestry dates back to the Ben Hasdai family that was known in Barcelona, Spain in the twelfth century. R. Joshua Sion was a devotee of the mystical group at Jerusalem known as the Holy Community of Beth-El. Ariel Bension informs us, on page 245 of his work *The Zohar in Moslem and Christian Spain*, that the Beth-El community was "founded by the descendants of some of the exiles from Spain; at first small but loosely held together, lacking cohesion and unity. As time went on, however, and under the guidance of devoted leaders, the group was transformed into a co-ordinated body possessing both authority and strength. Dominated by what may be called the categorical imperative of Ha-Ari's teachings, the prayers were made with Kavanoth-inner meditation . . . At first it had been the custom to carry meditation in a deep silence—the meditation on a single word, sometimes lasting for fifteen minutes. But with the introduction of the musical interludes the Kavanoth began to be performed during the intoning of a melody that was at the same time suggestive of the form which the meditation was to take. So true are these tunes in searching out and expressing the emotions of souls dwelling on the mystic meaning of the prayer, that even the listener, uninitiated though he may be, feels himself transported into the realms of thought, where dwell those who commune with the Infinite." This mystical communal atmosphere exerted a lasting influence on Bension throughout his life as is evident in his later literary activity.

The collector was educated by his father in the academy called "Qasad-El," which was established by his maternal grandfather. He was also educated at the institute called "Tifereth Jerusalem" and at "Beth-El," Bension acquired a wide knowledge of Talmud, Codes, and in mystical studies. At the age of fifteen he wrote a story entitled "Hanolad Be-Qedusha"—"He Who Was Born in Holiness," which was published in a series of five instalments in the publication known as *Ha-Yehudi*, in London.

Bension spent some time with his father's relatives in Algiers before he continued on his journey to western Europe, where he studied at universities in Germany and Switzerland. He pursued courses in history, philosophy, literature, and Asiatic philology. He was granted a doctoral degree in philosophy and semitic languages at the University of Berne and then he returned to the Holy Land. Subsequently he married Rachel, the daughter of Raḥamim Mizrahi. After his first wife's demise he married Ida Siegler of Montreal. It was due to this second marriage that the Canada connection was established so that the Bension manuscripts and texts eventually became the first collection of Hebrew manuscripts ever to be discovered in Canada. The young Ariel Bension was the first Sephardi of the Holy Land who is known to have pursued studies in the universities of western Europe. Bension served as Rabbi to the Jewish community of Betulia, Serbia for one year before the advent of the First World War. He worked in the service of the Zionist Organization from the beginning of the year 1920. Afterwards he served as an emissary for the Keren Ha-Yesod until the end of his life. He was especially active in this capacity in the Sephardic communities of Iraq, India, Indo-China, North Africa, Spain, Portugal, South America, and Egypt among other communities. He was successful in acquiring an ideological and financial commitment for the future building of the Land of Israel from the Jewish members of the aforementioned communities. Bension was also successful in gaining sympathy and esteem for the nationhood of Israel and for the Zionist cause from figures of prominence in the world political arena and from men of letters in many of the countries which he visited. The Indian poet Tagore was numbered among those sympathizers influenced by Bension.

Ariel Bension was also active on behalf of the Jewish Sephardic Organization in his travels throughout the diaspora. He co-ordinated the Sephardic organization's efforts together with those of other Jewish organizations that worked for the national aspirations of the Jewish people. Bension commenced these activities at the assembly of the Eleventh Zionist Congress which was held in Vienna. On that occasion he was chosen as the honorary secretary of the Executive that was given the task of assembling an international conference which would bring the Jewish nationalistic idea to reality. He participated in the Fifteenth Zionist Congress as a representative of the Jews of Argentina. Between his travels he engaged in communal activities in the Holy Land. Bension participated in the founding of the Rabbinic Academy "Maḥzikei Ha-Torah," in Jerusalem. Bension also was responsible for the redemption of land in Netanya, Israel. The Bension quarter of the town was named for him.

Ariel Bension published articles of a scholarly nature in publications such as *Haṣfirah*, *Ha-Or*, *Ha-Ḥerut*, and *Ha-Olam*, in his student days and thereafter, in Hebrew, German, and English. Special attention was paid to his article on the mysticism of Maeterlinck, in the publication *Ha-Olam*, in 1914. He also wrote on "The Sephardi Hassidism in the Land of Israel," "On the question of the Arabs and the Jews," which was written in English, "An Essay on Yemen," and "Echoes of the Inquisition" among other articles.

Bension's books include *Ḥatunat Ha-Mavet—Marriage with Death*, which appeared in Hebrew and German and served as an introduction to his work "Raphael," which remained unpublished. He also wrote the following books which were published, *Sar Shalom Sharabi*, in Hebrew and in English, and *The Zohar in Moslem and Christian Spain*, in English, a portion of which was produced in Hebrew, and for which the author was elected as a fellow of the "Real Academia de la Historia" of Madrid. This last work was originally published in London in 1932, and reprinted by the Sepher-Hermon Press Inc., New York in 1974. Ariel Bension is also mentioned in Gershom Scholem's *Major Trends in Jewish Mysticism*. The scholarly credentials of the collector of our manuscripts and texts, as well as his eclectic interests coupled with his extensive travel in behalf of Sephardic Jewry, are sufficient in themselves for us to acknowledge that this private collection is indeed an extraordinary find and that its Sephardic character is manifest. His Moroccan ancestry from his father's side of the family also supports the centrality of Moroccan material in the collection. It seems evident that we possess only a portion of this scholar's collection of manuscripts and texts. It is indeed a tragedy that he passed on, in Paris, on the ninth of November 1932, at the age of fifty-two. Had he been granted a longer life his literary productivity would have been even more prolific. Rabbi Dr. Ariel Bension was survived by his daughters from his first wife, namely Miriam, the wife of Simon Sassoon, and Hannah, the wife of Abraham Kohen. It is our hope that this volume will again bring the collector, scholar, rabbi, mystic, and indefatigable worker for the cause of Zion, to the attention of the reading public. We remain indebted to him for his collection.

Introduction

The historical and political background

The Bension Manuscripts and Texts of the Harry R. Cohen Memorial Collection have been designated as Sephardic. An explanation of the term "Sephardic," will help the reader comprehend the character of the entire collection. The term "Sephardic" has generally referred to those Jews who hailed from the Iberian peninsula, which includes Spain and Portugal, and all countries surrounding the Mediterranean Sea, and who came under the influence of the traditions of the Babylonian rabbinic leaders known as "Geonim" during the period of Mohammedan rule of these areas. In our age the term "Sephardic" has been broadly applied to most Jews hailing from Afro-Asian countries. The contemporary application of the term "Sephardic" to all Afro-Asian Jews is not in the purview of the collection. The Bension collection is primarily concerned with the literature and personalities of descendants of Jews who lived in Spain and Portugal before the expulsion of 1492, and of Jews who were indigenous to North Africa.

The Mohammedan influence was dominant throughout southern Europe and the Maghreb from the eighth century until the thirteenth century. During this period there was much commercial and cultural interaction between the populations of Iberia and North Africa. This was especially true of the cultural atmosphere that pervaded the Jewish communities of both areas. This glorious period in Jewish history is characterized as the Golden Age of Spanish Jewry. Major strides were made in the fields of Jewish philology, lexicography, liturgy, poetry, philosophy, rabbinic law, and mysticism.

Many of the illustrious teachers of the Jewish people appeared in this period on both sides of the Strait of Gibraltar. Among them were Bible commentators such as the members of the Ibn Ezra family; grammarians such as Rabbi Judah ibn Kuraish of Tahert, Rabbi Dunash ben Labrat of Fez, Rabbi Judah Ḥayudj of Fez, and Rabbi Menaḥem ben Saruk of Tortosa, Spain; poet-philosophers such as Baḥya ibn Pakuda, Solomon ibn Gabirol, and Rabbi Yehuda Halevi; and then there were the legal interpreters and codifiers such as Rabbi Isaac Alfasi of Fez, Rabbi Moses ben Maimon known as Maimonides, Rabbi Moses ben Naḥman known as Naḥmanides, and Rabbi Solomon ben Adret of Spain. Often, as was the case in the Middle Ages, each scholar was a master in several fields of endeavor. Thus Maimonides was a philosopher and an eminent jurist, while his income was derived from practice of the medical profession. Nahmanides was an astute commentator of the Bible while he was also known as an outstanding legal commentator and leader of a major mystical school in Gerona, Spain.

Moorish rulers of Spain encouraged a liberal atmosphere in the intellectual exchange of ideas and served as patrons of the arts and sciences of their day. In fact, the "lingua franca" of the scholarly world from the tenth through the thirteenth centuries was the Arabic language. The master works of such luminaries as Saadya Gaon, Baḥya ibn Pakuda, Maimonides, and other Jewish writers, which originally appeared in Arabic, had to be translated into Hebrew in order that they could be accessible to a wider reading public in the thirteenth century.

The adjoining provinces of Languedoc and Provence, the home of Provençal Jewry in southeastern France, served as adjacent allies to Spanish Jewry in the pursuit of Jewish culture. This district in southern France, whose inhabitants were the happiest of those under Christian rule in Europe, was also a bridge between the intellectual Jewish currents of northern and southern Europe. The Provence, blessed with a perpetual spring season, was the haven of a multitude of Jewish scholars who established schools where philosophical texts were translated into Hebrew in such centers as Beaucaire and Narbonne. Prominent among Provençal scholars were members of the Tibbon family who were translators of philosophical texts, the Kimḥi family of grammarians and Bible commentators, the philosopher-translator Shem Toḅ ibn Palqera, and the Talmudic commentators Rabbi Abraham b. David of Posquieres and Rabbi Zeraḥia Halevi.

The Provence was the major battleground in the "Hundred Years' War" of culture that ensued between the liberal religious pro-philosophical group referred to as the Maimunists (Jewish Rationalists), and the conservative, religious anti-philosophical anti-Maimunists. The philosophical camp viewed the study of philosophy as a natural ally to traditional Jewish study and piety while the anti-Maimonidean camp viewed philosophical study as a foreign element that was inimical to the preservation of traditional Jewish study and values. The battles which began after the death of Maimonides, in 1204, were not resolved because the Jews were expelled from the Provence and all of France in 1306. Many of those who were expelled made their way to Spain and North Africa.

At the close of the thirteenth century a new influx of scholars from northern Europe, which was under Christian influence, began to converge on the cultural centers of Spain. Some were driven from the Rhineland by the Rindfleish massacres of 1298, which uprooted over a hundred Jewish communities. In 1290, the sixteen thousand Jews of England were the first of their people on the European continent to be the victims of an official edict of expulsion. Most of them made their way to northern France. Every possible calumny that could be charged against the Jews was perpetrated in the thirteenth century under the crusading Pope Innocent III, such as the ritual blood libel. Jews were made to wear special badges, marking them as pariahs in Christian society. It is true that occasionally anti-Papist Christian rulers favored the Jews. Subsequently Jews came to Andalusia from northern France where they had been victimized by the pogroms that were current during the period of the Crusades. These newcomers from the north who came to Spain were known as Ashkenazim. An overwhelming number of northerners moved eastwards to the provinces of Bohemia, Moravia, and Silesia in central Europe and eventually penetrated eastern Europe. The theory is prevalent that those who are descended from most east European Jews are the children of the early Jewish settlers of the Rhineland and northern France.

The Ashkenazi traditions of the northern Europeans who came to Spain were markedly different from those of the Sephardim of the Iberian Peninsula. The origins for Ashkenazi traditions, excluding those practices that were added during the period of domicile in northern Europe, have been traced to the Holy Land. During the period after the destruction of the Second Temple in 70 C.E. many Jews journeyed to Italy. After living in Italian communities for hundreds of years the Jews were invited by Christian noblemen of northern Europe during the tenth century, to settle in northern France and the Rhineland and to help establish centers of trade. More often than not they migrated in the form of nuclear communities. Thus, the Ashkenazi traditions are traced to Israel while the Sephardi traditions are traced to the great Talmudic academies of Sura and Pumbedita in

Babylonia, today known as Iraq.

Despite the differences in traditions, the Hebrew language served as a common bond between Jews throughout Europe. The following incident will demonstrate that indeed this was the case. When Rabbi Asher b. Yeḥiel, the famous student of Rabbi Meir of Rothenburg, arrived in Toledo, Spain at the beginning of the fourteenth century, he was immediately accepted as a rabbinic leader. There he led a Talmudic academy and delivered his lectures in the Hebrew language which was comprehensible to all his students. We can assume that the overwhelming number of students were Sephardim. Rabbi Asher was representative of those Ashkenazi scholars who entered the Sephardic world because of expulsion from northern Europe.

At this point in our cultural travelogue the historical significance of the Bension Sephardic Manuscripts and Texts begins to become apparent. The collection contains a manuscript volume of the Responsa of the aforementioned Rabbi Asher b. Yeḥiel. Responsa are the answers that a rabbinic scholar gives to Jewish legal questions that have been addressed to him by individuals, communities, or other rabbinic scholars who may be seeking his guidance.

Although Rabbi Asher was educated in the Rhineland by Ashkenazi masters, he became the adopted teacher of the Sephardim in Toledo, Spain. He served as a vital cultural link between the Talmudical traditions of the Franco-German schools of the Tosaphists, those who added their comments to the Talmudic texts from the twelfth until the fourteenth centuries, and the Talmudical academies in Spain. It appears that his principles of Talmudic interpretation were compatible with those of the Sephardim. The collection contains an early manuscript volume of the Responsa of Rabbi Solomon ibn Adret of Barcelona, who was acknowledged as the greatest halakhic authority in Spain in the early part of the fourteenth century, and a comtemporary of Rabbi Asher b. Yeḥiel. The great Sephardi codifier of the sixteenth century was Rabbi Joseph Caro. He stated that in all his halakhic decisions he was guided by three luminaries of Jewish law, namely, Rabbi Isaac Alfasi, Rabbi Moses ben Maimon, and Rabbi Asher b. Yeḥiel. Thus we note that Rabbi Asher's absorption into the spectrum of Sephardic culture was complete.

Rabbi Asher's son, Rabbi Jacob, was representative of the first generation of children of Ashkenazi parents from northern Europe who came to settle in Spain, and who were subsequently influenced by the teachings of Spanish Jewry. Rabbi Jacob Bal Ha-Turim, as he was called because of his codification of Jewish law in four books called Rows-"Turim," cites the rulings of the Sephardic rabbis such as Rabbi Solomon ibn Adret side by side with the rulings of his father, Rabbi Asher, and other northern European Ashkenazi Talmudic authorities. The collection contains a late fifteenth century printed edition of Rabbi Jacob's "Tur" Shulḥan Arukh—Code of Jewish Law. Rabbi Jacob passed on in 1340. A famous halakhic work on Jewish liturgy which was produced by his contemporary, Rabbi David Abudarham, is also included in the collection in a printed edition of the late fifteenth century.

We mentioned earlier that the Jews of France were expelled in 1306. On several occasions they were invited to return to France and shortly thereafter they were again expelled. A similar opportunity was offered to the Jews by the German principalities. However, a more disastrous fate was to greet the Jews in German lands than even that visited upon them during the Rindfleish persecutions. A band of ruffians massacred many Jewish communities in the

Armleder persecution of 1336-1338. In the next decade the Black Death plague was blamed upon the Jews who, according to rumor, were acting in consort with the Moslems to poison the wells of Christian Europe. The fourteenth century has been regarded as the blackest in the history of northern European Jewry.

Unlike their co-religionists of northern Europe the Jews of the Iberian peninsula passed the fourteenth century in relative tranquility. However, suddenly the sky fell in on Spanish Jewry in 1391. We will briefly outline the events that led to the debacle of 1391 which did not reach its climax for the Jews of Spain until the issuance of the edict of expulsion in 1492, and for the Jews of Portugal in the year 1497.

While the Mohammedans controlled Spain for about three centuries, they did not exercise any uniform control, which was characteristic of the political history of this period. They were divided into a number of smaller states perpetually quarreling amongst themselves. The ruling Almoravid dynasty was toppled by the fanatical Almohads (both were of Berber origin) of North Africa in the middle of the twelfth century and this contributed to a further weakening of the political hold of Islam in Iberia. The Almohads' invasion caused repercussions in the Jewish communities. Maimonides left Spain for North Africa and the Kimḥi family moved from Spain to the Provence. We can conclude that other Jews also left Spain at this time. The Christians who held some parts of northern Spain seized the opportunity to go on the offensive which became known as the Reconquista, in the first decade of the thirteenth century.

By the second decade of the thirteenth century only the kingdom of Granada was under Moorish control. The majority of Jews who lived in Aragon, Castile, Leon, Portugal, and Navarre were now under Christian domination and they faced the full brunt of anti-Jewish legislation and the prejudices that Christians promulgated and perpetuated wherever they ruled in Europe. In this age of turmoil it became increasingly difficult for rulers to allow for a climate of free intellectual exchanges. The splendor of the golden age of Spanish Jewry began to dim.

The economic factor of the growth of a merchant class in the cities became a new force for the rulers to contend with. Christian merchants viewed Jewish merchants and tradesmen as competitors and the former sought favored status at the expense of the Jews. Occasionally the kings sought the support of the townspeople as a check against the nobility. Furthermore, the kings used the Jews as tax farmers and treasurers to secure funds that were needed by them to live opulently and to conduct military campaigns. This gave the Christian element further reason for disliking the Jews. The convergence of all these factors served to cause the first outbreaks against the Jews in 1391. Ferrand Martinez, the father confessor to the Queen-Mother of young King Henry VII, began to stir up mobs against the Jews from city to city. The Jewish communities of Seville, Cordoba, and Toledo, amongst others, were almost annihilated. Many individuals were given the choice between baptism or death. A significant number chose baptism hoping thereby to live as Jews in secret while protecting their positions which had been secured over hundreds of years of settlement. While some chose martyrdom rather than to submit to baptism, others were able to flee to North Africa. Some Jews who arrived in the Maghreb had already lived as Christians. Upon their arrival, Rabbinic tribunals sought methods by which the unfortunates could be restored to their people. Rabbi Isaac bar Sheshet and Rabbi

Simeon b. Zemaḥ Duran, of Algiers were among those rabbis who dealt with this problem at the end of the fourteenth century.

The New Christians were a source of great disturbance as they rose in privilege and in importance. Thus, the Inquisition was instituted to ferret out those who were regarded as insincere Christians. In order to facilitate their work the Christian clergy requested the rulers to remove Jews and Mohammedans from the kingdom. The edict of expulsion issued in Spain in 1492, forced the Jews to leave their wealth behind while they had to seek domicile in new lands. Jewish notables interceded with Ferdinand and Isabella, but to no avail.

Isaac Abrabanel, an advisor to the rulers of Spain and Portugal, left for Italy upon expulsion. While Italy was more favorably disposed to the Jews than the other western European powers heretofore mentioned, the various duchies and the Papal States subsequently instituted inquisitions and expulsions. One of the reasons that Jewish notables left for Italy as a place of refuge was that the Italian princes required their financial expertise. Many others turned to the rapidly expanding Turkish empire. Large Sephardic communities were established by the Megôrashim—those expelled were thus designated—in Salonika and Constantinople. Eventually some used this route as a stepping stone to settlement in the Holy Land.

A major portion of over 150,000 Jewish emigrés made their way to the shores of North Africa. Entire communities of the Megôrashim transplanted themselves to Fez, Debdou, Meknès, Tangiers, Tetuán, Salé, Safi, Tunis, Algiers, Tripoli, and a host of other communities along the shores of the Maghreb. Often ransom had to be paid for the Jews who were carried across the Strait of Gibraltar when their vessels were accosted by pirates who abounded in those waters. While some Muslim communities perpetrated rape and pillage against these unfortunates when they were thrust upon their shores, the overwhelming number of North African communities were very happy to receive these new settlers. It should be noted that a severe famine prevailed in Morocco in 1492. The Sultans looked upon these newcomers as a constructive adjunct to the native Jewish population. The economic and political sophistication of the industrious newcomers was looked upon as a real asset to the future development of North Africa.

While admittedly there were some marked differences in outlook between the Megôrashim and the native Jewish population known as Toshavim, there were also similarities. The Jews of Spain and North Africa shared many religious traditions drawn from a common Sephardic heritage that was nurtured in a Moslem environment in Spain and in the Maghreb. Students from North Africa frequented the rabbinic academies of Spain and liaison was established between Jewish families on both sides of the Strait of Gibraltar. It was natural for Spanish Jewry to flee to a place like Morocco because of the geographic proximity and a common sharing of traditions.

In the following years Castilian Jewry did succeed, in great measure, in preserving the distinct customs and halakhic traditions that they brought with them from Spain by establishing their own synagogues and by living in accordance with their traditions. In fact, in many communal matters the Castilians were able to win over the native born North African Jews to their ways of thinking and practices. In other matters a friction continued to persist between both Jewish groups.

A new spirit of cultural and commercial rejuvenation was infused into the indigenous

Jewish communities by the newcomers. While we may be certain that the emigrés from Spain could not take their gold and silver with them they were able to transport their spiritual treasures, their scholars, and their literature. This was especially the case in the area of philosophical literature. While the philosophical traditions of Aristotle and the Neo-Platonic school had finally received wide acceptance on the European continent at the end of the thirteenth century by Jewish and Christian scholastic circles, they were not popularized in North Africa, where a more conservative religious atmosphere prevailed. It remained for the Megôrashim to disseminate philosophical texts and studies. Among the manuscripts in the Bension collection there is a copy of Maimonides' "Moreh"—*Guide of the Perplexed*; also there are two manuscripts of aphoristic literature which were popularized by philosophic writers.

While many refugees settled in North Africa, not all remained there. In the early sixteenth century, we find the Maghreb becoming a way station to the Holy Land. One of the many celebrated personalities who came to Fez and subsequently journeyed to Palestine was Rabbi Jacob Berab. He studied in Spain with the famous Rabbi Isaac Aboab who was the author of the popular homiletic work Menorat ha-Ma'or. In the collection there is an early printed edition of this work. Rabbi Berab sought refuge at Tlemcen and later he became rabbi at Fez. After disseminating Torah learning in Morocco for a number of years he arrived in Safed in 1534. Rabbi Jacob Berab was also regarded as a teacher of Rabbi Joseph Caro, the celebrated author of the Shulhan Arukh—Code of Jewish Law. Other famous scholars who journeyed from Spain to Morocco and then eastward at this time were Abraham Zacuto and Rabbi David ibn Abi Zimra; the latter finally settled in Egypt.

We would be guilty of presenting an unbalanced historical picture if we viewed the conditions under which the Jews in the Maghreb lived as having been appreciably more satisfactory than the conditions of their settlement in Spain until the end of the fifteenth century. Two factors which undoubtedly contributed to the decision of the family of Maimonides to leave Cordoba for Fez in North Africa in c. 1150 was the religious policy of the ascendant Almohad movement, which did not tolerate the existence of non-Muslims and discouraged the study of philosophy as inimical to the true interests of Islam. During the reign of Abu Ya'Qub Yusuf (1165-84) the resurgence of Almohad fanaticism in Fez resulted in a new wave of forced conversions. Those who refused to be converted were put to death. At this time Maimonides left Fez for the Middle East. It is apparent that many families departed Morocco for Spain and the Provence when conditions became unbearable. Members of the ibn Danan family are representative of those Moroccan Jews who crisscrossed the Strait of Gibraltar as the exigencies of the times no doubt required. A further deterioration in the condition of Moroccan Jewry took place during the reign of al-Mansur (1184-1199) when he imposed upon the Jews, whether or not they were converted, the wearing of a distinctive badge called the Shikla because he questioned their sincerity to live by the rule of Islam. During the reign of al-Ma'mun (1227-1232) the Jews were permitted domicile in Morocco. However, shortly after, they were massacred at Marrakesh. Only when the Merivid dynasty replaced the Almohads in 1269 did Jews come to settle in Morocco in appreciable numbers. During the reign of the Almohads Jews sought refuge in the Christian territories of southern Europe and in the East. The Jews were favorably received by Christian rulers in northern Spain, in the territories of Aragon, Catalonia, and in Majorca.

The Jews of Morocco enjoyed relatively good conditions during the reign of the Merinid Sultans from 1269 to 1438. The Jewish ambassadors of the Christian kings of Spain were well received and native Jews were taken into the service of the sultans. The Moroccan Jews played a prominent role in the Sahara gold trade and in the exchanges with Christian countries. An indication of the tranquility of this period was the appearance of a Moroccan Jewish philosopher Judah ben Nissim ibn Malka who was active in the second half of the fourteenth century.

In the fifteenth century, as the Merinid dynasty began its decline, the Jews began to suffer. For the first time in Moroccan history the institution of what European Jewry was to refer to as a "ghetto" was introduced to the Jews of Fez, as they were enclosed in the walls of the mellah, in 1438. In the political upheaval that marked the fall of the Merinid dynasty, in 1465, many Jews were murdered or forcibly converted. Some families fled to Spain only to return to Morocco a generation later because of the general expulsion of Spanish Jewry. When Muḥammad al-Shaykh al-Wattasi came to power in 1471, he permitted the Jews who were forcibly converted to return to Judaism. He was the founder of the Wattasid dynasty that ruled the territories around Fez and he was the ruler who welcomed those who were subsequently expelled from Spain and Portugal.

The Portuguese began capturing port cities along the North African coast in 1415 with their taking of Ceuta. By the beginning of the sixteenth century Portugal occupied part of the Moroccan coast on the Atlantic Ocean, while Spain conquered cities off the Moroccan coast on the Mediterranean at the end of the first decade of the sixteenth century. Surprisingly, the Portuguese employed the Jews who were expelled from their lands as negotiators and political emissaries to the Muslim rulers. Other Jews who lived under the Wattasids of Fez and the sharifs of Marrakesh were the principal negotiators of the peace settlements between the Muslims and the Portuguese. Even more astonishing was the fact that Spanish and Portuguese Jewish exiles were engaged by the Moroccan rulers as ambassadors to the courts of Iberia. These Jews apparently prevailed upon a number of their co-religionists who had earlier publicly opted out of Judaism while remaining Jews in secret in order to remain as New Christians in Spain and Portugal, to settle in Morocco where they could return to Judaism.

The New Christians who were known by a variety of appellations such as Morranos, Conversos, Anusim, and Chuetas came to Morocco in the sixteenth century from the Iberian Peninsula, the Azores, and the Canary Islands, and some may even have returned from the Americas. Centers for reconversion to Judaism were established in the major cities of Morocco.

The first Sherifian dynasty known as the Sa'dis ascended the throne of Morocco by conquering Marrakesh in 1525 and Fez in 1549. The Sa'dis defeated the Portuguese army in 1578 and from that time Portuguese influence began to decline in North Africa. The Netherlands became the hub of commerce in northern Europe and the city states of Italy played that role on the Mediterranean. Moroccan Jewry served the Sa'di dynasty in both centers of the commercial world. Samuel Pallache, a Jew, arrived in the Netherlands and signed the first alliance pact between Morocco and Christian Holland.

The cultural background as revealed in the manuscripts

Among the masters of mystical literature in Spain

during the thirteenth century were Naḥmanides and his contemporaries, Abraham Abulafia, Shem-Toḇ ibn Gaon, Joseph Gikatilla, Moses de Leon, and Naḥmanides' student, Rabbi Solomon ibn Adret. This coterie of scholars represented the Jewish esoteric tradition which stood in opposition to the Maimonidean rational philosophical system and its adherents. In the Collection there is a fragment of a manuscript of the classical commentary of Naḥmanides on the Decalogue *Ms. 301*. The author presented his rational insights alongside his mystical interpretations of the biblical texts.

The Zohar, Book of Splendor, was traditionally associated with the mystical teachings of Rabbi Simeon Bar Yoḥai of the second century. This text continues to be part of the trilogy that is venerated by Moroccan Jewry: namely the Bible, Talmud, and Zohar. The Zohar and its associated literature were brought from Spain to Morocco. The forced geographic movement of thousands of Jews from Spain at the end of the fifteenth century began to spawn a number of dynamic systems and movements in Judaism. Such a revolution took place in Jewish Mysticism, but it did not achieve its full expression until the appearance of Rabbi Isaac Luria in the mystical community of Safed, in the Holy Land, after the second half of the sixteenth century. His system became known as Ari Kabbalism or Lurianic Kabbalism.

The dynamic concepts of spiritual exile and redemption of the soul took on new dimensions because of the recent mass physical exile that the Jews had to endure under the Spanish expulsion. An age of suffering was considered preamble to the final redemption. The chief exponent and literary figure of Lurianic Kabbala was Rabbi Ḥayyim Vital who had lived in North Africa and eventually sat at the Ari's feet in Safed. Rabbi Ḥayyim Vital was among the unwitting popularizers who made Kabbalism go public. In previous centuries only the select initiates could delve into this esoteric wisdom. The need for Tikkun—self improvement—was so urgent and the time so propitious, that the secrets had to be made available to every Jew. It was a matter greater than physical survival; it was a matter of salvation. The collection contains a manuscript copy of Ḥayyim Vital's classical work called Etz Ḥayyim—the Tree of Life.

The social phenomenon that accompanied the rampant mystical manifestations was the Messianic movement. The communities of North Africa were vulnerable to the Messianic tides that swept Europe during the days of Shabbetai Ẓevi. Long after the Messianic fervor had subsided on the European continent its embers were kept burning by its devotees in the Maghreb. Undoubtedly the mystical literature of Spain and the new esoteric expression of Lurianic Kabbalism had fired the imagination of the Jewish masses. Among several of the documents in the Bension Collection that contain mystical elements, the manuscript numbered 46 in the "Yalkut Roîîm" volume is of special interest. The author of this text uses the biblical passage "Blot out the memory of Amalek" (Deut. 25:19) to demonstrate his view that the year 1688 is significant for Messianic events. The Holy Name of God is computated together with the Hebrew terms "Timḥe" and "Zekhr" and the term "Yimlokh"—He will reign. The implication is that the enemies of Israel will be blotted out and God will manifest His glory in the year 1688.

The tradition that Elijah the prophet revealed himself to saintly scholars is noted in *Ms.85*. Examples of mystical elements that appear in poems and prayers are found in the collection. A poem by R. Jacob Ibn Ẓur, on the Ten Sephirot and the Holy Names of God, appears in *Ms. 84*.

A mystical prayer for protection when travelling in a dangerous area under siege is recorded in *Ms.177*. It reads as follows: "May the names of Sandalphon and Uriel strive to save me from the enemy and from those who lie in wait for me on my journey." Another prayer, which is supplicatory in nature and which possesses mystical elements, appears in *Ms.241*. After mentioning the merit of the scholars, saints, matriarchs, and patriarchs, the author adds "for the sake of the Ôfanim and Seraphim, Ḥashmalim, Tarshishim and the Holy Ḥayyôt, may you separate from me, your servant, the son of your maidservant, all those who would despise me and harm me."

A new figure appeared in the Maghreb who was responsible for the dissemination of the new mystical studies. He soon became an institution; he was called the Ḥaḥam Kôllel. He was a rabbi well versed in Kabbala, who journeyed forth as an emissary from the Kabbalistic centers of Safed, Tiberias, and Jerusalem to collect donations for their maintenance. He lectured on mystical themes, he provided the latest news that he amassed during his travels, he played an important role in stimulating the Hebrew book trade, and he brought glowing reports about the religious centers in the Holy Land, thus keeping the Messianic hope alive in the far flung communities.

The Ḥaḥam Kôllel was a vital force for injecting Zionistic fervor into Moroccan Jewry. This Zionism, which was based more on religious than on secular motives, prepared the Moroccans psychologically for mass migration to Israel. Unlike the European Jews who had experienced a major holocaust, the stimulus for North African Jewish aliyah was based on Messianic yearnings.

If a Ḥaḥam Kôllel died during his journeying he would be regarded as a saint and his burial site would become a place for religious pilgrimage. These pilgrimages to the graves of the saints throughout Morocco as well as the daily recitals of Zohar were, in some communities, regarded as ways to ward off the evil forces and demons known as Jinns, to restore health, and to help the Moroccan meet the daily adversities of mellah existence. Talismans and amulets were also popular as protection from the "evil eye." The text of an amulet which was intended to protect one from plagues appears pasted on to *Ms.18*. Similar practices won wide-spread appeal among large segments of east European Jewry until the advent of the twentieth century. Practical Kabbala was more pronounced, while the theoretical studies of speculative mysticism, which characterized the Spanish schools of Kabbala, were being pursued with zeal because of the influence of the new school of Lurianic Kabbala. In *Ms.269*, R. Raphael Moses Elbaz asks R. Solomon Ibn Ẓur to extend aid to R. Mordecai Elbaz. Among the latter's virtues it is noted that he "devotes himself to Torah study constantly and especially to the study of Zohar." In *Ms.220*, R. Menaḥem Serero informs R. Jacob Ibn Ẓur that R. Habib Toledano is sending R. Jacob a copy of a mystical work called Sefer Zerubbabel. R. Menaḥem says that he would appreciate R. Jacob's comments after he has read the work. R. Menaḥem notes that this work was composed by the author of Pirkei Haikhalôt, the Talmudic master R. Ishmael Kohen-Gadôl.

A providential aid to the perpetuation of Jewish literature at the time of the expulsion was the invention of printing. A golden age of Hebrew printing was attained in Italy in the first half of the sixteenth century, thanks to the efforts of the Soncino family, Samuel Latif, and Samuel Zarefati. Non-Jewish printers in Italy, such as Daniel Bomberg, engaged Jewish scholars to aid in choosing the best of the available manuscripts as the basis for the printed text. Turkey, in Constantinople and Salonika, took second place in the Hebrew printing field after Italy. In Portugal, Eliezer Toledano had published Hebraic and rabbinic works before the edict of expulsion.

The art of printing was brought to North Africa by the Spanish and Portuguese emigrés. The main location for the publishing of Hebrew books in Morocco was at Fez during the second decade of the sixteenth century. A Hebrew printing establishment was founded at Tunis in the third quarter of the eighteenth century and at Oran, Algiers in the middle of the nineteenth century. It was not until the end of the first quarter of the seventeenth century that Hebrew books were published at Amsterdam. The early printed works of the Bension collection that have been identified came from Ferrara, Lisbon, and Amsterdam. It is perhaps understandable why the works of Jewish scholars in Morocco were published in Amsterdam. They obviously had contacted the Sephardim who were prominent in the publishing industry in the Jewish community in Amsterdam. Among the leaders in the Hebrew printing field in Amsterdam was Manasseh Ben Israel. The principal centers of Hebrew publishing moved from southern Europe to central and eastern Europe by the middle of the eighteenth century.

Another intellectual "spin-off" resulting from the Spanish expulsion was the development of an historical sensitivity as Sephardic scholars of the post-expulsion period began to write chronicles about the unfortunate events they had experienced as eye witnesses. These scholars analyzed the calamitous events which had brought down the curtain on a thousand years or more of domicile in Spain. They memorialized the martyrs and left a record of the accomplishments of their co-religionists of earlier periods until their own time for posterity. Among these historians were Abraham Zacuto, who wrote the Sefer Yuḥasin which listed those personalities who brought glory to Spanish Jewry; Yehudah Ibn Verga who moralized about the reasons for the calamity in his work Shevet Yehudah; and the work Emek ha-Bakha, 'Valley of Weeping,' which was composed by Joseph Ha-Kohen.

The historical method of the Sephardim was perpetuated and given greater depth of expression by Moroccan Jewry. The repeated attacks upon the mellahs gave impetus to record the events that led to the martyrdom of co-religionists and the pillage of synagogues. The instability of the political situation in Morocco during the years 1640-1680 had its repercussions in the misfortunes that befell the Jewish communities. At Fez, Bu-Beqir, acting in behalf of the ruler who was a religious fanatic, ordered the complete destruction of all synagogues and schools of the Jews of that city. Among the synagogues that were destroyed are the following: the synagogue of the Megôrashim, the Atazi synagogue, and the synagogue of R. Isaac Abirgil, as well as the synagogue of the Toshavim. Only two were spared, the synagogues named after R. Saadya Rabuḥ and R. Jacob Roti. The same policy was promulgated in Tetuán among other communities.

One historical-legal document in the collection, *Ms.43*, gives an account of the pillage of the synagogue of the Toshavim in the mellah of Fez, in the year 1647. R. Isaac Ṣarfati was instrumental in preventing the complete destruction of the synagogue by paying a ransom to the attackers. The document is signed by the leaders of the Jewish community since it involved the sale of synagogue ritual vestments which were purchased by R. Isaac Ṣarfati. The latter served as the Nagid—political leader of the Jewish community of Fez—during the middle of the seventeenth century. The leading religious figure of this period was R. Saadya ibn Danan who supported the efforts of the aforementioned R. Isaac in implementing communal legislation against those who informed on the Jewish community to the governmental authorities. Another figure of this period (c. 1649) who appears in *Mss.141* and *144* is R. Ezra di Paridosh, who was a celebrated scribe gifted in the use of metaphor. His signature appears on two dowries composed at Marrakesh in 1649.

Other personalities of this period who appear in *Mss. 194* and *199* are the rabbis of Tetuán, Ḥananiah Arubash, Jacob Halevi, and Isaac Abudarham. R. Immanuel b. Menaḥem Serero (c. 1610-1680) of Fez, who was empowered by Isaac ibn Maman to act for him in matters pertaining to the estate of his late brother Moses ibn Maman, according to *Ms.199*, was appointed a judge during the lifetime of his paternal uncle, the famous Saul b. David Serero. These documents, which were composed in 1647, concern the estate of the late brother of Isaac ibn Maman. The aforementioned R. Jacob Halevi was known as a Kabbalist; he was author of a book on responsa called "Beit Yaakov," and a writer of elegies and liturgical pieces.

Rabbi Jacob b. Joseph b. Danan of Fez was active as a scribe during the ministration of R. Saul Serero (c. 1606). Rabbi Jacob was subsequently elevated to a judgeship in the rabbinic court of Fez. He composed a work on Jewish law which was quoted by subsequent scholars. R. Jacob ibn Danan signed a legal document, *Ms.172*. This document is especially interesting since it obliges one to reflect on the legal status of the Jew in relation to his Mohammedan counterpart.

The Charter of Omar, which was formulated in the ninth century and codified by Al-Mawardi, gave Jews the legal status of Dhimmi Ahl el Kitab, protegés of Muslim society. Among the advantages offered to the Christians and Jews, who were regarded as "people of the Book"—the Bible, were the right to live and the declaration of their property as inviolable. These rights were not always available to the Jews of Europe under Christian canon law. However, even in Islamic society there were limitations; Jews and Christians were not permitted to own a horse, which was regarded as a noble beast. A donkey, which was a lowly beast of burden, presented no problems of ownership. A mule as an article of transaction could pose a problem since it was part horse. Therefore, when Gideon ibn Sa'id Ha-Kohen purchased a mule from Yaḥya b. Abraham ibn Arwaḥ for one hundred and eighty uqiot in 1624, a clause had to be inserted stating that both parties agreed that if a Muslim should initiate a claim for the mule in a Muslim court and he won his claim, then Yaḥya, the vendor, would restore to Gideon, the purchaser, sixty uqiot, which was one-third of the original price. If Gideon won the case the loss that he might incur in payment for his legal defense might accrue to the total price of the animal plus an additional twenty uqiot. If the court expenses should exceed this amount then Yaḥya would be liable to pay half of any additional amount.

R. Saul Serero, who was active in the early part of the seventeenth century, served more than fifty years as a rabbi in Fez. His ministration extended from 1602 to 1655. After the demise of R. Samuel ibn Danan, R. Saul Serero was the Chief Rabbi of Fez for the next thirty years. A rabbi of Algiers, R.S. Ẓror, said of him that he was unique in his generation and the law was always decided in accord with his opinion. He is known for his halakhic work called "Urim Ve-Thumim." In it he informs the reader that his name was changed, because of illness, to Samuel.

Chronicles were composed by the leading scholars of the seventeenth and eighteenth centuries. Specimens composed by R. Saul b. David Serero and R. Samuel b. Saul ibn Danan are noted in *Ms. 87*. In the latter's chronicle a statement is attributed to the Talmudic sage Ḥanina b. Dosa which justifies the function of the chronicler; namely, that the tribulations of Israel should be recorded as well as the miracles. Every aspect of human existence was considered by the chroniclers to be a part of some divine plan and was accorded historical importance. Even such minute details as the formation of clouds in daily weather reports, especially during periods of famine and drought, were not considered too mundane to be recorded.

R. Saul b. David Serero writes in *Ms.87* about a famine that transpired between 1604 and 1606 at Fez, which took the lives of about three thousand souls, including that of R. Jacob ibn Attar. A lamentation was composed on the twentieth day of Adar 1606. During the second decade of the seventeenth century an incident is reported concerning one called Ḥamdun whose sons were killed by brigands. Ḥamdun wanted to blame the Jews and pour his wrath upon them. R. Saul Serero reported the incident to the king's officials as well as to the Nagid, R. Jacob Roti, who accompanied the king. After many bribes were paid safety was assured. The movements of the royal retinue are also meticulously recorded.

On another occasion, R. Saul Serero states that brigands, about ten of them, tried to enter his home through a window, but his brother David saw them and the brigands started shooting arrows. R. Saul and his brother thereupon threw stones at them until they fled. Conditions were so bad at Fez that R. Saul Serero moved to Ṣefrou. He also reported the upheavals of the community in Tafilalet where the majority of Jews suffered death, pillage, and starvation during a siege. Others were sold into slavery and the synagogues were destroyed. The Nagid was either hanged or crucified. The death of King Mulay Abdallah is reported. An earthquake was noted to have occurred on the twenty-second of Iyar 1625.

Samuel b. Saul ibn Danan, writing on Thursday, the tenth of Tevet 1724, reports a famine that lasted for three years, from 1721 to 1724, and a drought that continued for four years. The price of wheat was quoted at one hundred and thirty-five uqiot. A circuit of fasts was meticulously observed. A great penitential convocation took place in 1723 at the communities of Meknès, Salé, and Ṣefrou, as Torah scrolls were brought forth. Subsequently, rain fell for three days, whereupon the price of barley was reduced and wheat was quoted at sixty uqiot. The chronicler reports that the misfortune at Fez was indescribable.

Another chronicler of the seventeenth century was the illustrious scholar R. Saadya ibn Danan who is noted in *Ms.258*. The copyist of R. Saadya's chronicle was Immanuel b. R. Joshua Serero, in the month of Ḥeshvan 1724. Some of the excerpts are given as follows, "I have it in my grandfather R. Samuel ibn Danan's hand that the Castilian expulsion was in 1497. Lest I forget the date I have recorded it here. Also he [R. Saadya's grandfather] recorded that the expulsion that occurred to the Toshavim of the old city of Fez took place in 1438. The mellah suffered an expulsion in 1465." Another excerpt from Saadya ibn Danan reports an earthquake to have taken place at Fez on the seventh of Adar II 1636. As a result of the panic that followed, people grabbed weapons and attacked one another in confusion. A solar eclipse was recorded and the amount of sunlight was measured. Stars were seen in the afternoon on the twenty-eighth of Nisan 1630. A great quake was felt on an early morning in 1624, whereupon a great number of houses and towers were demolished in the old city of Fez and about three thousand, five hundred people were killed. More people were injured after the quake because of the weakened conditions of the houses. It was regarded as a miracle that not one Jew was killed although their houses were demolished, especially as their houses were not so well constructed as the houses of the non-Jews. A reason is given for recording this event. "To make known to future generations the magnitude of this miracle that occurred." The author is Saadya b. Abraham b. Samuel ibn Danan.

Additional natural occurrences are reported. On Wednesday, the eve of Shavuot 1624, the sky darkened and small creatures, the upper portion of their bodies appearing to be like locusts and the bottom like worms, fell from the sky. Simultaneously, a storm of large (hail) stones also fell. The weight of one stone was given as four uqiot. People who were in the marketplace were injured by the falling stones. One stone came through the window of R. Moses Almosni's house and broke a vessel. It was reported that a lion entered the Giza gate of the old city of Fez and killed one donkey and took another with him. "It is not known whether this is true but most of the non-Jews say that it transpired."

An almanac type of forecasting is offered for the cities of Morocco based on when the New Year falls. Brigands will abound and wars will be fought. The end of the year will be appreciably better than the early part of the year. Plentiful rain will reduce the price of wheat. The day on which the New Year will occur will affect weather conditions, health conditions, and whether difficulties will be encountered with the crops.

The chronicler, Immanuel Monsano of Fez of the eighteenth century, appears as the author of *Ms.275*. He commences his chronicle with the usual lament about how unfortunate are the times in which he lives. The excerpts deal with the years 1738-1760. Reports are given as to the scarcity of rain and to details of the fasts and services that were held. Then he adds, "The head of the academy, and the leading rabbi of the community, delivered a lecture. The message stressed that denial of rain is directly related to the sin of neglecting Torah study, since Torah study leads to proper actions." The speaker apparently also stated that another moral lapse that causes the rains to cease is gossip and the improper exercise of speech. Public violation of the Sabbath laws, especially by liquor vendors, is also a factor not to be discounted. An enactment was instituted to the effect that even if a liquor vendor was seen by only one witness to be violating the Sabbath by selling his wares then he should pay a fine which would be used to help the poor. The scholar noted another moral lapse which needed correction. Jewish women working in Fez for non-Jews remained there day and night and on the Sabbath. They should henceforth behave in accordance with the code that Jewish women are accustomed to live by. It was further decided that an emissary should make the women return. If the women remained adamant in their refusal then the ruler should intervene to oblige them to adhere to the enactment.

The political situation is also described. King Mulay La-Muztadi acceded to his throne in the month of Tammuz 1738 (at Meknès) and was declared king at Fez on Friday the eighth of Av. The non-Jew Maḥmad ibn Abu ibn Sa'id suffered a terrible death at the king's hands at Meknès. There was tranquility in the land during Mulay La-Muztadi's reign.

Immanuel Monsano reports the following: "On Sunday, the sixteenth of Shevet 1740, while we were engaged in Torah study we were informed that King Mulay La-Muztadi had fled to Fez. The entire city was in an uproar because of the reign of terror that would follow, especially for the Jewish populace, which was the usual course of events during unsettled times. That same day R. Jacob Monsonyego was wounded in the arm and head and lost much blood. The king fled the city in an easterly direction when he saw no relief. Mulay Abdallah was then declared king. This is the third time that he rules."

His supporters went to return the king who fled, arriving at Meknès in the month of Tishri 1740. The Al-Wadaya rebelled against the king for two months and refused his offer of amnesty because they did not trust him. A prayer is added that the Messiah might come. Finally, we learn, a reconciliation between the king and the Al-Wadaya was effected.

In the year 1758-59 no rain fell. After the usual fasts and prayer services some rain fell. Prayers of thanksgiving were then recited. When the rain ceased the non-Jews asked the Jews to pray for rain. Following the prayer service the people went to the cemetery to pray at the graves of the saints. Psalms were recited at R. Judah ibn Attar's tomb. R. Elijah Ha-Ṣarfati gave a lengthy discourse. That afternoon R. Saul ibn Danan addressed the people. On a subsequent occasion R. Elijah addressed the people in the morning and R. Raphael Ibn Ẓur addressed them at the afternoon service.

The city of Fez was conquered by King Muḥammed ben Mulay-Abdallah on Friday, the twenty-sixth of Av 1760. Afterwards a cannon was brought to the mellah and it was fired in the cemetery. The king was curious to see what distance the missile would attain.

In the seventeenth century, Moroccan Jewry had settlements in a number of communities in the Holy Land, at Jerusalem, Tiberias, Hebron, and Safed. In a number of eastern Mediterranean countries such as Egypt, Syria, Lebanon, Greece, and Turkey, Moroccan nuclear communities maintained their own synagogues, customs, and rabbinic leaders. It is probable that the North African scholar R. Ishmael Ha-Kohen Tanuji, author of the text Sefer Ha-Zikkaron which appears in the Bension collection, functioned as a rabbinic leader to North African Jews in Egypt during the first third of the sixteenth century.

The Algerian scholar R. Ḥayyim Capusi (1540-1631), who is mentioned in *Ms.85*, is another who is representative of the movement of scholars from Northwest Africa to the Eastern Mediterranean. R. Ḥayyim made his way to Egypt where he served in a rabbinic capacity in later years. He arrived in Egypt during the sixth decade of the sixteenth century. He is referred to as Ba'al Nes, the one to whom a miracle had occurred, as a result of a controversy which he had with the scholar R. Beẓalel Ashkenazi, compiler of the work Shitah Mekubbeẓet, concerning a suit for a debt. R. Ḥayyim sided with the defendant in the suit. Subsequently, he became blind and an aspersion was cast upon him that his blindness was due to a bribe he had taken. However, his sight was soon restored and R. Ḥayyim felt that he was vindicated in the dispute. The synagogue where he prayed received the appellation Ba'al Nes.

The illustrious Moroccan scholar and mystic R. Ḥayyim ibn Attar, author of the celebrated commentary on the Pentateuch Or ha-Ḥayyim, left Morocco for the Holy Land at an advanced age, in the eighteenth century. He took many disciples with him since he was desirous of opening an academy there. More disciples were added to his venture during his stopover in Italy. The unsettled economic and political situation in Morocco during the fourth decade of the eighteenth century was sufficient reason for R. Ḥayyim ibn Attar to make his exodus. R. Ḥayyim Joseph David Azulai, the prolific author and bio-bibliographer of the second half of the eighteenth century, studied under R. Ḥayyim ibn Attar. The former was a descendant of R. Abraham Azulai, the famous mystical scholar of Marrakesh. R. Ḥayyim Azulai is the author of the oft-quoted bio-bibliographical work Shem Ha-Gedolim, which is cited in *Ms.85*. He was the first Jewish scholar to study the Hebrew manuscripts of Italy and France systematically.

The last dynasty of Sharifs to rule Morocco until our own day is that of the Alawids. They rose to power in the seventeenth century during a period of political chaos which marked the end of the dynasty of the Sa'dis. Many chronicles are available that report on the activities of this dynasty. These rulers are noted in some of the chronicles that appear in the Bension collection. Mulay al-Rashid, who ruled between 1660 and 1672, was regarded as the founder of the dynasty. He received much support from the Jews and he subsequently adopted a favorable attitude toward them. Mulay Ismail, the brother of Mulay al-Rashid, was viceroy in Meknès while his brother ruled from Fez. When his brother died in Marrakesh, Ismail, with the help of the Jews, secured the sultanate for himself. The Jews fared better than even most of the Muslim population during Mulay Ismail's long rule, from 1672 to 1727.

The situation of the Jews began to deteriorate at the end of Mulay Ismail's reign when his sons fought over the ascendancy to the sultanate which was based in Meknès. Usually these stormy periods were of short duration until a ruler was finally installed. However, the thirty years following Mulay Ismail's death, 1727 to 1757, were marked by anarchy and suffering for the entire population. A vivid report of these events is noted in a chronicle which appears in *Ms.275*. This disorganized state of affairs gave France and Spain a golden opportunity to extend their influence in Morocco. The Jews dwelling in the towns in the interior began a movement to the big cities and the coast because of the lack of security.

There arose a number of rabbinic scholars who were prolific authors and who directed the religious life of Moroccan Jewry during the period that overlapped the reign of the aforementioned Mulay Ismail and the period of strife which followed, from 1672 to 1757. It is important to note that the religious life of Moroccan Jewry was not just confined to attendance at the synagogue on the Sabbath or even thrice daily. Rather the religious leadership played a decisive role in legislating on all aspects of daily life such as marriage, divorce, and inheritance as well as regulating the production and distribution of all food supplies, especially meat products which are subject to many dietary laws. The regulation of weights and measures and the establishment of fair pricing also came under rabbinic scrutiny, as is noted in *Ms.108*. The rabbinic courts were the formulators of the proper documentation for various legal situations such as certification for religious functionaries, bills of divorce, bills of debt, and legal forms for a variety of commercial transactions. The adjudication of property rights between individuals as well as all that which pertained to communal property rights came under their scrutiny. Occasionally enactments were made for the material and spiritual wellbeing of the inhabitants of the various communities.

Often as a result of persecutions and exorbitant taxes many rabbinic leaders of the various communities were obliged to leave. This resulted in an absence of rabbinic leadership to serve in the rabbinic courts and to educate young men who would be able to meet the future needs of the Jewish community. Some communities were fortunate in having distinguished scholars who stayed on and supervised activities at the rabbinic courts while they single-handedly directed studies at rabbinic academies. Communities which were in dire need of rabbinic leaders would often send pleas to larger communities to send a scholar of note to settle in their community. Thus, the responsibility for the perpetuation of the educational system was also the responsibility of the rabbinate.

Dynasties of scholars were nurtured in several families. These families are constantly reappearing in the hundreds of documents of the Bension collection, particularly in the "Yalkut Roiim" volume. Several of the personalities that were especially active in the major Moroccan communities during the first half of the eighteenth century will now be introduced. Among the most illustrious rabbinic scholars of Fez were the following three: Rabbi Judah ibn Attar, Rabbi Jacob b. Reuben Ibn Ẓur, and R. Samuel ibn Elbaz.

Fez and Meknès— seventeenth and eighteenth centuries

Rabbi Judah ibn Attar lived from 1655 to 1733. He was known by the title "Rabbi al-Kabbir,"—The Great Rabbi of Fez. R. Judah was a disciple of R. Vidal Ha-Ṣarfati and R. Menaḥem Serero of Fez. He was appointed to serve as judge together with his masters in the year 1698. Due to the persecutions that took place in Fez he moved to Meknès in 1701. He joined the rabbis Moses Toledano and his brother Ḥabib in deciding judicial matters before returning to Fez in c. 1704. The only judges of the rabbinic court in Fez at this time were R. Judah ibn Attar and R. Samuel Ha-Ṣarfati because other scholars had left and had not as yet returned to Fez. During his ministration as head of the court and as a judge he did not receive compensation from the community but he was self-employed as a silversmith. He was well versed in the customs of Castilian Jewry as well as being erudite in all areas of Jewish Law. Therefore, all the Moroccan communities turned to him with their queries. R. Judah collaborated with his younger colleague Jacob Ibn Ẓur in publishing the enactments of the Spanish exiles in Fez and in enacting new legislation which served as a basis for subsequent development in Moroccan Jewish law. In the Bension collection Rabbi Judah ibn Attar is noted in over forty-five separate documents and texts. R. Judah demonstrates great concern for his younger colleague, R. Jacob Ibn Ẓur, and had a high regard for R. Jacob's scholarly attainments. R. Solomon Elijah Ibn Ẓur recorded in *Ms.85* that the prophet Elijah revealed himself to R. Judah ibn Attar.

Rabbi Jacob b. Reuben Ibn Ẓur (1673–1752), appeared to suffer the exigencies of a more unsettled life than did his older colleague, R. Judah ibn Attar. In spite of his wanderings from Fez to Meknès (1720–28) and then to Tetuán (1738–40), R. Jacob was able to manifest prolific output in many literary directions as well as in the field of jurisprudence. Whereas R. Judah succeeded in achieving some financial stability, R. Jacob was always seeking ways of lessening the oppressive financial burden which was his to bear. Others usually seemed to be getting the better of him in matters of finance. Yet he was strong-willed and his temperament was such that he would rather suffer than succumb to those who attempted to lord it over him.

An indication that this indeed was the case can readily be noted from a very revealing correspondence in the collection, *Ms.227*, wherein the reason as to why R. Jacob Ibn Ẓur felt obliged to leave Fez, where he enjoyed such prestige, for Meknès, is alluded to. R. Judah ibn Attar, who is the writer of *Ms.227*, takes pain to keep R. Jacob's confidence and for this reason his essential motive for leaving Fez is not revealed. Yet R. Judah notes in a nebulous manner that a disorganized state of affairs affecting the Jewish community is the cause.

R. Judah is against R. Jacob's departure for Meknès. However, he refuses to have him write to the Nagid of Fez to initiate a process of conciliation and appeasement. He implies that it is the Nagid who should initiate the process of reconciliation, since R. Jacob suffers much privation because of the situation. He concludes the correspondence with his view that because of the personalities involved, no real improvement in relations will result until R. Jacob confronts the Nagid face to face. R. Judah seems to hint that R. Jacob Ibn Ẓur should make some effort to confront the Nagid so as to end his exile (at Meknès). He writes that he will only intervene in the dispute when R. Jacob returns to Fez.

R. Jacob Ibn Ẓur knew personal tragedy in the untimely death of his two sons who were named after his late father, the scholar R. Reuben. The Bension collection contains letters of consolation in *Mss.21* and *37* to R. Jacob on the passing of his sons. R. Jacob also suffered the loss of his precocious son-in-law, R. Menaḥem II Serero, at the age of twenty-six, which is noted in *Ms.35*.

A most revealing correspondence concerning this family in later years may be found in the collection. It is a response to Aaron Ibn Zur's desire to acquire a family tree, a Ktav Yuḥasin, on the occasion of the forthcoming marriage of his daughter. This information was composed in a letter on Purim day, 1876 by his brother, who desired anonymity. The writer describes the family as having originated in Castile and he commences with R. Moses Ibn Ẓur, who was known as Abraham the Hebrew, as the first scholar of note who was situated in Morocco. The writer regards the disclosure of this information as a disturbance of the dead and he asks that the letter should be destroyed after the contents are revealed, presumably to the groom's father, Mordecai ibn G̣o. For the entire text see the contents of *Ms.244*.

R. Jacob Ibn Ẓur, who was also known by the name Yaabeẓ, was the acknowledged Master of Jewish law by all the sages of his generation. In *Ms.19*, the leading rabbis of Meknès speak with the highest regard for R. Jacob's authority. R. Mordecai Berdugo states that the custom of Castilia remains the final guide for R. Jacob Ibn Zur and the former will do nothing until he receives permission from R. Jacob Ibn Ẓur. R. Mordecai Berdugo asks R. Jacob Ibn Ẓur to clarify a dispute but he will surely abide by R. Jacob's decision because of the esteem in which he is held, see *Ms.262*. In *Ms.117*, R. Jacob Toledano states that "the scholars of the West relied upon R. Jacob Ibn Ẓur." See also *Mss.118* and *119* where R. Mordecai looks to R. Jacob for guidance. In *Ms.63* the writer states, "that the law is in accord with R. Jacob (Ibn Ẓur) everywhere."

R. Jacob was an undisputed master of the popular metaphoric style of liturgical poetry of his age. He was a prolific composer of poetic constructions, several of which appear in the Bension collection in *Ms.84* while others are alluded to in R. Jacob's correspondence with R. Menaḥem Serero in *Ms.105*. According to R. Ḥ.J.D. Azulai, R. Jacob was also accomplished in the field of practical Kabbala. One of the poems that R. Jacob composed on the mystical theme of the ten sephirot and the holy names that are related to the sephirot, in twenty-six verses equal in number to the Holy Name of the Almighty, appears in *Ms.84*. R. Menaḥem Serero asks for R. Jacob's comments on a mystical work called Sefer Zerubbabel which was composed by the author of Pirkei Haikhalôt, the Talmudic master, R. Ishmael Kohen-Gadol. This correspondence appears as *Ms.220*. In his prose writings he shows an historical sensitivity. He also possessed an exhaustive knowledge of the traditions of Castilian Jewry.

Although R. Jacob Ibn Ẓur never made any one community his permanent home he immediately functioned as the highest authority in every community in which he sojourned. While he studied under the same masters as did R. Judah ibn Attar, namely, the rabbis Vidal Ha-Ṣarfati, and Menaḥem Serero, he always showed deference to his older contemporary. R. Judah was quick to capitalize on R. Jacob's abilities by having him serve as a judge in Fez. The signatures of R. Judah and R. Jacob that appear together on several court documents in the collection are representative of this period of R. Jacob Ibn Ẓur's activity in Fez. (See *Mss. 67, 196, 231* and *252*.)

When R. Jacob Ibn Ẓur moved to Meknès much correspondence passed between him and his colleague R. Judah ibn Attar. Some letters were of a personal nature while others involved litigations. (See *Mss. 28*, *33*, *62*, *65*, *69*, *70*, *73*, *162*, *171*, *188*, *193*, *207*, *242*, *250* and *257*.) R. Jacob Ibn Ẓur had his share of controversies and personality clashes with such figures as R. Jacob ibn Malka, R. Jacob Toledano, R. Samuel Azawi, and the Nagid of Fez among others. In *Ms.35*, R. Jacob Ibn Zur blames R. Jacob Toledano as being the cause of his wanderings and of his migration to Tetuán because he could not make a living in Meknès owing to R. Toledano's manipulations.

Towards the end of his life he ordained five of his students who subsequently became known as the "Court of Five at Fez." They were (1) Samuel Saul b. R. Jacob b. Danan (1700-1766); (2) R. Ephraim b. Abraham Monsonyego (1710-1780), who subsequently served as a judge in Tetuán; (3) R. Raphael Oḅed Ibn Ẓur (1710-1769), the son of R. Jacob Ibn Ẓur; (4) R. Elijah b. R. Joseph Ha-Ṣarfati (1715-1805); and (5) R. Matitya b. R. Menaḥem II Serero, R. Jacob's grandson. Thus R. Jacob Ibn Ẓur ensured a rabbinic leadership for the future generation. He also left many responsa in his work called "Mishpat u-Ẓedakah be-Ya'aqov," which is a good source for history of this period. He left much poetry as well. His liturgical compositions are sung by Moroccan Jewry till this day. Many of his works are still in manuscript. R. Jacob Ibn Ẓur is noted in more than sixty documents and correspondences in the Bension collection. The pre-eminence of Fez in Moroccan Jewish life ended with the death of R. Jacob Ibn Ẓur in 1753. The rabbis of Salé, Ḥayyim Toledano, Aaron the son of Judah Halevi, and Jacob Bibas, sent a letter of consolation to R. Raphael Oḅed Ibn Ẓur on the passing of his father. R. Raphael is mentioned as a successor to his father in this epistle which appears in *Ms.132*.

R. Samuel ibn Elbaz (1698-1749) was in his mid-thirties when he was appointed a judge in Fez together with R. Jacob Ibn Ẓur and R. Shalom Edery. His first wife was the granddaughter of R. Neḥemia Ha-Kohen, whose sons, Moses and Shem Toḅ, died martyrs' deaths. Subsequently, R. Samuel inherited the authority over the synagogue in Fez that had belonged to R. Neḥemia, established a school there, and in turn passed it on to his sons, R. Judah, R. Moses, and R. Jacob. R. Samuel Elbaz was shown deference by his colleagues on matters pertaining to Jewish law. The names of members of this scholarly family are noted in thirty-two separate documents in the Bension Collection. R. Samuel composed many works in the field of Jewish jurisprudence, among them decisions that he rendered in responsa as well as novellae on several tractates of the Talmud.

R. Samuel b. Abraham Ha-Ṣarfati (1660-1713), who was the cousin of R. Vidal II Ha-Ṣarfati (1631-1703), was a contemporary of R. Judah ibn Attar and served as a judge together with R. Judah at Fez. On the seventeenth of Tammuz 1707, the rabbis Judah ibn Attar, Samuel Ha-Sarfati, and Abraham ibn Danan signed a court document affirming Saadya Lahakhusin's ownership of a portion of an upper storey of a house that the latter had purchased from a non-Jew named Musa. The wife of the Jew David b. Tata o.b.m. made a claim against this property. Saadya was now protected by the rabbinic tribunal from any claims that David's wife might make. This is the subject of *Ms. 17*.

On another occasion R. Samuel Ha-Sarfati joined R. Judah ibn Attar, R. Vidal II Ha-Ṣarfati, R. Saadya b. Mîmun Aflalo, and R. Isaac Ha-Ṣarfati in attesting to the financial need of R. Isaac Melamed who was a scholar of Jerusalem. The aforementioned rabbis signed a court document, which appears in *Ms.192*, stating that financial aid should be made available to R. Isaac whenever he came to Fez. During the period in which this document was composed the economic situation in Fez was unfavorable for the Jews, while the non-Jewish population fared much better. The expression "the maidservant inherited the role of the mistress," was used by the rabbis to characterize the relations between Muslims and Jews and the conditions under which they lived. The rabbis pray that the scholar will receive his due as economic conditions improve.

R. Samuel Ha-Ṣarfati was a co-signer with R. Judah ibn Attar, R. Abraham ibn Danan, and R. Jacob Ibn Ẓur of a court document that was drawn up on the seventeenth of Tammuz 1709. On that occasion the community of Fez was in need of funds so it leased a concession to R. Daniel Toledano thereby realizing the necessary funds. All the particulars of this transaction are noted in *Ms.196*.

R. Samuel was a scion of the illustrious Ha-Ṣarfati family which claimed descent from the twelfth century Tosafist of Northern France, Rabbi Jacob Tam, otherwise known as Rabbenu Tam, who was the grandson of the celebrated Biblical and Talmudic commentator, Rashi. R. Samuel Ha-Ṣarfati's paternal grandfather was the famous scholar R. Vidal I Ha-Ṣarfati (1550-1620), whose son Issac II (d. 1660) served as the Nagid at Fez. R. Vidal I was a contemporary of the author of the Shulḥan Arukh, R. Joseph Caro, according to *Ms.85*. R. Samuel authored many halakhic works as well as a text on the aggadic portions of the Talmud entitled Petaḥ Ainîîyim. He also wrote an exegetical work on the commentaries of Rashi and Naḥmanides entitled Nimukei Samuel. There are more than forty-five citations of the members of this illustrious family in the Bension collection, with biographical source material available on them from the mid-seventeenth century. Signatures on legal documents in the collection bear the names of many scholars from this prestigious family.

R. Jacob, the son of Joseph ben Malka, served as a scribe of the rabbinic tribunal in Fez in the year 1717, and was still active as the head of the rabbinic court in Tetuán c. 1771. However, his irascible nature brought down the ire of his contemporaries who were the leading scholars of the age, see *Ms.133*. Among those who attempted to discipline him for his presumption were R. Jacob Ibn Ẓur, R. Shalom Edery, R. Samuel Elbaz, and R. Abraham Alel. Even R. Judah ibn Attar did not go unscathed from Jacob b. Malka's barbs.

R. Jacob b. Malka is mentioned in several documents and correspondences in the Bension collection. Immanuel Monsano's letter of consolation to R. Jacob b. Malka upon the murder of his son Samuel in c. 1760 is found in *Ms.255*.

R. Samuel b. R. Saul b. Danan (1668-c.1730), who served as the chief Ritual Slaughterer in Fez, was the composer of a chronicle on the history of the Jews of Fez between the sixteenth and early eighteenth centuries. This work was called Divrei ha-Yamim. The Chronicle Serero which is found in *Ms.87* includes some chronicles which were composed by Samuel b. Saul ibn Danan as well as by R. Saul Serero. More than thirty documents in the Bension collection note the members of this family, that was indigenous to Morocco centuries before the Spanish expulsion.

The Edery family is mentioned in the Bension collection in a dozen different documents. R. Shalom Edery, who served as a judge at Fez, was a contemporary of R. Judah ibn Attar and R. Jacob Ibn Zur. He was active between the years 1707 and 1736. R. Shalom's signature appears on several documents in this collection.

The Zikhri family was represented in Fez during this period by R. Ḥananiah b. R. Isaiah ben Zikhri. R. Ḥananiah left Fez to settle in Meknès, where he served as a scribe for the rabbinical courts at the beginning of the eighteenth century. He was also a composer of liturgical poetry. Members of this family are noted in several documents of the Bension collection. R. Hananiah b. Zikhri and R. Abraham b. David Ḥasin are the signatories to *Ms. 113*, in a correspondence from Meknès to R. Jacob Ibn Ẓur at Fez, in behalf of R. Samuel Maymeran. R. Jacob is asked to intercede with R. Shalom Edery to pay more for a piece of property even though the sale had been consummated a long time before.

The leading authority of Jewish law at Meknès during the time that R. Judah ibn Attar was active in Fez, was R. Moses Toledano (1643-1723). R. Moses inherited the leadership of the rabbinic court from his father, R. Hayyim, in the year 1680. R. Moses' younger brother, R. Ḥabib (1658-1716), was active as a judge in the year 1703. Both brothers remained childless. R. Ḥabib's first wife was the daughter of R. Shemaya Maymeran. R. Ḥabib's student, who was regarded as the next scholar of prominence in Meknès, was R. Moses Berdugo, also known as the Mashbir. He inherited the post of chief of the rabbinic court of Meknès upon the death of R. Moses Toledano, and died in 1731, when he was succeeded by R. Moses Adhan. The latter died in the year 1737.

The aforementioned brothers Moses and Ḥabib Toledano are not the only members of the larger Toledano family to be mentioned in twenty-two separate documents of the Bension collection. There were also four other Toledano brothers: R. Daniel, R. Barukh, R. Ḥayyim, and R. Jacob, the sons of another R. Moses Toledano whose father was R. Barukh. Two of these brothers, R. Ḥayyim and R. Jacob Toledano, are mentioned in several documents of the collection. R. Ḥayyim Toledano (1690-1750) was able to pursue an intensive Torah education because of a bequest that he received from his late uncle Ḥayyim's estate. He became a judge in 1723 and succeeded the late R. Moses Adhan in the position of chief judge of the court in Meknès in the year 1737. He composed works in the area of Jewish law and elegies.

R. Jacob Toledano surpassed his brother Ḥayyim in prestige and achievement. R. Jacob, who was also popularly known as the Moharit, served as the chief judge of the rabbinic court in Meknès from the year 1750, as well as being the leader of the community. He placed his relatives in the most influential positions, incurring the wrath of other scholars who became jealous of his power which he wielded for over forty years. He was the acknowledged halakhic authority from 1750 until his death in 1771.

R. Mordecai Berdugo, who was known as Harav Hamarbiz, is as often mentioned in this collection as is the aforementioned R. Moses Berdugo, the Mashbir. The latter was R. Mordecai's father-in-law and teacher. R. Judah Berdugo, a brother of R. Mordecai, was a colleague of R. Ḥayyim ben Attar, author of the celebrated Biblical commentary Or ha-Ḥayyim. R. Mordecai and his brother R. Judah served as judges in Meknès. R. Mordecai passed away in 1763. The greater Berdugo family is noted in this collection in twenty-five separate documents and correspondences.

Salé—
seventeenth and eighteenth centuries

Some of the outstanding scholars from Salé who are mentioned in the collection are R. Joseph Saba, R. Mordecai Ha-Kohen, R. Jacob b. R. Joseph Bibas, R. Samuel Azawi, and R. Jacob ben Shaiya. The first three are signatories to the same document, *Ms.175*, that orginated at Salé. R. Mordecai died in the year 1717. R. Jacob Bibas was born at Tetuán but eventually left for Salé where he was appointed a judge. He married a great-granddaughter of R. Vidal II Ha-Ṣarfati of Fez and she bore him two sons, R. Joseph and R. Ḥayyim. There are nine documents in the Collection which refer to members of the Bibas family. R. Samuel b. Moses Azawi also signed *Ms.189* with R. Jacob Bibas and R. Joseph Ṣaba of Salé. R. Samuel Azawi served as the ritual slaughterer and scribe to the rabbinic court of Salé and was there appointed to a judgeship aided by the rabbis of Fez and Meknès. R. Samuel, however, manifested an argumentative nature, particularly to scholars who were of a higher stature than he. The same scholars of Fez and Meknes who referred him to the judgeship now tried to have him removed, especially R. Jacob Ibn Ẓur who bore him particular enmity.

Moses Ben-Ẓur, who was a distinguished citizen of Salé, was the uncle of R. Jacob Ibn Ẓur. Moses died in the year 1706 and left three sons, Shalom, Jacob, and Judah. R. Shalom, who was considered a scholar in Salé, wrote and signed *Ms.129* to R. Jacob Ibn Ẓur, as well as *Ms.256*. R. Shalom was considered to be the greatest grammarian of the West as well as a proficient poet.

Tetuán—
seventeenth and eighteenth centuries

R. Ḥasdai Almosnino was a leading scholar and judge in Tetuán at the beginning of the eighteenth century until his demise in 1728. After R. Isaac Bibas left Tetuán, R. Ḥasdai and R. David Ha-Kohen (the latter serving as head of the rabbinic court until his death in 1708), were the only scholars left. After R. David's death, R. Ḥasdai remained the sole spiritual leader of authority in Tetuán. The dearth of scholars to lead the people was due to persecution and excessive taxation, particularly between the years 1700 and 1705. R. Ḥasdai Almosnino guaranteed spiritual leadership for the future in Tetuán by preparing the following students to serve as rabbinic judges: R. Menaḥem Anhori, R. Moses b. Zimra, R. Abraham Abudarham, and R. Isaac Nahôn. The Bension collection contains documents from R. Ḥasdai (*Ms. 23*) and his student R. Isaac Nahôn (see *Ms. 128*). R. Jacob Maragi, who was a resident of Tetuán at this time, was a celebrated Kabbalist who published commentaries on the Zohar.

Ṣefrou—
seventeenth and eighteenth centuries

Although the city of Ṣefrou had a smaller Jewish population than either Fez or Meknès, it could boast a high level of scholarship during the eighteenth century due to the efforts of the erudite sage, R. Moses b. Ḥamo. R. Moses was active in judicial matters during the last quarter of the seventeenth century as can be attested to from *Ms.197*, where R. Moses corresponds with R. Menaḥem Serero. That same document permits us to receive some insight as to the nature of the organization and curriculum at R. Moses' Academy in Ṣefrou. He states, in a postscript to *Ms.197*, that he is presently studying the Talmudic Tractate Hullin with his students after the morning service. At midnight he has another study session with more than twenty advanced scholars. R. Moses also corresponded with R. Vidal II Ha-Ṣarfati and R. Judah Uziel of Fez, contemporaries of R. Menahem Serero. R. Moses was the undisputed authority in every area of the communal life of Sefrou. He also possessed a zealous disposition which obliged him to rebuke all those who were in violation of the law irrespective of their position. Whenever R. Moses arrived in Fez for a visit the whole community was electrified by his personality and his homiletic ability.

Among R. Moses ben Ḥamo's students who served as spiritual leaders in the eighteenth century were his son R. Yeshua ben Ḥamo, R. Samuel b. Ḥota, R. David B. Shitrit, R. Meir D'Avila, R. Joseph b. Attia, R. Joseph Gabbai, R. Mas'ūd b. Joseph b. Rabuḥ, and R. Yaḥya Banon. R. Moses b. Ḥamo died at an advanced age in the year 1707.

Marrakesh and Demnat—
eighteenth century

R. Isaac Delouya of Marrakesh, who was highly regarded by the rabbis of Fez and Meknès and who left many notable students, died in 1711. Among his students were R. Solomon Amar of Demnat and R. Abraham Azulai of Marrakesh. R. Solomon and R. Abraham passed away in the same year, 1735. They both composed Halakhic works and were proficient in Kabbalism. R. Abraham Azulai engaged in Kabbalistic practices while he also composed works on Ari Kabbalism. Another student of R. Isaac Delouya, at Demnat, was R. Mordecai Attia, who also received instruction from R. Solomon Amar. R. Abraham's student R. Jacob Pinto wrote commentaries on the Zohar. He is mentioned in *Ms.4* of the Bension collection. His descendant, the Ḥaḥam Kôllel R. Moses Pinto, is mentioned in connection with fund raising for the great academy of the Jewish community of Tiberias in the Holy Land. There were many descendants of Moroccan scholars who served the interests of the Sephardi communities after they settled in the Holy Land. This epistle, which was written in the month of Shevat 1828, is part of a collection of letters which are called Kitvei Ha-Qodesh (letters from the Holy Land) requesting aid for the communities of Safed and Jerusalem as well as Tiberias.

The fourth letter in *Ms.4* is particularly interesting in as much as it concerns the Sephardic communities of Jerusalem who sent their emissary on behalf of the members of the community of Ashkenazim Midrash Perushim, the eastern European community of Jerusalem in search of funds in the year 1842. This epistle was signed for the Kôllel Ashkenazim Midrash Perushim at Jerusalem, by Natan the son of Menaḥem Mendl. This may not have been so unusual since the Sephardim who had the facility of the Arabic language were more successful in establishing an economic base than were the Ashkenazim who settled in the Holy Land during this period. It was also not unusual for Ashkenazi emissaries to come to the Moroccan communities for aid. This can be noted in the third letter in *Ms.4* where it mentions funds needed to rehabilitate synagogues damaged during earthquakes.

All the communities—
eighteenth and nineteenth centuries

During the second half of the eighteenth century the members of the "Court of Five at Fez" who were ordained by R. Jacob Ibn Ẓur, namely, R. Samuel Saul ibn Danan, R. Ephraim Monsonyego who later established himself at Tetuán, R. Raphael Oḇed Ibn Zur, R. Elijah Ha-Ṣarfati, and R. Matitya Ṣerero, were joined in their efforts by the scribe of the court, R. Immanuel Monsano, who died before 1770. R. Immanuel appears in his official scribal capacity in *Ms.121*. R. Immanuel Monsano is also the author of a chronicle that appears in *Ms.275*. He is noted in several other documents and on some occasions together with his brother, Abraham Monsano, see *Mss. 116* and *237*. Other members of this family that are mentioned in the collection are Yehonatan Ish Ṣion the son of Beẓalel, Barukh Monsano, and Ḍavid Monsano.

R. Raphael Oḇed Ibn Ẓur, the son of the aforementioned R. Jacob Ibn Ẓur, was called Oḇed by his father when he was a youngster. The name Raphael must have been added as a result of an illness from which he recovered, *Ms.105*. He received a portion of the income from his father's synagogue at Meknès, which was contested by R. Jacob Toledano. Apparently, R. Raphael Oḇed Ibn Ẓur was no more successful in his business ventures than his father had been. R. Raphael Oḇed informs R. Moses ibn Maman, in *Ms.190*, that he suffers a multitude of misfortunes as well as economic privation. He lost his possessions because he gave capital to entrepreneurs to invest for him; his goal in business ventures is not wealth but merely the ability to acquire that which would permit him to purchase the basic necessities; he is destitute and is located at the house of study at Meknès. He had been offered a stipend by that community which was available for resident scholars and after refusals had finally succumbed and taken it, but only as a loan. Eventually, we learn, the stipend was reduced because business conditions were bad. Raphael Oḇed refused to take any more stipends while he viewed his poverty as a sign of Divine chastisement.

He asks R. Moses Maman to extend a loan of two hundred uqiot to help him support his family, especially as the holiday season is approaching. He offers to compose a bill of debt and to give his land in Meknès as collateral. He has his eye on another business scheme (not unlike those which previously placed him in a situation of adversity) which someone would invest and manage for him. He expects that he will be able to live off the profits. For more bibliographical information on these members of the Ibn Ẓur family, see *Ms.35*.

After the passing of R. Raphael Oḇed, in the year 1769, his son, Samuel Ibn Ẓur, was elected as a judge to the court in Fez, in his father's stead. R. Samuel was still active in that capacity in the year 1782. There is a letter of consolation, *Ms.77*, which was sent by R. Ephraim Monsonyego and R. Judah b. Abraham Coriat, both of Tetuán, to R. Samuel Ibn Ẓur on the passing of his father. Another letter of consolation, *Ms.78*, was sent to the rabbis Matitya Serero and Samuel Ibn Ẓur by the rabbis Jacob, Solomon, and Moses Toledano and R. Solomon Tapiero of Meknès.

Contemporaneous with the activities of the "Court of Five" at Fez was the "Court of Three" at

Meknès which consisted of R. Solomon b. R. Eliezer Toledano, R. Moses b. Daniel Toledano, and R. Yekutiel b. R. Mordecai Berdugo. They succeeded the eminent R. Jacob Toledano, who passed on in 1771. R. Jacob, R. Solomon, and R. Moses Toledano were the signatories to the aforementioned letter of consolation, *Ms.78*. R. Moses Toledano also sojourned at Salé for a time because of the pestilence and famine which affected Meknès. He lost his first wife in the pestilence and in the ensuing years the rest of his family succumbed. R. Ḥayyim b. R. Judah Toledano, who resided in Meknès for a time, was an uncle to the aforementioned Moses and Solomon. R. Ḥayyim subsequently moved to Salé in 1750, where he served as a judge for thirty years. He wrote many Halakhic works and he composed a memorial book noting Moroccan scholars who passed on between 1714 and 1773.

Several documents of the Maymeran family appear in the Bension Collection. R. Moses Maymeran of Meknès and his son Ḥayyim were noted scholars who composed Halakhic works. R. Moses was a son-in-law of R. Jacob Toledano. A dispute between R. Moses and R. Jacob Toledano is noted in *Ms.35*. R. Ḥayyim was born in 1765 and although he passed on at the age of twenty he received wide acclaim for his erudition and he composed works in several areas of Jewish scholarship.

The Dahan family appears in eighteen documents of the collection. The spelling of the name may vary, i.e. Dahan, Adhan and Bendahan, and it is listed in the Index of Names under Dahan as well as Adhan. R. Moses Adhan who served as the head of the Rabbinic Tribunal in Meknès until 1737, was to serve as a conciliator in the dispute between the Nagid of Fez and R. Jacob Ibn Ẓur. R. Jacob was in self-imposed exile in Meknès because of that clash of personalities, which is noted in *Ms.227*. In the same correspondence it is noted that Mas'ūd ibn Adhan, together with R. Jacob Aspag and Saadya Lahaboz, wrote to Fez to get the notables to persuade R. Jacob Ibn Zur to write to the Nagid so that he would be able to return to Fez. R. Mîmun Adhan is mentioned in several documents. In *Ms.96* he joined R. Jacob Toledano in writing to R. Samuel Elbaz concerning a claim made by Isaac ibn Haroush against Ḥayyim ibn Magiruz. In *Ms.71* a note of consolation is added marking the recent demise of R. Mîmun ibn Adhan in Fez, on Saturday evening, the seventh of Ḥeshvan 1756.

Two interesting documents in the Bension collection which give additional information concerning some of the vicissitudes of members of the Adhan family are *Mss.250* and *251*. R. Judah ibn Attar inquires of R. Jacob Ibn Ẓur about certain deeds belonging to the descendants of Isaac and Ephraim ibn Amara which are supposed to be in R. Jacob's possession. These deeds will have a bearing on whether the descendants of the late Levi ibn Amara will be able to claim a courtyard containing a ritual bath or whether it will remain in the possession of R. Joseph Adhan in the form of a pledge. The latter needs to produce the pledge in order to redeem himself with its value because he and his two brothers are being held by a non-Jew who has confined them on his property for more than two weeks. The non-Jew also caught the young son with the intention of converting him to Islam. They were freed by the non-Jew on the condition that cash would immediately be made available to him. Joseph Adhan is sending his eldest son, Mîmun, to R. Jacob for the documents since the case involves redemption of captives. In *Ms.251*, R. Judah ibn Attar informs R. Shalom ibn Lakhraif that a decision was rendered in favor of R. Joseph Adhan.

The Ḥasin family was also active in Meknès during this period. One of the outstanding members of this family was R. David b. R. Aaron b. Ḥasin who was born c. 1730 and passed on after 1790. He was the student and son-in-law of R. Mordecai Berdugo of the previous generation. R. David was famous for his outstanding liturgical poems which were published in his liturgical work "Tehila Le-David." R. Abraham b. David ibn Ḥasin of Meknès was a signatory to *Mss. 113, 180* and *181*.

One of the rabbinic leaders of this generation in Ṣefrou, was R. Saul Yeshua Abitboul. He is the writer of a letter of consolation and a poem to R. Samuel Ibn Ẓur, on the passing of his father, R. Raphael Oḇed Ibn Ẓur, which is *Ms.208*. R. Saul Yeshua composed works pertaining to the laws of ritual slaughter in accord with Maaravic custom. He passed on in the year 1802. In *Ms.13* which was written in 1871, enactments pertaining to the practice of ritual slaughter and the examination of the lungs of animals are recorded. These enactments were formulated in Ṣefrou by R. Amor Abitboul and R. Amram Elbaz in the year 1847. Some of the enactments were that the slaughterer's knife and the lungs of animals must be examined by two people, one is insufficient. Also ritual slaughterers shall not use their occupation as an excuse for not attending morning services at the synagogue, since henceforth no slaughtering shall commence before the conclusion of morning services. The Abitboul family perpetuated an unbroken chain of leadership at Sefrou throughout this period. The members of the Abitboul family are noted in several documents of the collection.

The leading scholar at Salé during this period was R. Eliezer b. R. Samuel D'Avila. His father, R. Samuel b. R. Moses who was born in Meknès, studied under R. Hayyim ibn Attar I, and married the latter's granddaughter. R. Samuel left Meknès because of the excessive taxes that were levied on him and he made his home at Salé. R. Samuel's aspiration to travel to Jerusalem was realized as *Ms.135* testifies. In that epistle R. Samuel informs R. Jacob Ibn Zur that he has purchased several books for him and states that they should be paid for. R. Eliezer, who was called "Rav Adda," was born in 1714 and he married the daughter of R. Elijah Halevi b. Susan of Salé, at age fifteen. Although R. Eliezer died at the age of forty-seven, in 1761, he was a prolific scholar. Many of his works were posthumously published by his son-in-law.

R. Eliezer D'Avila appears in *Ms.47*, where his mother disputes with him over the estate of his late father, R. Samuel. R. Eliezer agrees that half of the properties should be given to his mother in accord with the custom of the enactment of the Jews of Castile. However, he claims that he has no properties available to give to his mother since they were sold to realize money for her maintenance and to pay off his father's debts.

Another dispute involving the inheritance between members of the D'Avila family of an earlier generation is recorded in *Ms.118*. R. Mordecai Berdugo wrote to R. Jacob Ibn Ẓur concerning this dispute. R. Moses b. Jacob D'Avila of Meknès, who was apparently a grandson of the late R. Judah D'Avila, was engaged in a litigation with another grandson, named Judah D'Avila, over wine barrels that once belonged to the late R. Judah D'Avila. R. Mordecai Berdugo asks R. Jacob Ibn Ẓur to endorse either R. Mordecai's decision or R. Jacob Toledano's decision in the same dispute, In *Ms.119* R. Mordecai Berdugo notes that R. Jacob Ibn Ẓur decided with him against R. Jacob Toledano.

R. Moses ibn Ḥamo wrote to R. Menaḥem Serero, in *Ms.197*, explaining that R. Jacob

D'Avila, who was a party to a dispute, was unable to participate in the proceedings because of ill health. Therefore, he should not be cited for obstructing justice. This R. Jacob D'Avila, who had a son called Meir, may also have been the father of R. Moses D'Avila who was the grandfather of Eliezer b. Samuel D'Avila.

Among the leading rabbinic scholars of Tetuán during the second half of the eighteenth century was R. Judah b. R. Abraham Coriat. We have already mentioned that R. Judah was a co-signer with R. Ephraim Monsonyego of a letter of consolation written to R. Samuel Ibn Ẓur on the passing of his father, see *Ms.77*. Many of the literary works produced by R. Judah were destroyed in the reign of terror of Al-Yazid in the year 1790. R. Judah passed on c. 1788, but his son, Isaac, was able to salvage some works which he took to the Holy Land. R. Judah is also mentioned in *Ms.155* as one of the judges in Tetuán together with the rabbis Judah and Solomon Abudarham. R. Judah Abudarham passed on after 1780. Members of this family of the previous generation are noted in *Ms.252*; namely, R. Samuel Abudarham and Joseph Abudarham. The subject of that document is Abraham ibn Amara who was in trouble with the ruling authorities and was obliged to call in bills of debt in order to realize money by which he could redeem himself. It is probable that the author of the liturgical work Sefer Abudarham (a printed edition appears in the Collection) was R. David Abudarham of the fourteenth century, a Spanish antecedent of this family which resided in Tetuán.

Another scholar of eminence in Tetuán during this period was R. Judah Halevi. He may be identified with R. Judah Halevi who was at Salé during this period, as may be noted from *Mss. 130* and *132*. R. Judah did move about from one community to another throughout his lifetime. After leaving Tetuán the first time he made his way to Algiers where he involved himself in controversy with the chief of the rabbinic court, R. Jacob b. Na'îm but he returned to Tetuán and established an academy. Then he left Tetuán again with the desire to get to the Holy Land and made his way there via Gibraltar, where he remained for five years and established another academy. He did not get to the Holy Land, however. Indeed, in 1790, he desired to return to Tetuán, but a storm brought him to Algiers. This turn of events was fortunate, since the persecutions of Al-Yazid's short reign (1790-1792) began soon afterwards. R. Judah lost all his possessions that remained in Tetuán while he tarried at Algiers. Subsequently, he made his way to Livorno, Italy, and then he returned to Gibraltar.

R. Judah Halevi's family achieved prominence at Gibraltar in the generations that followed. Ha-Ẓeḅi Me'at Devash, who was a book dealer in Jerusalem during the third quarter of the nineteenth century, informs R. Raphael Ibn Ẓur of Fez that the books he had ordered will be sent to the Halevi family at Gibraltar once they are available. These transactions are recorded in *Mss.264*, *145*, and *238*. The last two correspondences mention Moses Halevi as the agent for the transactions. R. Judah Halevi's last journey to Gibraltar, where he stayed until his demise, was that travelled by many Moroccan Jews after the persecutions of 1790; especially by those Jews who lived in Tetuán which was in close proximity across the Strait of Gibraltar.

Leading scholars—
nineteenth century

R. Samuel Ibn Ẓur of Fez, who was also known as Solomon Samuel, had two sons, R. Jacob Ibn Ẓur and R. Raphael Ibn Ẓur. The subject of his estate after his demise is found in *Ms.31*. This document was composed in Fez, in the month of Heshvan 1791. At that date Jacob Ibn Ẓur is reported to be a bachelor while Raphael is married and their mother is the third party to share in the estate. All three are agreed never to dissolve the estate. Jacob is given permission to pay for his future marital expenses from it. Both sons have made available to their mother half of what they each received. The remainder of the document stipulates how the perpetuation of the estate in future generations is to be ensured.

R. Jacob Ibn Ẓur, who served as a rabbi at Fez, passed on in the year 1850 at about the age of seventy years. R. Jacob had a son called R. Solomon Elijah Ibn Ẓur (1821-1873). R. Solomon Elijah Ibn Ẓur is mentioned in *Ms.3*, in a letter of reconciliation that was sent by Abraham b. Saul ibn David ve-Joseph to R. Solomon in the year 1864. R. Abraham appeals to R. Solomon not to let false statements that were made against him become a reason for accusing him of taking letters of correspondence that belonged to R. Solomon Elijah and to the latter's grandfather R. Solomon Samuel for whom he was named. R. Abraham also writes that R. Solomon Elijah is married to his sister. In the concluding portion of this epistle, Abraham discusses a litigation in which he is involved. It appears that R. Jacob, the father of R. Solomon Elijah, refuses to adjudicate because R. Jacob is wroth with Abraham. Finally, R. Jacob Serero is obliged to decide the matter. R. Raphael Ibn Ẓur, the brother of R. Jacob Ibn Ẓur, also had a son called Solomon, who passed on in 1843 at the age of thirty-seven. Although R. Solomon was not appointed as a judge, he was considered to be among the leading scholars of Fez.

R. Solomon Elijah Ibn Ẓur is mentioned in thirty-one different documents in the Collection. A member of the celebrated Ḥasin family of Meknès, who were prolific poets, namely, Aaron Ḥasin, corresponded with R. Solomon in 1860, in *Ms.7*. Often many scholars turned to R. Solomon to render Halakhic decisions for them. Among them were Elijah b. Haroush, in *Ms.8*; see also Samuel ibn Elbaz, *Ms.10*. R. Judah Berdugo, of Meknès, who left Morocco for the Holy Land, turned to R. Solomon asking him to render a decision which would enable him to realize the cash which the former needed and which could be available from R. Judah's portion of his grandfather's estate. However, his late grandfather had stipulated that the estate should remain in perpetuity. R. Judah suggests that R. Yedidia Monsonyego is also available to R. Solomon for consultation. This case is discussed in *Mss. 11* and *265*. R. Judah also offers to sell R. Solomon books on Responsa literature at a fair price. Other authorities who turned with their queries to R. Solomon Elijah Ibn Ẓur were R. Matitya ibn Zikhri, in *Ms.12*; R. Raḥamin Joseph G̣ayni, of Ṣefrou, in 1871, in *Ms.13*; and R. Raphael Maman, of Meknès, in *Ms.270*.

R. Solomon Elijah Ibn Ẓur cultivated many other interests. He copied historical information as well as biographical and bibliographical material, as may be noted from *Ms.85*. In the same document, R. Solomon Elijah states that his grandfather, R. Solomon Samuel Ibn Ẓur, informed his father, R. Jacob Ibn Ẓur III, that he saw R. Joseph Caro's signature. R. Solomon Elijah received a letter from Judah Zarmon in 1866, *Ms.52*, wherein the latter requests that a copy of an historical work called "Divrei ha-Yamim" which is supposed to be in the possession of R. Rahamim G̣ayni of Ṣefrou, should be made available to him. This work was in the nature of a diary of events that transpired from the Castilian expulsion until the nineteenth century. R. Solomon Elijah also copied a collection of tales and aphorisms called Divrei Ḥakhamim Ke-Dôrbônôt, which appears in *Ms.36*.

R. Solomon Elijah Ibn Ẓur's son, R. Raphael III Ibn Ẓur, succeeded his father as rabbinic leader at Fez, c.1875. In *Ms.120*, Raphael is identified as R. Solomon's son. R. Solomon Elijah was often referred to in correspondences as "Ham-Melekh Shlomo, "King Solomon and his son Raphael were often addressed as "Ham-Malakh Raphael," the angel Raphael. Elijah b. Jacob Kasis, who served as an emissary for the Jerusalem community, was also engaged in the book trade as can be ascertained from *Ms.32*, which was written to R. Raphael Ibn Ẓur, in 1863. R. Raphael's purchase of books is also noted in *Ms.54*. Joseph Sasson is the Jerusalem book dealer who corresponds with him in 1880. Ha-Ẓevi Me'at Devash, of Jerusalem, sends books to R. Raphael via Gibraltar through the agency of Moses Halevi, as is noted in *Ms.145*. See also Ms.232 and *Ms.264* which deal with the acquisition of books. Elijah Kasis wrote three other correspondences pertaining to his function as an emissary, to the rabbis Raphael III Ibn Ẓur and Jacob Ha-Kohen, in *Mss. 44*, *45*, and *48*. The writer sent regards to a number of personalities in Fez who were contemporaries of R. Raphael III Ibn Ẓur. Among them are the following: R. Solomon Ibn Ẓur, the Nagid Abraham, R. Abner Ha-Ṣarfati, R. Joshua Serero, R. Samuel Ha-Kohen, R. Israel Maymeran, Menaḥem Ṣaba, R. Jacob Dahan, Azuz Ha-Kohen, Aaron Ha-Kohen, and Matitya Serero.

R. Raphael III Ibn Ẓur was the recipient of many requests to come to the aid of the destitute, as in *Ms.56*; to aid emissaries, as in *Ms.101*; and to resolve disputes or to respond to queries of a Halakhic nature. In *Ms.55*, Moses Turgeman of Tiberias, in the Holy Land, asks R. Raphael to uphold a claim to an estate on behalf of the former's family. R. Raphael III Ibn Ẓur and R. Abner Israel Ha-Ṣarfati wrote a decision in a paternity suit against the seductor. He was flogged and fines were exacted from him. This court document, which appears in *Ms.146*, was written in 1876. The rabbis of Ṣefrou, Ḥayyim Elijah Gayni, Raphael Moses Elbaz, and Yekutiel ibn Elbaz ask R. Raphael III Ibn Ẓur to serve as interim overseer of the estate of the late Raphael Ha-Kohen, in *Mss. 203* and *204*. R. Raḥamim Joseph Gayni writes to R. Raphael asking him to render a decision in a difficult litigation. The former expects that R. Raphael's review of the matter will finally lead to its resolution. This is the subject of *Ms.200*.

R. Raphael Moses Elbaz wrote to R. Raphael Ibn Ẓur in Tammuz 1877, concerning the case of a husband who alleges that his wife is rebellious. Since the dispute reached a stalemate, R. Raphael is asked to try to achieve a compromise and if this fails then the latter should try to finalize the litigation as he sees fit. This case is reported in *Ms.245*. In *Ms.246*, R. Raphael Moses Elbaz again turns to R. Raphael Ibn Ẓur to serve as a final arbiter. The issue involves one who wants to challenge a communal enactment which prohibits a stranger from marrying a woman of the community. In *Ms.247*, R. Raphael Moses Elbaz enquires of R. Raphael Ibn Zur concerning the custom in Fez governing the acquisition of groves, fields, and gardens. He wants to know whether the owner also acquires the right of domicile therein, the question having been prompted by a Jew receiving land in pledge from a non-Jewish owner. Can he exercise the right of domicile over it and thereby prevent the non-Jewish owner from utilizing it as he sees fit? Another Halakhic query was posed by Joseph

Sasson, an emissary from Jerusalem, of R. Raphael, in *Ms.248*, in the year 1877. The former was travelling amongst the towns of the Rif when a question concerning a levirate arose. A minority opinion was referred to from the only work available, the code Even ha-Ezer. Joseph, however, desires a more sound basis for rendering a lenient opinion and he asks R. Raphael Ibn Ẓur to provide it with despatch. Rabbi Raphael III Ibn Ẓur's son Solomon III is mentioned in *Mss. 99* and *100*.

R. Elijah b. Joseph Ha-Ṣarfati was blessed with a longevity which spanned almost all of the eighteenth century, from 1715 until 1805. He studied with R. Judah ibn Attar and he was one of the Court of Five scholars of Fez who were ordained by R. Jacob Ibn Ẓur before the latter's demise. Subsequently, he served as the leading Halakhic scholar of Morocco during the last quarter of the eighteenth century. R. Elijah ordained R. Jacob Ibn Ẓur, the son of Solomon Samuel Ibn Ẓur and the great grandson of R. Jacob Ibn Ẓur, who had ordained R. Elijah.

R. Elijah Ha-Ṣarfati composed an aggadic work called "Simu Lehem," when he was fifteen, which appears in *Ms.107*. R. Elijah had two sons, R. Israel Jacob Ha-Ṣarfati who died at an advanced age in 1826 and R. Raphael Menaḥem Ha-Ṣarfati who passed on in 1843. The latter served as Nagid.

A letter of adulation which was written in honor of R. Elijah Ha-Sarfati and his son Jacob appears in *Ms.18*. An emissary, Israel Jacob Halevi, pleads with R. Raphael Ha-Ṣarfati to aid his plight by rendering a judgement against the Nagid of Meknès who has made an unjustified claim on a portion of the emissary's collection for the needs of the destitute of Meknès. The emissary states that he appeals to R. Raphael to deal with the issue since it requires the attention of the highest Halakhic authority and he imagines that only R. Raphael has the power to render a judgement in such a case. This subject is dealt with in *Ms.236*. This same emissary corresponded with R. Raphael in *Ms.103*. In this epistle he sends regards to Joseph, R. Raphael's son. In *Ms.89*, an appeal is made to R. Raphael by R. Judah Elbaz to convince an intransigent debtor to make payment.

A plea by the Rishon Le-Ẓion, the Sephardi chief rabbi of Jerusalem, R. Ḥayyim Abraham Gagin, to Raphael Ha-Ṣarfati of Fez, in behalf of the former's son-in-law, R. Judah Zacut, is the subject of *Ms.147*. R. Judah who is the son of the illustrious mystic R. Moses Zacut is in need of financial aid to support his large family and the writer asks R. Raphael to use his office to extend all possible aid to him. A copy of the introduction to R. Moses Zacut's work, Iggerôt ha-Ramaz is found in *Ms.151*.

On another occasion a plea was sent to R. Raphael Ha-Ṣarfati to grant protection to a widow who is in transit, to help consummate the levirate responsibilities. The writer asks that she should be chaperoned by persons of high moral character and that her needs should be provided until she arrives at her destination. Also R. Raphael is asked to forward letters to all those communities where the widow will stay that they should prepare for her arrival. This plea is reported in *Ms.148*, which was composed in 1834-35.

Samuel Halevi ibn Yulee corresponded with R. Raphael Menaḥem Ha-Ṣarfati on the tenth of Kislev 1841, from Gibraltar. Information about the whereabouts of the son of R. S. Aflalo is made available. R. Raphael is also reminded to concern himself with a litigation which involved the wealthy Isaac Ben Zaqen in order that justice may be served. This correspondence is the subject of *Ms.152*. A plea for charitable aid is addressed to R. Raphael Ha-Ṣarfati, who is designated with the appellation Ḥam-Malakh, by Zikhri Meshash. As Passover is soon approaching, Zikhri is depending upon the merciful nature of R. Raphael to help him in his moment of economic adversity. This letter is the subject of *Ms.222*. In *Ms.239*, R. Ḥayyim Toledano extends an invitation to R. Raphael Ha-Ṣarfati to stay with him when he arrives at Meknès. R. Hayyim refers to the close relationship that existed between his father of blessed memory and R. Raphael. The writer sends greetings to R. Raphael's son Joseph.

R. Israel Jacob Ha-Ṣarfati, the brother of the aforementioned Raphael, had a son called Solomon. Solomon's son, R. Vidal III, who lived from 1797-1856, was a profound rabbinic scholar and Talmudist who also served as a judge. In *Ms.149*, R. Ḥayyim Ḥaluah who wrote to R. Ḥayyim David Ibn Zimra also addresses R. Vidal III Ha-Ṣarfati. R. Vidal III had an illustrious son called R. Abner Israel (1827-1884) who served as a rabbinic judge at Fez. He was the author of responsa and he is known for his historic work called Yaḥas Fez which contains information about the generations of scholars of Fez from the seventeenth century until his own time. He wrote this work in 1879 at the request of members of the Kol Israel Ḥaverim (Alliance Israelite) Society who enquired about the origins of the Jewish community of Fez. R. Abner Israel was well versed in philosophy and mysticism and is noted in ten manuscript documents of the Bension Collection.

A letter was sent by the communal leaders of Ṣefrou to the rabbis of Fez concerning fund raising irregularities that arose during an emissary's visit. The writer was R. Raphael Maman who wrote to the rabbis Saul ibn Danan, Solomon Elijah Ibn Ẓur, and Abner Israel Ha-Ṣarfati concerning the funds that were collected by the Jerusalem emissary R. Barukh Pinto. This correspondence is found in *Ms.39*.

On another occasion the rabbis of Ṣefrou, namely Raḥamim Joseph Gayni, Raphael Moses Elbaz, and Saul Elbaz ask the rabbis of Fez, R. Solomon Elijah Ibn Ẓur and R. Abner Israel Ha-Ṣarfati to aid in settling prior claims against an estate which creditors are now suing. This document appears in *Ms.57*. In the month of Tishri 1876 R. Abner Israel Ha-Ṣarfati and R. Raphael Ibn Ẓur rendered a decision and sentence against one who was accused in a paternity suit. This case is recorded in *Ms.146*.

Moses b. Aaron Attia composed a poetical collection called "Yashir Moshe" with an introduction wherein he moralizes about the function of speech and how it is ennobled by religious poetic compositions. He also was asked to compose appropriate verse for a pleasant Arab melody so as to elevate the melody from its secular state to the holy. The poems were accompanied with an explanation of the terms. This work was given a seal of approval by R. Abner Israel Ha-Ṣarfati. For the content of the individual poems refer to *Ms.224*.

Joseph Sasson, a book dealer of Jerusalem, had R. Abner Israel as a client as can be ascertained from *Mss. 54* and *232*. Joseph also sent regards to R. Abner in a letter that the former sent to R. Raphael Ibn Ẓur, as may be noted in *Ms.248*. The emissary Elijah b. Jacob Kasis sent his regards to R. Abner in his correspondences to the rabbis Jacob Ha-Kohen and Raphael Ibn Ẓur in *Mss. 32* and *48*.

A letter was prepared by the rabbis of Fez in the month of Tammuz 1838 introducing an emissary of Tiberias to the region of Tafilalet. Among the rabbis, Ḥayyim Abraham Ha-Ṣarfati is mentioned. On this occasion the rabbis proclaimed a malediction and excommunication on all those who would refuse to extend aid and a blessing upon those who would grant such aid. This correspondence is the subject of *Ms.240*.

R. Matitya Serero (1718-1788), who was ordained by his grandfather R. Jacob Ibn Ẓur (d.1753), had seven sons who became scholars. They were the following: R. Saul; R. Menaḥem (1744-1780); R. Joshua (d. 1814); R. Ḥayyim David, who passed away at the age of seventy-seven in 1826; R. Jacob, who died at the age of eighty-two; R. Judah, who died in a plague in 1835; and R. Naḥman. While the rabbis Saul, Joshua, Ḥayyim David, and Jacob were appointed as judges, it was Ḥayyim David Serero who was the most illustrious. Two correspondences concerning R. Ḥayyim David appear in the collection; *Ms.2* contains a letter which R. Ḥayyim David wrote to Mas'ūd Arwaḥ asking that a reconciliation should take place between the latter and R. Abraham Pariente, and in *Ms.184* R. Ḥayyim David was asked to render an Halakhic decision in a litigation.

R. Jacob Serero adjudicated a litigation for R. Abraham b. Saul ibn David Ve-Joseph, according to the text of *Ms.3*and he is noted as one of the authorities of Fez who prepared a letter introducing an emissary of Tiberias to the area of Tafilalet, in 1838, as it is recorded in *Ms.240*. Jacob Serero and Reuben Serero served as judges together with Jacob Ibn Ẓur III when they signed an edict against unfair pricing in the city of Fez. This information is found in *Ms.108*. A letter of consolation which appears in *Ms.260* was sent by the scholars Amor Abitboul and Amram Elbaz of Ṣefrou to the mourners R. Reuben Serero, R. Matitya Serero, R. Shalom Serero, and to R. Joshua Serero on the passing of R. Jacob Serero o.b.m., in the year 1855.

Joshua Serero's son, the aforementioned Reuben, served as a judge in Fez and signed a court document in 1851, together with R. Judah Elbaz and R. Yedidia Monsonyego, in a ruling concerning the erection of a structure that blocked the public throughfare. This document is found in *Ms.202*. Reuben passed on in 1856. Another Joshua Serero who was active c.1860 is noted in *Mss.32*, *44*, *48*, and *260*.

R. Saul Serero and his contemporary R. Samuel Ibn Ẓur both pleaded with R. Solomon Toledano (in separate documents but on the same page, 176a, which contains *Mss. 126* and *127*) to expedite the cause of justice in a case which still has not been adjudicated. In the year 1788, R. Elijah Monsano was disputing with his uncle Ḥayyim Monsano over property. The rabbinic court in Fez could not deal with the matter, since the authorities were related to the litigants; so the case was to be adjudicated in Meknès. However, since the parties to the dispute from Fez did not arrive in Meknès, the rabbis of Tetuán, namely R. Solomon Toledano, R. Solomon Abudarham, and the young R. Abraham Monsonyego, turned to the rabbis of Fez to adjudicate the matter. The rabbis of Fez, Samuel Ibn Ẓur and Saul Serero, still insist that the rabbis of Meknès should complete the judgement. This material is noted in *Ms.155*.

R. Judah ibn Attar II (c.1725-1812), the son of R. Obed b. Attar and the grandson of the Great Rabbi Judah ibn Attar, was a contemporary of the aforementioned R. Saul Serero. R. Judah was appointed as a judge together with R. Saul and he acceded to the position as chief judge in Fez, c.1810. Prior to their period of rabbinic leadership, during the reign of Muḥammad ibn Abdallah (1759-1790), a tranquil atmosphere had prevailed in Morocco, and Marrakesh became the center of political activity. Jews served the interests of the government in areas of diplomacy. This atmosphere was marred when Mulay al-Yazid, Abdallah's son, succeeded his father and instituted a reign of terror which lasted for two years, from 1790 to 1792. During this terrible time when the majority of the prestigious Jewish citizenry and the rabbis of Fez fled, R. Judah ibn Attar II stayed with the remaining Jews and has left us an eye witness account of the occurrences.

Anti-Jewish hatred, unknown to such an extent since the Almohad persecution in the days of Maimonides, led to the demise of a multitude of Jewish communities and the decimation of the Jewish population. Muslims who tried to save Jews were subjected to torture when Mulay al-Yazid learned of their activities. This ruler eventually died as the result of a wound and his reign was brought to an abrupt end.

A litigation which arose out of the conditions of these tumultuous times is recorded in *Ms.111*. As a result of the pillage which transpired during the days of the arch-enemy Ṣahiq Tamia Ġalul, the inheritors of a creditor known as R. Aaron Ha-Kohen o.b.m. were unable to collect certain debts that were owed to their ancestor. Eventually these notes of indebtedness were unearthed during the reign of the Sultan Mulay Suleiman, who ruled from 1792 to 1822. A judgement was rendered in favor of the descendants of the creditor. A more recent decision was cited concerning a similar case which was adjudicated in the presence of the rabbis Saul Serero, Judah ibn Attar II, and Raphael Ibn Ẓur. The last two were recorded as having been dead at the time that this document was written.

R. Raphael Aaron Monsonyego who served as a judge in Fez, and who enjoyed longevity, (d.1840), was blessed with a son, R. Yedidia Monsonyego, who was one of the most prolific authors of the nineteenth century. R. Yedidia, who also served as a judge in Fez, passed away in 1868. He once wrote a letter of reference for R. David Monsano who was in need of financial support (recorded in *Ms.6*), alluding to the fact that a scholar named Saul was the cause of David's tribulations.

R. Yedidia served as a judge together with R. Solomon Ibn Ẓur, as is apparent in *Mss. 11* and *265*, where R. Judah Berdugo asks that R. Solomon should take counsel with R. Yedidia concerning Judah's claim to an inheritance. This query was written in 1862. In *Ms.268* a plea is made to the rabbis Yedidia Monsonyego and Solomon Elijah Ibn Ẓur to render a decision on behalf of a dead orphan. R. Solomon Elijah Ibn Ẓur notes in *Ms.85* that R. Yedidia Monsonyego discusses the problem of tribulations that the corpse undergoes in the grave after death in the latter's work "Kupat Rokhlim." In *Ms.110* a letter of a Halakhic nature which was sent to R. Yedidia is recorded. R. Yedidia's son-in-law, who is anonymous, attributes a booklet of Halakhic riddles in the form of responsa to the former's authorship. It is described in *Ms.191*. The name of Yedidia Monsonyego is found in an incomplete poetic text which appears as *Ms.102*.

In the community of Meknès the Berdugo and Toledano families continued their hegemony throughout the nineteenth century. One of the outstanding figures of the Berdugo family during this period was R. Raphael Berdugo (1747-1822). In a judgement which was rendered by the rabbis of Meknès, Matitya Berdugo, Abraham Amor, and Jacob Berdugo, in 1867, they cited the authority for their decision as R. Raphael Berdugo. This judgement was sent to the rabbis of Fez in connection with the case of a man adjudged as unfit to take a second wife on the grounds that he would be unable to support two wives. All the details are recorded in *Ms.243*.

R. Joseph Elmaleh (d.1823), who was appointed chief of the rabbinic court in Salé-Rabat before 1788, corresponded with R. Raphael Berdugo on certain matters and about certain cases in Jewish law which were of mutual interest to both scholars. R. Joseph asks R. Raphael to intercede in a case involving an inheritance which was being disputed. In another matter R. Joseph states that he agreed with R. Raphael's decision. A fuller treatment of the correspondence is given in *Ms.167*.

R. Raphael Berdugo shared leadership in Meknès with R. Barukh Toledano (1738-1817), with whom he often became embroiled in vehement dispute, and with R. Petaḥiah Mordecai Berdugo (1764-1820). R. Samuel b. Waîsh was also reckoned as one of the leading scholars in Meknès at this time. In *Ms.184*, Abraham, the son of Samuel b. Waish, wrote to R. Ḥayyim David Serero of Fez asking for his learned opinion in a matter pertaining to Jewish law. Abraham states that he wrote the letter on behalf of his father who could not write at night.

There were other scholars in Meknès who deserve to be mentioned although members of neither the Berdugo nor the Toledano families. Among them are R. Benjamin Laikhraif, who is mentioned in *Ms.18* and R. Raphael Maman, whose son R. Shalom was also a scholar of note. R. Raphael Maman responded to the rabbis of Fez as to why an emissary's funds were held back for a prolonged period, in *Ms.39*. On three other occasions R. Raphael Maman wrote to R. Solomon Elijah Ibn Ẓur concerning litigations which involved a daughter's share in her father's estate (*Ms.270*), a divorcée who claimed her settlement was unjust (*Ms.271*), and a short note concerning some litigations (*Ms.273*).

R. Samuel Halevi ibn Yulee who lived in Meknès was also known to have made his residence in Tangier and to have settled in Gibraltar. In a correspondence to R. Raphael Menaḥem Ha-Ṣarfati of Fez (*Ms.152*) R. Samuel Halevi wrote, in 1841, that he was in Livorno. The letter was, however, written upon R. Samuel's arrival at Gibraltar. R. Raphael is reminded about a litigation which involves the prosperous Isaac Ben Zaqen, to which he should direct himself. R. Samuel Amar who served as a rabbi in Meknès (d.1890) and composed responsa is noted in *Ms.153*, where the writer pleads, for him to extend aid to R. Jacob Ha-Kohen who needs to raise funds for his daughter's forthcoming marriage. R. Samuel Amar had a son, R. Shalom, who excelled in the rabbinate of Meknès. R. Abraham Amar was also a rabbinic scholar in Meknès according to *Ms.243*.

One of the outstanding rabbinic scholars of the nineteenth century was R. Raphael Moses Elbaz of Ṣefrou, who died at the age of seventy-three in 1896. R. Raphael Moses was a prolific author in the fields of Halakha and Liturgy. At the age of twenty-eight he was already a judge of the rabbinic court in Ṣefrou. R. Raphael Moses Elbaz joined the rabbis Raḥamim Joseph Ġayni and Saul Elbaz in pressing a claim on behalf of some creditors of Ṣefrou who had prior claims against an estate. The rabbis Solomon Elijah Ibn Zur and Abner Israel Ha-Ṣarfati of Fez are asked to pursue the matter in the interest of justice. This correspondence appears in *Ms.57*.

The signatures of the rabbis Raphael Moses Elbaz and Judah Ha-Kohen appear in *Ms.155*, a copy of an older legal correspondence that was dated 1788. Apparently, an old dispute about property amongst members of the Monsano family, had never been concluded. It was probably brought to the attention of the rabbis Elbaz and Ha-Kohen by descendants of the disputants. This signature of R. Raphael Moses Elbaz is significantly different and appears to belong to a much earlier period in his legal career than do his signatures in *Mss.203*, *204*, *245*, *246*, and *247* which were written many years later to R. Raphael Ibn Ẓur.

There are two more correspondences by R. Raphael Moses Elbaz which contain his unique signature and which are of interest. In *Ms.268*, Raphael Moses wrote to the rabbis of Fez, Yedidia Monsonyego and Solomon Elijah Ibn Ẓur, to right an injustice that had been perpetrated against a dead orphan, since the court was the proper caretaker of the orphan and the widow. In *Ms.269*, R. Raphael Moses asks R. Solomon Elijah Ibn Ẓur to extend aid to the former's relative, Mordecai Elbaz, who is frugal, and an avid student of Torah and Zohar. In the same correspondence an enquiry is made concerning one who paid his debt late, whether an additional penalty should be paid.

In the second half of the nineteenth century a number of Moroccan rabbinic scholars left to settle in the Holy Land. One of these was R. Joseph b. Moses Arwaẓ of Rabat. He settled in Jaffa where he served as chief of the rabbinic court for the community of Sephardim. In *Ms.41* we learn that R. Joseph Arwaẓ, now serving as an emissary for the Moroccan community in the Holy Land, wrote to R. Raphael Ibn Ẓur of Fez on the eighth day of Iyar 1876, informing him of the trials and tribulations which hindered his mission. There were individuals who would prevent a successful fund raising effort from being realized he says, and the destitute of the Moroccan Jewish communities in the Holy Land suffer as a result. R. Joseph Arwaẓ's signature is accompanied by a seal which contains writing composed in three languages, namely, Hebrew and Arabic, with the Roman initials J.A. inscribed in a wreath at the Seal's center.

At the age of thirty R. David Ben Simeon left Rabat in 1854 for Jerusalem, where he helped to establish an organized community for Sephardim of the west (Morocco). He was also instrumental in the building of synagogues and schools. He served as chief of the rabbinic court from 1860 to 1880 when he passed away. His son, R. Raphael Aaron Ben Simeon, became a leader of the community after his father's demise and was sent in 1887 and again in 1891 as an emissary to Morocco.

R. Raphael Ḥayyim Moses Benaim left Tetuán for the Holy Land in 1860 and he settled in Tiberias. After he was appointed a member of the rabbinic court he was sent to Morocco as an emissary. When he arrived in Gibraltar he was appointed to serve as the rabbi of that community.

Other Moroccan scholars made their way to Tiberias. R. Raphael Maman (c.1810-1880) left for the Holy Land at a young age and aspired to rabbinic positions, serving in Tiberias and then in Safed. R. Solomon b. R. Jacob Toledano was born in Meknès in 1835 and he travelled to Tiberias in 1858, where he was subsequently appointed to the rabbinic court as a judge. He was sent afterwards as an emissary to Morocco. He was destined never to return to the Holy Land since he passed on in the community of Taza in 1877. R. Raphael Ohana was also born in Meknès, in 1850, and he made his way to Tiberias in 1865. Later he served as an emissary on several occasions. He passed on in 1902 and was buried in Safed.

Many scholars and saints were desirous of settling in the Holy Land, but the function that they fulfilled for the masses of Jews who needed them often prevented them from ever reaching the promised land. This function was akin to the role that the "Rebbe," the Ḥasidic master fulfilled for eastern European Jewry. The famous Moroccan mystic R. Jacob Abi-Ḥasira of Tafilalet was such an individual, whose renown as a holy man reached far and wide. He commingled moments of solitude with caring for the needs of the destitute, which is reminiscent of R. Israel Ba'al Shem Tob̄, the founder of Hasidism. When R. Jacob attempted to make his way to the Holy Land the Jews who needed him placed obstacles in his path. He was only able to get as far as Egypt, where he passed away on the twentieth day of Tevet 1880 at the age of seventy-two years. The day of his death has been celebrated ever since as "Hilula," a holy celebration.

The influence of Europe and the United States

The efforts of France and Spain to extend their spheres of influence into North Africa were met with opposition from the sultans of Morocco at the beginning of the nineteenth century. Mulay Suleiman, who ruled from 1792 to 1822, was under the illusion that by significantly reducing trade with Europe he could stop the foreign powers' attempts to dominate Morocco. Since Jews were actively involved in foreign trade they were suspected of being in the service of the European powers and as a result repressive measures were applied against them. Jews who were previously granted special privileges to dwell in prosperous communities were now obliged to live in ghettos known as 'mellahs.' While Tunisian and Algerian Jewry were gaining more rights, the Jews of Morocco were obliged to conform to all the disabilities of the pact of Omar which relegated them to second class citizenship.

The juridical disabilities that were enforced during the early nineteenth century encouraged pogroms against Moroccan Jewry. Epidemics that occurred in 1799 and 1818 also took their toll. It was not surprising that many individuals who could leave for the Holy Land did so not only because of their fervent love for their ancestral homeland, but also because local conditions in Morocco were most undesirable compared to the more liberal atmosphere that prevailed in other countries where Jews took up domicile. Moroccan Jews migrated to the Americas and some returned to Spain and Portugal to establish communities for the first time since the expulsion of 1492. Subsequent rulers of Morocco still turned to their Jewish subjects to render service in the fields of diplomacy and commerce. This policy was pursued during the reigns of Mulay Abd al-Raḥman (1822-1859), Mulay Muḥammad ben Abd al-Raḥman (1859-1873), and Mulay al-Ḥasan (1873-1894).

European Jewry began to look southward to the plight of their fellow religionists after the middle of the nineteenth century. The appalling conditions under which the Jews lived in Morocco at this time caught the attention of the famous English Jew of Sephardic extraction, Sir Moses Montefiore, whose philanthropy was legendary. At an advanced age he journeyed to Morocco to see if he could ameliorate the conditions of his co-religionists, and as a result of his efforts the Sultan Mulay Muḥammad issued a proclamation called Dahir, on the fifteenth of February 1864, which was to ensure equality before the law to all his subjects. It was, alas, shortlived.

Included among the manuscripts in the "Yalkut Roĩim," volume compiled by Ariel Bension, is a printed issue of the Hebrew publication "Ha-Libanon" (Vol. 3, No. 9, pp. 129-144), dated the eleventh of Iyar 1866 which contains an article reporting the arrival of Sir Moses Montefiore in the Holy Land, on the eleventh of Nisan 1866.

On that occasion he planned a Jewish quarter for domicile outside the Old City of Jerusalem. The article appears in *Pr.133 5* (Pr.-printed rather than manuscript document.)

Occasionally other Jewish organizations and prestigious individuals took a cue from the precedent established by Sir Moses Montefiore and tried to intervene with the ruling authority of Morocco on behalf of the Jews. The Anglo-Jewish Association of London tried to have the Sultan issue a new Dahir about ten years after the first was issued and revoked. Among the concerned individuals who attempted to improve the condition of Jews of the Maghreb were Dr. Albert Cohen in 1860, Ḥayyim Gedaliah in 1864 and again in 1888, and Mr. Marcus of Boston, Massachusetts in the United States, in 1885. The organization that played a decisive role with an eye to the future development of Moroccan Jewry was the Paris based Alliance Israelite Universelle, known in Hebrew as "Kol Yisrael Ḥaverim." The Alliance was also in the vanguard of those who labored for the improvement of the legal status of the Jews in the Maghreb.

The Alliance organized a network of educational institutions in Morocco. The first school was opened in Tetuán in 1862. The schools served to bridge the cultural gap by giving the young the wherewithal to meet the challenges of modern western society. The schools also served as focal points whereby many other services were made available to local Jewish communities. The Alliance schools were not welcomed by all quarters of the rabbinic leadership. Some rabbis regarded the introduction of secular studies as an effort that would oblige students to neglect their religious studies.

The proceedings of the sixth meeting of Kol Israel Ḥaverim appears in printed form in *Pr.73.5*. Among the participants are the following: the aforementioned Dr. Albert Cohen, Rabbi Artoum of the London Sephardic community, the Chief Rabbi of France, and the official Nissim Shamama of Tunis, amongst others. A review of the year's previous activities, a financial report, and a record of the number of members is given. America begins to play a role and the B'nai Brith Organization is mentioned. It is reported that Serbian Jews desire to colonize the Holy Land but funds are not available for this purpose.

In *Ms.206* there appears a correspondence from Ish Ẓa'ir of Fez to the Alliance Israelite Universelle in Paris. The writer commends the organization for undertaking the publishing of the responsa of R. Asher b. Yeḥiel. Ish Ẓa'ir reports that internal Jewish communal politics in Fez are holding back the appointment of the two delegates who are to come to Paris. He also requests the appointment of a resident representative for Jewish matters to be stationed in Fez. In his opinion this would be an effective way of improving the condition of the Jews. The writer states that the community of Fez will be unable to raise funds for Jewish causes as did Gibraltar, because economic conditions have deteriorated considerably.

Morocco became a French Protectorate in 1912. Subsequently, the state of affairs which had prevailed between the Muslims and Jews for twelve centuries was upset by the arrival of the French. They became a third force, and drove a wedge between Jews and Moslems. Since the source material of the Bension collection concludes at the end of the nineteenth century I shall conclude the historical sketch at this point.

The purpose of this introduction has been to give the reader an historical perspective for the Bension manuscripts and texts. The Sephardic character of the collection has also been elaborated upon. Space was devoted to the political events in Morocco because a significant part of this collection deals with life in Morocco from the seventeenth century until the nineteenth century. Since a dearth of source material is available for this historical period the collection is all the more valuable. It will be noted that Moroccan Jewry played a dynamic role in the preservation and perpetuation of Sephardic culture in the four hundred and fifty years following the Spanish expulsion. The cultural values of the native Jewish population of Morocco which were conserved in an unbroken chain of tradition, dating back to the days of the destruction of the Temple, were given vigorous expression when they were amalgamated with the Spanish Jewish heritage of the pre-expulsion period. This process of conservation of cultures was accomplished under very trying political and social conditions. The next section will deal with the source material of the manuscripts and texts in detail.

The manuscripts in the Yalkut Roîîm volume

The two hundred and seventy-five manuscript documents and correspondences described in this section were originally collated in the volume designated "Yalkut Roîîm." The compiler, who was in all likelihood Dr. Ariel Bension, had inscribed in ink at the top of the first page of this collection "Yalkut Roîîm, part III." The volume contained 356 pages. We are confronted with an unresolved mystery as to what has happened to the other two bound volumes of manuscripts.

The title "Yalkut Roîîm" means "Collected writings of the shepherds." The term "shepherds" refers to the rabbinic leaders of Moroccan Jewry. The manuscripts did not appear in the book in any organized sequence. In fact, while the pages were numbered in ink, often half of one page would appear several pages later because of the way the manuscripts were sewn into the text. Blank pages were also numbered.

In order to serve the needs of scholars and interested students, and to aid in the method of reproduction, each separate manuscript has been removed from the original volume and placed in an individual case. It is hoped that this method of handling the manuscripts will aid in their preservation. Those desiring to use copies of the manuscripts described in this section for their research should prefix the manuscript number for which they are asking with the letters B.C.Y.R.Ms. The symbol B means Bension, C means Cohen, Y means Yalkut, R. means Roîîm, and Ms. means manuscript. Printed documents are given the prefix "Pr." rather than "Ms."

The page numbers referred to in this section are based on the pagination found in the volume wherein the documents were originally bound.

Ms. 1
Pp. 1a, 8a, 8b, 7a, and 7b

A rhymed letter of adulation

This is a manuscript copy of a letter of praise written in honor of an unnamed scholar who was one of the leading judges of his age. The pages are not given in proper sequence, as was explained in the introduction to this section. It appears on pages 1a, 8a, 8b, 7a, and 7b in its proper sequence. The copyist who transcribed it also transcribed *Ms.2* which is found on pages 9a and 9b.

Ms. 2
P. 9a and b

A copy of a correspondence from R. Ḥayyim David Serero to R. Mas'ūd Arwaḥ

The first three stanzas of the epistle commence with the first two letters 'Mem' and 'Samekh' of the name Mas'ūd, according to the Hebrew spelling, and they conclude with the last three letters 'Ayin,' 'Vav,' and 'Daleth,' which comprise the last three letters of the name Mas'ūd. In the last paragraph of page 9a, R. Abraham Pariente is mentioned. The writer, R. Ḥayyim David Serero, attempts to bring a reconciliation between R. Abraham and R. Mas'ūd.

Ms. 3
Pp. 4a—6b

A letter of reconciliation called Divrei Shalom Ve-emet

This letter of reconciliation is written to R. Solomon Elijah Ibn Ẓur, the son of the Torah scholar R. Jacob Ibn Ẓur, by Abraham the son of Saul Ibn David Ve-Joseph. The writer intends to set the record straight as well as to achieve a reconciliation. That is why he calls the letter Divrei Shalom Ve-Emet, which means "Words of Peace and Truth."

Abraham claims that he was falsely accused by R. Solomon Elijah. He appeals to the latter not to believe these false accusations: "R. Samuel (R. Solomon's sister's husband) informed me of that which you accuse me, namely, that I took letters of correspondence that belonged to you and your grandfather, Solomon, of blessed memory, which would destroy a long friendship." Abraham's son is ill. He asks R. Solomon to recite prayers in behalf of his son; since R. Solomon is descended from such an illustrious line of rabbis his prayers will have especial merit.

Abraham does not hesitate to exhort R. Solomon to improve his own character. On page 5a, the writer states that R. Solomon Ibn Ẓur is married to his sister. He also prefaces a poem of friendship, "Shir Yedidut," that he includes in the letter in honor of R. Solomon. The writer gives his full name as Abraham bar Saul David Ve-Joseph, in acrostic form. The authorship of the poem he attributes, however, to R. Raphael Jacob Ibn Simḥon, who was still living when this letter was composed. The poem consists of twenty-two lines. The letter was written in the month of Iyar 1846 (see page 6a). The writer states that his epistle was not concluded for quite a while after it was commenced since his son had already recovered from his illness before the letter was sent. In the last part of the letter the writer discusses a litigation in which he was involved with one called Abraham Ibn Zaqen. It was finally decided by R. Jacob Serero. R. Jacob Ibn Ẓur, the father of R. Solomon, refused to judge the case on an earlier occasion because he was angry with the writer.

Ms. 4
Pp. 10a—15b

A ms. copy of a collection of letters called Kitvei Ha-Qodesh pertaining to Ḥalukah

The collection of letters is called Kitvei Ha-Qodesh because all the letters relate to the needy communities in the Holy Land. The first letter of this collection commences with a short *excursus* on Jewish history leading to the religio-historical importance of Tiberias. The one who is mentioned in connection with fund raising for the great academy of the Jewish community of Tiberias, which is in dire need of funds, is the Ḥaham Kollel R. Moses Pinto, the son of Isaac, o.b.m., who is descended from R. Jacob Pinto. The latter composed the work "Miqdash Melekh." The date of this epistle is given as Shevat 1828. The debt had grown to over 300,000 gerush. The conditions were exacerbated by plagues of locusts.

The second letter in this collection was written to the members of the community of Tetuán. They are informed that the great academy of Tiberias is maintaining the traditions that were set in Tiberias from the days of the Talmudic masters. Many misfortunes have created a great need for money for food and clothing and to pay debts including the interest that had accrued. The emissary who was sent was called R. Abraham ha-Cohen Duwayk. The date of this epistle is given as 1834 and it was written at Tiberias.

The third letter is to the scholars and communal officials of Fez, from Safed, the location of the tomb of R. Simeon bar Yoḥai. Money is needed to repair the holy synagogues, in particular, the synagogue called "Ba'al Teshuvot," where repentant sinners gain forgiveness. The structure is falling into great disrepair. R. Ḥayyim Ashkenazi is sent to the diaspora to raise the funds necessary for the rehabilitation project. The latter is a descendant of the author of "Pitḥei Levahoh" and "Ḥiddushei Shnei ham-Meôrôt." The leaders of Fez are asked to accompany the aforementioned emissary from house to house and that one gerush be donated for every member of the household to this special reconstruction fund. This letter is dated in the month of Elul 1835, and it is signed by the rabbis of Safed.

The fourth letter is from the Sephardic communities of Jerusalem for the community of Ashkenazim Midrash Perushim, consisting of three houses of prayer and study. The misfortunes that have befallen the community include natural calamities such as an earthquake in Galilee as well as physical attacks from marauders. Great losses have been incurred both in money and in people, particularly by the Ashkenazim. The scholar R. David Devash, who was a Sephardi and a Jerusalemite, has been sent as an emissary. The communities are asked to extend him hospitality and to help him in his fund raising endeavor. The letter is signed for the directors of the Kollel Ashkenazim Midrash Perushim in the month of Tammuz 1842, at Jerusalem, by Nathan the son of R. Menaḥem Mendel of blessed memory.

The fifth and final letter by this copyist is from the rabbis of Safed to Shalom b. Malka asking him to receive the emissary R. Simeon Ha-Kohen and to extend to him all necessary aid and financial support in his endeavor to collect money to help rebuild the city of Safed.

Ms. 5
P. 16a

A ms. copy of a letter sent by R. Raphael Jacob Ibn Simḥon on behalf of R. Samuel Koskaso

The first four lines of this letter contain a poem commencing with the acrostic which spells out the name Raphael. It was written by R. Raphael Jacob Ibn Simḥon on behalf of R. Samuel Koskaso who has fallen upon hard times and requires financial aid. This letter of reference is written to the Jewish communities to help R. Samuel pay his debts. The epistle concludes with the prayer that the Messiah should come and that he shall remove the burden of the tax collectors.

Ms. 6
P. 16b

A ms. copy of a letter written by R. Yedidia Monsonyego on behalf of R. David Monsano

R. Yedidia Monsonyego writes this letter extolling the virtues of R. David Monsano. The writer compares R. David to the biblical David who suffered tribulations because of Saul's enmity. R. Yedidia notes that R. David suffered economic adversity because "two kings cannot wear one crown." R. David Monsano was forced to seek his fortunes elsewhere because of Saul. The writer asks that financial support should be extended to R. David Monsano.

Ms. 7
P. 18a

A correspondence with a poetic introduction from Aaron Ḥasin to R. Solomon Ibn Ẓur

This epistle, which was sent from Meknès to Fez by Aaron Ḥasin, commences with ten lines of verse beginning with the Hebrew word "Eḥad"—the singular one, and concludes with other forms of the word "Eḥad." It was composed in praise of R. Solomon Ibn Ẓur, to whom this correspondence was sent. The date of this epistle is the fifth of Kislev 1860. The writer informs R. Solomon at length of his weakened physical and mental condition and of his inability to visit him but he is filled with desire to correspond with him. Aaron adds his signature and begins each paragraph with a letter of his name thereby forming an acrostic spelling Aaron.

Ms. 8
P. 19a

A plea for a legal decision to be rendered speedily because one of the litigants is leaving for the Holy Land

Elijah ben Haroush writes to R. Solomon Ibn Ẓur of Fez, asking him to render a speedy decision in a pending litigation which will otherwise involve a loss of money. One of the litigants is leaving shortly for the Holy Land.

Ms. 9
P. 20a

The original emissary became ill and another is appointed in his stead. A campaign to extend aid to him is organized

The emissary, R. Abraham Ḥayyim Pinto of the Jerusalem Kollelim, sends word from Rabat that he is bedridden and unable to complete his mission to collect funds, so he is appointing R. Barukh Pinto in his stead. He is so ill that he should have aborted his plans while he was still at Tangier. A campaign is now organized by the rabbis at Fez to aid R. Barukh in his mission. The community of Debdou is also advised to follow the practice of Fez in this matter while the same applies to outlying villages. Even if any emissaries should appear from the Kollelim of Hebron, the emissary from Jerusalem shall take precedence. This letter was composed at Fez, in the month of Kislev 1857.

Ms. 10
P. 21a

An Halakhic query concerning a sale with an option to repurchase, but the inheritors are not stipulated

This query was sent to R. Elijah Solomon Ibn Ẓur, of Fez, by R. Samuel Ibn Elbaz of Ṣefrou. A house was sold by David ben Elijah Moses Ha-Kohen, his mother, and his brother, to Azuz Ha-Kohen with a provision that the vendors could repurchase the house at the same price, in the fifth year from the time of purchase. The aforementioned vendors, excluding David, are deceased and the agreement did not include their inheritors. R.J. Caro states this ruling in Hoshen Mishpat 209:6; namely, that the descendants shall also be included in the terms of the transaction. The Maharshakh, Part II, No. 32 and Beit Judah, Ḥoshen Mishpat, No. 14, state that at the time of the original transaction the term "to me and to my inheritors," should have been included. R. Samuel Elbaz asks R. Elijah Solomon Ibn Ẓur to contact Azuz, who now resides in the latter's jurisdiction, to resolve the matter, perhaps by reaching a compromise.

Ms. 11
P. 22a

An Halakhic query concerning an attempt to remove a conditional element in a deed of land given as a gift

Land was given by R. Judah Birdugo's grandfather to his father with a condition stipulating that it should not be used as a payment for a claim on a marriage contract, nor should it be sold or given as a pledge. It should always remain as a family inheritance so that future generations might benefit from the land's produce. Judah has left Morocco and settled in Jerusalem, but while on a visit to Meknès, his brother granted him his portion of land as a gift according to law. He wants to sell it because he really needs the money and since he resides in the Holy Land he wants to assure the purchaser that no claim will arise against the sale by any of the other relatives.

R. Judah argues that the original contract does not actually contain the aforementioned stipulation, even though it might be claimed that such a stipulation is indeed implied. He feels this is particularly the case, as the proper legal form of stipulating a condition, a "T'nai Kafull," a double stipulation [an agreement stating both alternatives and their eventual consequences], is not given. This is not a case of actual claimants as the present situation stands. Therefore, R. Judah turns to R. Solomon Ibn Ẓur of Fez to render a decision on the matter. R. Judah reminds R. Solomon that R. Yedidia Monsonyego is also available to R. Solomon for consultation. Incidentally, Judah offers books on Responsa literature to R. Solomon at a fair price. He also informs R. Solomon that a speedy response would be appreciated since he is obliged to return to the Middle East. [This letter was sent prior to another letter on the same subject which was sent in 1862. The second letter appeared in the original volume on page 334a, *Ms.265*.]

Ms. 12
P. 23a

An Halakhic query asks whether a woman subject to a levirate marriage, whose prospective husband is presently a minor, can be sustained by the dowry which is possessed by a third party

R. Matitya Ibn Zikhri sends a legal query to R. Solomon Elijah Ibn Ẓur concerning a woman subject to a levirate marriage but whose prospective husband is presently a minor. Can she be sustained from the dowry that her husband never took and that is now found in the possession of a third party? This would be in accord with Moram [Rema] in his amendment to Even ha-Ezer, chapter 160:3. Or can she not use the dowry for her support until the levirate marriage comes into force when the prospective husband becomes of age? This view would be in accord with R. Joseph Caro. R. Matitya states that he has heard that R. Solomon agrees with the former authority and wants to know if such is indeed the case? He asks for a speedy reply.

Ms. 13
P. 24a

An Halakhic query asking if one partner marries must the other refrain from business transactions. Also an enactment concerning ritual slaughter

This letter was addressed to R. Solomon Ibn Ẓur of Fez by R. Raḥamîm Joseph Ġayni of Ṣefrou in the year 1871. The date is given in two different ways in this epistle. After two introductory paragraphs the writer poses a legal question and supplies an answer himself in the third paragraph. The question is posed in the following manner: "If one of two partners weds, must the other partner refrain from transacting any business during the traditional seven days of post-nuptial festivities, just as one would be obliged to in the case of seven days of mourning? The work "Pri Ḥodosh Matei Aharon" is cited in the answer given, which states that if the younger of two brothers who are business partners marries, the older brother may transact the business, only the bridegroom must refrain.

In the last paragraph of the letter an enactment is presented concerning the ritual slaughter of animals and fowl. The main points of the enactment are as follows:

"(1) Because people make light of the examination of the knife of the ritual slaughterer and of the animal's lungs, henceforth at least two people shall examine the knife and at least two people shall examine the lungs.

(2) No ritual slaughter of animals or fowl shall commence before the hour when the morning services are completed, since those who are in the service of the abattoir use this as an excuse not to attend morning services.

(3) Any ritual slaughterer violating the aforementioned enactments by slaughtering or examining lungs unaccompanied by another individual will mean this animal being declared unfit for human consumption. These rules do not apply to the slaughter of fowl which the ritual slaughterer can be trusted to do himself."

These enactments were made in Ṣefrou, in the month of Iyar 1847. The undersigned were R. Amor Abitboul o.b.m. and R. Amram Elbaz o.b.m. This letter is more informative in nature than the usual type of inquiry. The writer supplied documents that were apparently of interest to R. Solomon Ibn Ẓur. Another document that was requested by R. Solomon could not be found by the writer. The latter states that he will not eat anything but fowl, even on the Sabbath, unless the aforementioned enactments are fulfilled and he is present during their implementation. He states that he will not buy meat from the butchers on any occasion. The writer gives his signature as Raḥamim Joseph Ġayni.

Ms. 14
P. 25a

A court action legalizing the transfer of land from a non-Jew to a Jew for the welfare of the Jewish community

Unscrupulous people are taking advantage of the poor by building shops on land that belongs to the non-Jew Al-Ḥawaja. This individual places all the purchasers of the shops at his mercy by ignoring all claims that they bring against him. He acts in this manner because he desires to destroy all those structures which house these shops. Sometimes he dismantles them and then claims the material as his own. The shopkeepers can do nothing to stop him and they suffer a complete loss.

This document depicts a court action legalizing the transfer of the land to R. Joseph Almosnino who has acquired it from the aforementioned Al-Ḥawaja. R. Joseph will sell the shops to the vendors at a fair price. Whoever refuses to abide by this arrangement loses the shops which revert back to Joseph. There is also the danger of a precedent being established whereby other unscrupulous people will appropriate land, as Al-Ḥawaja did, unless it is bought from him. It is noted in an addendum to this document that the chaotic political situation justifies this action being taken. This document was composed in the month of Nisan 1757 at Fez. The three rabbis who served as the tribunal were Saul Ibn Danan, Raphael Oḅed Ibn Ẓur, and Elijah Ha-Ṣarfati.

Ms. 15
Pp. 27a and 26b

An Halakhic exposition on succession to rabbinic leadership when a leader is temporarily incapacitated

Rabbi S. Atazi acceded to the role of rabbinic leader when his predecessor was temporarily incapacitated. The latter is now able to resume his duties and Rabbi S. Atazi's future role is in question. The author of this legal opinion disagrees with the decision of the authority to whom he writes who had argued that a compromise should be achieved similar to that which prevailed at the accession of R. Eleazar b. Azariah and R. Gamliel. He had based his decision on the version of the Talmud in the Propes edition, which requires that the honor of the second authority should be taken into consideration.

The author of *this* expositon refers to the decision rendered by R. Joseph Caro in his codes, Oraḥ Ḥayyim, 153:22, and Ḥoshen Mishpat, 149. "If one lost the right to perform a ritual, the honor for which he paid in the past, because he is poverty-stricken, that right shall be returned to him when he again has the money to pay for the honor. The one who had the honor in the interim loses it completely." R. Caro's view is in accord with the Mordecai, Pereq Ḥezqat, No. 533. It is also in contradiction to the Propes edition of the Talmud.

A further proof favoring the first appointed rabbi over the second is the case of the High Priest when temporarily disqualified. When the condition which disqualified him passes he is restored to his previous position to the detriment of the one who replaced him. A further distinction is made by the author: when a monetary loss is incurred, such as in this situation, Rabbi S. Atazi should not even be considered. Whereas, in the performance of rituals, as was cited by R. Caro, no loss of money is involved.

Ms. 16
P. 28a

A certificate for one to serve as a ritual slaughterer, given at Fez, for a resident of Debdou

A beautifully hand-written certificate, issued in Fez, authorizes Yamin Kohen ben Isḥak of Debdou to serve as a Ritual Slaughterer. The candidate must agree to review all the laws thereto pertaining according to the ruling of Maharil and Maharash. The reason for issuing such a certification is given in the text as follows: "Villagers who required the services of a Ritual Slaughterer would ask a sojourner if he was well-versed in the laws pertaining to Ritual Slaughterer whereupon he would answer in the affirmative, even if he was totally ignorant and he would then be guilty of providing the Jewish community with prohibited food. In order to avoid this situation, the scholars of an earlier period made a requirement that a Ritual Slaughterer was to present a document from them attesting to his ability and knowledge."

Ms. 17
P. 29a

A Jewess collects a debt from the niece of King Mulay Rashid which results in complexities

The wife of David ben Tata engaged in commercial dealings with some non-Jews. One of them was known as Musa ben Abd Laziz against whom she had a claim in the non-Jewish court. She has also acquired the right to collect a debt from Lala Sharif, the niece of the King Mulay Rashid. Lala had sold the wife of David half of an upper floor in exchange for the amount of the loan that she owed. The non-Jew, Musa, bought the other half of the upper floor.

A Jew known as Saadya Lahakhusin ben R. Moses purchased the half that belonged to the non-Jew. The undersigned rabbinic tribunal comprising the rabbis Judah ibn Attar, Samuel Ha-Ṣarfati, and Abraḥam ibn Danan gave assent and support to Saadya's legal right so that no one should register a claim against it. Even if the owners of the land raised sufficient funds within the year from the date of this decree, they should not disturb the purchaser, nor should he be obliged to return the land to them. This document was composed at Fez, the seventeenth day of Tammuz 1707.

Ms. 18
P. 30a and b

A letter of adulation written in honor of R. Elijah Ha-Ṣarfati and his son Jacob

This epistle was written in honor of R. Elijah Ha-Ṣarfati and his son R. Jacob. A poem in honor of the former appears on page 30a and a second poem in honor of the latter appears on page 30b. R. Solomon Abitbol is mentioned as the one who was to deliver the letter. R. Benjamin LaKhraif, who was alive on this occasion, is also mentioned. Some remarks attributed to R. Ḥayyim Alfandari, from the introduction of his commentary to Genesis, are noted. An additional text pasted on to page 30b contains the text of an amulet which was intended to protect one from plagues.

Ms. 19
P. 31a and b

The rabbis at Meknès intervene in a judgement rendered by the rabbis at Fez

R. Jacob Ibn Ẓur rendered a decision in a certain matter.

R. Samuel Labaz is also involved in this litigation. One of the disputants has refused to abide by the judgements of R. Jacob Ibn Ẓur and the matter has been brought to the attention of the rabbis of Meknès, namely, R. Ḥayyim Toledano, R. Jacob Toledano, and R. Mordecai Berdugo, all of whom signed this document. They speak with the highest regard for the authority of R. Jacob Ibn Ẓur and are chagrined at the disregard and disrespect that is being shown to him. The attackers who demean R. Jacob Ibn Ẓur falsify the judgement and produce weak testimony in their defense, they say. All this time R. Samuel has remained silent according to his pious nature when he might have been able to illumine the matter with his testimony. R. Samuel, by his silence, has given approval to those attacking R.

Jacob Ibn Ẓur. R. Samuel is exhorted not to remain silent. The rabbis of Meknès state that they will assemble all the arguments pro and con including the ruling of R. Jacob Ibn Ẓur and they will send them to all the rabbinic scholars so that the matter will finally be decided by the majority. They assert that it is a breach of judicial procedure that litigants should interfere in the decision-making process of the rabbinic courts. If R. Samuel feels that his wrath justifies his silence then steps should be taken to appease him so that he will report the necessary information. If, however, he does not accept the counsel of the rabbis of Meknès then they will be forced to exercise all measures to uphold the honor of R. Jacob Ibn Ẓur.

Ms. 20
P. 32a—33b

A controversy concerning a Torah scroll

On the Intermediate days of the Passover Festival, in the year 1734, the author of this text accompanied Yaabeẓ [Rabbi Jacob ibn Ẓur] to the synagogue of R.Y. Busidan to collect a Torah scroll which was to be taken to Yaabeẓ's synagogue from which it had been borrowed. It belonged to R. Ḥayyim ibn Magirẓ who was also of the party with a whole assembly of people. When they entered the synagogue, they opened the ark, and asked the incumbent reader, R. Ḥayyim Al-Atabi, to point out the right Torah. Al-Atabi claimed he didn't know which it was, a most improbable state of affairs. Two hours later the sexton was brought and he also claimed not to be able to identify the scroll. The man who prepared the parchments said that he wasn't able to identify it either, so another Torah was given in its place.

Subsequently R. Ḥayyim [Al-Atabi] wrote to his brother Mîmun who normally shared his duties as reader in the synagogue but who was on a visit to Meknès at the time, whereupon Mîmun began to spread slander against Yaabeẓ. Yaabeẓ, he said, had waited for him, Mîmun, to leave for Meknès before claiming that the scroll should be returned to his synagogue, and Yaabeẓ had forced Ḥayyim ibn Magirẓ into returning the scroll against his will. All these damaging statements were made against Yaabeẓ but none of the scholars or communal leaders reprimanded R. Mîmun.

In response to the aforementioned attacks, on the eighth of Iyar, witnesses testified that for more than a year Ḥayyim ibn Magirẓ had wanted to return the scroll to Yaabeẓ's synagogue. He had procrastinated, however, because he wanted to be accompanied by R. Moses ibn Maman so that he could save face. But R. Moses was always preoccupied and so the Torah had not been returned until the present. Upon R. Mimun's return from Meknès he begged forgiveness from Yaabeẓ for treating the latter unjustly. Yaabez was magnanimous in accepting the apology, which was in accord with his forgiving nature, and Ḥayyim ibn Magirẓ returned to pray at Yaabeẓ's synagogue which had been the place of prayer of his forebears.

[The story behind the controversy over the Torah, as gleaned from the manuscripts, is an interesting one. Ḥayyim's grandfather, Hanun ben Magirẓ, had prayed with Yaabeẓ from the time that he moved his residence from Al-Arsa to the Mellah until his death, at which time Yaabez eulogized him as he had Ḥanun's wife at her passing. Ḥanun's son, Mas'ūd, also frequented Yaabeẓ's synagogue until his death and Ḥayyim himself had celebrated his Bar Mitzva there. Only after Yaabeẓ had left Fez and established his residence at Meknès, had Hayyim moved to the synagogue of R. Mîmun Al-Atabi. Eventually Yaabez returned to take up residence again in Fez and because there had been a period of misfortune and famine during his absence Yaabeẓ was not surprised to find Ḥayyim no longer among the worshippers; many had died or moved away. Then one day Yaabez noted Ḥayyim's name among the parties involved in a litigation. He inquired if Ḥanun was his grandfather. When this fact was established, he convinced Ḥayyim he should return to the synagogue of his forefathers according to the legal tradition. The Torah Scroll was to be returned as well.

So eventually R. Mîmun was ordered to return all the vestments belonging to Ḥayyim's Torah.]

This judgement was rendered in the tenth of Iyar 1734.

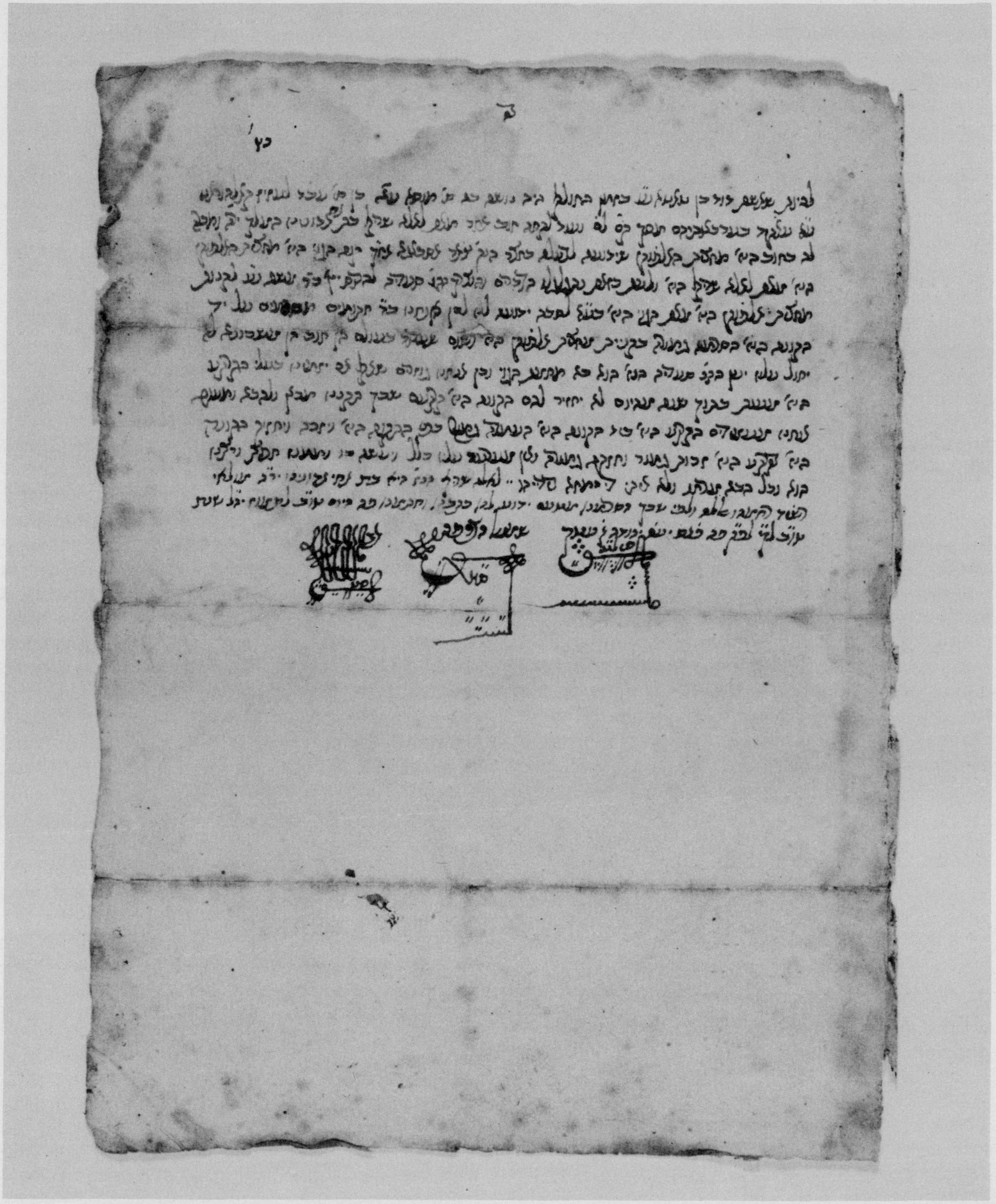

Ms. 17
A document concerning a debt owed by the niece of King Mulay Rashid, written in Fez in 1707

Ms. 21
P. 34a

A letter of consolation to Rabbi Jacob Ibn Ẓur on the death of his son Samuel

This letter was written to Rabbi Jacob Ibn Ẓur consoling him, his wife, and his daughter-in-law on the untimely passing of his son Samuel, may his memory be a blessing. The letter was signed by Samuel ibn Adhan.

Ms. 22
P. 35b

A correspondence from R. Jacob Ibn Malka to Rabbi Jacob Ibn Ẓur

R. Jacob ibn Malka informs R. Jacob Ibn Ẓur that in spite of his many duties and the exigencies of time he has been able to prepare certain documents which have been signed by rabbinic authorities, and he sends them through a messenger. He apologizes for being tardy in his response to an earlier letter by R. Jacob Ibn Ẓur. However, two weeks passed before R. Jacob Ibn Malka received R. Jacob Ibn Ẓur's letter. The former states that his function as teacher to many students prevents him from devoting more time to the transcribing of documents.

Ms. 23
P. 36a

A scholar demands that certain legal actions in a litigation should be taken before a final judgement is rendered

R. Ḥasdai Almosnino is involved in a case where the litigants are R. Joseph Ha-Ṣarfati and his uncle. The uncle, R. Joseph, who previously resided in R. Ḥasdai's community Tetuán is now living in Fez. R. Joseph had also abandoned the members of his family who now suffer privation. The rabbis of Fez and Meknès have brought the matter under litigation to a settlement by having the uncle pay R. Joseph a stipulated sum of money. R. Ḥasdai notes that he had more evidence that was pertinent to the case but since the matter has already been resolved by the rabbis of Fez and Meknès he will not forward it. However, R. Ḥasdai feels that the case will not be closed until the uncle (who is referred to as "the scholar") pays an additional sum of fifty uqiot of silver, which would cover the amount due to R. Ḥasdai for the services that he rendered in the case heretofore. This demand is just since the other rabbis have already received payment for their services rendered and Joseph is too poverty-stricken to make the payment. The rabbis are asked to relay this information to the uncle. R. Ḥasdai asks that in order to insure that the settlement is a lasting one, the uncle should pardon R. Joseph for any indiscretion that might have arisen during the litigation. The author states that he is in mourning.

Ms. 24
P. 37a

A letter of consolation to Abraham Monsano

The brother of Abraham Monsano has passed away. The author of this letter of consolation to Abraham Monsano is Abraham Alfasi. After an introductory paragraph, the author writes four paragraphs. The first paragraph consoles the wife, the second the children, the third the relatives, and the fourth the whole house of Israel.

Ms. 25
P. 38a and b

A case involving the expiration of tenancy in a domicile and property claims

The following case was adjudicated by R. Jacob Ibn Ẓur on the twenty-fourth day of Elul 1747. Jacob ben Amozag, who was abroad, is at present a tenant of Menaḥem ben Amozag. The period of occupancy of the suite had run its course, when Jacob claimed that he still owned a percentage of two courtyards while another portion of his total claim had been sold against his will by his brother Joseph. He said that even if proof could be brought that Joseph had acted for him legally and with his knowledge, still only a portion thereof had been sold. Therefore, Jacob insisted that he still had a percentage in the courtyard that was not sold. Subsequently, Jacob admitted that he was paid additional money by Menaḥem so that he really had no claim to a percentage in either the longer or the smaller courtyard as he had previously asserted.

In the outcome, Menaḥem waives the monetary claim for the apartment that was owed to him by Jacob according to the terms of the lease for one year of domicile. Menaḥem also waives any claims for back rent that was due to him from Jacob after the year expired, until the present. Menaḥem further renews the lease for Jacob for two more years, rent-free, provided that Jacob promises never to make further claims on properties which are no longer his.

Ms. 26
P. 39a

The rabbis of Meknès wish to apply a ban against another community for money that should be forthcoming

R. Solomon ben Moses Maman wrote this letter in Judaeo-Arabic and Hebrew to the Rabbis Jacob Ibn Ẓur and Moses Birdugo, at Meknès, concerning the emissary R. David Gabbai, of blessed memory. The aforementioned rabbis of Meknès claim that R. David left money with somebody in the other community and if the money is not forthcoming then they will declare a ban against the community. R. Solomon replies, "Let it therefore be known that the emissary did nothing without first consulting with me. I want to testify that he gave not a penny to anyone except the Master David Abirgil to whom he gave twelve mitkalin. Ten of the twelve were returned while a contract was made in the name of Solomon ben Lisha for the remaining two. A contract of indebtedness was made which I signed. In truth, forty or fifty mitkalin were given to R. Elazar Delouya. The aforementioned David [Abirgil] is not a liar or a thief, God forbid, and he is prepared to send the balance of the money. However, we must wait until he completes a transaction involving the sale of arak and raisins when the market price is higher."

Ms. 27
P. 40a and b

Two prayers of supplication and one liturgical poem

On page 40a, two prayers of supplication appear. The first was composed by one called Reuben. The second prayer of supplication at the bottom of the page was composed by R. Yaaḅeẓ, of blessed memory.

A Liturgical poem appears on page 40b. It was composed by one called Abraham. The writing on 40b is quite faded.

Ms. 28
P. 41a

A Jew owes a non-Jew money and the Jew must collect a loan to ease his burden which affects the property of R. Jacob Ibn Ẓur

Rabbi Judah ibn Attar wrote this letter to R. Jacob Ibn Ẓur concerning R. Aaron ibn Haroush. The last-named owes money to a non-Jew called ben Azzim Adda. The time to pay the debt has arrived but Aaron does not have the money available to make the payment. Azzim Adda is putting him under pressure but he is ill and has no recourse to money except by calling for the payment of a debt of 500 uqiot of silver which is owed to him by R. Jacob Ibn Ẓur. When Aaron told Azzim that the properties enumerated in the bill of debt as a guarantee more than equalled the value of the money owed, Azzim was happy to accept this in payment. These are the places enumerated in the bill of debt: one sixth of the courtyard adjoining the synagogue wherein the descendants of R. Immanuel Monsano pray, one sixth of R. Jacob's synagogue, and one sixth of the courtyard called Zar Asiban. The non-Jew wants to have the option to sell these properties or to realize dividends therefrom. R. Judah notes that the property of the courtyards is for sale; however, not the synagogue property, as is stipulated in the bill of debt. This communication is dated Shevat 1721.

Ms. 29
P. 42a

A request for a document of transference of property to be drawn

Rabbi Judah ibn Attar writes to R. Jacob Ibn Ẓur on Adar II, 1720, upon the request of Aaron ben Moses ben Samuel. One known as Israel Ben Shaiya, the son of the scholar R. Jacob, has written a letter to Aaron in his own name and in the name of his brother Reuḅen's wife (who dwells at Tafilalet) stating that Reuḅen has granted permission to transfer to Aaron the pledge of property which is located in Fez, in the courtyard of R. Solomon ibn Amiel. The value of the pledge is sent through the agent Jacob ibn Garton. It is Aaron's desire that a document of transfer be drawn by R. Jacob Ibn Ẓur stating that Aaron has acquired the pledge and that Israel shall assume the responsibility for his brother Reuḅen and the latter's wife. If Reuḅen will put his assent to the transfer in writing, then this should be submitted so that R. Jacob Ibn Ẓur can formalize the document. When the procedures are completed, the final document of ownership should be sent to Aaron through the agent. The monies that are made available for this transaction are also mentioned at the end of the letter. R. Judah also wants a reply to the letters that he sent to R. Jacob Ibn Ẓur in the previous week.

Ms. 30
P. 43a

A plea to the rabbis to innovate and support methods of fundraising for the Jerusalem community as the emissary is encountering difficulties

One who signs his name as David Ha-Katan writes to the rabbis informing them of many difficulties that he encounters in fundraising for Jerusalem. He asks them to support such an effort but says that if it will cause difficulties then the effort should not be expended. Help will be available from another place. Some practices are suggested for fundraising. On joyful ritual occasions such as weddings and Brit Milah (circumcision), it would be appreciated if money could be donated for Jerusalem. The communal reader should remind the people; also the synagogue treasurers should put in more effort.

Ms. 31
P. 44b

The inheritance and perpetuation of the estate of rabbi Solomon Samuel Ibn Ẓur O.B.M.

This document, which was written in Fez, on Ḥeshvan 1791, was signed by R. Abraham ben David Ohayun and Rabbi Saadya. The two sons of the rabbinic scholar Solomon Samuel ibn Ẓur were Rabbi Raphael and his brother Jacob. The latter who was a bachelor, desired to formulate a contract to deal with the terms of the estate which their late father had left for them and their mother. They agreed never to dissolve the estate until parted by death. Jacob would be permitted to draw upon the estate for marital expenses since he was still unmarried. If any party violated this agreement by desiring to dissolve it, he would forfeit half of the rights which accrued to him both before and after the death of his father. Also each one would make available his half for the use of his mother. The liability would be limited only to those items that came under the terms of this agreement. If anyone should die, to be survived by daughters only, the latter were to be sustained from the estate until such time as they married, at which time they would be entitled to a proper dowry from the estate. If any one of the brothers died without leaving an heir then all these benefits would accrue to the surviving brother. The brothers would be unable to pass on their rights to a female heiress. If either brother died then his wife would be sustained by the estate until such time as she remarried. If she did remarry then she might take only 15 mitkalin of silver.

Ms. 32
P. 45b

A letter of greeting from Jerusalem to Fez which deals with the purchase of books

This letter was written from Jerusalem by Elijah ben Jacob Kasis to Rabbi Raphael, referred to as Ham-Malakh (The Angel), in Sivan 1863. The author states that he recites prayers for R. Raphael's family when he visits the graves of the Saints and he recites blessings at the Kotel ha-Maaravi (Western Wall of the Temple). The books that were requested by R. Solomon Alaluf for Rabbi Raphael are unavailable, including the work of Harav Ḥukkei Ḥayyim, since the author's son is presently abroad as an emissary for the Jerusalem community. Regards are sent to R. Solomon Ibn Ẓur, R. Jacob Ha-Kohen, ha-Nagid R. Abraham, Rabbi Aḇner Ha-Ṣarfati, R. Joshua Serero, R. Samuel Ha-Kohen and his brothers R. Moses and R. Isaac, and to R. Israel Maymeran.

Ms. 33
P. 46a

A son has a claim against his father, the amount of which can be ascertained by a document held by R. Jacob Ibn Ẓur

This is a document signed by the rabbis Judah ibn Attar and Abraham ibn Danan of Fez written to R. Jacob Ibn Ẓur requesting that he supply information from a legal document that he possesses. This information will substantiate the amount of a claim by Joseph ben David Elmaleh against his father, David, for his portion of his deceased mother's estate. David has admitted that the document that requires him to pay the money of his departed wife to his son is in the possession of R. Jacob Ibn Ẓur. Since the son is not aware of the amount that is due to him and what the father wants to give him seems a small amount, strife has ensued between father and son. R. Jacob can help to resolve the matter by sending the document to either one of the two judges.

Ms. 34
P. 47a and b

A document of sale of a Jewish communal enterprise in Fez when the community needed funds

The Jewish community of Fez was in need of money, so the rabbinic court, consisting of R. Judah ibn Attar, R. Mîmun Alfasi, and R. Moses ibn Maman, acted for the community and arranged for the sale of a communal enterprise to Abraham ben Maḥlouf ben Yitaḥ for 1,200 uqiot. This document was drawn in the month of Elul 1729. The terms of the contract are spelled out as follows: Only Abraham or those he designates may engage in the sale of alcoholic beverages. If he agrees to permit Saadya Lehaboz and Moses ibn Reuḇen ben Susan to serve as vendors they may do so. Any other person selling alcoholic beverages will be obliged to pay 10 uqia for each one hundred kilo. Those who prepare them for private consumption will pay five uqiot, and for those alcoholic beverages produced from raisins, figs, dates, almonds, and rice one uqiot for each one hundred kilo. For dealers in charcoal, one quarter of an uqia and olive oil; one quarter of an uqia whether it is pressed out in the olivepress or it is brought into the Mellah. Different amounts payable are enumerated such as one hundred and ten uqiot to Isaac Porat, sixty uqiot to Moses Ibn Susan, and two hundred and seventy uqiot to be paid to R. Moses ibn Maman as agent of the community. Even if the purchaser should benefit beyond the sum of three thousand uqiot the agreement must still be honored. On page 47b, in an addendum, we are informed that the original transaction with Abraham ben Yitaḥ as the buyer was nullified. R. Judah Bibas replaced Abraham ben Yitaḥ as the purchaser with all stipulations of the contract remaining the same as before except that the price rose to thirteen hundred uqiot. Seven hundred uqiot was to be paid to Abraham ben Yitaḥ with the balance going to whomever the community should designate. The latter transaction took place in Fez, on the third day of Tishri 1729. The addendum to the earlier document was signed by R. Jacob Ibn Ẓur.

Ms. 35
Pp. 48a—49a

R. Jacob Ibn Ẓur is asked to return a confiscated article to a litigant after a dispute is settled. R. Jacob Ibn Ẓur sends a correspondence to R. Jacob Toledano

R. Jacob Toledano sent a short correspondence to R. Jacob Ibn Ẓur concerning a monetary dispute between one called Saiyag and Judah ben Zazun. R. Toledano states that since the litigation has been settled R. Jacob Ibn Ẓur should return an article belonging to Judah ben Zazun which was previously confiscated because of the latter's non-payment. R. Jacob Ibn Ẓur's correspondence to R. Jacob Toledano also appears. This letter is dated from Fez to Tetuán, Tishri 1741 and in it R. Jacob Ibn Ẓur complains that R. Jacob Toledano has spoken harshly of him because he has left a percentage of income from his synagogue in Meknès to his son R. Raphael Oḅed without informing R. Toledano. A quarter of the income was allotted to R. Toledano, although he is claiming that only an eighth part was allotted to him. R. Toledano has therefore referred to R. Jacob Ibn Ẓur as a cruel person. The latter claims that it is a most natural act to guard one's own son's succession in preference to someone who is not related. Besides, R. Toledano has been given a percentage towards his income apart from other sources of income that are available to him. R. Jacob Ibn Ẓur argues that if he had left out his son and given all to R. Toledano, then everyone would consider that he had wronged his son. The only one R. Jacob Ibn Ẓur has been cruel to is himself, he states, as he enumerates a variety of transactions concerning himself where R. Jacob Toledano did not act fairly.

One such occasion transpired on the death of R. Mîmun ben Nissim when R. Toledano persuaded R. Jacob Ibn Ẓur to lend him close to two thousand uqiot and promissory notes were drawn for this transaction which were in R. Ibn Ẓur's possession until the time for payment arrived. R. Toledano used guile to secure those notes, claims R. Ibn Ẓur, and the money remained in the other's possession unjustly for many years. On another occasion, says R. Jacob Ibn Ẓur, he held the promissory notes of one R. Meir Bibas and had refused to give them to R. Toledano, but the latter pleaded that they should be placed with him and as a result R. Jacob Ibn Ẓur was unable ever to collect a penny on the notes. Once during a dispute R. Toledano had with R.M. Maymeran, in Meknès, he asked R.J. Ibn Ẓur for money which was given in payment for a loan. R. Toledano gave some volumes of codes in return which made up only a portion of the loan. R. Ibn Ẓur wanted to return the books, but they were refused. Once when R. Ibn Ẓur travelled to Meknès he left money belonging to some orphans with his son-in-law, R. Menaḥem Serero, o.b.m. R. Toledano persuaded R. Serero to receive promissory notes for the money. When R. Serero passed away, R. Ibn Ẓur went to Fez where he found two sacks full of promissory notes. R.J. Ibn Ẓur confronted R. Toledano with the notes whereupon the latter admitted that they were his and he offered to sell them and to pay R.J. Ibn Ẓur, but in the event he never paid a penny. R. Jacob Ibn Ẓur had a bill of debt against R. Solomon Al-Mishaeli which was held by R. Ibn Ẓur's cousin, R. Judah, the brother of the departed, called Isaac. R. Toledano asked to be able to collect the debt whereupon he would share half with R. Ibn Ẓur. Instead R. Toledano made a deal with the one who held the debt, whereby he received all and R. Ibn Ẓur received nothing.

Jacob Ibn Ẓur faults R.J. Toledano as the cause of his wanderings and his migration to Tetuán because he couldn't make a living in Meknès due to R. Toledano's manipulations. Apparently he returned to Fez for a short time because of his insolvency. R. Jacob Ibn Ẓur's son, R. Reuḅen, was obliged to accompany his father in the latter's quest for financial stability. R. Reuḅen's wife was obliged to remain in Salé due to these circumstances. R. Jacob Ibn Ẓur informs us that his only grandson has been born, in Salé, and that he has not yet had a chance even to see him. Since his quest for economic self sufficiency is unsuccessful he refuses to have his daughter-in-law suffer hunger on his account. In spite of all his suffering R. Jacob is falsely accused of wronging R. Jacob Toledano. R. Toledano is maintaining that he should have the total income of R. Jacob Ibn Ẓur's synagogue in Meknès instead of just a quarter, while half goes to R. Ibn

Ẓur and the remaining quarter to the latter's son Ṛaphael. R. Jacob Ibn Ẓur retorts that R. Toledano owes him much money which has never been paid even though funds were available. Even if R. Toledano couldn't pay *all* of his debts he could at least pay a portion of them. If R. Toledano claims not to have available cash or movable property he still owns real estate, books, and scrolls of the Law which could be sold for cash. In the face of all this R.J. Ibn Ẓur has never made a claim against R. Toledano in court but R. Toledano has the temerity to call R.J. Ibn Ẓur a cruel man. The latter notes that justice would prevail if R. Toledano was obliged to sell his properties to pay his debts, rent living quarters, and suffer like those whose lot it is to be poor.

Ms. 36
Pp. 50a—52b

A ms. of the collection of tales and aphorisms called Divrei Ḥakhamim Ke-Dôrbônôt

[See also page 62a and b and *Ms.160* on pages 221a to 224b.]

The title of this manuscript, Divrei Ḥakhamim Ke-Dôrbônôt, is based on a verse which is found at the end of the biblical work, Ecclesiastes, 12:11. It means, "The words of the wise are like goads." It is a compilation of aphorisms of the philosophers and sages including riddles and a tale concerning the wisdom of R. Saadya Gaon which contains Judaeo-Arabic statements. In our collection called Yalkut Roĩĩm there are two such manuscripts. *Ms.36*, which is found on pages 50a to 52b, should have the additional pages 62a and b following it. The compiler of this collection mistakenly separated it from the other pages. The earliest copyist is noted as Yaabeẓ (R. Jacob Ibn Ẓur) who also provides comments on some texts. Yaabeẓ informs us (on page 52b) that he copied this text from an earlier manuscript which he expanded upon with comments and a more complete text than the original.

At the end of the third line of page 62a we are informed that "The material given until this point comes from Yaabeẓ while the texts given thereafter were copied by R. Solomon Elijah Ibn Ẓur." The signature of R. Solomon appears at the end of this manuscript, on page 62b.

There is another manuscript in the Yalkut Roĩĩm (pages 221a to 224b) which is almost identical to *Ms.36*; it is another copy of Divrei Ḥakhamim Ke-Dôrbônôt. This is *Ms. 160* which is identical to *Ms. 36* until page 62a, where Yaabeẓ is quoted as the copyist, except that Yaabeẓ is identified as Rabbi Jacob Ibn Ẓur and as "Yaabeẓ, the son of R. Reuḅen, of blessed memory." Thereafter a text is given which does not appear in *Ms. 36*. It is recorded as part of what is found of the manuscript copied by Rabbi Jacob Ibn Ẓur. Another copyist whose name follows is Yehonatan Ish Ṣion Monsano, the son of Rabbi Beẓalel, of blessed memory. There follows a copy of Abraham ibn Ezra's riddle on his poverty which was copied from a Ms. by Rabbi Elijah Ha-Ṣarfati. Page 224b is titled "Maalt ha-Emet" since the opening statement deals with the subject of truth and falsehood. A number of statements and anecdotes follow, one of which is attributed to the RASHBA, author of a volume of Responsa in the Bension Collection. At the end of *Ms.160*, on page 224b, the last copyist mentioned by the copyist of this manuscript is given as R. Immanuel Monsano, of blessed memory. Our final copyist is noted as Yehonatan Ish Ṣion Monsano, the son of R. Beẓalel.

Ms. 37
Pp. 53a—54b

A eulogy

This classical form of a Moroccan eulogy was written by one called Yehonatan. It may be surmised that he wrote this eulogy and letter of consolation for R. Jacob Ibn Ẓur, on the passing of his son Reuḅen, who was a colleague of the author. No other name is clearly indicated except that of the writer. A letter of consolation which was written to R. Jacob Ibn Ẓur on the demise of his son Reuben appears in *Ms. 21*.

Ms. 38
P. 55a

An Halakhic text dealing with an alteration to one's property which may infringe on private or public property

One has a cistern in his house and he wants to direct the water that is flowing into his courtyard into another cistern from which Reuḅen is drawing water. The owner of the courtyard can construct a conduit underground at a distance of at least three handbreadths removed from the wall of the house and at a depth of two or three handbreadths so that the clean water shall flow into his cistern. This procedure may be followed even in a courtyard held in partnership and even within four cubits opposite his partner's entrance. This decision was rendered by Maharam Mi-Trani, Volume two, No. 96 and by Keneset ha-Gedolah, No. 153. Another ruling, that of Maharam Galante, No. 85, states that water drawn from one well to another gives one property rights.

One who builds opposite a synagogue must allow for a greater distance (than from a house) because a synagogue requires more light. The Beit Yosef on the code Oraḥ Ḥayyim cited the Sefer Agudah who is mentioned by the Mahari-Weil in his Responsa, on this subject.

A case arose concerning one who wanted to build near a synagogue in Salonika and the matter was adjudicated in accord with the Agudah, i.e. a synagogue requires the allowance of a greater distance by the builder than from a private domicile. The measure of distance that must be maintained is discussed by the Maharad Egozi in his Responsa as being eight cubits. However, if there is sufficient light for the synagogue even with a four cubit separation that sufficeth according to R.M. Egozi. The Keneset ha-Gedolah in Responsum No. 154 is also in agreement.

Reuḅen and Simeon are neighbors who are dwelling near the public thoroughfare. Simeon builds a new addition to his house which protrudes into the public thoroughfare opposite Reuḅen's window. The latter claims that the new addition should be dismantled since it causes him the discomfort of being exposed to his neighbor's sight. Simeon retorts that he left the necessary four cubits vacant; but in order to remove the cause of the complaint he is prepared to build a fence around his addition. Reuḅen replies that if Simeon builds a fence he will obstruct Reuḅen's view of the length of the marketplace. The law is decided in Simeon's favor. Thus do we find the decision rendered by R. Levi ibn Habib in No. 44, of his work.

Ms. 39
P. 56a and b

A letter from the communal leaders of Ṣefrou to the rabbis of Fez concerning fundraising irregularities that arose during an emissary's visit

Raphael Maman writes to the three rabbis (of Fez) Saul ibn Danan, Solomon Elijah Ibn Ẓur, and Abner Israel Ha-Ṣarfati concerning the funds that were collected by the emissary from Jerusalem, R. Barukh Pinto, in the author's community. The author reports that the collected funds were sent a day earlier but he felt obliged to respond to the communication of the rabbis as to why the money was held up until this late date and as to why the sum is less than might be anticipated. It seems that R. Barukh wanted a larger sum than the community could produce at the present time. The writer mentions that he was among those who negotiated for the emissary with the leaders of the community whereby a compromise was reached but the emissary was not present on that occasion. The expenses incurred by the emissary would be deducted up to one fourth of the income from the collection. The emissary finally agreed to this arrangement after refusing to do so at first. The writer notes that the emissary did not lose any money, since more than a quarter of the total amount was added to the regular collection. When the community leaders had to settle with R. Barukh before his departure he refused to pay the twenty-five percent which had been agreed upon as the expense of his upkeep. The writer notes that he counselled the emissary not to behave in this way because his actions would reflect upon all the scholars of the Holy Land. People would say that these scholars were not trustworthy people. R. Ḥayyim Elijah and the author accompanied the emissary out of town and they continued to persuade him to take the money.

Shortly after the emissary took the money he sent it back to R. Ḥayyim Elijah, writing that he found less than the proper amount without an explanation as to why the amount was deficient. It is because of the highly improper conduct of the emissary that the money was subsequently withheld until a later date. Furthermore, every precaution was taken to see that the proper sum should be received by the emissary excluding the possibility of theft on the journey. R. Ḥayyim Elijah is too trustworthy to be doubted as to the sum that he placed in the pouch before he sent it to the emissary; in fact, he even added more money from his own pocket. Regards are sent to the rabbis and to the emissary (who is presently at Fez).

R. Ḥayyim Elijah added a postscript to the letter, which is found on page 56a. He states that Joseph Ha-Kohen can testify about the money that was sent. Also the emissary was given seventeen mitkallin as a loan. Another eleven mitkallin was given to him by Shalom Abitbol and another person called Abraham; additional money was given to him by Aaron Elbaz.

Ms. 40
P. 57b

Calamitous conditions and strife are recorded in an early sixteenth century correspondence

This letter is written by Aaron Ha-Kohen to one whom he regards as his master. The author reports on the diligence that Joseph, his son, has shown in his studies which will be to the satisfaction of the respondent. The author then describes the visitation of many natural and political calamities that have befallen him and some of his compatriots. Drought conditions prevail and a number of his colleagues have been imprisoned and beaten. Among them are mentioned R. Solomon ibn Daviera and R. Samuel ibn Saiivar. The latter's son is imprisoned because he entreated His Majesty the King concerning his suffering at the hands of the leader of the Jewish community, referred to as the Nagid. An allusion is made to Moses, the anniversary of whose death is commemorated on the date the letter was written. The author states that more could be reported but the time is not propitious. Aaron cannot comprehend why one called R. Shemaya, who is also a Kohen, rose up against him.

The script appears to belong to the first half of the sixteenth century. It is possible that it is the strife between the Megorashim and Toshavim in Morocco that is hinted at in this letter.

Ms. 41
P. 58a and b

An emissary informs R. Raphael Ibn Ẓur of the trials and tribulations which hindered his mission

This letter was written on the eighth of Iyar 1876 to R. Raphael Ibn Ẓur by the emissary of the Moroccan community in the Holy Land, Joseph the son of Moses Arwaẓ. The writer's signature is accompanied by a seal which is composed in three languages; namely, Hebrew, Arabic, and in the center of the seal a wreath wherein the Roman initials J.A. are inscribed.

This letter commences with two paragraphs of flowery introduction. In the third paragraph, Joseph apologizes to R. Raphael for not writing sooner; however, the tribulations of his journey prevented him from doing so. He then reports on some of the hindrances he has encountered on his fundraising mission.

When Joseph arrived in Debdou he stayed at the residence of Judah ibn Susan who was allied with the Kohanim. The Murçiano family, who apparently feuded with the Kohanim, made sure that Joseph's fundraising efforts would not be too successful. If anyone wanted to give a larger contribution the Murçiano family prevented them from doing so. The ones who will suffer from this dispute are the poor of the Moroccan Jewish community in the Holy Land. Joseph's journey to the villages of Arif was likewise unsuccessful since a libelous charge had been made that a Jew had murdered a non-Jew, so he feared to travel in that area. Joseph would not permit R. Judah Leib, his associate, to travel there either for the same reason. Joseph was therefore unable to meet R. Abner and R. Raphael (to whom this letter is written) and he begs for their pardon. He describes his journey as a very unsettling experience. Regards are sent to R. Ḥayyim Kohen.

Ms. 42
P. 58b

The rabbis of Fez are asked to assemble all properties pertaining to an estate and to forward them to the rabbis of Tetuán

This court document was sent by the rabbis Isaac ibn Walidûn and Isaac Nahon of Tetuán to the rabbis of Fez, in the year 1857, concerning an estate. Clara, the daughter of the late Yom Toḅ ibn Attar, was in the service of R. Judah Alaluf. Clara recently passed on and one who was not numbered amongst those who had her best interests at heart made a claim upon her estate. The rabbis of Fez are asked to protect the estate of the departed Clara, first, by supervising the accumulation of all her assets and then by sending them to the rabbis of Tetuán who will apportion them to her legal inheritors. Thus false claims against the estate or its inheritors will be thwarted.

Ms. 43
P. 59a

A legal document concerning the history of Fez in the middle of the seventeenth century

This legal document begins with a dirge which describes the pillage of the Mellah of Fez in the year 1647. The Arab destroyers vented their venom in particular against the synagogues. They wanted to level the synagogues completely and with this threat they extorted money from the Jews. They said they would not be satisfied until they were guaranteed a huge sum of money. The community agreed to sell a pair of silver Torah crowns, made by the artisan ibn Rivka, to the scholar Issac Ṣarfati, the son of the scholar Vidal, of blessed memory, in order to realize the sum of money that was needed. The sum that was agreed upon for the Torah crowns was four hundred and twenty uqiot, according to the old standard of currency. The legal formula for this transaction is then elaborated upon. The document was composed on the first third of Adar II, in the year 1647. The sum of one hundred and seventy uqiot was used to pay the ransom so that the synagogue walls would not be levelled and the remaining two hundred and fifty uqiot were given in payment for the Torah crowns which were held as a pledge by R. David Alkazabi. The Torah crowns were in the possession of the congregation that prayed in the Great Synagogue of the Toshavim. Among the five signers of this historic document were: 1. Shem Toḅ ibn Ramukh; 2. Saadya bar R. Samuel ibn Danan; 3. Abraham ibn Danan; 4. Benjamin Ha-Kohen bar R. Naḥman; 5. Ephraim Ha-Kohen bar Manasseh.

Ms. 44
P. 60a

A correspondence from Elijah B. Jacob Kasis at Ṣefrou to the rabbis Ham-Malakh Raphael Ibn Ẓur and Jacob Ha-Kohen of Fez

[See *Ms.32*, page 45b; *Ms.45*, page 61a; and *Ms.48*, page 66a for additional documents by the same author in the same hand.]

This letter was written by Elijah b. Jacob Kasis in 1868 to the rabbis Ham-Malakh Raphael and Jacob. He informs them that he has left money collected in Meknès with R. Israel Maymeran who is supposed to forward the sum of three hundred and one durham to the rabbis. The balance of six hundred durham should be sent by them to Tangiers, to Joseph Achriqi through R. Ḥayyim Yemin Ha-Kohen. The letter to Joseph should contain another letter which should be forwarded to his (the writer's) son. The writer suggests to R. Raphael that if the money is already available to be sent to Joseph then his letter to his son should be sent with it. If not, then the letter should be forwarded to R. Ḥayyim who will forward it to the son. He asks them to use good glue by which to secure the letter, since he has none available. The writer requests of the rabbis to whom he is writing, as well as of the Nagid Abraham, that they should prevent wayfarers from coming to Ṣefrou from Fez since they cause the writer a substantial loss. It has been the Nagid Abraham's practice to prevent wayfarers from coming in the past. The writer asks R. Raphael to hasten to fulfill all his requests, and he sends regards to R. Ham-Melekh Solomon, the Nagid Abraham, Menaḥem Ṣaba, R. Jacob Dahan, Azuz Ha-Kohen, R. Joshua Serero, and Aaron Ha-Kohen. The address to this document is

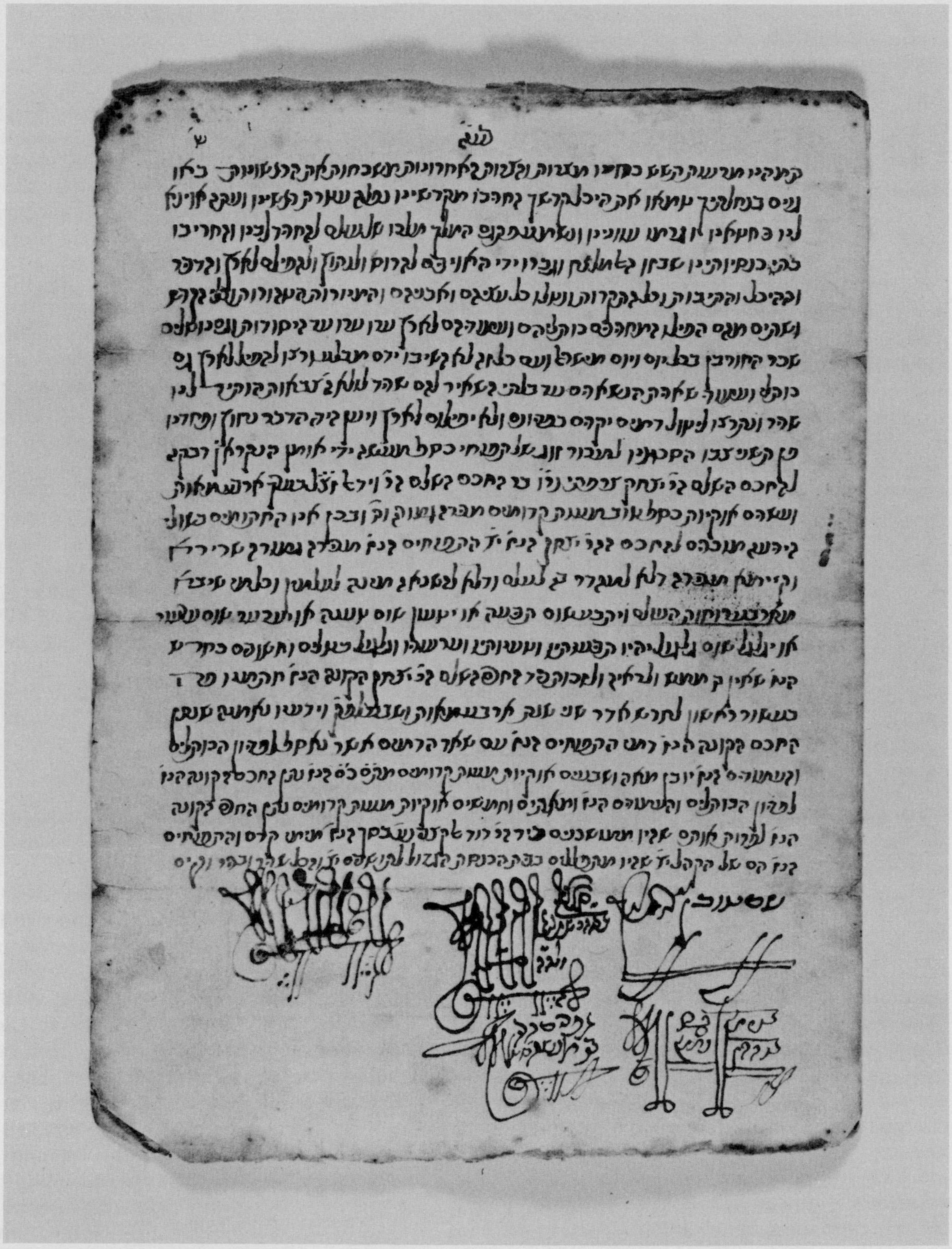

Ms. 43
A legal document concerning the history of Fez in the middle of the seventeenth century

found on page 67a according to the compiler's arrangement. Two lines of verse appear at the top of page 67b. Calculations follow on the rest of page 67b.

Ms. 45
P. 61a

A correspondence by Elijah B. Jacob Kasis at Ṣefrou to the rabbis Jacob Ha-Kohen and Ham-Malakh Raphael Ibn Ẓur of Fez

[See *Ms.32*, page 45b; *Ms.44*, page 60a; and *Ms.48*, page 66a for additional documents by the same author.]

Elijah b. Jacob Kasis thanks the rabbis for writing to him and for trying to send letters to Jebel Tor (Gibraltar). He states that he hopes to see them in the near future. He also thanks them for acquiring four durham from Moses ibn Na'im. The writer further informs them that because of preoccupations he was unable to write to R. Israel Maymeran concerning the money that the latter held (which was one of the subjects taken up in *Ms. 44*) and which would have been transmitted to them, nor has he written to Joseph Chriqi concerning the same matter. The money that is being delivered to the Nagid by the bearer of this letter comes from the hospitable innkeeper Aaron Elbaz, a supporter of Torah. Regards are sent to R. Ham-Melekh Solomon and to all the scholars, including Menahem Ṣaba, R. Jacob Dahan, the innkeeper Azuz Ha-Kohen, and to Raphael Elijah Elbaz, the son of Aaron Elbaz. On page 61 a whole page of calculations is given. On the other side of the page the address is given. [Page 62a and b which immediately followed *Ms.45* in the collection "Yalkut Roîîm" is the concluding page to *Ms.36*. See *Ms.36* for a description of the contents of this page.]

Ms. 46
Pp. 63a and 64b

A Kabbalistic Messianic Calculation

This is a Kabbalistic manuscript using the biblical text of "Timḥeh Zekhr Amalek" (Deut. 25:19) to point to the year 1688 as significant for Messianic events. The numerical value of Timḥeh equals 5,488 which also corresponds to four sets of six combinations of the word "Zekhr" as the author tabulates them. The sum total of the four lines is 5,448 as each line equals 1,362. In all probability this text dates from 1688. Page 63b contains mystical calculations based upon the Holy Name of God. Twelve lines of computation of the Hebrew letters of God's Name are set out six terms to a line which result in the numerical value of 72. Pages 64a and b contain alphabetical calculations of the Hebrew word Yimlokh, "He will reign." The implication is that God will reign and the enemy will be blotted out in 1688. Twelve lines with four terms to each line equals the number 48 as the Mem and Ḥet of Tamaḥ on pages 64a and b.

Ms. 47
P. 65a and b

A dispute over the estate of the late R. Samuel D'Avila

[This document commences on page 65b and concludes on page 65a. The compiler bound the page in the book in reverse order.] The document deals with a legal judgement concerning the claims of the widow of R. Samuel D'Avila against her son R. Eliezer D'Avila. The mother originally claimed that her son's half of the inheritance included Torah scrolls and Torah crowns, while the half that belonged to her and her daughters consisted of properties. R. Eliezer denied this to be the case and he took an oath. He agreed, however, that half of the properties should go to his mother in accord with the custom and enactment of the Jews of Castile. Presently he stated that he had no properties available that he could hand over to his mother since some had been sold to realize money for her maintenance and others sold to pay his father's debts. Additional properties belonging to his father had been deposited with the scholar and judge Jacob Gedaliah.

It was decided that these properties should be divided between mother and son, but the son subsequently refused to divide them. Instead he said that he would use them to pay a debt to B'nai Yeshurun, which never had been recorded in contractual form or in the presence of witnesses.

Ms. 46
A Kabbalistic
Messianic calculation.

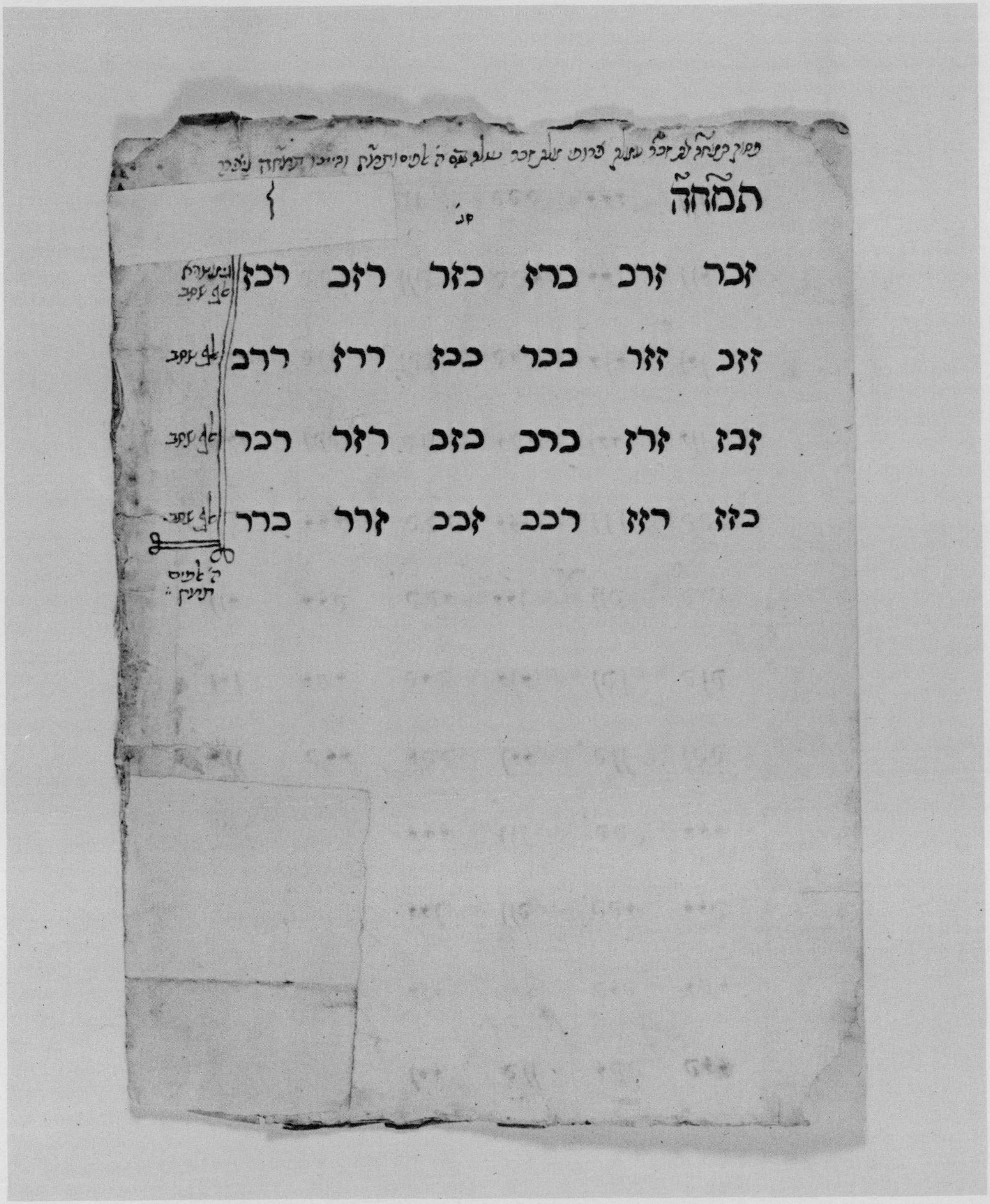

A judgement was rendered that if the creditors would file a proper claim and if it was a just one, then the mother would pay from her portion. If the son admitted that he owed the money to them, then he should pay only with his portion but his liability should not extend to his mother's portion. The mother should immediately take her portion from Jacob Gedaliah and use it for any purpose she deems fit.

The aforementioned document and judgement appears to be rendered by R. Jacob ibn Ẓur even though his name does not appear anywhere on this document. The script is characteristic of his style of writing.

Ms. 48
P. 66a

A correspondence by Elijah B. Jacob Kasis to the rabbis Jacob Ha-Kohen and Ham-Malakh Raphael Ibn Ẓur of Fez

[See *Ms.32*, page 45b; *Ms.41*, page 60a; and *Ms.45*, page 61a for additional documents by the same author.]

This is one of a series of letters sent by Elijah b. Jacob Kasis to R. Jacob Ha-Kohen and R. Ham-Malakh Raphael ibn Ẓur of Fez. Here he informs the rabbis that on his travels from Fez to Ṣefrou he was the guest of the munificent R. Aaron Elbaz of the latter city, who also aided him in the collection of charity. The writer excuses himself for not having corresponded earlier as he was preoccupied with the collection of funds. He expresses the hope that the rabbis to whom he writes have forwarded certain letters for him and that they have collected some monies from Jacob ibn Na'im. The author also asks these rabbis to speak with Hayyim Yamin Ha-Kohen concerning monies that should be forwarded to Joseph Achriqi. The author sends regards to R. Solomon, R. Saul, R. Mattitya, R. Abner, and R. Israel. Also regards should be sent to the prominent citizen Menaḥem Saba, to the scholar R. Jacob Dahan, and to Azuz Ha-Kohen. The author sends his best wishes for a speedy recovery to the daughter of the latter because when he last saw him she was ill. He also asks to be remembered to R. Joshua Serero. In a postscript he sends regards to Solomon Halevi and Aaron Ha-Kohen. On the other side of page 66a the address is given for this document. Four lines of biographical material are also given. [P. 67a is an address from Elijah b. Jacob Kasis to R. Raphael ibn Ẓur and Jacob Ha-Kohen of Fez. See page 60a for the document. It is really one and the same page. P. 68a is an address to the rabbis Abner Israel Ha-Ṣarfati and Raphael ibn Ẓur. It is pasted to page 59a as a reinforcement.]

Ms. 49
P. 69a

A query from Debdou concerning a complex problem involving real estate transactions

Simeon Jacob ben Susan, of Debdou poses a Halakhic query concerning real estate transactions and he asks the rabbis to resolve the matter. We are not informed as to who the rabbis are.

One who is designated as Reuḅen held land in partnership with his mother and sisters which he subsequently sold to another called Simeon, and guaranteed the value of the land for a certain sum. Reuḅen had additional land in partnership with Simeon. Reuḅen sold the additional land to a non-Jew but, in accordance with an enactment that land remains intact in the hands of the previous owners when it is treated as confiscated property with which one may not transact, the sale was not valid. The non-Jew sold the land to another Jew called Levi. Levi acquired the property rights from the vendors. The sisters of Reuḅen made a claim against Simeon and they wrested the land from him. Simeon arose and made a claim against Levi with his aforementioned property rights. Upon further examination it was learned that one-sixth of the aforementioned property rights belonged to Reuḅen. An evaluation was made as well as a proclamation concerning these property rights. The result was that Simeon possessed one part while Reuḅen's rights consisted of one part and one-half.

After some years, Simeon brought a claim against Levi because he said that he had found proof that the entire rights of the property belonged to Reuḅen. Levi responded that if in fact it was as Simeon claimed, then he would do whatever was necessary to restore everything to Reuḅen and that he, Levi, should be the recipient of one-sixth. Simeon claimed that the sixth was established to be his and if Levi didn't turn over the remainder then he, Simeon, would claim it according to law. The writer turns to the rabbis to whom he sent this letter to respond whether the law is in accord with Levi, in which case the sixth that Simeon took was in error, because he was of the opinion that Reuḅen's property rights extended only to a sixth, or is the law in accord with Simeon? This document was sent from Debdou in the year 1870.

A responsum concerning air pollution and property rights

Ms. 50
P. 70a

The question: Reuḅen possesses a structure that houses furnaces which is located near the home of Simeon. An oven is located therein which many people use for baking. Simeon suffers much physical and monetary damage because of the smoke that is emitted from the oven even when the wind is normal. The walls of his house have become blackened from the soot. Reuḅen wants to add another oven to the structure. Simeon, upon hearing of this, has made a claim to prevent the new oven from being added since he claims to suffer so much from the first one. A decision is requested.

The responsum: The law is in agreement with Simeon's claim and Reuben is unable to add an additional oven since the smoke is injurious even with a normal wind. Even though the property damage is slight, (a mere blackening of the walls) still Simeon can prevent Reuḅen from building any further additions. The authority of R. Joseph Caro is cited in Ḥoshen Mishpat, chapter 155. Also the Haggahot Maimoniyyot, chapter 11 of the Laws of Neighbors, law number 7, in the Maimonidean Code, is cited.

An introductory prayer to the Havdalah ceremony

Ms. 51
P. 70b

"He who established His covenant with our father Abraham, with our father Isaac, with our father Jacob, with Moses our teacher, the master of all the prophets, with Aaron the holy one of God, with Phineas with Elijah, with David and Solomon, may he save us and his whole nation the house of Israel from tribulations of the grave, from messianic pangs, from the war of Gog and Magog, from plunder, destruction, captivity, from all forms of poverty and plague, from thieves and wicked people, from bad moments, from evil decrees that come upon the world, protect us from all and be gracious unto us, for Thou O' Lord are good and forgiving and show abundant kindness to all who call to you. We entreat thee Our Lord and the God of our fathers, make our hopes end in peace, resolve all our dreams in peace" etc. The last three words of the prayer end in the following, "unto you silence is praise." Thereafter the traditional, "a cup of salvations" etc., follows. No authors or dates are indicated in this document.

A request for information about an historical chronicle and a copy of that work

Ms. 52
P. 71a

This letter was written to R. Solomon Elijah Ibn Ẓur in the year 1866 by Judah Zarmon. The writer requests that R. Solomon should secure information concerning a manuscript of an historical work that is in the possession of R. Raḥamim Ġayni of Ṣefrou. R. Raḥamim had promised to make a copy of this unique work available to the writer but nine months have gone past and he has not communicated about the work at all. The historical work "Divrei ha-Yamim" is supposed to contain daily reports about all the events that had transpired "in every generation from the expulsion from Castile until the present day." The writer of this letter asks R. Solomon to secure information about the content and nature of the work and from what year it begins; does it give daily reports of events? As soon as the work arrives, Judah Zarmon asks R. Solomon to hire the finest scribes gifted in Rashi script because they are so meticulous in their work that they will not permit errors to enter into their texts. Ten or fifteen pages should be copied and then sent through Samuel Ibn Ẓur. Judah asks to be informed of the cost of the copyists' work and he will pay well. When he has perused the ten or fifteen pages he will give the permission for the work to be completely transcribed.

Ms. 53
P. 72a and b

Testimony is given as to the operation of a sewage disposal system

A sewage system constructed by ham-Melekh Solomon is the subject of this document. Testimony is given as to the nature of the construction of this system and of its effectiveness in preventing solid sewage from escaping from it. The reply in testimony is that no raw sewage in solid form can escape from the system. Every part of the system is described. In this document a number of words are given in Judaeo-Arabic.

In the same scribal hand a vertical list of books is given on page 72b. Among the titles are the following: Mikneh Avraham, Melekhet Shlomo, Simḥat Yehudah, Ḥeker Lev, Ohalei Yehudah Naggar, Devar Emet, Zera Avraham, Elef Kesef, Oseh Shalom, Sha'ar Ha-Zekenim, Zekan Aaron, Siftei Renanot, Penei Maivin, Shoresh Yosef, Lev Maivin, Kehunat Olam, Yavo Ha-Levi, Minhat Zikkaron, and Derash Avraham. This document was composed in the second half of the nineteenth century.

Ms. 54
P. 73a and b

A letter from Joseph Sasson of Jerusalem to R. Raphael Ibn Ẓur of Fez concerning book purchases

The address of this letter appears on page 73a and the letter appears on page 73b. The letter was written in the year 1880 and was sent to R. Raphael Ibn Ẓur of Fez, by Joseph Sasson of Jerusalem. The writer notes that he wrote to R. Raphael a while ago and has not received any reply. Now Abraham ibn Simḥon and his son have come to make some acquisitions on behalf of R. Raphael. Other books, purchased previously, were sent through the emissary Maharam Suzan with a list denoting all the books that were purchased. The writer is in constant contact with the book dealers that they should supply him with the additional works that were requested by R. Raphael as soon as they are available. Payment for the books that were sent previously should be given to R. Jacob Ha-Kohen excluding three books that were sent as a gift. One book from Joseph Sasson is in place of the Sha'ar ha-Melekh that was requested but it was unavailable, and two books from R. Kubo, o.b.m. Also two books are sent for R. Abner. The writer wants to know if these have arrived.

Joseph entreats R. Raphael concerning R. Yeshua Halevi who apparently owes money for books that his son bought. The latter has been unable to pay due to illness. Therefore, Joseph asks R. Raphael to convey his regrets, and says that he has also reduced the price that he would have otherwise charged.

Ms. 55
P. 74a

A plea to R. Raphael Ibn Ẓur to uphold a claim to an estate

In Elul 1861, Moses Turgeman writes from Tiberias to R. Raphael Ibn Ẓur at Fez. He relates that in the year of the demise of King Mulay Maḥmad he and his son Jacob, of blessed memory, desired to go to settle in the Holy Land. However, this desire never materialized because of poverty and the illness and demise of his son. In spite of his poor economic condition Moses would not permit himself to live on gifts, although he had only enough to make ends meet from what he was able to earn.

The writer continues that he has been informed of the death of Maḥmoud Turgeman, may his soul reside in paradise, who was his brother-in-law (the brother of his wife). According to law, part of the estate of Maḥmoud should come to him. Meanwhile, one called Jacob ibn Zimra, a man of means, has taken that portion of the estate that should go to his, Moses', daughters. Moses has asked the permission of his daughters to claim the remainder of the estate for himself. Moses therefore appeals for justice for his daughters. He feels that since his wife has died he has no claims, but that his daughters' claim should be upheld.

Ms. 56
P. 75a

An appeal to help a poor bridegroom

This letter is written by Ha-Ẓevi Me'at Devash at Tiberias to Raphael Ibn Ẓur of Fez concerning the plight of an orphan, Ḥayyim Mîmun Boutboul. The grandfather of this orphan worries about his financial plight since he is to be presently married. The writer of this letter has taken it upon himself to quiet the grandfather's fears by applying to R. Raphael Ibn Ẓur to help the young man in his financial plight.

Ms. 57
Pp. 76a and b, 79a and b

Creditors in Ṣefrou make a claim against an estate. The rabbis of Ṣefrou ask the rabbis of Fez to aid in settling the matter of prior claims

This legal document is written to R. Solomon Elijah Ibn Ẓur and to R. Abner Israel Ha-Ṣarfati of Fez by three rabbis situated in Ṣefrou. The latter were R. Raḥamim Joseph Gayni, R. Raphael Moses Elbaz, and R. Saul Elbaz. [The compiler placed this document in the original compilation in such a manner that one part is on page 76a and the concluding part with three rabbinic signatures are on page 79b. The address of this letter is found on the reverse sides of pages 76b and 79a. They are actually one page.]

The creditors of R. Elijah, the son of Moses called Mulayl, who has been deceased for five months, want satisfaction of their claims on his land in lieu of non-payment of debts. A portion of the land is in the hands of the inheritors of Mulayl's wife in accordance with the ruling of the court in Fez. A half and an eighth of the upper levels of the structure are owned by the aforementioned R. Elijah but they were further placed as a pledge in the hand of R. Yeshua Elbaz for more than three years. Other adjoining attics were given in pledge to Simha, the widow of R. Salim ben Ḥamo, and the pledge ended up in the possession of Elijah ben R. Solomon ben Asulin for the two upper stories. Elijah Asulin also held debts against the estate. The creditors of Sefrou demand prior payment by having the land evaluated and apportioned. They should be paid before Elijah since they have prior claims. The rabbis who are addressed are asked to compel Elijah to come to court or to send his agent so that prior claims can be paid and justice done.

Ms. 58
P. 77a and b

An early seventeenth century diary of recorded documents and events

On page 77a a dowry is fully documented. The dowry was for the maiden Masuda, the daughter of Levi Magirz. It contained linens, a pillow, a tablecloth, pieces of silk fabric, and various garments that made up the bride's trousseau. On the bottom half of page 77a many names are recorded. Among them are the following: Isaac Ḥota, Moses Solomon Susi, Ephraim Jacob bar Moses, Jacob Maymeran, ——— Solomon Yomtoḅ Saadon, ——— Ephraim bar Solomon Susi, Benjamin bar Solomon Sa'id, ——— Abraham Slieman ibn Danan, ——— Judah ben R. Isaac Adhan, Solomon Moses Ab ——— Maman, ——— Akot, the daughter of R. Aaron Asbag, Ḥayyim Amozag, and Simḥah the daughter of R. Ab(raham) Alel.

There is another nuptial document on page 77b dated Shevat 1628. The bridegroom is the bachelor R. Abraham, the son of Joseph, the son of Isaac Maymeran. The bride is the maiden Bilyada, the daughter of Isaac, the son of the scholar R. Judah o.b.m., the son of Joseph, the son of Abraham o.b.m. Uziel. The witnesses to the marriage contract are R. Mîmun Bonfed and

R. Saul ben Ramukh. More biographical material is given on the second Joseph mentioned in this paragraph. This Joseph was the brother of R. Solomon Uziel, o.b.m. After the genealogical table of the newlyweds a note is added at the bottom of the page relating that Saul ben Ramukh bar Saadya was circumcised on a Friday, Vayish-laḥ, in the year 51.

Ms. 59
P. 78a and b

Liturgical poetry for festivals

The liturgical poems on page 78a are supplementary to the prayers called "Hoshana" of the festival of Tabernacles. The first prayer is a supplement to the prayer for the third day of Tabernacles, "Amẓaini Elohai Bemoadi Vaḥagigi." The first part of this prayer is missing; the top of this page begins with the sentence beginning with the letter 'Lamed' since the poem is composed in alphabetical sequence, and it concludes with the Hebrew letter 'Taf.'

The second prayer on this page is a supplement to the prayer for the fourth day of Tabernacles called El Pitḥakh Yarôn, which is found in the prayers of "Hoshana."

The third prayer appears on page 78b and it was composed for the Passover liturgy in the synagogue. No names or dates are discernible in the three prayers. The page and the script point to it as a product of the seventeenth century. [Page 79a and b belong to *Ms.57*.]

Ms. 60
P. 81a

R. Zevi Judah Berdugo serves as an emissary from the Holy Land to the Moroccan communities

This letter was written by Ẓevi Judah Berdugo to R. Raphael Ibn Ẓur of Fez, in the month of Sivan 1879. The writer has travelled from his home at Tiberias in the Holy Land to Meknès for the purpose of collecting funds for the poor of the Holy Land that are being supported by the charity funds of the holy Talmudic sage R. Meir Ba'al Ha-Nes. He also sends his regards to R. Abner Israel Ha-Ṣarfati of Fez. He mentions that the danger of bandits and the rigors of his journey kept him for arriving at his destination on time. He intends to be in Fez in a week and he asks R. Raphael Ibn Ẓur to begin a campaign for funds since the western communities have of late been neglecting to send the charitable support which is needed now more than ever. He prays for a safe return to Tiberias.

Ms. 61
P. 82a

A list of works composed by R. Ḥayyim Palaggi of Izmir, Turkey

Twenty-nine works published by the prolific writer R. Ḥayyim Palaggi, of blessed memory, are listed as they are mentioned in his luminous work "Ginzei Ḥayyim." The compiler of this list notes that some of the author's works were made available to him by the author's son.

Ms. 62
P. 83b

R. Judah Ibn Attar writes to R. Jacob Ibn Ẓur concerning a summons to court

R. Judah ibn Attar writes to R. Jacob Ibn Ẓur concerning a letter that R. Meir Gabbai received from Abraham ibn Joseph ibn Asaiyag asking him to appear before R. Jacob Ibn Ẓur for a Din Torah, a litigation. R. Meir refuses to go because many creditors hound him, among other reasons. However, R. Judah states that R. Meir is prepared to settle the matter if Abraham is prepared to come to the former's community (Fez). Otherwise Abraham will be obliged to wait until such time in the future when they will meet in order for the matter to be settled.

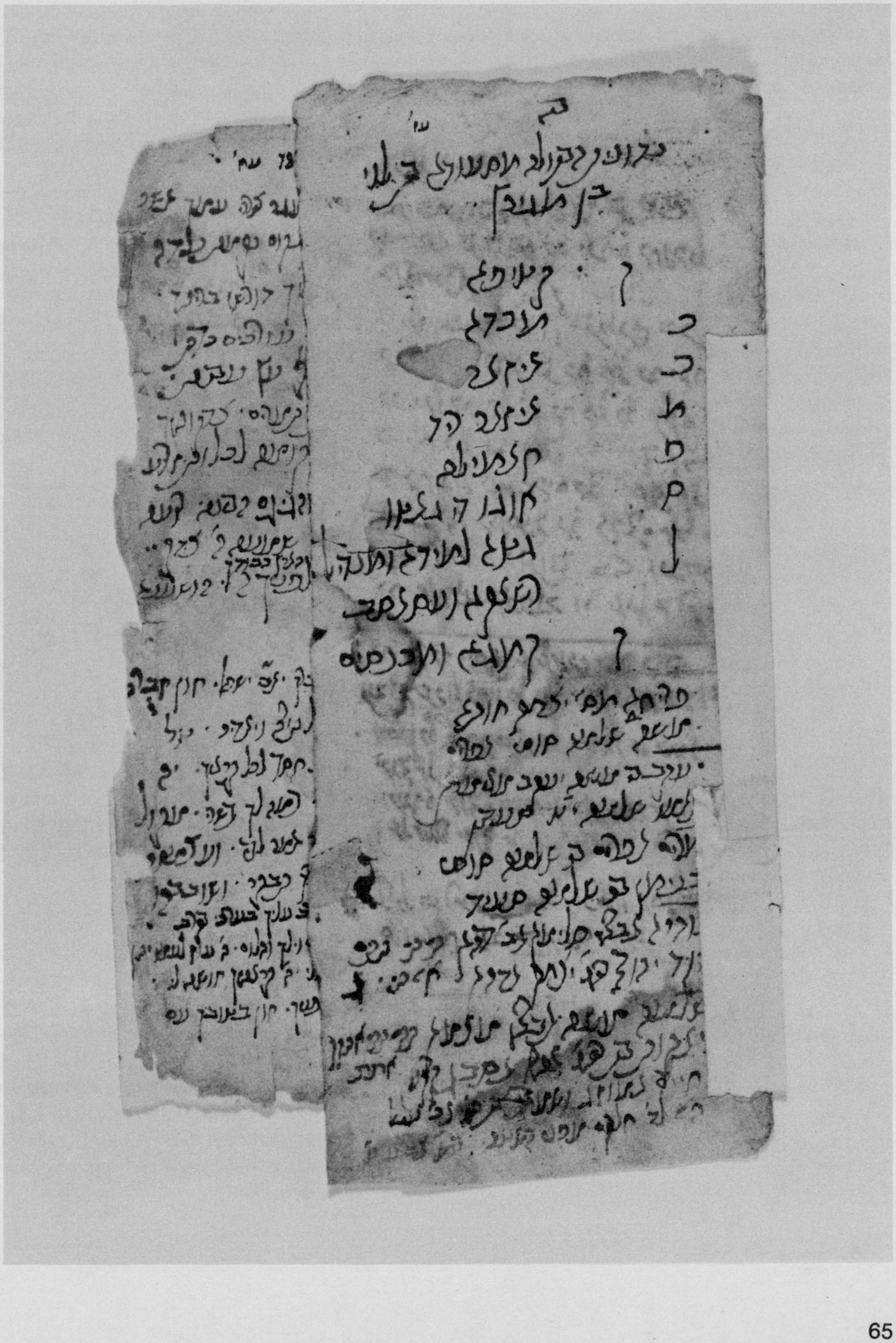

Ms. 58
An early seventeenth century dowry

Ms. 63
P. 84a and b

Two Halakhic queries to R. Jacob Ibn Ẓur. The first concerns a possible levirate. The second concerns an inheritance

[This letter commences on page 84b and concludes on page 84a.] Two halakhic queries are written to R. Jacob ben R. Reuben, of blessed memory, Ibn Ẓur, on Shushan Purim, in the year 1749.

The first query concerns a woman who gave birth to a baby prematurely at seven months and the baby died nineteen days later. The baby had hair and nails. The woman's husband died subsequently. Is she obliged to go through the levirate ceremony? The one who poses the question notes that the code Even ha-Ezer, chapter 166:4, deals with the subject.

The second query concerns an inheritance. A woman brought her possessions as her dowry to her husband's house upon her marriage. (Her husband can hold these possessions. However, upon her divorce or death he must restore in specie, all these possessions, and he is responsible for their loss or deterioration. This property is designated as Nikhsei Ẓon Barzel.) This woman has died and so has her husband, who was in another country. The woman had stated in her will that she wanted her niece, her brother's daughter, to inherit. The question posed is can the niece, who is poor, inherit the aunt's possessions? The anonymous person who poses this question states "that the law is in accord with R. Jacob (Ibn Ẓur) everywhere."

Ms. 64
P. 85a

A correspondence from Isaac Sabag to R. Jacob Ibn Zur

This letter is written by Isaac Sabag to R. Jacob Ibn Zur, at Fez. The writer informs R. Jacob about all the vicissitudes he has suffered: loss of limb, destitution, and the death of his son. He mentions the tribulations that transpired on his way to Marrakesh. He states that he was the beneficiary of the hospitality of R. Isaac Morigon, who supports poor wayfarers at his table. Three of them ask for alms from door to door. The writer mentions that he is ashamed to ask his host to aid his plight. The writer requests that R. Jacob ibn Attar should be asked to give aid to the members of the writer's family in his absence, since they are in a poverty-stricken condition. There was another person named R. Jacob Ibn Zur who died and the writer appeals to R. Jacob Ibn Ẓur to act on behalf of the widow. R. Jacob is asked to write to Elazar Arwah and one called David to help secure property that once belonged to Yaḥya Lekra for the deceased Jacob Ibn Ẓur's heirs. R. Moses Berdugo can't act for the heirs since he is at present very ill. The writer asks R. Jacob Ibn Zur to pray that he may return home safely from his journey.

Ms. 65
P. 86a

A correspondence from R. Judah Ibn Attar to R. Jacob Ibn Ẓur

This letter was written by R. Judah ibn Attar to R. Jacob Ibn Ẓur on the twenty-first of Adar II in the year 1720. R. Judah informs R. Jacob that he was chagrined to learn of R. Jacob's illness and he prays for his speedy recovery. The writer also informs R. Jacob of drought conditions (in Fez) which necessitated the declaration of fasts, public prayer recitals, confessions, and a procession to the cemetery where circuits were made in supplication. The wind began to blow just at the time of evening services and two hours later rain fell. R. Judah adds a postscript to his letter informing R. Jacob that two weeks ago he hurt himself in a fall in his house which is situated in the courtyard named after the late scholar Mas'ūd ben Ankab. [On page 86b an address to the people of Arif appears.]

R. Jacob Ibn Ẓur has prepared an Index to the Commentary Midrash Samuel on the Talmudic Work "Ethics of the Fathers"

R. Jacob Ibn Ẓur has compiled an Index To The Commentary Midrash Shmuel by R. Samuel Uẓedah on the Talmudic work "Ethics of the Fathers" according to the Venetian edition of the year 1575. R. Jacob informs us that he prepared this text for his uncle.

Ms. 66
Pp. 87a and 90b

The rabbis of Fez ask the community of Arif and its environs to extend financial aid to the agent of an emissary from Jerusalem

This document is written to the community of Arif and its environs by R. Judah ibn Attar. It was signed by R. Judah ibn Attar, R. Abraham ibn Danan, and by R. Jacob ben R. Reuḅen Ibn Ẓur in the city of Fez in the year 1718. It was sent to the prestigious citizens of Arif: R. Figo Bourbea, R. Aaron Larédo, R. Ḥayyim ben Shitrit, his son Mas'ūd, and R. Joseph ibn Shitrit. The rabbis of Fez ask that financial aid be given to the emissary from Jerusalem, R. Yom Toḅ Krispo, through the person of his agent R. Joseph b. Sa'id Abuzaglo. Due to his physical exhaustion R. Yom Toḅ is personally unable to travel to Arif. Since, for a prolonged period of time, no emissary has visited these areas the rabbis of Fez ask these communities to give a more substantial sum of money to maintain the institutions in the Holy Land. [The address to the community of Arif appears on page 86b.]

Ms. 67
P. 91a

R. Judah Ibn Attar responds to R. Moses Berdugo concerning a monetary claim made by Judah Monsano

This letter is written by R. Judah ibn Attar to R. Moses Berdugo of Meknès in reply to a letter received. R. Moses had mentioned that R. Judah Monsano had been awarded by the community a claim he had filed against Ephraim ibn Saadon and that Solomon b. Samuel was capitalizing on it. R. Judah ibn Attar says he has discussed the matter with the aforementioned Solomon, who maintains that Judah Monsano's claim against him is not proper since he is merely collecting what is his due and there are still expenses outstanding for which he should be paid.

Ms. 68
P. 92a

R. Jacob Ibn Ẓur is requested to make contracts available for a poor bride so that she can provide a dowry for herself

R. Judah ibn Attar writes to R. Jacob Ibn Ẓur concerning the daughter of Joshua, deceased, the son of R. Neḥemiah Ha-Kohen. She is poverty-stricken and has recently been married to Ya'ish ibn Asbag without bringing even a minimal dowry into the marriage. The groom is likewise penniless. Her mother has stated that R. Jacob Ibn Ẓur possesses contracts from her first husband Joshua which contain claims against the inheritors of the estate of his brother Shem Toḅ and his brother M. Kohen. R. Jacob Ibn Ẓur is therefore requested to find these contracts and to make them available to the bridegroom, Ya'ish, who is the bearer of this letter, so that he may commence litigation with the aforementioned inheritors.

Ms. 69
P. 93a

R. Jacob Ibn Ẓur at Meknès is asked to intercede with the brothers of a widow to grant her financial support

Rabbi Judah ibn Attar writes to his colleague, R. Jacob Ibn Zur, who is residing at Meknès, to intercede with the brothers of the widow of Moses Gabbai to grant her means of support. Her children are unable to support her, even though she raised them from the time that their father died. Her children are the victims of heavy

Ms. 70
P. 94a

taxation which has forced them to leave for other areas and they have since been set about by pirates and robbed of all that they possessed. Since the widow has decided to go to Meknès R. Jacob is asked to prepare her brothers for her arrival.

Ms. 71
P. 95a

The rabbis of Tetuán ask the rabbis of Fez to uphold the claim of Abraham Ibn Zeraḥ to the estate of his sister

This letter was sent by R. Jacob ibn Malka and R. Moses Bibas of Tetuán to the rabbinic judges of Fez, and signed by the former on the fourteenth day of Ḥeshvan 1756. The subject of this document is the claim of Abraham ibn Zerah called Musi, for his sister Donna, the widow of R. Yaabeẓ, whose legacy fell to him after she passed on. Abraham's brother Solomon was missing and therefore was not included in the legacy. Abraham claims that there were properties of the estate recorded in her marriage contract with her second husband apart from what was stipulated for her in her marriage contract with her first husband.

The rabbis of Fez are asked to support Abraham against R. Raphael Ibn Ẓur who is a stepson of Abraham's deceased sister. Both claim the right to receive all the monies that are due to her estate. Until such time as the rabbis render their decision all those monies should be held by R. Saul ibn Danan. Any monies that R. Raphael might have belonging to this estate should also be surrendered by R. Saul ibn Danan. All additional properties of a movable nature belonging to Donna, which are not stipulated in the marriage contracts, that are outstanding, should likewise be held by R. Saul ibn Danan.

The rabbis should inquire about the second marriage contract that was held by R. Samuel ibn Elbaz, which was also attested to by the elderly R. Joseph ibn Attar who accompanied her when she married her second husband. Therefore, the rabbis should request the marriage document of the widow of R. Samuel ibn Elbaz, and upon reviewing all the conditions set forth therein let them render their final decision on the matter. A note of consolation is added on the recent demise of R. Mîmun ibn Adhan, of Fez, on Saturday evening, the seventh of Ḥeshvan 1756.

Ms. 72
P. 96a and b

R. Saul Serero protests a ban placed by the Holy Land communities against the community of Tetuán for appropriating charity in times of need

This is a copy of a manuscript originally composed by R. Saul Serero to the rabbis in the Holy Land who have unjustly pronounced the ban against the community of Tetuán for withholding funds originally designated for charities in the Holy Land. The rabbis of the Holy Land are evidently not aware of the dire conditions and severe taxation prevailing in Tetuán in this most troubled of times. R. Joseph Bibas of Tetuán, who has been taken to task by the rabbis in the Holy Land has pleaded with R. Saul Serero to reply to them. R. Saul berates the rabbis in the Holy Land for rashly using the ban; particularly since rabbinic luminaries of earlier generations such as R. Joseph Colon, the Rosh, and Rabbenu Tam permitted funds earmarked for charity to be appropriated for other pressing purposes in times of distress. Furthermore, the resident scholars of Tetuán should have first been informed of the contemplated ban. This was the procedure followed when the rabbis in Morocco had to exercise a ban against the smaller communities; they always informed the scholars of that community first. R. Serero affirms the love of the western communities, especially Tetuán, for the Holy Land communities; but times are bad in the west so aid cannot be forthcoming at present. Three scrolls of the Law have already been sent to Algiers to be sold to pay obligations to the emissary of the Holy Land, Abraham Pariente. The letter concludes with the hope that times will become better and the western communities will again resume sending money to the Holy Land.

Ms. 73
P. 97a

R. Judah Ibn Attar implores R. Ḥabib Toledano to intercede with a non-Jewish creditor on behalf of Abraham Ibn Danan

This letter is written by R. Judah ibn Attar to R. Ḥabib Toledano on behalf of Abraham ibn Danan. In this troubled period ibn Danan owes a debt to a non-Jew, Leḥajj Adayl, who is demanding payment before the date the debt is due. The non-Jew is a candidate for a royal position as the third in charge of the chariots for the royal entourage. He therefore needs the money immediately in order to secure the position for himself. R. Jacob Ibn Ẓur and Aaron ibn Amozig will both testify that the non-Jew is demanding payment before it is due. The non-Jew is terrorizing R. Abraham who has been in hiding for three days. R. Judah implores R. Ḥabib to intercede with the non-Jew on behalf of R. Abraham. A letter that R. Judah had already sent to R. Jacob concerning money that could help to alleviate the present situation has gone unanswered. R. Abraham has asked R. Judah to write to R. Ḥabib to contact R. Jacob about the money. The address of this document, which is to Meknès has page 100a pasted on it.

Pr. 73.5
Pp. 98a—99b

The proceedings of the sixth meeting of "Kol-yisrael Ḥaverim," a report on organizational activities

This report was printed in the Hebrew language and published in Paris, Typ. L. Guerin, rue du Petit-Carreau, 26. A review of the activites of the past year of "Kol Yisrael Ḥaverim" is recorded. Among those present at this sixth meeting of the organization were Dr. Albert Cohen, Rabbi Artoum of the Sephardic community of London; N. Camondo, the Chief Rabbi of France; and the official Nissim Shamama of Tunis, amongst other personages. Seventeen months have passed since the previous meeting. The organization's statement of purpose is given as well as a record of its activities in various countries. America begins to play a role. Serbian Jews wish to colonize the Holy Land. There is not much money available for this purpose; 50,192 francs have been spent and 37,818 francs remain. The number of members is recorded as 4,610. Rabbi Kalisher is mentioned. The B'nai Brith Organization is also mentioned. "Kol Yisrael Ḥaverim" is popularly known by its French appellation as Alliance Israelite Universelle.

Ms. 74
P. 100a

A list of Halakhic citations

Maharashdam, Yoreh De'ah 169 does not render a lenient ruling like the Rashba and Ran. See Maharik, Shoresh Vav and Maharashdam, Yoreh De'ah 171, 173 and 181; see also responsa of the Rosh, Kelal 13:2. Terumat ha-Deshen, nos. 53 and 144.

See Maimonides, chapter nine of Zekhiya U'Matanah, "If one declared all his property to be holy or ownerless" where he renders a lenient ruling in accord with the Rashba, no. 65b; the responsa of the Ran . . . and Ḥoshen Mishpat, Ran in his father's name and nos. 213 and 212. The Ran in the first chapter of Nedarim (Vows) page 7. Shakh, Yoreh De'ah, at the end. Ḥoshen Mishpat, 124; Maimonides chapter nine of Ma'aseh Ha-Kôrbônôt, Darkhei Mo'am. Maimonides, chapter two, of Matnôt Aniiyiim. Ḥoshen Mishpat chapter twenty-seven, page 22b. Maimonides, chapter nine of Bikkurim and chapter ten, law 12, and chapter eleven, law no. 13. Ribash, no. 260.

Ms. 75
P. 101a

R. Jacob Ibn Ẓur receives an affirmative reply about one judgement, but in a second case one party remains intransigent

Two documents are found on page 101a and they are related. R. Menaḥem Attia sent the upper document to R. Jacob Ibn Ẓur. R. Jacob ibn Malka appended his reply below on the same page [see *Ms.76*] and sent it back addressed to the judges at Fez.

The letter on top of page 101a was written in

the month of Kislev 1722, to R. Jacob Ibn Ẓur by Menaḥem Attia in response to a letter received from the former. It deals with two different cases. The writer states that in regard to the first matter a compromise was finally achieved after the claimant was convinced that his claim was given proper consideration, especially since a decision had already been rendered on the matter by a scholar.

The second case involved one called Joseph ibn Gikito. The writer has informed the latter of the judgement rendered by R. Jacob Ibn Zur, but Joseph ibn Gikito has ignored it, saying that his dispute was with the widow and her child and that Menaḥem Attia has nothing to say about the matter. Menaḥem suggests to R. Jacob Ibn Ẓur that he should take the additional measures against Joseph. Perhaps they will help and he will be obliged to restore the money to the child and the widow.

Ms. 76
P. 101a

R. Jacob Ibn Malka asks R. Jacob Ibn Ẓur to exercise a ban against one who is contemptuous of the judgement rendered in the rabbinic court

This letter is written by Jacob ibn Malka to R. Jacob Ibn Ẓur at Fez asking the latter to apply the ban against Joseph ibn Gikito for acting contemptuously by disobeying the judgement issued by a rabbinic court. Joseph was obliged, according to the court's decision, to make payment to a widow and her child. Jacob ibn Malka charges the aforementioned Joseph as also being guilty of theft. He offers the testimony of R. Mas'ūd ibn Moiyal against Joseph. The writer awaits R. Jacob Ibn Ẓur's reply, together with R. Menahem Attia and the aforementioned Mas'ud ibn Moiyal. The writer asks R. Jacob to send the letter that he will prepare to R. Moses Berdugo for his signature so that the document will have even more authority.

Ms. 77
P. 102a

A letter of consolation to Samuel Ibn Ẓur

This letter of consolation was composed in the year 1769. It was sent to Samuel Ibn Ẓur on the passing of a male member of his family. The text consists of four stanzas. Each stanza commences with the word Petaḥ and concludes with the word Rav. The first two stanzas consist of four lines each, while the last two stanzas consist of three lines each. The letter is signed by Ephraim Monsonyego and Judah b. Abraham Coriat (at Tetuán). This letter of consolation was written on the passing of R. Samuel's father, (R. Raphael Oḅed Ibn Ẓur), according to the address.

Ms. 78
P. 103a

A letter of consolation

This letter of consolation is sent to R. Matitya Serero and R. Samuel Ibn Ẓur at Fez by four scholars from Meknès. Their four signatures appear in the following order, Jacob (Toledano), Solomon Toledano, Solomon Tapiero, and Moses Toledano.

P. 104a [See *Ms.82* on page 109a of which this page is a part.] A short list of contributors and their contributions are given on page 104a. The following names are noted: Moses Ha-Levi, one called Yom Toḅ, Judah b. Solomon, and the members of the committee of the Isle of Compagne. P. 104b [See *Ms.82* on page 109a of which this page is a part.] This is an introductory portion of a letter that was sent to the brothers Moses and Isaac Ha-Levi of the Isle of Compagne.

Ms. 79
P. 105a

A legal document issued by a rabbinic tribunal attesting to the acquisition of a burial plot

Shem Toḅ, the son of Abraham, of blessed memory, Ben Attar, has decided to acquire a burial plot near the place of his forbears, even though he probably has rights to be buried there anyway. The money that he will pay the treasurers of the Burial Society of Fez will thus be available for the poor. This document was drawn up by a

Rabbinic Tribunal after it was clarified that the plot had been paid for so that he might dig a grave, never to be prevented from doing so by any member of the community. This document was drawn up in the month of Marḥeshvan 1734 in Fez. The undersigned are in the following order, R. Jacob Ibn Ẓur, R. Shalom Edery, and R. Samuel Elbaz.

A Midrashic exposition based on a text in the Yalkut on the Book of Psalms

Ms. 80
Pp. 106a—107b

The verse which is being expounded from the Yalkut is chapter 32:1 in the Book of Psalms. The author develops the themes of Divine Judgement, Pardon, and Sin. The one who wrote this manuscript also wrote *Ms.81*.

An Aggadic exposition of a rabbinic text

Ms. 81
P. 108a and b

This Aggadic exposition of the rabbinic text concerns three books representing three groups of people: those who are wicked, those who are neither wicked nor righteous, and those who are righteous. The beginning of this text is missing. The script is in the same hand as that which wrote *Ms.80*.

A letter addressed to the brothers R. Moses Ha-Levi and R. Isaac Ha-Levi of the Isle of Campagne

Ms. 82
P. 109a

[See pages 104a and b which are part of this manuscript.]
This letter, which flows with rhyme and metaphor, was written to the brothers R. Moses Ha-Levi and R. Isaac Ha-Levi of the Isle of Compagne concerning a charity campaign. The community of Gibraltar is mentioned as having responded with beneficence. The members of the community of Fez, which is reported as being in a poor economic condition, have also pledged to give additional grants in spite of their bad situation. The letter hints that the Jews of the Isle of Campagne should also follow suit. Some pledges are recorded on the other side of this page. [See page 104a.]

A letter of consolation to Meknès

Ms. 83
P. 110a

No names are recorded in this letter of consolation. It is written "to console all the mourners of Meknès." This letter was written by the same hand that copied *Ms.1* and *Ms.2*.

A series of poetic compositions by R. Jacob Ibn Ẓur

Ms. 84
Pp. 111a—116b

A series of twenty-five poems are recorded on pages 111a to 116b. The following poems are included: (1) Yah Le-am Evyon; (2) Yah Adonai Godlekha B'mo Fi Amalail; (3) Yeḥi Hasdokh Le-dal Ve-dokh; (4) Yah Dror Zur; (5) Yonat Hen; (6) Ani El Adonai Eqra Yekonen Ereẓ Yeqara; (7) Lekha Ẓur Yeshuati; (8) Elohay Avi Ẓur Yeshuati; (9) Yaaqov Yagil Yisrael Yismaḥ; (10) Yaḥid U-Meyuḥad Bekha Evtah Lo Efhad; (11) Yah Ẓur Misgabi Sh'ay Et Nivi; (12) Sh'ay Shaddai Shma Koli Be-Siḥi; (13) Ait Oll Hamon Monai Maali Asira Anokhi La-Adonai Anokhi Ashirah; (14) Yaḥid Be-Ḥeldo Ain Milvado; (15) Yah Be-Vnot Ulamkha; (16) El Ḥai Nimẓa Ẓur Mahsi; (17) Yah Haray Na Le-Ainai Pe'er Binyan Bait Miqdash; (18) Yom Eqra Lekha Ẓur Norah; (19) Yimlokh Be-Arẓi Gezah Ish Parẓi; (20) Yah Mah Me'od Niflaita; (21) Yedaber Pi Teḥilot El Be-Zimra; (22) Elohim Ḥai Meẓiuto; (23) Rom Aneh Et Atirati; (24) Haẓmaḥ Le-Aiyda Lekḥa Nosa'at Ainekha.

Poem number sixteen is based on the thirteen principles of faith. Poem number seventeen was composed for the construction of a synagogue. Poem number twenty was composed by R. Jacob Ibn Ẓur upon his recovery from illness. He added three more stanzas for those freed from bondage, their safe return from sea voyages, and those who return safely from a caravan journey. Poem number twenty-one was composed on the ten sefirot and the Holy names that are related to the sefirot in twenty-six verses equal in number to the Holy Name of The Almighty. Poem number twenty-two, on the thirteen principles of faith as they appear in the prayer Adon Olam, is composed in thirty-two verses corresponding to the thirty-two paths of wisdom. Apparently additional pages followed in this collection of poems since the last page (116b) concludes with the Hebrew word "Nogah" which should appear on a following page which is missing from the collection. In most poems the author's name appears in acrostic form.

Ms. 85
P. 118a

Ms. containing biographical and bibliographical information culled from a variety of sources

The material in this manuscript was transcribed by R. Solomon Elijah Ibn Ẓur, the son of R. Jacob Ibn Ẓur. The work "Kupat Rokhlim" that was composed by R. Yedidia Monsonyego is noted as discussing the problem of tribulations that the corpse undergoes in the grave after death.

The writer states that R.Y. Caro was a contemporary of R. Isaac Ibn Ẓur and R. Vidal Ha-Ṣarfati and that the author's father, R. Jacob Ibn Ẓur, had it from his father, R. Solomon Samuel Ibn Ẓur o.b.m., that he saw R.Y. Caro's signature. R. Solomon Elijah records that the prophet Elijah revealed himself to R. Judah ibn Attar. Also that R. Neḥunya b. Ha-Kane composed a work called Seferha-Peli'ah. [See page 129b which is part of this manuscript page, for additional material.]

Ms. 86
P. 119a and b

Practical aspects and problems related to the scribal profession

[*The original manuscript was stolen from this collection, but a photocopy of it exists.*]

The importance of perfecting the skills of the artisan in performing tasks for preparing or repairing articles for holy use in religious rituals, is discussed by Uri, the son of David Levi, of blessed memory. Biblical and Talmudic texts are quoted in support of this viewpoint. The preparation of the parchment to best receive the ink when writing Torah Scrolls is elaborated upon. It is noted that R. Samuel Aboab, of blessed memory, was concerned that the concoction used to prepare parchments might become an obstruction between the parchment and the ink that comes into contact with it. This would invalidate the Torah Scroll for ritual use.

In the seventh year after the demise of the aforementioned R. Aboab, the author claims to have devised a method whereby it is unnecessary to apply some other material to the parchment to achieve the desired results. He states that he discovered this by experimentation even though he is not a scribe by profession. The method is then fully described.

The last section of page 119b deals with methods of correcting mistakes in a Torah Scroll. In the last paragraph the problem concerning the impression left by the Divine names of God is discussed and R. Samuel Aboab's concern in this matter is mentioned. [This page is not the conclusion of the subject matter under discussion since another page is indicated. That other page is found in our collection on page 128a and it is the conclusion of this manuscript.]

Ms. 87
P. 120a and b

Chronicle Serero

[*The original manuscript was stolen but a photocopy exists.*]

[See also pages 127a and b which are part of this manuscript.]

This chronicle includes tracts from earlier scholars who also reported on the historical incidents that transpired during their lifetimes. Among these scholars the names of Samuel b. Saul ibn Danan and R. Saul Serero are mentioned. The author also notes that some of the writings

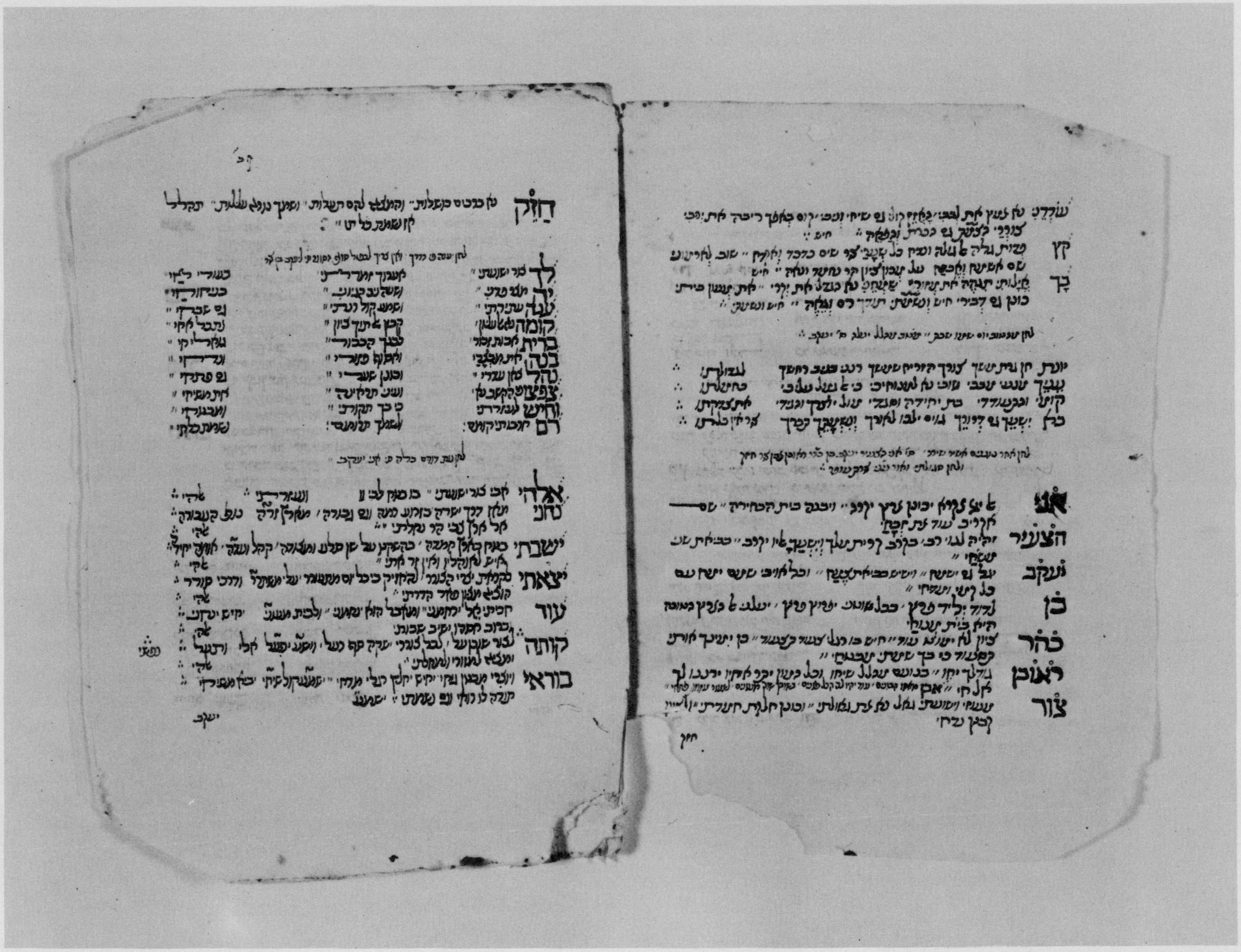

Ms. 84
Poetic compositions
by Rabbi Jacob Ibn
Ẓur

were the work of his grandfather. The author commences with a statement attributed to Ḥanina b. Dosa that the tribulations of Israel should be recorded as well as the miracles.

Saul b. David Serero begins by relating some misfortunes. A famine between 1604 and 1606 took the lives of about eight hundred dwellers in Fez. More than six hundred are mentioned as having been converted. The roads were dangerous because highwaymen abounded. Suicides were also reported. A lamentation was composed on the twentieth day of Adar 1606 for the community of Fez. The famine claimed the life of R. Jacob ibn Attar among close to three thousand souls who also succumbed.

Samuel (son of Saul ibn Danan) writing on Thursday the tenth of Tevet 1724 reports a famine that lasted for three years, from 1721 to 1724, and a drought that continued for four years. The price of wheat was quoted at 135 uqiot. Every year the "Ba-Ha-B" circuit of fasts was constantly observed and added to. Great convocations were observed in 1773 at Meknès, Salé, and Ṣefrou. Torah Scrolls were brought forth. Rain began to fall and continued for three days. The price of barley was reduced and wheat was quoted at 60 uqiot. In the month of Tevet the price went up again to 135 uqiot. The author informs us that the misfortune in Fez was indescribable. [Another part of the chronicle is found on pages 127a and b.]

Ms. 88
P. 121a and b

A case of inheritance involving the customs of Meknes and Ṣefrou concerning a widow's portion of an estate

[*The original manuscript was stolen but a photocopy exists.*]

[This letter continues on page 126b and the address is on page 121b.]
This letter is written by Amor Abitbol to R. Raphael Ha-Ṣarfati of Fez. The writer states that he accompanied R. Isaac Abitbol to appease R.Y. Elbaz, who swore that he had only received half of the money in question, the other half having gone to his nephew Mordecai Elbaz. After being spoken to he was prepared to return a certain amount from his portion.

R. Raphael is also informed of an enactment by the community of Meknès in the matter of inheritance laws, namely, that the inheritors have the prerogative of paying a widow only the value of her marriage contract when the estate is large. If, however, the estate is small they may divide it with the widow. An orphan has informed the writer that in his case he followed the ruling of Mahari Berdugo and only paid the value of the marriage contract. If a protest was going to be lodged then he would increase the amount. In the present case Mahari Elbaz and his nephew have permitted the orphan to take all that remained over the value of the wedding contract. The writer informs Mahari Berdugo that in this case the enactment of Meknès will not be in force since the woman was married in Ṣefrou. Even though they subsequently moved to Meknès the customs of Ṣefrou on these matters should prevail. The author states that he is aware that Mahari Berdugo is adamant in following the custom of Meknès. However, he should at least try to reach a compromise. In the earlier case, R.Y. Elbaz is vindicated. If it were possible to satisfy the orphan they would have done so. Now, however, the orphan can only be convinced to follow the law.
[This letter continues on page 126b.]

Ms. 89
P. 122a and b

An appeal is made to R. Raphael Ha-Ṣarfati to convince an intransigent debtor to pay his debt

[*The original manuscript was stolen but a photocopy exists.*]

R. Judah Elbaz writes to R. Raphael Ha-Ṣarfati asking him to use his good office to convince one called Abraham ibn Azuz to pay his debts to R. Elbaz. Abraham lived in an apartment belonging to the writer for some years after 1822. The apartment has now been sold but Abraham still has not paid his debt. In the year 1829 he was called to a judgement on this matter and Abraham sought the help of R. Jonathan, of blessed memory. The latter convinced the writer to let

Abraham pay his debt in installments because of the embarrassment involved. R. Raphael is informed that he will receive the bill of debt that will indeed show that such was the case. The aforementioned Abraham is still intransigent and therefore R. Judah Elbaz appeals to R. Raphael Ha-Ṣarfati for help since so many years have passed and Abraham does not comply.

On page 122b a list of names appear next to numerals. The days Thursday and Friday are indicated. Some of the names are R. Solomon Ibn Ẓur, R. Aaron, Moses and Elijah. Also the address to R. Raphael Ha-Ṣarfati of *Ms.89*, page 122a, appears here.

Ms. 90

P. 123a and b

A letter concerning an estate and other matters sent by Samuel Halevi ibn Yulee to R. Immanuel Monsano

[*The original manuscript was stolen but a photocopy exists.*]

This letter, which commences with an introduction in Hebrew followed by a Judaeo-Arabic text, is sent by Samuel Halevi ibn Yulee to R. Immanuel Monsano at Fez. Greetings are sent to R. Immanuel's daughter and his son-in-law R. David. Also Jacob Ibn Ẓur is alluded to. The writer informs R. Immanuel that he did everything in his power to oblige R. Jacob ben Simḥon to pay the money that he owed to the estate belonging to R. Abraham, the late father-in-law of R. Immanuel Monsano. R. Jacob did, however, place the money in the safekeeping of a third party until a copy of the will of the late R. Abraham could be made available. Samuel asks R. Immanuel either to send R. Ḥayyim D'Avila to testify or at least to make a copy of the will available so that the dispute can be resolved. The contract that is in the possession of R. Joseph Ohanah is still awaited.

Samuel informs R. Immanuel that the reason that he does not reside in his former domicile is because R. Sammai Masrafi made free lodgings available to him while the status of the previous dwelling was involved in a litigation. It is possible the case could be reopened so that there is an element of insecurity involved in living there. A book of accounts will be forwarded to R. Immanuel as soon as R.Y. Maragi has time to make certain corrections therein. The garment that R. Immanuel inquired about is not presently available, but another kind is available for purchase. The writer inquires if the book Maharam Zabara is available. If so it should be sent through the person of R. Solomon Edery or Joseph Almosnino who is coming to the writer's city. Samuel asks that the letter should be given to R. Moses Halevi.

Ms. 91

P. 124a

Ms. called Pinkas Patuaḥ

[*The original manuscript was stolen but a photocopy exists.*]

This manuscript deals with a litigation concerning a commercial transaction and it is completely written in the form of rhymed metaphor heavily borrowing its style from biblical narrative. No names are indicated in the body of the text. It appears that a non-Jew may also be involved in the litigation. See *Ms. 92* where a signature is given, since both texts are written by the same hand.

Ms. 92

P. 125a

An Aggadic exposition

[*The original manuscript was stolen but a photocopy exists.*]

This Aggadic exposition refers to three texts from the Book of Psalms, Ps. 5:10, Ps. 115:7, Ps. 149:6. Each text contains a form of the Hebrew word "Gronum." The subject deals with the merit of the righteous who are regarded as living even after their passing, and on the demerits of the wicked, who are regarded as dead even during their lifetime. Biblical passages and Midrashic texts are drawn upon in this composition which does not exceed a page in length. This manuscript is written in the same hand as *Ms.91* and it comes from the same booklet. A signature is given at the bottom of this exposition.

Ms. 93
P. 125b

A rhyming prayerful petition

[*The original manuscript was stolen but a photocopy exists.*]

This page which was written by the author of *Ms. 91* and *Ms. 92*, is part of a small collection of writings. It consists of about twenty-two lines of verse. The theme deals with a prayerful petition to the Almighty in times of trouble.

Ms. 94
P. 125b

A list of biblical passages containing the term "Shlosha"... three

[*The original manuscript was stolen but a photocopy exists.*]

The author of *Ms.91*, *Ms.92* and *Ms.93* compiled a list of eleven Biblical quotations which contain the word "Shlosha"—"three." This page appears on the other side of page 125b. The compiler inserted the page in such a way that it appears not to have pagination. [See *Ms.88*, page 121a.]

The conclusion of *Ms.88* is found on page 126b because of the way the compiler inserted that document into the book.

P. 127a and b

[The beginning of this document may be found in *Ms.87*.]

The chronicler, Serero, reports an incident (one of a series, we gather), concerning the two wicked sons of Ḥamdun, a non-Jew, who entered the Mellah and spent the night in the house of a divorcée whom they raped while a few immoral Jews offered a musical accompaniment. Some brigands, attracted by the music, entered the house, beat the Jews, and murdered the two sons of Ḥamdun as well as a third non-Jew who was with them. The author feared that the wicked Ḥamdun would spend his wrath on the Jews, himself included, in retaliation for the lives of his sons. The king was not in the city, the writer informs us. He himself sought refuge in the house of an Arab official to whom he reported all that had transpired. He then began to send messages to many of the officials of the realm and to the Nagid, R. Jacob Roti, who accompanied the king. After many bribes were given, his safety was assured. The wicked Ḥamdun appealed to the king who informed him that his charge was false. It was not the Jews but the brigands who killed his sons and, the Qadi of Fez added, the brigands would probably kill Ḥamdun too.

In the month of Ḥeshvan 1622, the king went to the city of Qazzar when he heard that his brother Mulay Maḥmad had been chased from there.

The brigands finally came to the author's home on the fifteenth of Kislev and tried to gain entry through the window. The author's brother, R. David, noticed about ten of them and was shot at by arrows but he and his brother cast stones at the intruders until they fled. The chronicler informs us that he went to Ṣefrou in the month of Kislev because of the violence in Fez. He remained there for fifteen days whereupon the community sent messages on his behalf from the king and officials to the Sheikh Ali, who ruled the village of Ṣefrou, to provide protection (an escort) to enable him to return to Fez.

On page 127b we are informed of upheavals in the community of Tafilalet and how the majority of Jews suffered death, pillage, and starvation during the siege of that community. Others were sold into slavery and the synagogues were destroyed. The Nagid was hanged.

On the eve of the new month of Sivan, King Mulay Abdallah became ill and on the night of the fourteenth of Sivan he died. After his burial, his brother Mulay Abd Almalkh, who was fifteen years old, was crowned in his stead. The political situation was stabilized and travel to Ṣefrou became safer except for the wicked Almatein who subsequently rebelled against the king in the month of Elul. After a Friday service the ninety-year-old Qadi was killed on his return from the king's palace. He was reported to have been favorably disposed to the Jews, and they mourned his passing. Apparently conditions grew worse for the Jews, since all the king's actions were now influenced by the official Ali ibn Musa. He took a certain fixed sum of tribute from the Jews.

On Sabbath eve, the twenty-second of Iyar 1625, there was a great rumbling and an earthquake.

[This document is the conclusion of *Ms.86* on page 119b.]

The question is posed as how to correct mistakes in Torah Scrolls when one encounters the Holy Names of God? After this subject is treated, the third point which is discussed is to find the most convenient way to prepare the scribal ink.

[This text is part of *Ms.85* on page 118a.]

Pp. 128a and 129b

This manuscript contains biographical and bibliographical information culled from a variety of sources by Solomon Elijah Ibn Ẓur, the son of R. Jacob Ibn Ẓur. Among the sources we have quotes from R. Hayyim David Azulai's "Shem ha-Gedolim," a famous bibliographical work, concerning Rashi, R. Solomon Izḥaki, acclaiming the latter as the most outstanding of French bible commentators. Also notes are offered on R. Hayyim Capusi, the miracle worker of blessed memory. He is mentioned as having served as a religious judge. The source of these comments was the aforementioned work "Shem ha-Gedolim."

Ms. 95
P. 130a

Western communities are asked to support the Holy Land communities who are economically distressed

This letter is written to R. Raphael Ha-Ṣarfati (of Fez) by Rabbi Abu Alafia, of Tiberias, to arouse the western communities to extend substantial financial support to the Holy Land communities. The need is particularly great since the price of barley has risen dramatically of late. The writer introduces the emissary Rabbi Moses Pinto, the son of the illustrious R. Isaac Pinto, of Tiberias, of blessed memory, who is delegated to collect the funds.

Ms. 96
P. 131a

The rabbis of Meknès ask R. Samuel Elbaz to provide information against a legal claim or else the claimant will exercise his rights within thirty days

This document is written to R. Samuel Elbaz of Fez by the Rabbis Jacob Toledano and Mîmun Adhan of Meknès concerning the claim of Isaac ibn Haroush against Ḥayyim ibn Magiruẓ. Isaac held a pledge against a portion of a courtyard called Ẓar Asbaga which Joseph ibn Amram ibn Tata sold for 700 uqiot of silver thereby forfeiting his rights to the courtyard. The time to make good on the pledge before it would become forfeited was on the twenty-eighth of Adar 1716. That date having arrived, Isaac made a claim to exercise his rights against the aforementioned Ḥayyim. On four subsequent occasions Isaac sent formal legal claims, but no response was forthcoming. On his arrival in Meknès Hayyim had stated that when he returned to Fez he would ask R. Samuel Elbaz to forward additional information which would support his case, but Ḥayyim had never taken this action and his stalling was making a mockery of justice. Now if a satisfactory answer was not forthcoming then within a month Isaac would exercise his claim to all parts of the courtyard. Both parties to the dispute had been instructed by the undersigned rabbis to write to R. Samuel Elbaz concerning the litigation, on the same day that this letter was written. This would insure that R. Samuel could forward a speedy reply and the matter could be resolved.

Ms. 97
P. 132a

A copy of a last will and testament

This will is a copy of the original that was drawn up for Solomon ibn David Murciano. Someone needed this copy but the reason why it was needed is not stated, apart from the fact that it was to be taken to another location. The father, who was ill, had this will drawn so that his children would not feud over his estate after his death. He therefore stipulated that it should be apportioned in the following manner. Provision was to be made for the first born son, Joseph, to receive the larger of two houses. Two separate upper stories were assigned to the younger son, David. Joseph received an additional sum of 30 pieces of silver.

The wife was to receive the value of her marriage contract in cash, and an additional part of the estate would be divided equally amongst her and her two sons. A smaller upper storey was set aside for the two younger daughters so that a domicile should always be available to them in the event of their prospective husbands divorcing them or leaving them widowed. Money was also set aside for their dowries. This copy was drawn up on the eighteenth day of Shevat 1874. The original was drawn up on the twenty-eighth day of Tishri 1873. The witnesses to the original will were R. Aaron Ha-Kohen, and R. Joseph ibn Aaron Ḥamo. The witnesses to the copy were Abraham ibn Jacob Ha-Kohen Skali and Solomon ibn Joseph ibn Ḥamo.

Ms. 98
P. 133a

A plea for a confirmation concerning a judgement rendered in a case dealing with inheritance which casts aspersions on the judgement of a scholar and an exhortation against introducing non-Jewish officials into legal action

Rabbi Mordecai Berdugo of Meknès writes to Rabbi Samuel ibn Elbaz (of Fez) concerning the report of the issuance of a judgement pertaining to an inheritance that the latter had rendered against Eli Pariente which casts aspersions on R. Jacob Toledano's judgement on the matter. If indeed the report is true then R. Mordecai asks R. Samuel to substantiate the matter by providing a written statement of the witnesses and their names. If the witnesses had already been cross-examined by the Rabbinic Tribunal (in Fez) then apparently nothing could be done to reverse the judgement. Even so why would the plaintiff be encouraged by R. Samuel to inquire of the non-Jewish authorities to force the defendant to comply? R. Samuel is asked to stop the non-Jews from interfering in the matter, "As if we have not sufficiently suffered by their actions." This letter was written about 1745.

Ms. 99
P. 134a

An emissary of the Holy Land corresponds, in transit from Ṣefrou, with R. Ham-Malakh Raphael of Fez

This letter which is in metaphoric style was written on the fifteenth of Tevet 1875 to R. Raphael by an emissary from the city of Safed. The writer, Abraham, informs R. Raphael that he is receiving the correspondences from the Holy Land that the latter forwards to him at Ṣefrou. He also alludes to the financial aid that is being made available to him. He inquires about the arrival of some funds that he sent. The writer sends regards to R. Raphael's son, Solomon, also to R. Jacob and to the innkeeper Maḥlouf and his son. The author relates that he is presently in a city of scholars, at Ṣefrou, and that he enjoys their hospitality. The address is found on the other side of the page.

Ms. 100
P. 135a

A letter from the Holy Land to rabbi Raphael Ibn Ẓur of Fez

This letter was sent by Abraham ibn Walid of Jerusalem in 1873 to R. Ham-Malakh Raphael Ibn Ẓur of Fez and it also mentions R. Raphael's son Solomon. The author apologizes for not being able to write sooner. He states that his brother and sister and her sons have just arrived from the west and he is busy caring for their needs. Concerning certain books he replies that Rabbi Ẓuf Devash has already sent them to Rabbi Raphael. He also mentions that Rabbi Eliyahu Amor, who is serving as an emissary in the interests of the Kôllel, will soon arrive in Morocco. In a postscript Abraham sends regards to R. Ish Ha-Ṣarfati, R. Mattityahu Serero and to R. Jacob Ha-Kohen. Abraham asks R. Raphael to send a letter in the former's name to the city of Taza concerning their contribution to the Jerusalem Kollel. The address is given on the other side of the letter, on page 139b, which is part of the same page.

A letter from the Holy Land to R. Raphael Ibn Ẓur (of Fez)

Ms. 101
P. 136a

This letter is sent to R. Raphael Ibn Ẓur asking him to aid an emissary who is referred to as R. Aryeh. The latter has been sent to collect funds for the purpose of building a synagogue in the Holy Land. The author expresses his regrets that he was not able to find a book that R. Raphael requested. It was called Torah Ḥadashah. The author of this letter states that he offers prayers for the health of R. Raphael at the tomb of R. Meir Ba'al Ha-Nes on the occasion of the anniversary of the death of the Saint. This letter is written in anticipation of the arrival of the aforementioned emissary in the west. The letter will be borne by Elijah Asulin who is returning to Fez after spending some time in the Holy Land. The letter cannot be too lengthy since Elijah Asulin has to leave immediately.

An incomplete poetic text

Ms. 102
Pp. 137a—138b

This incomplete two page text of poetic genre which is rich in metaphor appears to belong to a larger collection of texts. The only name that is inserted is that of Yedidia Monsonyego, which appears at the end of page 137a, before the last paragraph.

An emissary writes to R. Raphael Ha-Ṣarfati

Ms. 103
P. 140a

This letter is written to R. Raphael Ha-Sarfati, at Fez, by Israel Jacob Halevi. The latter appears to be an emissary and his flowery language seems to attest to his calling. He states that he is just completing his campaign in the community (which he does not name) and he is leaving for another community, Irbir, after Purim. He alludes to the aid he hopes to receive from R. Raphael. The writer sends regards to Joseph, R. Raphael's son. R. Yaira Ohana and R. Shalom Edery send their regards.

Laws concerning the collection of debts

Ms. 104
Pp. 141a—142a

This two-page digest of the laws related to the collection of debts is written very clearly although part of the text is torn away. The authorities of Jewish law who are cited are the commentators on the Code of Jewish Law known as the Shulhan Arukh, such as the Shakh, Sema, and Levush. Earlier authorities of the middle ages such as the Geonim and Maimonides are noted, as well as Talmudic sources.

A response is given to the query as to what point in time one attains his majority, in a lengthy letter written to R. Menaḥem Serero

Ms. 105
Pp. 143a—144b

This correspondence was written to R. Menahem Serero, at Fez, on the twelfth day of Adar, in the year 1719. The author is R. Jacob Ibn Zur who was situated in Meknes when he wrote the letter. The author informs us of his inability to take solid or liquid nourishment because of his illness and of his need to take medicine before prayer services and before recital of the Kiddush on Sabbath morning. Then he takes up the issue as to when one attains one's majority. Whether it is on the first or second day of the fourteenth year which is thirteen years and one day or thirteen years and two days. "It is obviously attained by the age of thirteen and one day and far be it for me to have stated that it was thirteen and two days. The next question is, must a full twenty-four hours of the first day transpire before the majority is attained or as soon as the first hour of that day commences is it attained?" The author admits to having erred because of the influence of his illness when it was noted that he stated that the day of birth was regarded as belonging to the thirteenth year when it is indeed common knowledge that it belongs to the fourteenth year. The name of Judah ibn

Maḥmias is noted as the messenger who transmitted the erroneous calculations of the author that misled R. Menaḥem Serero. Before the author had a chance to correct his error the messenger was gone. The writer mentions that his son Reuben fell and remained in a stupor for a long time but is now recovered. The writer asks R. Menaḥem Serero to transmit the former's advice to the sons of his master R. Vidal Ha-Ṣarfati, of blessed memory, that they should not initiate a litigation unless certain conditions can be met first.

The writer mentions that he had received information from R. Musa Halevi and R. Menaḥem Serero that two pairs of pants would arrive for him but only one pair has arrived and the matter is still in doubt. The writer inquires about the wellbeing of R. Menaḥem Serero's father who was beaten by a non-Jew. Concerning one Joseph b. Glaqon the writer says he refuses to intervene since he is closely related to him and that if he must be removed it is better to have someone else do it.

R. Jacob Ibn Ẓur mentions a new liturgical piece that he has composed; as soon as it is prepared he will make it available to R. Menaḥem. The writer notes that R. Menaḥem complains that the former never refers to the latter's children in his correspondences. R. Jacob responds that R. Menaḥem never inquires concerning the wellbeing of the writer's grandchild, Mattitya. R. Jacob informs R. Menaḥem that the latter's cousin Saul will soon be married to a young maiden, an orphan, of the Ben Ezra family. Saul was a son of R. Menaḥem's late uncle, of blessed memory.

A man has been charged with burning a pillow and R. Jacob says that as soon as the owners of the pillow are discovered the guilty party shall make restitution. Regards are sent by R. Jacob Ẓadok to R. Menahem.

R. Jacob Ibn Ẓur states that he composed a prayer of praise for recital at Yishtabaḥ (a juncture in the morning prayer service) and another liturgical poem for Kaddish. The latter poem deals with the commandments of the Ẓiẓit (prayer shawl) and Tefillin (phylacteries). These poems were chanted publicly on the new month of Adar, when R. Jacob's son, Oḅed, was publicly initiated into the performance of the aforementioned commandments. The writer informs R. Menaḥem that he includes a copy of these liturgical poems in the present letter, to be used especially for youngsters on their introduction to the commandments. R. Jacob requests that the poems be read on the occasion of the initiation of his brother's son called Reuben, which will take place either on the new month of Nisan or thereafter. Also David b. Pargon received a copy of the poems. If anyone who is a payytan (a master of liturgical compositions) desires to copy these poems R. Menaḥem is informed to tell David b. Siqron to make them available to them, for they were composed for the benefit of all. The letter is signed by R. Jacob Ibn Ẓur. The address appears on page 144a and the following six lines appear on page 144b. "From the money that you collected, give some to Esther Arzawiya, a linen curtain to Judah, a cousin, and buy for me two linen curtains with the remainder."

Ms. 106
P. 145a

A fragment containing the concluding part of a dissertation on a verse from the biblical tale of creation

A novel interpretation is given to the biblical verse, Genesis 2:20, "As for Adam, he did not find a helper who worked at cross purposes to him." The wisdom of man became apparent at the naming of various creatures that were brought before Adam. Man did not contend with God as to the naming of the various creatures, but he was in total agreement with Him. Although the angelic beings were not in accord with God's desire to create man in the first place, God saw the value in the wisdom of man. This paragraph appears to be the conclusion of a longer dissertation which might be in the nature of a biblical commentary.

Ms. 107
Pp. 146a—149a

An Aggadic work called Simū Leḥem

This manuscript contains an Aggadic work which was composed by the copyist R. Elijah Ha-Ṣarfati when he was fifteen years old. The work commences with an Aggadic exposition of a text in the

Talmudic tractate Mo'ed Katan, chapter Ve-Elu Megalḥim, "Whoever goes from the house of prayer to the house of study will merit receiving the Divine Presence." The next point discussed is an explanation of the text "The righteous are sitting with crowns on their heads (in the world to come)", and a contradictory text "The scholars, have no transquility either in this world or in the next world."

The remainder of the work deals with Aggadic material that is germane to biblical passages in the early chapters of Genesis. At the conclusion of the section on Genesis he identifies his father as Joseph Ha-Ṣarfati.

An edict against unfair pricing

Ms. 108
P. 150a

Three judges of the Rabbinic Court of Fez, acting for the community, have issued an edict against unfair pricing. The undersigned rabbis are R. Jacob Serero, R. Jacob Ibn Ẓur, and R. Reuben Serero. This legislation proscribes using dishonest weights and measures. The butchers are pointed to as prime violaters. Even if they increase the price only by pennies, they are guilty of theft and of robbing the poor. The members of the community have agreed by popular assent to the appointment of an inspector who will be responsible for checking all weights and measures and whether there is any overpricing. The appointee is R. Abraham ibn Niẓẓam, who shall be vested with complete authority. Whoever violates this law will be severely punished.

[Page 153b is part of 150a while the subject is totally unrelated. 150a was used for calculations and enumerations and was later given the number 153 by the compiler.]

A judgement concerning air pollution

Ms. 109
Pp. 151a—152a

[On page 151a two names appear; one masculine and one feminine. The man is Ḥayyim, (son of R. Mas'ūd, the son of Moses ibn Saadon). The woman is listed as Donna (daughter of Abraham, the son of Solomon ibn Sharbit). The names could have been noted for a number of purposes such as marriage, a betrothal, or a divorce and they seem to be entirely unrelated to the document upon which they were inscribed.]

The author is in agreement with other authorities with whom he was in attendance when they rendered their judgement that the owners of a furnace cannot add any additional ovens thereto even if they are willing to make certain adjustments so that the smoke will rise in a straight column and will not adversely affect anybody. The neighbors are acting within their rights when they try to prevent any alteration of the existing furnace. A decision was rendered on this matter in the Code of Jewish Law, chapter 132, by the Maharshakh. The author of Ḥut ha-Meshulash, responsum number 17, makes the point that even if modifications are made they can fall into disrepair and therefore no new installations shall be added. The judgements of Ramban and Rashba that are cited by R. Joseph Caro, in chapter 154, paragraph 16, of the Code of Jewish Law, are also against such installation. No names of rabbis or individuals contemporaneous to the time when this document was written, are mentioned. [Pages 151a and 152a are part of one page.]

A list of calculations and names

Ms. 109
P. 153b

While nothing appears on page 153a there is a list of names and accompanying calculations on page 153b. This list might enumerate a series of contributors to some charitable cause. Among those listed are the following: Joshua, Joseph ibn Attar, Moses Sabaḥ, and Isaac ibn Yitaḥ. [This page is the other side of page 150a.]

Ms. 110
P. 154a and b

A letter to R. Yedidia Monsonyego of Fez

This letter, which was sent to R. Yedidia Monsonyego, discusses a halakhic matter which is not easy to comprehend since the script is not easy to decipher. Some of the authorities that are cited are the Maharashdam, the Maharshakh, and the work Tumat Yesharim. It is conceivable that the subject relates to a litigation concerning properties.

The address appears on the other side of the letter.

Ms. 111
P. 155a and b

A responsum concerning claims made on an old loan by inheritors of the late creditor shall be honored if the upheavals of the times make it impossible for the original claim to be made

Many years before, a creditor, designated as X, had two bills of claim where land was stipulated as being pledged against a debtor, Y. Those who have now inherited the bills of claim after two generations want to make a claim against the debtor's family of inheritors, can they do so? The counter argument of the debtor's family, that the debts were probably paid because the creditors' family never made any claim during all those intervening years, does not stand because of the upheavals that transpired during the days of the arch-enemy Ṣahiq Tamia Ġalul. He it was who pillaged the area of the inheritors of R. Aaron Ha-Kohen and the records disappeared until they were unearthed at a later date. The creditor complained to the King Mulay Slieman and he was subsequently killed and his claims confiscated. The inheritors of the debtor tried to claim that their inheritance could not be tampered with in such a situation, whereas the inheritors of X claimed that since the land was placed as a pledge for non-payment the claim did stand. If the latter are vindicated, then they question whether they may claim the value of the produce from the date of death of Y, who received the loan initially?

The response is given in favor of the inheritors of X, the creditors, with regard to the debts. However, the rabbis are not so sure as to the claim on the produce. They base themselves on the Code, Tur Shulḥan Arukh, chapter 61, who bases himself on the Rosh, his father. The Beit Yosef, Rabbi Caro's commentary, is also mentioned. Also the Haggahot Ha-Tur 13:14 and the Rashdam are cited. A distinction is made in the aforementioned citations between an indication of falsification of a claim that has lapsed over a period of time, and one where the circumstances are such that the claim may still be pending because of upheavals which made the particular documents of proof previously inaccessible so that it could not be acted upon.

A more recent decision is cited which is more similar in its circumstances to the case before us. The judges in that case are the Rabbis Saul Serero, Judah ibn Attar, and Raphael Ibn Ẓur. The last two are recorded to have been deceased at this time. The year of this document is given as 1874. The signatories are Aaron Ha-Kohen Skali and Samuel Ġayni.

Ms. 112
P. 156a

A letter from the Holy Land to emissaries

This letter was sent by R. Samuel Ha-Kohen of the Holy Land to the emissaries R. Mimun Aflalo and R. Jacob ibn Danan in Fez, on the eighth of Ḥeshvan 1684. A part of the letter is written in Judaeo-Arabic words. A document from the widow of R. Azriel Ashkenazi has been sent to the emissaries. R. Samuel informs them that the monies will be personally apportioned. Some money has been sent with the emissary R. Hayyim Ashkenazi; other money with R. Moses Waqil and R. Maḥlouf ibn Ḥamo, but until now no response has been received from them. Additional funds should be sent to the judge R. Benjamin Duran, to the city of Algiers, upon the reception of letters with requests sent by the writer. It is important to avoid tardiness in these matters. A new emissary, R. Joseph Ha-Kohen, is being appointed in the hope that he will be blessed with greater success. Prayers are recited for all at the Kotel (Western Wall of the Temple compound) and in the academy during studies. The address is given on the other side of the page.

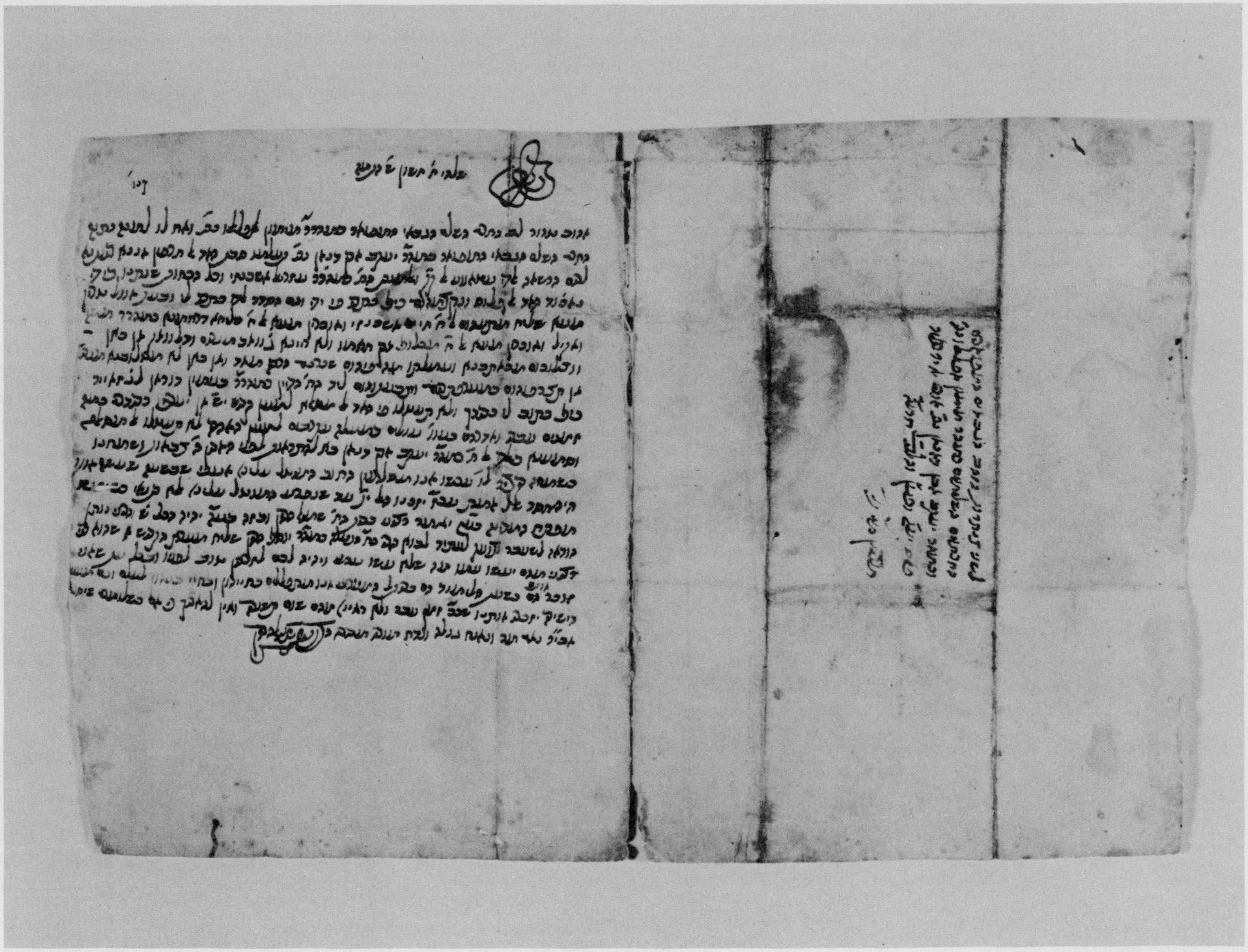

Ms. 112
A letter to emissaries
from the Holy Land

Ms. 113
P. 157a

An appeal on a sale that has already been consummated because the property sold far below the original price

This document is written to R. Jacob Ibn Ẓur asking him to intercede with R. Shalom Edery on behalf of R. Samuel Maymeran, the son of Jacob. The latter, Jacob, sold a piece of property to the grandmother of R. Edery at much below cost, between one half and one third of that which the seller paid for it himself. This was done because the Maymeran family was very pressed financially at that time. Therefore Samuel asks the undersigned to write to R. Jacob Ibn Ẓur to intercede on his behalf with R. Shalom. R. Samuel feels that only then will justice be done. The two undersigned are Abraham b. David Hasin and Hananiah b. Zikhri.

Ms. 114
Pp. 158a—159b

A scholar reproves the rabbis of Fez for not arousing the people to aid him financially

This letter is written to the Rabbis Elijah Ha-Ṣarfati and Matitya Serero of Fez by a scholar who is in great distress economically. The writer berates the aforementioned rabbis for not paying attention to his plight. He appears to be in transit or to have recently moved, since his books are not available for him to quote textual sources for his comments which, he claims, abound in rabbinic sources. He reproves the rabbis for not arousing the compassion of the populace to his needs. This activity on their part would serve to arouse the multitude to acts of charity. Furthermore, he has always helped those in need such as was the case when some had to journey from Fez to Larache. If the rabbis are desisting from helping him because they feel intimidated, he tells them that the very opposite should be the case. The people are wondering why the rabbis have not issued a call for aid. In the days of the Hasmoneans one feared intimidation, but not in "our days," he says. He states that he is prepared to sell whatever he possesses to pay his debts; however, more funds are needed. He informs his correspondents that the Nagid has placed additional taxes on him. A R. Jacob Halevi is also mentioned. The author of this letter may be R. Jacob Ibn Ẓur.

Ms. 115
Pp. 160a—164a

Novellae on Jewish law and a responsum

On pages 160a and 160b, novellae on the Codes of Jewish Law are recorded. The subject "Ain Shaliaḥ Le-Devar Averah" (the power of agency does not apply in the case of perpetration of transgression) is discussed.

On pages 161a and 161b the subjects "Ain Ma'avirin Al ham-Mitzvot" (one does not by-pass some objects used for mitzvah purposes to utilize other objects that come later) and "Ain Osin Mitzvot Ḥavilôt Ḥavilôt," are discussed.

On pages 162a to 164a a responsum is presented concerning one who interrupted the blessings of the Sh'ma in order to respond to a "Davar She-be-Qedusha" and then neglected to recite the blessing "Ga-al Yisroel" and immediately began to recite the Amida.

All the texts from page 160a through page 164a are written by the same hand.

Ms. 116
P. 165a and b

A correspondence from R. Mordecai Berdugo that includes two Halakhic queries

This letter is written by R. Mordecai Berdugo (of Meknès) to R. Abraham Monsano of Fez. He also sends greetings to R. Immanuel (probably a Monsano). A letter had been written, but returned and the present letter incorporates the contents of the previous letter as well. The writer adds that if a letter has already been sent to R. M. Adhan, at Tetuán, then another note should be sent concerning a Torah Scroll belonging to R. Elazar Zadok that is in the synagogue of R. M. Adhan. This letter should be so written as if R. Abraham Monsano initiated it himself. He should write that when he was in Meknès a plea was made to him to do so. Inquiry is also made concerning the wellbeing of Rabbi Yaabez who was known to have been ill. Greetings are sent to R. Samuel. The writer notes that he sent a decision to R. Jacob concerning Moses A Ṣayaig and he requests it or at least a copy of it. He also asks that a purchase of some material should be made for him, since he has heard that a scholar from the ibn Siqron family acquired it from one Levi ibn Laḥdav. The writer asks that it should be sent with R. Y. Rosilio and the former will make immediate payment or he will send the money.

R. Mordecai asks that the replies to two questions should be sent to him through Maharibeẓ (R. Jacob Ibn Ẓur) but if he is not free to reply then he should ask Maharsha (R. Samuel Elbaz) to do so. The first question concerns two partners; whether their contract is to be considered like all writs of obligation so that one cannot state "I bought your interest," or is it to be treated only like a deposit, in which case he can say that he paid half of it back? Then what force does the original contract have? If it is to have legal force, surely he should be able to collect even from inheritors or one who might have bought that portion of the partnership. R. Mordecai notes that this is an old dispute and it requires resolution.

The second question refers to two Jews who had houses in a courtyard belonging to a non-Jew. The two houses fell in and the non-Jewish owner of the courtyard wanted to take down whatever remained standing and to appropriate the beams. However, he said if there was a customer who would buy the courtyard he would not take down the remaining beams. Reuben, one of the two Jewish owners of the houses, lived in geographic proximity to the non-Jew, but Simeon had moved away. Reuben wanted sufficient time to inform Simeon and to ask whether he would like to buy the courtyard. The non-Jew was impatient and wanted to leave the city and said that if they did not acquire the courtyard immediately he would take everything apart. Reuben, pressed as he was, decided to buy the courtyard rights by himself from the non-Jew, excluding Simeon entirely. He had witnesses attest to the fact that this was his intention. Now Simeon has come with a claim against Reuben demanding that his rights in the courtyard should stand and saying that he will pay Reuben for half of it. Reuben has countered that Simeon has no claim, since if Reuben had not bought the rights, everybody would have lost the courtyard.

Rabbi Mordecai supposes a hypothesis. If a third party had bought the courtyard from the non-Jew, would that purchaser have acquired the courtyard with all its buildings levelled? Since this would have been the position for the non-Jew with respect to the building rights, the only rights that Reuben and Simeon should have extend only to the price of the bare land on which their buildings once stood.

[The text is cut off on top of page 165b. Only the last part of the famous signature of R. Mordecai Berdugo is visible, at the conclusion of the letter.]

Ms. 117
P. 166a

A plea to review a previous judicial decision which was reversed by rabbi Jacob Ibn Ẓur as a result of the submission of new evidence

R. Jacob Toledano writes this letter in response to an authority, who remains unnamed, concerning a transaction that became a subsequent case for litigation. The case concerns a gift that Re'SH'M gave to Re'SHa'kH. The latter was the previous year in Meknès. Then a dispute arose between Re'SH'M and R. M. Edery and those who inherited from R. Saadya Kohen. Presently, R. Toledano is asked to recall what transpired at the time that the gift was given. Was the gift given by the instrument of a document or was it given orally? R. Toledano replies that he doesn't recall whether a contract was formally drawn up or whether it was an oral transaction. His colleagues who joined him on that occasion also have poor recollections of those events. The writer states that a request to confirm a decision rendered by R. Ḥasan ibn Laḥsin has still not been responded to. The latter has been informed that R. Jacob Ibn Ẓur once wrote opinions on the case because new evidence had become available, thus making it like a new query and not the questioning of an earlier decision. R. Toledano asks the one to whom he is writing to seek one of the litigants who dwells in his vicinity who has a copy of the ruling that he (R. Toledano) and other scholars had rendered. Perhaps that litigant also has a copy of the ruling rendered by R. Jacob Ibn Ẓur? Even though the scholars of the west rely upon R. Jacob Ibn Ẓur, R. Toledano writes, perhaps another insight can be arrived at by his correspondent thereby preserving his own earlier decision. R. Toledano asks that a new ruling based on such an insight should be forwarded to him.

Ms. 118
P. 167a

R. Mordecai Berdugo responds to R. Jacob Ibn Ẓur concerning a dispute over an inheritance amongst the members of the D'Avila family

This letter is in response to a previous correspondence sent by R. Jacob Ibn Ẓur concerning an inquiry about wine barrels that one R. Judah D'Avila was said to have had in his possession. The wife of Moses, son of Jacob D'Avila, has replied saying that R. Judah left no more than three barrels in his storage from days gone by. Apparently, her husband, Moses, is a grandson of R. Judah D'Avila, as is the present claimant, Judah D'Avila. The aforementioned Moses has begun to curse vilely all those making inquiry into the extent of R. Judah D'Avila's estate. R. Mordecai Berdugo, wanting some factual information, has suggested that two people should enter the storage area to see for themselves that such is indeed the number of barrels, i.e. not more than three. R. Mordecai mentions that he has tried to achieve a reconciliation whereby Judah D'Avila would receive a certain number of barrels, because he wants to acquire the barrels elsewhere if necessary before the winepressing season is over, with R. Jacob Ibn Ẓur's permission. It seems that the Maharit (R. Jacob Toledano) also wrote a ruling on the matter which would leave Judah D'Avila empty-handed. R. Mordecai Berdugo asks R. Jacob Ibn Ẓur to decide either in accordance with the former's ruling or with the Maharit's ruling. In either case R. Mordecai requests a speedy reply. Both rulings are included in this correspondence. [An aspect of this case is discussed in *Ms.119*—page 168a, which is a subsequent correspondence from R. Mordecai to R. Jacob Ibn Ẓur.]

Ms. 119
P. 168a

R. Mordecai Berdugo has received a legal decision from Jacob Ibn Ẓur and he asks that R. Jacob help to achieve a compromise

R. Mordecai Berdugo informs R. Jacob Ibn Ẓur that he has received the latter's written legal decision and that he is happy to note that R. Jacob's decision is in agreement with R. Mordecai's account book and not on the first book as Harit (R. Jacob Toledano) would have it. The writer says that the custom of Castilia remains the final guide for R. Jacob Ibn Ẓur. The first woman involved pleaded with R. Mordecai to initiate moves that would produce a compromise. The writer states that he will not do anything until he receives permission from R. Jacob Ibn Ẓur. Therefore, the writer pleads with R. Jacob Ibn Ẓur that he call to the maiden Shazbona and persuade her to be willing to compromise. R. Mordecai has assured her that the result of the compromise would leave her with a higher sum, while R. Mordecai now notes that only a smaller sum would be available. R. Mordecai says that he will not act unless he can first hear what R. Jacob Ibn Ẓur intends to do. R. Mordecai suggests that it would be best if a compromise could be reached because Harit (R. Jacob Toledano) is stubborn while the women who are involved in the litigation are incurring losses. Therefore, R. Mordecai feels that R. Jacob Ibn Ẓur should persuade the second woman to be a party to a compromise which would bring the litigation to a quick conclusion. R. Jacob is asked to inform the writer as soon as he is able to convince the woman to agree to compromise.

Concerning the barrels [see *Ms.118*, page 167a] R. Mordecai states that he purchased five of them and when they arrive he will send them to R. Jacob Ibn Ẓur with the first sojourner. The writer signs as Mordecai Berdugo.

In a postscript R. Mordecai writes that when ReSHaKH comes to R. Jacob Ibn Ẓur he will speak at length concerning the matter and he will bring a document which R. Jacob should ignore or even destroy. The writer signs the postscript with his initials Marbiẓ.

Ms. 120
P. 169a

A correspondence from Raphael Halevi to R. Solomon Ibn Ẓur of Fez

Raphael Halevi commences his correspondence by noting that he has received a letter from R. Solomon Ibn Ẓur. He states that he is confronted with the problems of old age and that this affects his writing. The information that R. Solomon Ibn Ẓur has provided concerning R. Y. Simḥon's account is news indeed. The writer informs R. Solomon that on a number of occasions R. Hayyim ibn Danan has written to say that an illness of the eyes prevents him from engaging in more activity. The writer, Raphael, states that upon his return from Meknès he will communicate with him. R. Solomon's report that Mas'ūd "built his house" (got married) is again news. Raphael extends blessings to R. Solomon Ibn Ẓur's only son who bears the same name as the writer, i.e. Raphael. The writer reminds R. Solomon that when he was in Rabat he wrote that he was not intending to return to Fez.

Ms. 121
P. 170a and b

A classic legal document of guarantorship involving the Ben Shaiya family drawn up by R. Jacob Ibn Ẓur

This legal document was formulated by R. Jacob Ibn Ẓur in the month of Adar 1744 at Fez. The principals who agreed to serve as guarantors are Reuḅen the son of R. Jacob b. Aḥarpi, who is known as Ben Shaiya, and Samuel the son of Mas'ūd ben Aḥarpi, called Ben Shaiya. These men admit that they received a certain sum of money from Masuda the daughter of Israel ben Aḥarpi, called Ben Shaiya. They agreed to make payment to an orphan, Luna, the daughter of Musa ben Aḥarpi, called Ben Shaiya. An attic was given as a pledge by the aforementioned Reuḅen and Samuel to the aforementioned Masuda. It is adjacent to the yard owned by David b. Amozag in the Mellah of Fez, with all other rights of tenancy applying to her.

Apparently this document was drawn up with only one witness in attendance. Thus R. Immanuel Monsano and Elijah ben Zimra have certified this document thereby correcting this situation. The addendum which was written for this correction also states that one called Israel, the son of Saadya (a brother of the aforementioned Reuḅen) acted on behalf of his uncle, while Samuel acted for himself. Those present reiterated all the foregoing with Masuda in the presence of the court.

Ms. 122
P. 171a

An enactment by the community of Ṣefrou concerning the dispensation of charity

The Rabbis Ḥayyim Elijah (Ḡayni) and Saul ibn Elbaz write to the rabbis Raphael Ibn Ẓur and Aaron Ha-Kohen of Fez concerning an enactment that the elders of the community of Ṣefrou have passed with regard to charitable contributions. Whenever a scholar arrives from Fez for a charitable collection he should present an official receipt issued by the rabbis of Fez for the amount of money which the community of Fez gave to him. He will automatically receive one-third of that amount from Ṣefrou. This does not apply to what individuals should desire personally to give the emissary.

Ms. 123
Pp. 172a—173b

A court action guarantees a compromise

Mordecai ibn Abraham ben Zazun brought a claim against Mîmun ibn Ayush ben Halfon based on a bill of debt that the latter owed the former for the purchase of an item in the sum of 300 uqiot. Mîmun brought a counter-claim against Mordecai saying that the item he purchased was defective and as a result he incurred losses. A mediator has now been able to negotiate a compromise between the contending parties. The terms of the compromise stipulate that Mîmun should pay one hundred and forty uqiot over the amount that was already paid to Mordecai, thereby freeing himself from any subsequent claims that might be made. Mîmun also agrees to drop any counter-claims. However, since Mîmun is fearful that Mordecai will violate the terms of the compromise, the latter has stated in the presence of a rabbinic tribunal that he agrees to uphold the terms of the compromise and has engaged in legal forms to show his intentions. The agreement between the parties is now formulated in a legal document. Dates are stipulated for Mîmun to complete his payments to Mordecai, who is also reminded of Mîmun's devotion in not handing Mordecai over to the authorities for producing a faulty product. The court will act in this matter with the power of "that which the court declares ownerless so shall it remain." If any protest is registered against the compromise then Mordecai accepts upon himself the punishment of the Nazirite vows of Samson, which only Mîmun's goodwill will be able to invalidate. If any court certifies any claims against the compromise, such claims shall be declared null and void in accord with Maimonides' ruling. All this was completed on Sunday, the twenty-fifth day of Nisan 1725 at Fez. The undersigned are Moses Asulin and Jacob the son of R. Joseph of blessed memory, Busida.

A formal statement is added on page 173b stating that even though this document deals with a compromise, where a formal renunciation of all protestations that would make this arrangement null and void is not necessary, still the undersigned include such a renunciation with the power of "that which the court declares ownerless shall be ownerless." The undersigned to this addendum are the rabbis Judah ibn Attar and Shalom Edery.

Ms. 124
P. 174a

A letter of reference asking that assistance be extended to Jacob Halevi

This letter is written introducing R. Jacob Halevi to Ḥayyim and to Joseph Lamdiyoni and asking them to come to his aid. The writer has never had occasion to meet those to whom he writes but he has heard much about them. They are apparently communal leaders and men of substance who could grant aid to Jacob Halevi. This correspondence probably originated in the Holy Land. **[Page 179, which is blank, is part of 174a.]**

Ms. 125
P. 175a

An emissary from Safed arrives in Ṣefrou and communicates with R. Jacob Ibn Ẓur at Fez

This letter is written in a beautiful script by Moses Israel, a messenger from the city of Safed, to R. Jacob Ibn Ẓur of Fez, informing the latter of his arrival in Ṣefrou ten days earlier. The writer informs R. Jacob that on Sunday he will journey to Meknès. The writer also wants R. Jacob to correspond with R. Jospeh ibn Ḥamo to inform him that he should arrive at Ṣefrou to accompany the writer to Meknès. The writer also reminds R. Jacob Ibn Ẓur concerning R. Jacob Ha-Kohen of Gibraltar (the name Gibraltar is written in Judaeo-Arabic as Jebel Tor), that he should inform him concerning charitable donations for R. Simeon bar Yohai, of blessed memory. Regards are sent to R. Judah ibn Attar and he is asked to forgive the author of this letter for not writing to him personally.

Ms. 126
P. 176a

R. Saul Serero makes a plea that action against injustice be taken by R. Solomon Toledano

This letter is written in a cryptic form concerning a very delicate matter which has still not been adjudicated in the courts, although a long time has passed. R. Solomon Toledano is asked to attend to the matter so that the machinery of justice will be activated. The letter is signed by R. Saul Serero.

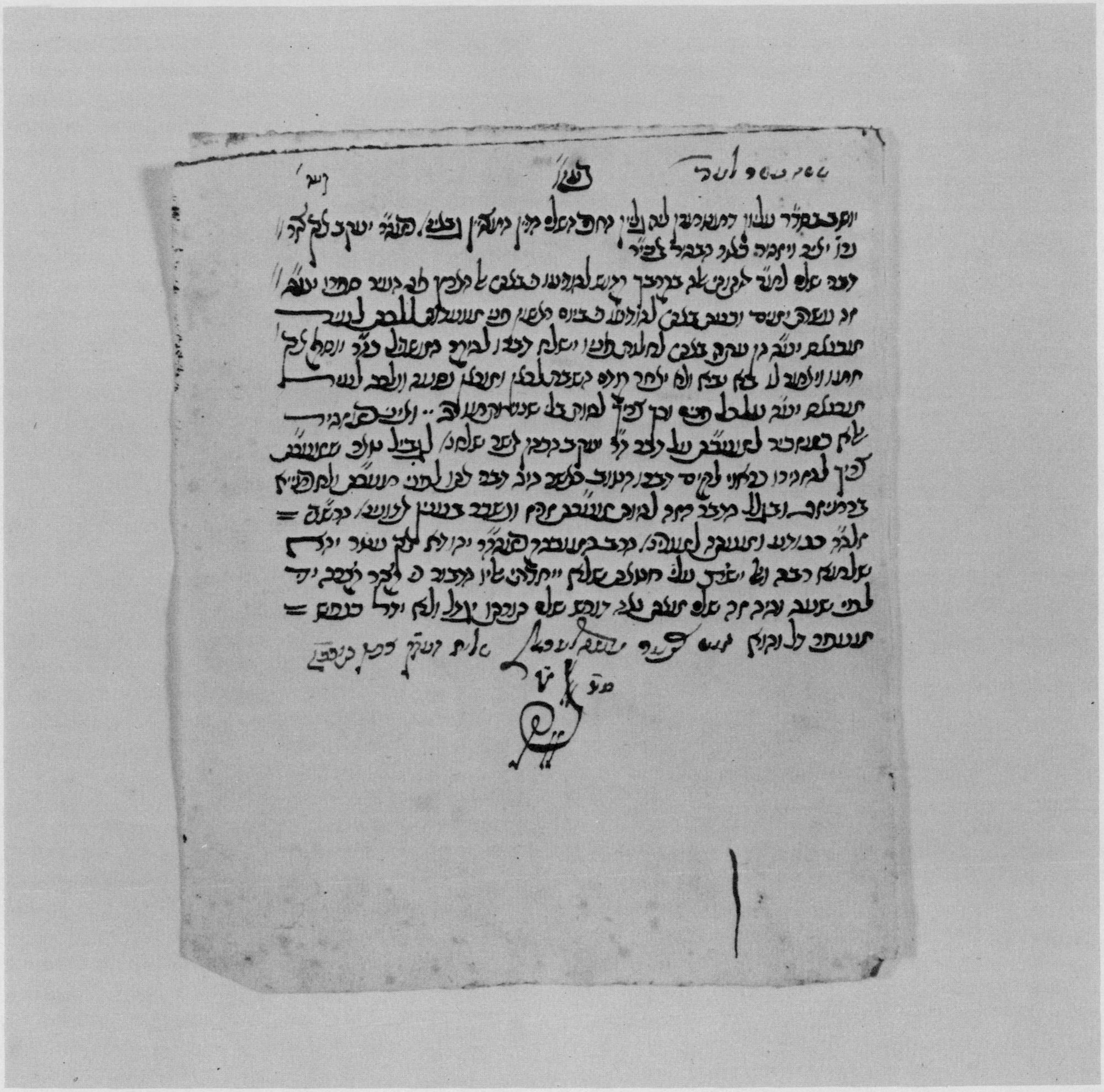

Ms. 125
A letter from an emissary just arrived in Sefrou to Rabbi Jacob Ibn Zur in Fez

Ms. 127
P. 176a

R. Samuel Ibn Ẓur sends his appeal to R. Toledano about the same case mentioned in Ms. 126

[This letter is written on the bottom of the same side of the same page 176a as *Ms.126*.] It is from R. Samuel Ibn Ẓur to R. Solomon Toledano appealing for his support for the cause of justice in this case and asking him to expedite the matter in order that injustice should not continue to be done to an innocent party.

Ms. 128
P. 177a

The Rabbis of Meknès are requested to act on behalf of a case of forced widowhood

This letter which is written to the rabbis of Meknès, R. Moses Toledano, R. Jacob Ibn Ẓur, and R. Moses Berdugo, by Isaac Nahôn, concerns the case of a woman who has been thrust into a situation of forced widowhood (called "Igun" in Hebrew). This matter has already been brought to the attention of the aforementioned rabbis by the author of this letter on some other occasions. However, no response has been forthcoming; perhaps the exigencies of time have prevented such a response. When the parents of the woman heard that R. Saadya Halevi and R. Shem Toḇ ibn Walid were leaving the community for Meknès they asked them to intercede on her behalf that she might be granted justice. Thus, R. Isaac Nahôn, the writer of the letter, asks the rabbis to begin to act on the matter.

Ms. 129
P. 178a

A letter to R. Jacob Ibn Ẓur asking him to help press a claim for Aaron Halevi of Safed

This letter was sent by Shalom Ibn Moses Ben-Ẓur to R. Jacob Ibn Ẓur, at Meknès, on Sunday evening, the twentieth day of Adar, 1730. He appeals to R. Jacob concerning a litigation by one Aaron Halevi of Safed who had a claim against his nephew but refused to press it as long as he could earn a living. However, now that he is poverty-stricken he has no recourse but to press his claim. The writer asks R. Jacob to study the case and, if the claim is true, to expedite the matter. Also R. Moses Berdugo is asked to give his opinion on the case.

Ms. 130
P. 180a

An appeal to help a widow and her daughters is made to R. Samuel Ibn Ẓur

R. Judah Halevi states that he has already written to Samuel Ibn Ẓur before concerning Sa'îda, the widow of R. Judah Ibn Ẓur, of blessed memory, and also the widow of R. Reuḇen Tamakh and her daughters who are suffering from starvation. The entire community is suffering from famine. The widow of R. Reuben is concerned about the future welfare of her daughters, lest they should meet with death or some other terrible fate because of the adversity that prevails. The author is appealing to R. Samuel to aid the unfortunate widow and her daughters. A second subject is also brought to the attention of R. Samuel: a query that is being sent by R. Jacob Bibas. [This query is presented on the same page 180a, below R. Judah Halevi's letter.]

Ms. 131
P. 180a

R. Jacob Bibas poses his query to R. Samuel Ibn Ẓur concerning a claim that another should pay

R. Jacob Bibas had made money available to a widow who was in need. However, one Moses Kohen who was supposed to deliver the money to her used it to transact business dealings for himself. R. Jacob Bibas is not well off economically and the times are especially difficult with everything so expensive. R. Jacob expects the money to be claimed from the aforementioned Moses and made available to the woman.

Ms. 132
P. 181a

A letter of consolation to R. Raphael Ọbed Ibn Ẓur on the demise of his father, R. Jacob Ibn Ẓur

This letter of consolation is sent by the undersigned, Ḥayyim Toledano, Aaron the son of Judah Halevi, and Jacob Bibas, to Raphael Ọbed Ibn Ẓur, the son of R. Jacob Ibn Ẓur, on the death of his father. The aforementioned rabbis (of Salé) eulogize the late great Rabbi Jacob Ibn Ẓur in accord with his many talents and the excellence that he manifested in all those fields of endeavor. They offer consolation to the bereaved family and praise R. Raphael as the one who will succeed his late father. In a one line postscript mention is made of some books that were placed in safekeeping and it is asked whether they should be forwarded to R. Raphael. This letter was written in 1753.

Ms. 133
Pp. 182a—183b

A court action reprimanding a scribe for assuming the authority to serve as a judge

This document is a court action rendered in agreement with the communal leaders against Jacob ibn Malka who for many years assumed judicial power by signing his name to responsa and legal documents without having received any authority to do so. Since he was a scribe he utilized the opportunity to add his signature to legal documents that he had occasion to compose, thereby giving the impression that he was appointed as a judge with the other undersigned judges.

A decree is thus handed down that Jacob ibn Malka shall never add his signature to any legal decision or responsum either by himself or with other scholars. Nor shall he communicate with scholars of other countries concerning any matters pertaining to law. He shall not exceed his authority as a scribe of the court in accord with the practice of other scribes who are in the service of the court. He is only permitted to arbitrate and to compose documents of arbitration. If he violates any of the aforementioned terms then he shall be judged accordingly and the Nagid, the lay leader of the Jewish community, Samuel Halevi ibn Yulee, shall order him to pay a fine as he sees fit. This court document is dated Ḥeshvan 1732 at Fez. The rabbis signing the documents are R. Judah ibn Attar, R. Jacob Ibn Ẓur, R. Shalom Edery, R. Abraham ibn Alel, and R. Samuel Elbaz. The document is affirmed by R. Moses ibn Maman, R. Aaron ibn Saadon, R. Judah ibn Moses, R. Moses b. Abraham ibn Ashikh, R. Moses ibn Shitrit, R. David Aspag, and R. Israel Adhan. The two signatures certifying this document are those of Joseph Siqron and Mîmun b. Joseph Busîdan. The document gives the following background information.

When the Great Rabbi (Judah ibn Attar) died, the rabbis instituted a practice that two lectures should be recited each day at morning and afternoon services in his memory for a period of thirty days. R. Jacob ben Malka did not attend either to lecture or to listen, nor did he even visit the cemetery. This was considered an affront since R. Judah ibn Attar, as holder of the title Av Bet Din (head of the court), and as the greatest rabbi of the generation, was considered to be the great master and all his students (including R. Jacob ben Malka) were obliged to pay respects to his memory.

Three months later Jacob ibn Malka called all the scholars and communal leaders to his synagogue to hear *his* lecture. He used the occasion to insult the scholars by intimating that he was superior to all of them, adding that the members of the court were also his inferiors. He afterwards lobbied members of the community to give him a document stating that he had legal standing as a judge. However, they were not persuaded to do so. He also asked them to attest to his impeccable character. In fact, incidents were enumerated to demonstrate the opposite.

Jacob was known, for example, to have contradicted the rulings of the head of the court, and on another occasion he had cursed the grandson of the Rabbi. In the year 1731 the Rabbi (Attar) rendered his response to a query from Ṣefrou which he signed together with the members of the court, but when the document reached the hand of Jacob ibn Malka the response was contradicted and the decision reversed. On many occasions Jacob ibn Malka had been noted for his insulting manner. At one time he had received a stipend from the community but when his negative attitude became evident it was taken from him. Even then he would not acknowledge that the stipend was a grant, but viewed it as a debt owed to him by the community.

In this document Jacob is further warned that if he persists in claiming that he has been wronged and removed from his position, then this court ruling will be sent abroad to Amsterdam and Venice to be published, publicized, and spread throughout the world. This second document was composed in the first month of Adar 1734, at Fez. The undersigned are Jacob Ibn Ẓur, Shalom Edery, Abraham Alel, and Samuel Elbaz.

Pr. 133.5
Pp. 184a—191b

An issue of the Hebrew journal Ha-Libanon, vol. 3 no. 9, pp. 129-144

This issue of the Hebrew literary periodical, *Libanon*, published in Paris and dated the eleventh of Iyar 1866, contains the following articles. (1) A report on the arrival of Sir Moses Montefiore in Jerusalem on the eleventh of Nisan 1866. Sir Moses plans to build a Jewish quarter of domicile outside the old city of Jerusalem during this visit. (2) An article announcing the publishing of a work on the crowns that appear over certain letters in Hebrew scripture, called Sefer Tagin. (3) An article discussing the customs of the Jews of Aden on the Day of Atonement and on the Feast of Tabernacles. The writer of the article, Jacob Halevi Sapir, visited this community and he recounts his experiences as well as describing the poverty-stricken condition of the people. (4) The fourth article offers historical information about Jewish medieval scholars of France. The writer is Eliakim Carmoly. Two short articles (5) and (6) follow containing scholarly notes. (7) A halakhic (Jewish legal) exposition on priorities of the performance of certain deeds under special circumstances, when limited funds are available, is discussed by Alexsander Aran. The final article (8) is an installment on Arabic ethical proverbs, in Hebrew translation, with a commentary. The editor of this publication is Yeḥiel Brüll.

Ms. 134
P. 192a

A plea to the rabbis of Fez to enforce a judgement against a runaway husband if he refuses to return to his wife

This document is written to the rabbis of Fez and to the scholar R. Moses Grimeau asking them to render justice on behalf of a woman, Miriam, the daughter of R. Joseph Navôt. Her husband, R. Isaac, the son of R. Daniel Sas, has made her a living widow for the past five years by abandoning her and her small son without any financial support. An earlier correspondence to the rabbis depicted the abject condition of this neglected wife. The writer of this document notes that on this same day the woman found her husband to be unfaithful to her. The rabbis of Fez are asked to ascertain the matter for themselves and to convince the husband to return to his wife. If he refuses then the rabbis are asked to call upon the Parnasim (public officials of the Jewish community) to use their persuasive powers, or even to flog him in accord with rabbinic law. A non-Jew named Muhammad Al-Ḥaji, who is the bearer of this letter, is placed at the service of the rabbis for this purpose. If the husband remains intransigent then the rabbis are asked to ensure that he will pay the full value of her marriage contract which is in the amount of 4500 golden denari, her dowry and, in addition, all the unpaid support that is coming to her from previous years. Also a proper bill of divorce should be forthcoming. The two signatories to this document are Judah Ayush and Abraham Apil, of the city of Argil (Arzila), in the year 1735.

Ms. 135
P. 193a

A letter from the Holy Land to R. Jacob Ibn Ẓur concerning the purchase of books

Samuel D'Avila, the author of this letter, has arrived in Jerusalem from Salé. He informs R. Jacob Ibn Ẓur, at Fez, that payment for books previously purchased should be made to the writer, since he himself has already paid for them in the interim. R. Solomon ibn Danan is mentioned in this letter. The titles of the following books are mentioned as having been purchased: Sefer Turei Zahav, Sefer Mageenai Areẓ and Sefer Ein Ya'akov. [This letter is difficult to decipher because the script is light and faded.]

Ms. 136
P. 194a

A response to a rabbinic plea for the collection of a creditor's claim

This letter is in response to an earlier correspondence from R. Jacob Ibn Ẓur to the writer concerning a claim brought against Messrs. Yamin and Abraham ibn Aḥyo by a creditor. The writer of the letter, Maḥlouf ibn Joseph bar Alzera, confronted the debtors who had no funds available to make payment. However, the debtors were able to send 100 uqiot which is a portion of the debt. The money was given to R. Ḥayyim ibn Mas'ūd ibn Magirẓ, who dwells in R. Jacob Ibn Ẓur's community at Fez, and who is presently in the author's community, with instruction to hand it to the creditor.

Ms. 137
P. 195a

A plea to R. Judah Ibn Attar to help the cause of justice by making a debtor pay a creditor who is in financial difficulty

This letter is written to R. Judah ibn Attar of Fez, on behalf of David Sasportas, who is engaged in business transactions. David extended a loan to a young man called Isaac ibn Yahya who dwells in Fez. The latter promised to pay the debt to David Sasportas in the amount of 140 weights of silver, as stated in the bill of debt. Meanwhile, David's creditors are pressing him for payment of a debt owed to them. Therefore, R. Judah ibn Attar is being called upon to come to David's aid against Isaac ibn Yaḥya who is described as a thief and a perjurer. The signature that concludes the letter is that of Saadya Chouraqi.

Ms. 138
P. 196a

A plea by the rabbinic court of Fez that charitable aid be extended to a scholar of Morocco

This plea is directed to the scholars and communal leaders of all communities that charitable aid should be made available to R. Abraham Ha-Ṣarfati, the son of R. Vidal Ha-Ṣarfati, of blessed memory. Furthermore, R. Abraham should be treated with deference since he is the scion of a distinguished family and only recently he has fallen on bad times. This document was composed in the year 1731, and it was signed by the rabbis Judah ibn Attar, Jacob the son of Reuḅen Ibn Ẓur, of blessed memory, and Shalom Edeṛy.

Ms. 139
P. 197a

A dowry from the mid-seventeenth century, in the tradition of the Toshavim

This dowry is part of a booklet which records several dowries which are dated circa 1649. The other dowries appear on pages 197b, 198b, 198a, and 202a and b. The subjects of this dowry are the bride, Shazbona, the daughter of R. Elazar Al-Barazani, and the groom, Judah, the son of Joseph Gabbai. A list of the items that the bride brought to her husband's home comes to the sum of 2200 uqiot of silver. This document is in accord with the traditions of the Toshavim, those Jews who were indigenous to Morocco. The date on this document is the fourth day of Nisan 1649, at Marrakesh and it was written by Shalom Aḅṭah.

Ms. 140
Pp. 197b and 198a

A dowry stipulating that the marriage contract will be in the Castilian tradition which reverts back to the tradition of the Toshavim after five years

This dowry is for the bride, Mani, the daughter of R. Judah, the son of R. Solomon Ha-Kohen. The groom is Judah, the son of Joseph ben Simon. The figure for the value of the dowry is placed at 3200 (uqiot). This dowry stipulates that the marriage contract will follow the Castilian tradition for the first five years, after which it will follow the tradition of the Toshavim, Jews indigenous to Morocco. The movable properties in the dowry cannot be removed for five years without the express consent of R. Judah, the father of the bride. After the five years the bride's consent will be required. This document was written on Sunday, the fourth day of Nisan, in the year 1649, at Marrakesh.

Ms. 141
Pp. 198b and 199a

A third dowry recorded in the dowry booklet

This dowry is for the maiden Aliya, the daughter of R. Shalom ibn Azrawa, who was to marry the groom, R. Ḥayyim ibn Solomon ibn Zorihin. The sum total of the dowry came to 4000 (uqiot). This contract was composed at Marrakesh, in the year 1649. The signature of R. Ezra De Pardosh the scribe appears at the top of page 199a. [The same signature of R. Ezra De Pardosh the scribe appears on page 202b with another signature preceding it. Pages 198a and b and 199a and b are part of the same page.]

Ms. 142
P. 199b

A contract of mutual agreement for the purpose of marriage

The principals in this mutual agreement for the purpose of marriage are the prospective groom, Abraham, the son of R. Joseph ibn Ḥarbon, and Miriam, the daughter of Abraham ibn Mamushat. Abraham has to declare that he is not presently betrothed to any other maiden, nor has he agreed to enter into a prospective marriage with any one else. Furthermore, if he should be the cause of any obstacle to the marriage taking place he agrees to pay fifty uqiot of silver. Similarly if the bride will not be given to the groom in marriage at the appointed time agreed upon, then the bride's father agrees to pay the groom fifty silver uqiot for his disgrace. This document was drawn up on Monday, the twenty-sixth of the month of Nisan, in the year 1649. A piece of land was given as a gift by Leḡima, the mother of the groom.

Ms. 143
P. 200a and b

A court document containing testimony concerning a Jewish bandit

Abraham, the son of Moses called Ḥazit, and Isaac Slieman ben ATurgeman, of Tafilalet, came before the Rabbinic Tribunal in Fez to register a complaint against Yom Tob̤ ibn Saadon bar Yissakhar, a gangster terrorizing the area of Tafilalet by committing the most vile kinds of crimes. He has engaged in immoral sexual acts to satisfy his lust thereby causing many husbands to divorce their wives. He also is known to function as an informer against the Jews to non-Jewish leaders and the Jews suffer the consequences. A case in point is the suffering he has brought upon the people of Ṣefrou, and this is well known to those who dwell at Fez. His lust for money has contributed substantially to the suffering of the Jews.

When the Jews turned to the king for aid Yom Tob̤ was incarcerated and forced to pay a fine, but after he was freed from prison, he threatened to inform further against the Jews to revenge his imprisonment. The aforementioned men who testified against him at the rabbinic court claim that he wants *them* to bear false testimony against those witnesses who earlier spoke against him, namely, against R. Maḥlouf ibn Simḥon, R. Moses, the latter's son, and R. Ayush b. Attias. They state that they will not bear false testimony. In fact, they maintain that any testimony they might have given heretofore must be suspect as having been given under compulsion.

Afterwards, Mordecai Boutboul of Tafilalet came to the court at Fez and testified concerning the character of Yom Tob̤ saying that he was responsible for causing monetary losses to many Jews all the time that he was in Tafilalet. Another who testified against Yom Tob̤ was Joseph the son of Abraham, the son of Shitrit, of Tafilalet, now residing in Fez, who stated that Yom Tob̤ informed on the Jews, thus causing them monetary losses.

Ms. 144
P. 202a and b

A dowry in the tradition of the Toshavim

This dowry is part of the booklet of recorded dowries [see *Mss. 139* to *141*, on pages 197-199]. The name of the bride is given as Simḥa (daughter of R. Slieman ibn Meshash) and that of the groom as R. Joseph (son of R. Mîmun ibn Ḥarbon). The total amount of the dowry is valued at 4800 uqiot of silver. The custom of the Toshavim is to be followed. This document was composed on Wednesday, the seventh of Nisan 1649. The father of the groom has also given land to his son. Two signatures appear at the end of this document. The first signature, although blurred, appears to be that of a person called Jacob Halevi, while the second signature is that of Ezra Di Paridosh, the scribe whose signature is found on the top of page 199a of *Ms.141*. In all probability this document was composed in Marrakesh. [The page on which this document appears is part of pages 197a and b.]

Ms. 145
P. 203a

Ha-Ẓevi Me'at Devash corresponds with R. Raphael Ibn Ẓur concerning the purchase of books

This letter was sent by Ha-Ẓevi Me'at Devash of Jerusalem to Raphael Ibn Ẓur, of Fez on the twelfth day of Ḥeshvan 1873. The writer mentions that two volumes of the Code, Ḥoshen Mishpat (on civil law) with all the commentaries, as well as the work Netivot Mishpat and the book Keẓot ha-Ḥoshen, were until recently unavailable, but now he has been able to acquire them. He has also acquired the Code Even ha-Ezer. The price for books has increased. A certain edition of the Scriptures is still unavailable.

The books which are being sent by the writer to R. Raphael are arriving via Gibraltar through the agency of Moses Halevi. Two other books that are arriving are Ginzei Ḥayyim and Birkhat Mo'adekha L'Ḥayyim, Part II, by the author Ḥayyim Palaggi, of blessed memory. They are being sent by the son of the author of those works, R. Abraham Palaggi, head of the Academy, at Izmir, Turkey. In a postscript the writer informs R. Raphael that the aforementioned R. Abraham Palaggi sent his father's books to R. Raphael, but that the latter never responded or sent any money. The author's stamp appears on this letter. It has a picture of the Western Wall of the Holy Temple compound at its center, with the writer's name and domicile at Jerusalem stated on the border of the seal.

Ms. 146
P. 204a

A legal document concerning a paternity suit

This document, which is signed by the rabbis Abner Israel Ha-Ṣarfati and Raphael Ibn Zur of Fez, was written on the twenty-fifth day of Tishri 1876. After the death of her husband Joseph, a woman called Leah and her two daughters were given refuge at the home of the valorous woman Simha, the daughter of the late Hillel ibn Samuel, and a relative. Leah was soon discovered to be pregnant. Leah testified that she became pregnant from Moses, the son of Judah ibn Samuel, and that she had had no sexual relations with anyone else. Moses was sent for and he admitted to having had relations with Leah, except that he claimed that she seduced him at the house of the aforementioned Hillel. He stated that he thought that she was a wayward woman. Leah claimed that Moses seduced *her*. The court, after having established his guilt, punished him severely for taking advantage of the woman and for not marrying her. He was flogged and fines were exacted from him. [Calculations appear on page 204b as well as the name of Jacob ibn Simḥon.]

Ms. 147
P. 205a

A plea by the Rishon Le-Zion, R. Hayyim Abraham Gagin, to R. Raphael Ha-Ṣarfati to aid his son-in-law, R. Judah Zacut

This letter is written by the chief rabbi of Jerusalem, R. Hayyim Abraham Gagin, to R. Raphael Ha-Sarfati, of Fez, concerning the plight of the former's son-in-law, R. Judah Zacut. The latter is the son of the illustrious mystic R. Moses Zacut. R. Judah Zacut is in a poor financial condition and he must support a large family of some ten souls. He is obliged to journey and ask for economic support from others. The writer asks R. Raphael to extend all possible aid to his son-in-law. The letter is signed by the writer.

Ms. 148
P. 206a

A plea for protection in transit to be extended to a widow who will enter a levirate marriage

This letter was written to R. Raphael Ha-Sarfati, at Fez, on the eve of the New Moon of the month of Tevet 1834-35. It concerns a woman whose husband has been dead for twelve years. The writer notes that a candidate to perform the levirate rite was found in the town of Onaba, but because he was still too young she was not sent to him. Subsequently, another two candidates have been found in the same town, who are of age, and therefore the widow must be sent there so that the levirate responsibility can be fulfilled. Besides, since the woman has been existing in her solitary state for a number of years it is only just that she should be able to remarry. Those who are able to fulfill the marital rites are reported to be bachelors.

Money is being made available to send the widow to Fez from whence she would travel to the aforementioned town so that the levirate responsibility can be consummated. The writer asks R. Raphael to make sure that the widow is properly chaperoned by persons of high moral character and that her needs are provided for until she arrives at her destination, especially since she is a very chaste and religious woman. Rabbi Raphael is asked to send letters to the various places to prepare for the widow's arrival.

Ms. 149
Pp. 207a and 208a

A copy of a letter sent by R. Ḥayyim Ḥaluah to R. Ḥayyim David Ibn Zimra

This is a manuscript copy of a letter rich in metaphor that R. Ḥayyim Ḥaluah wrote to R. Ḥayyim David ibn Zimra. This epistle commences with verse which incorporates the name of the Radbaz in the following form, Ḥayyim David ibn Zimra. The writer also addresses R. Vidal Ha-Ṣarfati in the paragraph following the opening section of verse. In the third paragraph greetings are sent to R. Jacob (Ibn Ẓur) and R. Abner (Ha-Ṣarfati). The writer is presently on a sea voyage in his travels for charitable purposes. He asks for the rabbis' blessing and support in his hour of need.

Ms. 150
P. 209a and b

A traveller who settled in the Holy Land writes a disparaging report about conditions there

This letter is written to R. Raphael Ḥa-Ṣarfati of Fez by R. Ḥayyim Romano of Hebron. R. Ḥayyim, who is a recent arrival in the Holy Land, describes conditions there. He notes that disorganization is rampant in its various communities. The leadership, which is fractionalized, has only one purpose and that is to pay off the local rulers. The welfare of the many is neglected by the weak leaders. The writer is confident that ultimately God will avenge the ill treatment of his people. This letter was sent from Ṣefrou, in the year 1842. [Editor's note: R. Ḥayyim Romano was known to have travelled to Gibraltar after establishing residence in Hebron. See *Ms.152*, page 212a for additional information on R. Ḥayyim Romano.]

Ms. 151
Pp. 210a—211b

A manuscript copy of the introduction of Iggerot Haramaz

This introductory part of the work Iggerot HaRaMaz was composed by Maharam Zacut, i.e. R. Moses Zacut, of blessed memory. The name Moses and the name Zacut appear respectively at the beginning and end of the fifteenth line of page 210a. The author was a Kabbalist and a Halakhist, a Jewish legal scholar. The Kabbalistic quality of this introduction is apparent. The metaphoric quality of the language is also evident.

Ms. 152
P. 212a

A correspondence from Samuel Halevi Ibn Yulee to R. Raphael Menaḥem Ha-Ṣarfati, of Fez

This letter was written by Samuel Halevi ibn Yulee, residing temporarily at Jebel Tor (Gibraltar), to R. Raphael Menaḥem Ha-Ṣarfati of Fez, on Tuesday, the tenth of Kislev 1841. The writer inquires about the well-being of R. Raphael's son Joseph because R.S. Aflalo, who is at Gibraltar, has asked the writer to discover his whereabouts. The writer reports that when he was in Livorno he inquired about Joseph from the local gentry, as well as from the Italians, Roumanians, and others, and that many who knew him did not know his present whereabouts. When he arrived at Jebel Tor the writer encountered R. A. Bîton, who had not been well and who informed him that the emissary R. Ḥayyim Romano, of Hebron, who is presently in Tetuan, having departed from Gibraltar before the writer's arrival there knew the son to have been in the Holy Land and to be a prosperous scholar of note. R.A. Bîton did not write concerning Joseph because of his poor health. Additional information concerning the son can be derived from R. Ḥayyim Romano if R. Raphael Menaḥem would write to him. The writer also reminds R. Raphael about a litigation concerning the prosperous Isaac Ben Zaqen to which he should turn his attention so that justice will be done. The writer offers to elaborate on the matter at length.

Ms. 153
P. 213a

An appeal is made to R. Samuel Amar to aid the scholar R. Jacob Ha-Kohen in raising funds for his daughter's forthcoming wedding

The writer appeals to R. Samuel Amar to aid the scholar R. Jacob Ha-Kohen in his plight to raise money for his daughter's marital needs. Since the scholar Jacob is not an aggressive person he requires the help of others to intercede on his behalf in this effort. The writer of this letter, who remains anonymous, was apparently from Jerusalem as was the aforementioned Jacob Ha-Kohen.

Ms. 154
P. 215a

A letter of adulation and a prayer of well-being written to Reuben Ibn Ẓur by Elijah Utmazgin

This letter of praise and prayer for well being was written by Elijah Utmazgin to Reuben Ibn Ẓur, on the seventeenth of Shevat, 1879. Apparently Reuḅen is not in the best of health. Blessings are recited for Solomon and Esther, the son and daughter of Reuben. [Page 226a is part of this letter. The writer's name appears on both pages. The bottom of page 226a is used for miscellaneous notations.]

Ms. 155
P. 216a

A dispute concerning real estate involving the Monsano family and the communities of Fez and Meknès

This document commences "A copy of a letter from Meknès" and was sent to the following judges of Tetuán: R. Judah Abudarham, R. Judah Coriat, and R. Solomon Abudarham. The litigation concerns R. Elijah Monsano who is disputing with his uncle, Ḥayyim Monsano, and a cousin over property which seems to be related to an inheritance. The rabbinic court in Fez has not been able to deal with the matter since the authorities are related to the disputants, and are thus disqualified. R. Elijah Monsano had invited the parties to deal with the matter in Meknès, but apparently the parties from Fez had failed to appear in Meknès, even after they had been invited on several occasions. Thus, the rabbis of Tetuán, R. Solomon Toledano, R. Solomon Abudarham, and the young R. Abraham Monsonyego have turned back to the rabbis of Fez to adjudicate the matter where both parties have now agreed the matter shall be dealt with. The rabbis of Fez, Samuel Ibn Ẓur and Saul Serero, ask the rabbis of Meknes to complete the judgement, in the year 1788. This document was certified by Judah Ha-Kohen and Raphael Moses Elbaz on a subsequent occasion, because the matter was not adjudicated until many years later.

Ms. 156
P. 217a and b

The Nasi complains to the rabbis of Fez about the breakdown of authority and the injustices of the times

This letter was written in Judaeo-Arabic to the rabbis of Fez, Raphael Ibn Ẓur, Isaac ibn Danan, and Solomon ibn Danan, on the fourth of Ḥeshvan 1880. The writer (the Nasi) complains about the injustices that are rampant in the jurisdiction of the above-named rabbis and further, blamed them on these rabbis and other members of the community. One such incident reported to the writer by Jacob Oḥana concerned the injustice perpetrated by Judah ben Agrir. Judah had gone to the ruler to inform on a Jew who owed him nothing more than rent. What is more, he bribed the ruler with twenty Reál and the man was put in prison for four days without a trial and then locked out of his house. All this transpired on the eve of the New Year. False witnesses were also produced, among them, Joseph ANizzam, who was forced to tell lies.

On another occasion Mîmun b. Haroush told Elijah Kaṣiba to take a kilo of meat for him. Elijah didn't take the meat and was beaten for it until he was near death. Then there was the neighbor of Jacob Ohana's aunt who received a flogging when ben Agrir tried to force him to attend a rabbinic court. When he refused the claimant, David Edery, demanded that they go to the ruler. The aforementioned ben Agrir forced him there bodily. After hearing David Edery's complaint the ruler imprisoned the plaintiff and refused to let him go.

All of the aforementioned troubles have arisen because disputants go to the ruler instead of to the rabbinic courts. The Nasi, head of the Jewish community, registers these complaints with the rabbis who now undertake to intercede in the matter to help this unfortunate Jew who has the highest references from Meknès.

Ms. 157
P. 218a

An Halakhic query is posed

The query is as follows: "can a man divorce his wife on the condition that she cannot marry until a set time passes?" This question is posed by Solomon Susan. No reply appears to this short query.

Ms. 158
P. 219a

A litigation that resulted in a compromise

This legal document was written in Ṣefrou, on the day of the new month of Marḥeshvan 1868. It was signed by the judges of Ṣefrou, the rabbis Hayyim Joseph Gayni and Ḥayyim Eliyahu. It discusses a dispute between David, (son of Jacob, son of Waḥnish) and Moses (son of Abraham, son of Siso). The aforementioned David has presented a business contract and demanded that Moses make payment on the principal and the dividends according to its terms. Moses, on the other hand, claims that he has incurred many losses and that the conditions of the contract are therefore null and void. However, he has been informed that the law is in accord with him with regard to profits provided he swears that he didn't make any. Moses further claims that he left sacks as security with David who has sold them without Moses' knowledge or permission. Moreover, a number of the sacks that he gave to David are missing. After much bickering they have compromised in the following manner: Mahlouf, Moses' brother, has bound himself to pay a sum of forty mitkalim (one mitkal equals ten of the smallest coin denomination of the realm) to David. David has dropped his claim against Moses and accepted responsibility for the lost sacks. All further claims are dropped.

Ms. 159
P. 220a

An aged scholar writes concerning a litigation

This letter was written by R. Ḥayyim Joseph Gayni of Ṣefrou to R. Raphael Ibn Ẓur of Fez, on the twenty-sixth of Kislev 1881. The writer states that his hand is not steady because of the weight of his years and he will therefore not write more than is necessary. His subect is a litigation. The actions of one of the parties is prompted by economic privation, he says, otherwise the claim would not be bothered about. [It is interesting to compare the writer's signature here with that in *Ms.158*, page 219a, since there is a difference of thirteen years between them.]

Ms. 160
Pp. 221a—224b
P. 226a

A manuscript copy of the work Sefer Divrei Ḥakhamim Ke-Dôrbônôt

This work is a compilation of aphorisms of the philosophers and the sages. [For a full treatment of the material in this manuscript see a description of another copy of this work in this collection, *Ms.36*, pages 50a to 52b and 62a and b.] This copy was composed by Jonathan Ish Ṣion Monsano, the son of Beẓalel, of blessed memory. The scholar Judah Uziel and his contemporary, the scribe Ezra De Paridisi, are mentioned on 224b.

A blessing composed by Elijah Utmazgin for Reuben Ibn Ẓur, which belongs to *Ms. 154*, page 215a, appears on page 226a.

Ms. 161
P. 227a and b

The settlement of an estate by a mother and her daughter has implications for the daughter's forthcoming marriage

R. Solomon Kohen (son of R. Jacob Kohen o.b.m. Skali, of Debdou) died, leaving a widow, Masuda (daughter of Salem Ha-Kohen) of Fez and a small daughter, Esther. Masuda's marriage contract was in accord with the customs of Castilia whereby she was obliged to divide the whole estate, movable and immovable property, in half between herself and her daughter. After a time Masuda married Judah (son of Simon ben Betito, called Askouri) and brought as her dowry that remaining from her first husband's estate. There remained in Debdou a certain amount of movable property and land.

Now her daughter Esther has attained a marriageable age and become betrothed to Joseph (son of Mordecai Ṣaba o.b.m.) of Fez. However, Joseph has discovered that his bride-to-be has only about twenty uqiot for her dowry and he wants to break the engagement, even though he is promised her portion of what remains of the estate in Debdou.

There is no alternative but to divide in half also that portion that the mother has taken, and what is in Debdou must also be equally divided between mother and daughter. Originally, the mother took the best part of the estate for herself and left the daughter that part which would only realize its true value over a period of time because it was in a more remote place. Masuda and her second husband, Judah, now persuade the groom not to break the engagement, promising to withdraw all claims to any further part in the properties at Debdou and to give all of it to Esther for her dowry.

[Although there is no signature appearing in this document, which was written in Fez, it undoubtedly bears a resemblance to the writing and style of R. Jacob Ibn Ẓur. Compare it with *Ms.121*, page 170 where R. Jacob Ibn Ẓur's signature appears.]

Ms. 162
P. 228a

R. Judah Ibn Attar asks R. Jacob Ibn Ẓur to convince a party to a litigation to accept a judgement achieved by mediation

This letter was written by R. Judah ibn Attar to R. Jacob Ibn Ẓur, *circa* 1720. R. Judah states that he served as a mediator between David Arwaẓ and Jacob Monsonyego [here the page is torn and words are missing] concerning the rights to a courtyard and the rights pertaining to synagogues which R. Jacob Ibn Ẓur will note in a document which has presumably been brought to him by Jacob Ha-Kohen. R. Judah wants R. Jacob Ibn Ẓur to add his signature to the document. Another matter, pertaining to overseeing the interests of the orphans of Abraham ibn Danan who are involved in a judgement with ———ibn Amara, is brought to the attention of R. Jacob Ibn Ẓur. R. Judah would like him to act as a mediator in behalf of the orphans. Finally, R. Judah closes with a postscript concerning Jacob Monsonyego's refusal to accept the result of the aforementioned mediation. He asks R. Jacob Ibn Ẓur to persuade him to accept the judgement which is just.

Ms. 163
P. 228a

A letter of reference for one who collects funds for the redemption of captives

This document, which was written in the year 1721, is found on the lower part of page 228a. The letter on the upper part of the same page was sent to R. Jacob Ibn Ẓur. [It is most probable that this letter, which appears on the lower part of the page, was written by R. Jacob Ibn Ẓur. A comparison of the style of handwriting found in this letter with that found in *Ms.35* clearly indicates that R. Jacob Ibn Ẓur is the writer of this letter.] It is written by Jacob Ibn Ẓur for the scholarly R. Abraham Halevi (son of Barukh Halevi, a descendant of the author of the Tosafot Yom Toḇ) who is engaged in collecting funds for the redemption of captives. The writer asks that every comfort, hospitality, and charitable offering be extended to this lofty guest as he travels for the worthiest of causes. If he, in turn, should appoint an emissary, then similar treatment should be accorded the emissary. It appears that R. Abraham Halevi comes from the Holy Land.

Ms. 164
P. 229a

The transmission of contracts from Fez to Meknès

This letter is written by R. Judah ibn Attar to the rabbis of Meknès concerning three contracts that had been placed in his possession for safekeeping. One of these contracts had been written for Mas'ūd ben Isaiah who resided in Meknès. One day the son of the aforementioned Mas'ūd, Samuel, had approached him asking for the contracts because he was acting for his mother. R. Judah did not have the contracts with him at that time so Samuel asked that they be sent to Meknès as he was leaving Fez. The contracts found their way into the possession of a young man, Judah ibn Jacob Ṣaba and subsequently into the possession of R. Reuben ben Isaiah at Meknès. The rabbis of Meknes are now asked to obtain Mas'ūd's contract so that it might be forwarded to his wife before Reuben ben Isaiah leaves Meknès. Mas'ūd has left the area for a distant place, so the contracts had been sent to Reuben, who is his son-in-law, according to the instructions of Samuel. Originally, a letter had been brought from the mother by her son Samuel instructing that the contracts be sent to her but, R. Judah ibn Attar notes, it is not the practice to engage in these legal transactions with a woman and therefore the son was sent to act in his mother's stead. The rabbis of Meknès are asked to oblige Reuben, the son-in-law, by surrendering the contracts to his mother-in-law.

Ms. 165
P. 230a

R. Mordecai Berdugo asks R. Jacob Ibn Ẓur to support his decision to free an Agunah, based on the testimony of one witness

This letter is written by R. Mordecai Berdugo to R. Jacob Ibn Zur concerning the case of an agunah, a woman of the town of Armil who is prevented from remarrying until her husband's death can be substantiated. The writer asks R. Jacob to support his decision to permit her to remarry. There is only one witness who can testify to the husband's death although normally two witnesses are needed. At first R. Mordecai wanted to prohibit her from marrying by contending that the testimony of one witness was insufficient. However, he now feels that one witness is sufficient. R. Mordecai asks R. Jacob to offer arguments in support of his decision. R. Abraham Monsano will bring this letter to R. Jacob Ibn Ẓur. [The address of this document serves as the backing to page 235a.]

Ms. 166
P. 231a and b

Two supplicatory prayers by Yaaḅez (R. Jacob Ibn Ẓur), and one poem by R.Y. Najara

The first of two supplicatory poems is by Yaaḅez, of blessed memory, commencing with the words "Hashem Yoshev Ha-Kerubim"—"Lord who dwells amongst the cherubim." The second supplicatory prayer pertains to the thirteen attributes from the prophet Micah. It commences with the words, "Hashem Yaḥid Um-Yuḥad Ain Arokh Ailekha"—"God thou art uniquely One, nothing can be compared to You." It is composed by R. Jacob Ibn Ẓur and written in the acrostic form of the author's name. A third poem commencing with the words "Ḥida Tamah" is written on page 231b. It is composed by R. Y. Najara, of blessed memory. The page is in a poor condition. [Additional poems in the Bension collection, by R. Jacob Ibn Ẓur, appear in *Ms.84*, pages 111a to 116b.]

Ms. 167
P. 232a

A correspondence concerning some legal matters and misunderstandings which have arisen between the Jewish communities of Fez and Meknès

R. Joseph Elmaleḥ writes this letter to R. Raphael Berdugo concerning misunderstandings between Jewish communities on certain matters and also about some cases in Jewish law which are of mutual interest to both scholars. The writer states that he is replying to a previous letter from R. Raphael although he intended not to send any additional letters since these letters only tend to exacerbate the situation of strife that earlier letters produced. R. Elmaleḥ states that his decision in one case was based on the ruling of R. Y. Asulin who will respond to R. Raphael and to the scholars of Meknès on another occasion. R. Elmaleḥ asks that the rabbis of Meknès should respond by writing their views on the matter so that there should no longer be misunderstandings between the two communities of Meknès and Fez. A parable is introduced to demonstrate that the leaders should not repeat the follies of those whom they lead by increasing the existing strife.

A disgraceful act perpetrated by the community of Salé against two emissaries from Jerusalem is reported. One emissary is Isaac Amzalag and some scholars of Rabat were also involved. Comments are made about the dispute such as, "the falsifiers turn truth to folly. It doesn't pay to fight for justice against a majority who support injustice." The writer states that it is difficult for a court to reverse a decision which has already been handed down in another court. Concerning a decision rendered in a case involving a widow and one called Mahlouf, the writer states that he agrees with R. Berdugo's decision. To serve the cause of justice R. Berdugo is asked to intercede in a case of a disputed inheritance involving R. Y. Leg̣imi, who acted unjustly to his younger brother.

Ms. 168
P. 233a and b

A business transaction between a Christian and a Jew which is guaranteed by other Jews who become totally responsible for the completion of the transaction

Many commercial terms in this document are of a Spanish origin. The case involves one called R. Abraham who had once entered into a small business transaction with a Christian when no contract was necessary. However, when Abraham entered into a bigger transaction with the same gentile, a contract became necessary to protect his interest, especially considering that he was a stranger in the land. He persuaded some wealthy Jews to guarantee the contract for him against any false claims that might arise and paid them a large sum of money for this service. These arrangements were made with witnesses in the presence of the non-Jew. The persons acting as guarantors, known by the name Ibn Susan, have written to R. Abraham telling him to acquire the merchandise from the gentile. He has responded that he will not deal directly with the gentile anymore and since they have committed themselves to the transaction, it is *their* job to deal with him. The guarantors say that Abraham should at least send an agent to act on the matter.

Abraham retorts that they are not only agents guaranteeing a transaction but by their silence at the time of their agreement with him they have tacitly admitted full responsibility for the transaction. Otherwise, R. Abraham says he would not have set up this transaction at all.

It is finally agreed that R. Abraham will no longer have to deal directly with the Christian, since an agent cannot change the terms to which he originally agreed without accepting total liability. This is in accord with the ruling of R. Joseph Caro, in chapter 184 of the Code, "whoever gives money to his agent to act for him on a specific date and the agent doesn't comply on time then he accepts all liabilities that are incurred." There are many more citations that could be noted, but there is no point in reciting them here. The document concludes with the hope that the wealthy guarantors will perform the right action for R. Abraham, who is not in good economic circumstances. [The first part of this document appears to be missing.]

Ms. 169
P. 234a

A query about access rights

The controversy taken up in this document centers around whether an original real estate settlement included the right of access or not. Four individuals were parties to the original settlement, which involved houses and other real estate. The conclusion reached is as follows: if, when the houses were assigned to each party, land for access was part of that evaluation, then no further claims to access rights can be made. If, however, no such rights were included then a consideration must now be made for such rights to be extended.

Ms. 170
P. 234b

A list of tombs

The names of the departed who appear on this list of tombs is as follows: the scholar R. Y. Ha-Kohen, his son Abraham, and the latter's son, the scholar Yaḥya; the scholar Isaiah Ha-Kohen and his wife; R. Jacob Ha-Kohen and his daughter; the aged R. Solomon Attiya, and the scholar R. Mas'ūd, his son; the scholar Joseph Attiya; R. (Aziz) ibn Haroush; the scholar Isaac Israel; R. Hayyim ibn Gigi and the first wife of Aaron ibn Gigi; R. Reuben ibn Siso and his wife; the daughter of Shalom ibn Siso; R. Mîmun ibn Gazi; R. Mahlouf ibn Shitrit and his wife; the second wife of Jacob ibn Shitrit; the scholar R. Shalom ibn Rabuḥ; R. Abraham Rabuḥ and the wives of the scholar R. Abraham ibn Rabuḥ; R. Isaac ibn Danan and his wife; R. Joseph ibn Adhan and his wife; R. Isaac ibn Elbaz; Mahlouf ibn Shitrit and his wife and R. Salman Abirzil and his wife.

Ms. 171
P. 235a

A letter from R. Judah Ibn Attar asking that economic aid be made available to R. Isaac Rotî who is faced with an extraordinary situation forced upon him by an apostate

After R. Judah ibn Attar has related the adversities which his community (of Fez) faces, he continues this letter to the rabbis Jacob Ibn Ẓur and Moses Berdugo (at Meknès) on behalf of R. Isaac Rotî. R. Isaac is forced to travel abroad in his old age to seek funds because an apostate Jew has made false claims against his family. R. Isaac's son, Joseph, once acquired an article from the apostate, which he had been given for safekeeping but had been stolen. The matter was brought before the non-Jewish court and the judgement rendered was that Rotî would have to pay a stipulated amount of money by a certain date. A number of additional expenses had also been incurred. R. Isaac had neglected to mention his great need to R. Judah when travelling through his area because of his shame, but he had been informed of the old man's plight by the son. Therefore, R. Judah writes this letter to the rabbis at Meknès asking them to come to the aid of R. Isaac Rotî. This letter was written in the year1719.

A transaction involving the sale of a mule

Ms. 172
P. 236a

This legal document records a transaction involving Gideon ibn Sa'îd Ha-Kohen who acquires a mule from Yaḥya the son of Abraham ibn Arwaḥ for 180 uqiot. The vendor has already received the payment and Gideon has acquired the animal. They hereby agree that if any non-Jew should win a claim in the non-Jewish court against Gideon for owning the animal then Yaḥya shall restore to Gideon 60 uqiot from the amount of the sale, but Gideon will lose the remaining 120 uqiot. If the non-Jew does not win his claim in the non-Jewish court then any loss that Gideon might incur in payment for his legal defence may accrue to the total price of the animal, plus an additional 20 uqiot. If the expense should exceed the amount then Yahya agrees to pay only half of the additional amount. Both parties agree to this stipulation. (This provision was necessary because a mule is half a horse and Jews were not allowed to keep horses, only donkeys. The horse was considered a noble animal and only non-Jews were allowed to own them. Therefore, it was possible that Gideon might be challenged in the courts for owning a 'half-noble' animal.)

The contract stipulated that any payments due under its provisions should not be subject to the law of the remission of debts in the Sabbatical year. The responsibility for fulfilling all its terms should also apply to those who stand to inherit the principals involved in the transaction. This contract was composed on the twenty-first day of Tammuz, in the year 84 (according to the dating of contracts), *circa* 1624. This document was signed for the benefit of Gideon, in Fez, by Jacob the son of Joseph ibn Danan. The document was certified by the latter signing his name, Jacob, a second time.

Novellae on Rashi's Talmudic Commentary pertaining to the monetary options available to the wife upon the husband's death

Ms. 173
P. 236b

Rashi, the eleventh century commentator, offers two ways to explain the statement of the master, R. Abba in the Talmud, pertaining to the options available to the widow as to how she may receive what is due to her monetarily upon the death of her husband. Either she receives the monetary value stipulated in her marriage contract, or R. Abba maintains that she receives an equal portion to that which each son receives besides what she receives as the value of her marriage contract, called the Ketubba. This second view is maintained even though the amount that each son would receive exceeds the value of the marriage contract. The wife still receives both.

Another way to explain the text is that the sons will give her a portion equal to their portion and she forfeits thereby what she would have received from the Ketubba. According to this explanation the widow would stand to lose much, but this would depend on the situation. For instance, if there were to be more children and the land which she will acquire is limited to what the husband possessed at a particular time, then she stands to lose a great deal, unlike the sons who would not have a time limitation placed on them. However, it is also possible that the number of heirs could be reduced through death before the demise of the husband, in which case the widow would conceivably receive more money than was originally anticipated.

A chronicle, commencing from Rosh Hashanah, 1775

Ms. 174
P. 237a

The first thirteen lines of this document record the rainfall between the Jewish New Year and the month of Tevet. On the day after the minor festival of Ḥanukah a public fast is declared because the rain supply is far from ample. The non-Jews in Fez cry to God for rain all the eight days of Ḥanukah and they ask the Jews to pray for rain. The gentiles have stopped planting seeds because of the lack of rain. A Torah is brought forth during the morning service and scriptural reading for fast days is also read at the afternoon service.

On the fifth of Tevet a public fast is again declared and psalms are read. Afterwards the entire community, comprising thirteen synagogues, recite the prayer "Shma Kolenu"—"Hear Our Voice," on their way to the cemetery. They arrived at an open area near a stone wall where R. Jacob Qanizal is buried. The people wept there as the author of this chronicle exhorts them, using a text from the Jerusalem Talmud and a verse from the Song of Songs. Prayers are directed to the saintly ones in paradise and sentences from Job are recited as the rain begins to fall. The people also go to the tomb of the venerable R. Vidal Ha-Ṣarfati to recite Psalms.

Ms. 175
P. 238b

A plea to the judges of Fez to attempt to bring about a reconciliation between a husband and his wife; if it can't be done then a divorce should be given

The scholars of Sala write this letter in the form of a court document to the rabbis of Fez in reply to an earlier correspondence. The case pertains to R. Moses, the son of Isaac Ibn Ẓur, and the marital problems that he has had with his spouse. The husband wants to grant a divorce to his wife, while she is desirous of a reconciliation regretting that she originally wanted a divorce. The wife has asked that an agent be appointed to plead for her and to respond to the claims that her husband is filing against her. If the husband refuses to arrive at a reconciliation, then the claims he is making should be investigated by the rabbis of Fez with the presentation of witnesses under oath.

Afterwards a monetary settlement should be made based on what the wife brought to the marriage and what may be deducted therefrom, based on the husband's claims against her; this should be accounted together with the value of the marriage contract. Thereafter her portion of the estate should be reduced according to a fixed percentage. If the husband will be reconciled, the wife states that she will be prepared to go anywhere with him without any hesitation. She will in any event abide by the decision of the judges of Fez. This document was signed on the twenty-second day of Sivan 1710, at Salé. Three signatures appear on the document: those of Mordecai Ha-Kohen, Joseph Ṣaba, and Jacob Bibas. (These three were famous scholars in Salé during this period.) A postscript is added stating that the marriage contract should be paid according to the custom of Castilian Jewry in the event of divorce. He must pay the full amount of her marriage contract but if he does not have the money available, then he is obliged to support his former wife until he pays the full value of her contract.

Ms. 176
P. 239a and b

An emissary of Jerusalem writes to R. Solomon Ibn Ẓur of Fez

Raphael Halevi, who was an emissary from Jerusalem, writes to R. Solomon Ibn Ẓur. He explains his tardiness in replying to R. Solomon's earlier correspondence as due to his preoccupation with collecting donations. R. Solomon had sent fifteen uqiot which is now acknowledged. R. Abraham Simḥon and members of his family are mentioned in this letter. [The letter was written the day following the festival and the address for this letter, which was sent to Fez, is found on page 239b. This writer is also the author of *Ms.178* and *Ms.183*].

Ms. 177
P. 240a and b

Prescriptions for physical and spiritual ailments

This text gives antidotes for those who drink too much wine, those suffering from diarrhea, women who suffer an issue of much blood during the menstrual period, women who are sterile, people with worms in the stomach, and sufferers of excessive coughing and other congestions of the chest. A recital of a mystical prayer for protection when travelling in a dangerous area which is under siege is recorded. This prayer, which was transmitted by a mystic, reads as follows: "May the names of Sandalphon and Uriel strive to save

Ms. 172
A legal document recording the sale of a mule to a Jew by a gentile

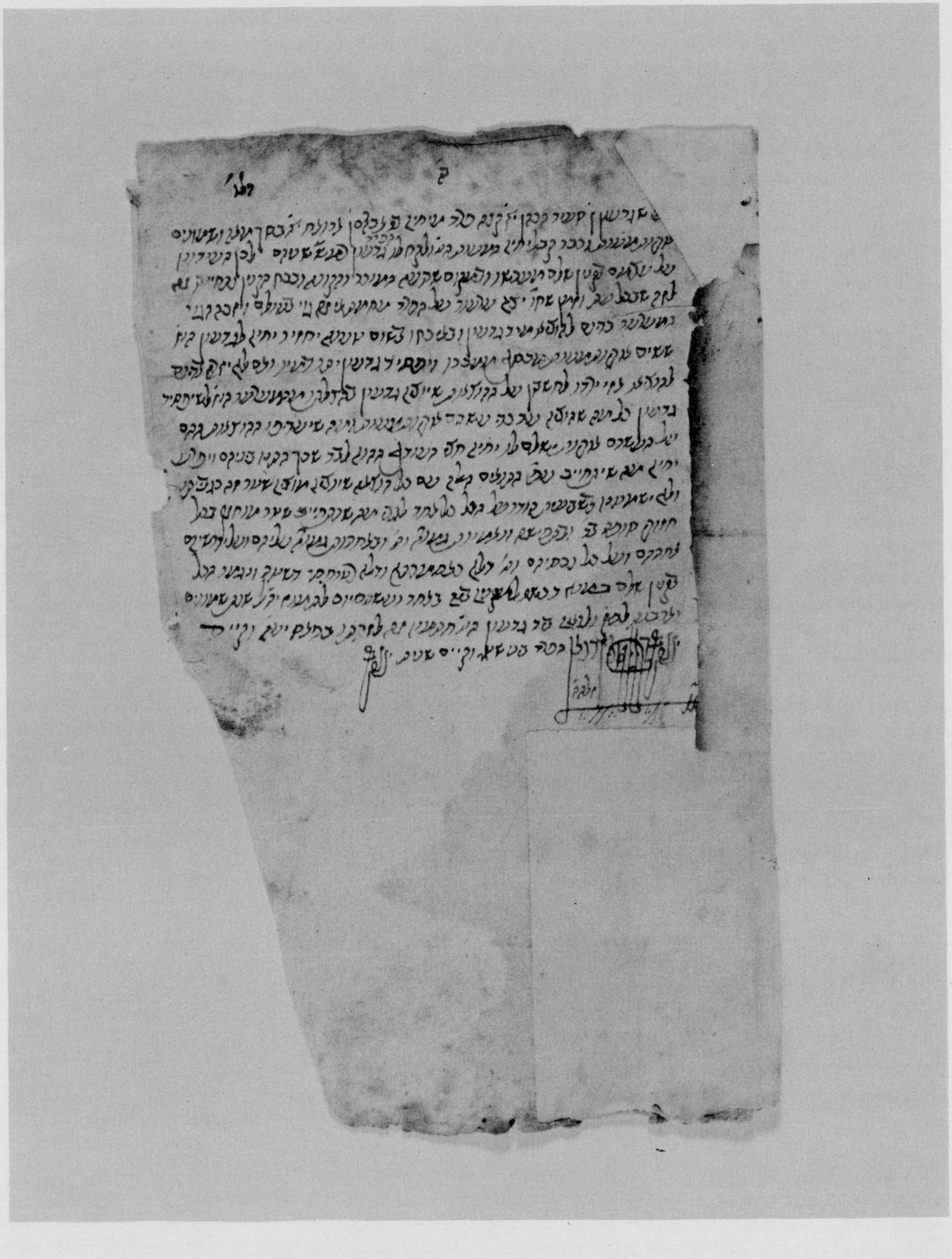

me from the enemy and from those who lie in wait for me on my journey." Antidotes are given for those who must pass stones and a prescription is noted for a woman to become pregnant who has no blood flow during her menstrual cycle. A formula is also offered for one to meet with success. [No names or dates are given on this page.]

Ms. 178
P. 241a and b

An emissary from Jerusalem relates the hospitality that he enjoys in his travels

The writer of this letter is the same Raphael Halevi, an emissary of the Kollel in Jerusalem, who is the writer of *Ms.176*, page 239a and b—and *Ms.183*. He writes this letter to R. Solomon Ibn Ẓur of Fez. He mentions having received a letter from R. Solomon Ibn Ẓur wherein the latter inquires about the treatment Raphael is receiving on his journey to collect charitable contributions. Raphael responds that the Jews of the West (Morocco) are very hospitable and the good treatment that he receives from them is in accord with the traditions of earlier generations. Even though many people are themselves impoverished they are happy to make donations. The scholars among them are of good standing and are careful to give citations for their statements. Raphael sends regards to the brothers, senior Abraham and senior Solomon ibn Simḥon, and to the young Mas'ūd. On the top of page 241b four lines are written wherein Raphael asks that a certain type of unavailable stone be sent to him which he will pay for on his return trip. (The stone was probably used in preparing knives for the slaughter of fowl and cattle.) He asks that regards be sent to Jacob, the son of the emissary R. A. Kizri. The address to R. Solomon Ibn Zur, at Fez, is found on this page.

Ms. 179
P. 242a and b

A prayer to be recited in times of distress, and scriptural verses for proper names

[The compiler of the collection reversed the pages. Page 242a should follow page 242b. It appears that there was at least one more additional page preceding the one before us.]

The copyist commences with a prayer which one who is in distress is advised to recite twelve times, followed by a supplicatory prayer with some Kabbalist elements which is given in full on page 242b. At the bottom of this page proper names are listed alphabetically with scriptural verses that pertain to them. This list is given in full and is completed on page 242a (which should actually be page 242b). Both texts are the product of the same copyist.

Ms. 180
P. 243a

The court in Tafilalet is asked to guarantee the consummation of a transaction

R. Jacob, a creditor, has sent an agent to Tafilalet to collect a debt in the amount of 340 uqiot. However, because of the danger of robbery on the roads he has not sent the contract itself with the agent but only a copy of it. The undersigned asks that upon full payment to the agent a legal document should be drawn up by the court of the city attesting to the fact that the payment was made and that once it has been made it should be recorded in the original contract. This statement is signed by Mîmun ibn Walila and by Abraham, the son of David ibn Ḥasin.

Ms. 181
P. 243a

A business transaction between two parties in Fez and Meknès

The undersigned to this document are Mordecai ibn Malkạ and Abraham, the son of David ibn Ḥasin. [The latter was also a signatory to *Ms.180*, the document at the top of page 243a.] They testify, by this document, to the sale by R. Jacob Halevi to Ḥayyim b. Mas'ūd ibn Ḥanun ibn Magiriẓ, who dwells in Fez, of a deed that was paid for by Ḥayyim in the sum of one thousand uqiot. This document, which was composed on the fifteenth of Adar 1733, at Meknès, was confirmed by the signatures of Barukh Monsano and Elazar Bahalul.

The addendum to this document, which is signed by R. Jacob Ibn Ẓur, informs us that a certain sum was subtracted from the one thousand uqiot by the evaluation of the courtyard of Amram ben Tata in the sum of one hundred and twenty uqiot, for his partnership with the aforementioned Ḥayyim ibn Magriẓ.

Ms. 182
P. 243b

A debtor vows to pay his loan in installments and he uses the income of a business venture to pay the creditor until that arrangement dissolves

Dinar, the son of Tata, the son of R. Amram, may his soul repose in paradise, owed the sum of one thousand, three hundred and forty uqiot to R. Jacob Halevi (son of Samuel, of blessed memory) who is an inhabitant of Salé. Dinar agreed to pay it in installments. The sum of two hundred uqiot was to be paid at the end of the month of Iyar and a further oath was made to make that payment on time. Dinar agreed to pay an additional six hundred uqiot whenever the creditor desired it from that day forward. The remaining five hundred and forty uqiot was to be paid by the end of the month of Tammuz. Both parties agreed to the following conditions: that whatever monies accrued from the merchandise sold by the debtor would be transmitted in the form of merchandise to his creditor. The creditor would sell the merchandise and whatever profit accrued would be divided equally among them. The creditor would take the principal in payment of the debt, but if any losses were incurred then they would be shared equally.

Shortly thereafter the commercial arrangement that existed between both parties was dissolved and the only binding element between them was the oath that Dinar agreed to reaffirm in the presence of a court concerning the debt that still remained. Dinar now admits his willingness to reaffirm that oath at the pleasure of R. Jacob and to fulfill all the terms of indebtedness that the oath implies. This document was composed on the first day of the week (Sunday), the twentieth day of Tevet 1717, at Fez. The document was signed and affirmed by Jacob, the son of Joseph, the son of Malka. The signature of Aaron Halevi ibn Safed appears in a lighter shade of ink at the end of the document as one who served as a witness.

Ms. 183
P. 244a and b

An emissary informs R. Solomon Ibn Ẓur of the difficulty he is encountering in collecting funds that have been pledged

Raphael Halevi, an emissary from the Jerusalem Kollel, thanks R. Solomon Ibn Ẓur for tobacco that he sent to him and says he is responding to R. Solomon's last letter. He also tells R. Solomon about his difficulties in collecting for the Holy Land. Every person, he says, sets an amount for his donation but when he comes to collect it they say, "You will have it in two or three days." Raphael then took an oath that he would not eat anywhere until the money vouched was paid, but the people still put him off, stating that money was not available. However, about half of the money has been collected. While the writer would like to leave the area, the residents want him to stay until all the money has been collected. Raphael goes on to say that he wonders why R. Solomon sends him no news, and that he has heard that another R. Raphael has had a dispute with an Ashkenazi. The news that R. Judah Ha-Kohen gave a lecture on the first text in "Ethics of the Fathers" and other texts as well is related. Regards are sent to R. Solomon's mother and also to R. Jacob ibn Simḥon. [See also *Ms.176* and *Ms.178* for two other letters by Raphael Ḥalevi.]

Ms. 184
P. 245a

A Halakhic opinion is asked of R. Ḥayyim David Serero

This letter was written by Abraham (son of Samuel ibn Waish) to R. Ḥayyim David Serero on behalf of his father who was not able to write at night. The case concerns two people who are involved in a dispute about an oven on which a legal decision has already been rendered. The disputants implored the writer's father that R. Ḥayyim's legal opinion should be sought on the matter. One of the owners of the oven is Abraham ibn Siso who is a good friend of the writer's father and a God-fearing man. Therefore the writer asks R. Ḥayyim to expedite the matter as quickly as possible, to sign his own response to the query, and to deliver it to Ayush ibn Malul, the partner of Abraham ibn Siso, who is presently in R. Ḥayyim's vicinity.

Ms. 185
P. 245b

A prayer of entreaty called Bakashah

This prayer consists of thirteen lines followed by two signatures. The text commences with the words "Yishtabah Shimkha La'ad, Rom Va'adon Ha-adonim," and concludes with, "Yisrael Hiv dil ḤeVel Le-ait Na'asa Ke-Ḥefṣo Kol." [This is really a separate page from 245a but the compiler pasted them back to back.]

Ms. 186
P. 246a

The rabbis of Fez are informed that the community of Debdou is inhospitable to scholars

Elijah ben Reuben Elmalieḥ writes to the rabbis Jonathan Serero and Abraham Raḥima ibn Danan, at Fez. After a flowery introduction the writer asks forgiveness for not writing sooner but his many tribulations prevented him from doing so. He writes that when he arrived in Debdou he stayed at the home of a scholar called Abraham Ozen who was not particularly hospitable to the writer, so he made his own arrangements for lodging. The writer suggests to the rabbis at Fez that scholars should not be sent from Fez to Debdou because the people are inhospitable to visiting scholars. He further states that he relates only a small part of what he is enduring. He asks that his brother Abraham should not bother himself to enter into a judgement but asks that the rabbis should respond to this letter.

Ms. 187
P. 247a

A correspondence to R. Judah Ibn Attar relating to the acquisition of books

This letter is written by Musa b. Shalom Levi to R. Judah ibn Attar, who resides at Fez. The writer sends his blessing to R. Judah and to the latter's son. [A portion of this letter is obliterated.] R. Judah was present with R. Samuel Ḥalfon on a Saturday night when the decision on a case concerning an agunah, a fettered wife, was being discussed and at that time a purchase was made of a volume of Maimonides' code containing the commentary Kesef Mishneh, for the sum of 70 uqiot. The money should now be paid to R. Solomon Kaspi because R. Judah promised to pay the amount on R. Samuel's behalf. If it is not paid now then a note should be written stating that the next person who arrives at Fez is to be given the money.

The writer inquires if by chance the work Beit Shmuel and the Shakh, on the code Ḥoshen Mishpat, also the book Tosaphot Yom Tob̥, in the Amsterdam edition, are available? R. Mordecai Aṣban will pay their price for the writer since R. Mordecai is presently in Fez and has been informed that such a transaction might transpire during his stay. This letter was sent from Tlemcen.

Ms. 188
P. 248a

A plea for a Jew who served as a guarantor on a loan and who is presently oppressed by the children of the deceased non-Jewish creditor until payment of the loan is made

This letter is written by R. Judah ibn Attar to R. Jacob Ibn Zur concerning the bearer of the letter, Isaac ibn Mahlouf Abitbol, who is in a poor economic situation and whose brother, Abraham, took a loan from a non-Jew. Abraham lives in R. Jacob's vicinity. Isaac was a contracting guarantor, a'reb Kabb'lan, for the aforementioned transaction. The non-Jew recently passed on and his children rose against Isaac and held him and his wife as hostages, even torturing them. They are willing to free Isaac and his wife if Isaac will pay the amount of forty uqiot to them. Isaac's wife is being held by them as a hostage until Isaac returns from his brother Abraham with the stated amount.

R. Judah now asks R. Jacob to intercede on behalf of Isaac by speaking to Abraham to make the stipulated amount available so that the husband and wife may be freed. Isaac and his wife have already incurred many expenses which would equal the amount of forty uqiot. They have not disclosed Abraham's whereabouts to the creditors so they will not be able to demand the whole debt from Abraham. Therefore Abraham would best be advised to send the money requested lest Isaac's wife sends the creditors to him to get herself freed. Isaac and his wife have achieved the best compromise for all concerned so Abraham should send the money. This document was signed by R. Judah ibn Attar, on the tenth of Adar 1720.

Ms. 189
P. 249a

The rabbinic tribunal of Salé asks that the rabbinic tribunal of Fez free one from performing his levirate duties because of his poverty-stricken condition

This legal document which was signed by the rabbis Jacob Bibas, Joseph Saba, and Samuel b. Moses Azawi of Salé, is sent to the judges of the rabbinic tribunal at Fez. The aforementioned rabbis send their opinion stating that Maḥlouf Aḅiẓror (son of Mîmun) should be freed from performing his levirate duties with the woman Rachel, the daughter of the late Mas'ūd Aludi. The aforementioned Maḥlouf should only be obliged to participate in the Ḥaliẓa ceremony, which would free him and the woman Rachel from the levirate duties. The overriding reason for their decision is that Maḥlouf already has a wife, sons, and daughters, and they all suffer from destitution. If he should be obliged to take an additional wife his economic situation would become even more serious. This document was composed in 1716.

Ms. 190
P. 250a and b

Raphael Oḅed Ibn Ẓur writes to R. Moses Ibn Maman asking that a loan be extended to him

Raphael Oḅed Ibn Ẓur informs R. Moses ibn Maman of Fez that he suffers a multitude of misfortunes, too numerous to record on paper. Even if he did record them, he fears that they would be read by those who were not intended to know about them. He states that he did not heed the advice of his masters and he went in ways against which they had warned him. He lost his possessions because he gave his capital to entrepreneurs to invest for him. He accepts God's judgement and declares that he never sought benefit in his life except for his basic necessities. Whatever monies he had, he used for his travelling expenses.

He is now destitute and located in the House of Study in Meknès. That community had offered him the stipend that they make available to resident scholars, but he had refused it on several occasions. The people of Meknès insisted that if he did not accept the stipend they would be given a bad name for not supporting scholars. He had finally been persuaded to take the stipend but only as a loan to be repaid. This money he received every Friday, but eventually the amount of the stipend had been reduced to nothing at all because business conditions were bad. The writer decided not to take any more stipends even if they were available, when times improved. Friends had implored him to take the stipend but he had refused because he views his poverty as a sign of Divine chastisement.

In his letter he asks R. Moses Maman to extend a loan of two hundred uqiot to help him support his family. He has his eye on an investment which someone would manage for him and expects to live off the profits. He assures the prospective creditor (R. Maman) that he will repay the loan. He has agreed to compose a written contract of obligation for the loan, putting up land in Meknes as collateral, and will repay the loan immediately on demand. He states that if R. Moses Maman agrees to extend the loan, it should not be sent through R. Samuel Elbaz for then the writer will not receive it. Rather, it should be sent through their mutual acquaintance R. Moses Gabizon, who will in turn send it through R. Ephraim Monsonyego. If R. Moses Maman agrees, he will give the contract of obligation to R. Ephraim. He ends by saying that he needs the money urgently for the support of his family for the coming holidays. The letter is signed by Raphael Obed Ibn Ẓur.

Ms. 191
Pp. 251a—259a

A booklet of Halakhic riddles in the form of responsa

This booklet contains amusing queries which may be characterized as riddles on subjects of Jewish law. In fact, the first page, 251a, has the Hebrew word for riddles, "Ḥidot," as a title. The work is attributed to R. Yedidia Monsonyego, of blessed memory, by his son-in-law who remains anonymous. The author utilizes the literary form of Responsa literature. The responsa refer to the works of the medieval Halakhists known as Rishonim. Among them Maimonides, Ravad, the Responsa literature of R. Solomon ibn Adret, and the Code of Jewish Law of R. Joseph Caro, as well as his encyclopaedic work Beit Yosef, are mentioned.

On page 251a the author informs us that his son inquired about how one can be permitted to remarry his wife whom he divorced after she subsequently married another person, when this is contrary to biblical law? The writer responds that this query is already treated by R. Solomon ibn Adret in his Responsum, number 1,209, and the writer elaborates. Later authorities, designated Aḥaronim, such as the Leḇush, are also noted in the response to the first query. The second question which appears on page 251b pertains to a hypothetical case of a legally married woman who was unfaithful to her husband yet was permitted to live with him according to the law. The response is given that if she was a minor at the time of her marriage, in accord with the Ravad's view that the seduction of a minor is not considered a culpable act, then her husband can legally retain her as his wife. This view is recorded by R. Joseph Caro in chapter 175 of Even ha-Ezer. Several cases pertaining to the relations between men and women are discussed. They are followed by several cases that relate to matters in civil law. It is apparent that this type of Halakhic work was composed to sharpen the student's mind. [Page 257 sides a and b are blank.]

Ms. 192
P. 260a

A testimony from a rabbinic court that a particular scholar from the Holy Land shall be entitled to financial assistance

This document, which was signed by the following scholars of Fez; R. Vidal Ha-Ṣarfati, R. Judah ibn Attar, R. Samuel Ha-Ṣarfati, R. Saadya b. Mìmun Aflalo, and R. Isaac Ha-Ṣarfati, is a testimony to the bonafide need for financial support for the scholar R. Isaac Melamed of Jerusalem. The scholar has showed them a letter which notes his misfortunes. They further state in this document that financial aid should be extended to R. Isaac in accord with his station whenever he comes to Fez. Apparently, at the time this document was written the economic situation in Fez was not at all good for the Jews, but the Arabs were faring much better. The expression "The maidservant inherited the role of the mistress," (the former referring to Hagar the maidservant of Sarah, the mistress) is used by the rabbis to characterize the relations between Arabs and Jews and their respective conditions at this time. It seems that the scholar from the Holy Land could not receive adequate funds on this occasion. The rabbis pray that economic conditions will improve so that the scholar will receive his proper due.

Ms. 193
P. 261b

One who desires to take another wife is warned against doing so. He is to be told to return to his wife and to give her financial support

In this correspondence R. Judah ibn Attar replies to the rabbis Jacob Ibn Ẓur and Moses Berdugi of Meknès, that upon receiving their letter he called for the wife of Mîmun ibn Didi and for her brother Abraham ibn Shaprut and he read the letter to them. R. Judah states that Mîmun has no legal basis for taking another wife, since his present wife is of sound mind and body and also is pregnant by him. Mîmun's claim that his daughter is a cripple is unfounded and R. Judah has testimony to prove that the opposite is the case.

Mîmun will not be able to take another wife until his present wife gives birth. If a healthy male child is born then he cannot take an additional wife. If a female child is born then a judgement will be rendered and he will be informed what course of action to pursue. Meanwhile the wife is making a counter claim of abandonment and non-support against her husband from the time that he left (for Meknès). The writer asks the rabbis Ibn Ẓur and Berdugi to compel the husband to return to his wife immediately. The letter was here concluded but before signing it, the writer added an additional eight lines testifying to the woman's good state of health and reporting that both she and her brother testified to her being pregnant. Meanwhile, the husband must send his wife financial support since she is penniless.

R. Judah mentions another case in the same letter concerning R. Jacob Ibn Ẓur. The widow of R. Isaac ibn Amara has implored R. Judah to write to R. Jacob to entreat the Nagid about a sum of money that he levied upon Solomon ibn Amara. The latter has struggled to find the wherewithal to pay a portion of the sum and her plea is that the Nagid should be asked to forego the remainder of the sum.

Ms. 194
P. 262a

The rabbis of Tetuán ask the rabbis of Fez to aid R. Isaac Ibn Maman in acquiring his late brother's estate

This document which is signed by the following three rabbis of Tetuán, R. Isaac Abudarham, R. Jacob Halevi, and R. Ḥananiah Arubash, is sent to the rabbinic scholars of Fez concerning an estate which belonged to R. Moses ibn Maman, of blessed memory. The latter's brother, Isaac ibn Maman, an elderly gentleman who comes before the rabbis of Tetuán, is very poor. He informs them that his late brother Moses, who resided in Fez for many years, left an estate to him. However, the courtyard which belonged to Moses was given in pledge to the king for the sum of four hundred uqiot. Isaac asks that the pledge be paid and the balance be paid to him. The rabbis of Tetuán ask the rabbis of Fez to expedite the matter, since R. Isaac is in dire need of the money and is otherwise unable to support himself. This document is dated Wednesday, the second third of the month of Ḥeshvan, in the year 1647. [See page 268a for another document signed by R. Ḥananiah Arubash, in the same year, which is related to this document.]

Ms. 195
P. 263a

A letter from the rabbis of Fez to all communities to alleviate the plight of a fellow Jew. Also a note to the judges of Sefrou

This letter was composed for the honorable Mîmun ben Amozig by the following rabbis of Fez who signed it: R. Judah ibn Attar, R. Jacob b. R. Reuben Ibn Ẓur, and R. Shalom Edery. Mîmun is one of the leading taxpayers of Fez, known for his benevolence. Now his economic misfortunes require that he ask others to aid him, but as he has never been in this predicament before, nor is he forward because of his plight, the rabbis are asking others to come to his aid in accord with his station. The date of this document is 1731. The rabbis Jacob Ibn Ẓur and Shalom Edery sign a postscript to the scholars and judges of Ṣefrou and to R. Judah Ṣaba and R. David Ḥarar saying they should make a speedy response to this letter.

Ms. 196
P. 264a

The community of Fez draws up a contract to sell a concession because it is in need of funds

This document was drawn up on the seventeenth day of Tammuz, 1709. It is signed by the following rabbis of Fez: Judah ibn Attar, Samuel Ha-Ṣarfati, Abraham ibn Danan, and Jacob b. Reuben Ibn Ẓur. Since the community of Fez is in need of cash, it is selling a concession involving the sale of fruit for the processing of alcoholic beverages, to R. Daniel Toledano, (son of the scholar R. Phineas, of blessed memory) for twenty litres of cochineal. The period of the concession is one year from the first day of Tishri. The terms set forth are that the purchaser, the aforementioned R. Daniel, will collect from every purchaser the weight of grapes one uqia and from every purchaser of a talent weight of raisins, figs, and dates, and any other produce from which liquor can be produced, one half uqia, according to the old system of currency. This price schedule applies when the weight of grapes is measured to potfuls. However, if it is in the volume of basketfuls and if it weighs up to one and one half talents, then one uqia shall be paid. If it is found to weigh more, then one uqia, according to the earlier system of currency, shall be paid for each talent. These terms are in accord with the community's decision. The community will protect the purchaser of the concession from any claims that might be laid against him.

Ms. 197
Pp. 266a and 265b

A scholar writes that one of the parties to a dispute was unable to participate in a judgement for reasons beyond his control and not because he wanted to obstruct the cause of justice

[This correspondence which was written by R. Moses ibn Ḥamo (of Ṣefrou) to R. Menaḥem Serero (of Fez) commences on page 266a and concludes on page 265b; which is really part of the same page.] A response is made to R. Menaḥem's letter which had been received by the writer a day before. R. Menaḥem stated that R. Jacob D'Avila was guilty of obstructing justice by not appearing before the court (at Fez). R. Moses states that this charge is without foundation because the letter signed by R. Mîmun has just been received by the writer. Furthermore, R. Jacob thought it best to remain at home for the Sabbath as he was not in good health. On Tuesday he began his journey but he was turned back midway by people from R. Serero's own community who informed him that those who would dispute him would soon arrive in his town. They also noted his poor physical condition.

When R. Jacob returned home it was suggested that he send his son, Meir, in his place with all the proper testimonies, but he still insisted that he would go himself to R. Serero's community. R. Moses Ḥamo asks that the matter be resolved quickly. After a careful examination of the evidence R. Moses feels confident that it will be found to be in R. Jacob's favor. The deceased woman about whom the controversy revolves has apparently nullified all the conditions of the marriage contract that pertain to the Megôrashim (exiles of the Castilian communities). The signature of this document, which is found on page 265b, is followed by a postscript wherein the writer asks that a message should be transmitted to his friend, R. Joshua, requesting a copy of the Talmudic tractate Niddah. It seems that a student has asked to borrow that text and the writer has already lent two copies to others. Now he relates that he studies the tractate Ḥullin after the morning service in the academy. At midnight, another study session is held with the participation of more than twenty scholars, among whom are excellent students who analyze the subject well. There are also average students who stand and study together. Again the writer requests that a copy of the Talmud tractate Niddah be sent to him, and if it is in a bad condition R. Moses says that he will repair it. He signs the postscript with the words, "also these are the words of Moses."

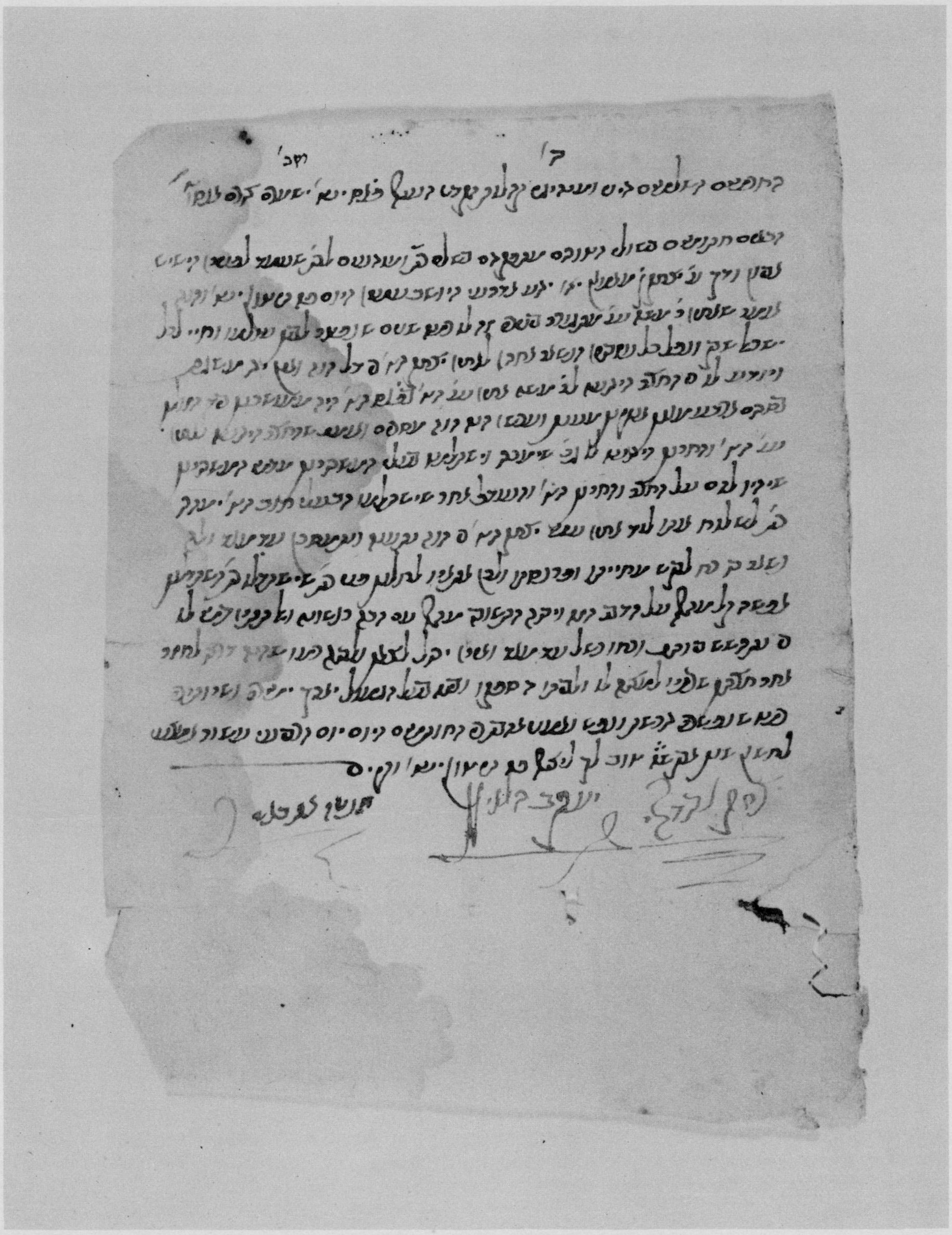

Ms. 194
A document signed by three rabbis of Tetuán in 1647 concerning the settlement of an estate

Ms. 198
P. 267a and b

R. Judah Ibn Attar writes to the scholars of Meknès concerning one who violated a pre-marital agreement. R. Jacob Malka concurs with R. Attar's judgement

This document was written by R. Judah ibn Attar on the nineteenth of Iyar 1728. However, the matter was held off until the twenty-third of Iyar when the incident was better substantiated, so that the letter was not sent until afterwards. A postscript is written to this effect with a second signature by R. Judah ibn Attar.

The case involves Elazar ibn Asulin who became betrothed to a widow against legal practice and not in accord with the wishes of his relatives because he was already engaged, in Fez, to the daughter of Levi ibn Amara. In accord with practice, a high penalty must be paid if he violated the terms of that arrangement. Elazar's brother, Moses ibn Asulin, a guarantor of the pre-nuptial contract, was very angry over his brother's actions, especially as he had a monetary obligation arising from the matter. Because he suffered from an ailment which prevented him from travelling on animals, he was personally unable to confront his brother. Another brother, Mas'ūd, went to confront Elazar and to oblige him to nullify his relationship with the widow on the strength of R. Judah's letter, in which the rabbis of Meknès were asked to persuade Elazar to divorce the widow. If he refused, then he should pay his brother Moses for the latter's indebtedness on his behalf and also the fiancée who would be disgraced by his actions. In a postscript dated the twenty-third of Iyar, R. Judah states that the brother Moses had heard things that might require the rabbis of Meknès to secure a bill of divorce by force. In spite of his ailment Moses had decided to travel to confront Elazar.

[An opinion on the case by R. Jacob b. Joseph b. Malka follows on the same page, 267a, and continues on the top of page 267b.] Jacob agrees with R. Judah ibn Attar that there are grounds to force Elazar to withdraw from "the wicked woman who ensnared him." He has violated a rabbinic enactment which requires that one who marries must do so under the jurisdiction of the local scholar. Furthermore, the marriage ceremony was performed by the bridegroom himself, without the benefit of clergy, in the presence of ten young sheep (young boys) who came from the communites of Meknès, Fez, and Salé, which are all under the jurisdiction of the aforementioned enactment. One who has violated the rabbinic enactment may be beaten until he submits.

Apart from the above he has been guilty of disgracing his elder brother and shaming his fiancée. He cannot marry, in any case, until he makes restitution to his brother Moses. Elazar is also regarded as a scholar and he has disgraced his calling by his actions, as well as besmirching the honor of his family. Therefore, his relationship with the widow should be nullified in accordance with the opinion of the Tur (in chapter two of Even Ha-Ezer). However, the fact that the widow was married two or three times previously should not be the basis upon which Elazar is forced to withdraw from her. Rabbinic literature states that if one marries a woman who is not fitting for him then Elijah (the prophet) forces him to withdraw from her. The widow had previous husbands who died while they were married to her and this would justify the nullification of Elazar's marriage to her. An opinion is expressed that when a woman is divorced from three husbands it is a basis for nullification of a subsequent marriage. R. Jacob b. Malka indicts Elazar for abandoning a maiden from a good family in favor of a wealthy widow. He notes that tradition has unkind things to say about one who marries for an ulterior motive such as the acquisition of money. The signature of Jacob b. Malka is given at the conclusion of this document.

Ms. 199
P. 268a

A court document from the rabbis of Tetuán granting the power of attorney to Immanuel Serero on behalf of Isaac Ibn Maman

This document was composed by the rabbinical authority of Tetuán and signed by R. Ḥananiah Arubash and Jacob Ha-Kohen b. R. Gideon Ha-Sofer on Wednesday, the twelfth day of Ḥeshvan, 1647. Isaac ibn Maman empowers R. Immanuel of Fez (son of R. Menaḥem Serero, of blessed memory) to act for him in all matters pertaining to the estate that Isaac inherited from his late

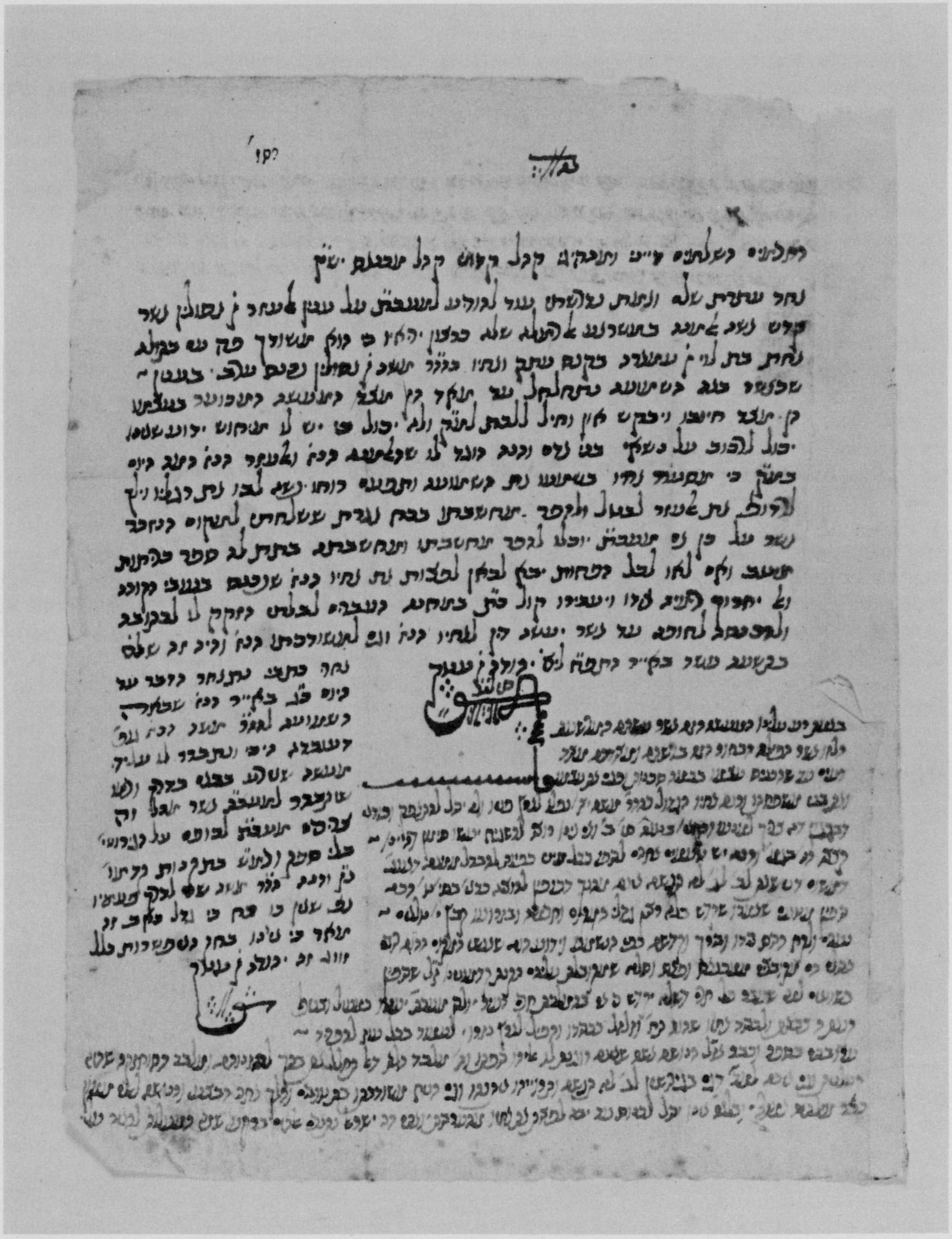

Ms. 198
A letter written by Rabbi Judah ibn Attar to the scholars of Meknès in 1728 concerning a violation of a pre-marital agreement.

brother, Moses ibn Maman, both with regard to movable and immovable property. R. Immanuel can rent, give, or take on pledge and sell the courtyard and properties that belonged to Isaac's late brother. The address to the rabbis at Fez is found on page 268b. [See *Ms.194*, page 267a, for another document with the signature of R. Ḥananiah Arubash which pertains to the subject of the estate which Isaac ibn Maman inherited.]

Ms. 200
P. 269a

R. Raphael Ibn Ẓur is asked to render a decision in a difficult litigation. The writer cites another case dealing with the exercise of authority over property in the postscript

Rabbi Raḥamim Joseph Ġayni writes to Rabbi Raphael Ibn Ẓur, of Fez. The introductory portion of the letter includes a prayer for peace and the advent of the Messiah so that the Jews will no longer suffer persecution. Regards are sent to Maharash Ibn Ẓur and a prayer is offered for his health. The writer informs R. Raphael of the arrival of R. Ḥayyim ibn Zikhri who is coming to inquire about a legal matter. He brings with his many written statements from the rabbis of the city of Ḥeleb. R. Raḥamim asks R. Raphael to review the judgement in all its minutest details as quickly as possible. As for himself he no longer wants to have anything to do with this bad situation. He expects that R. Raphael will finally bring the matter to a conclusion by rendering his judgement.

In an addendum, R. Raḥamim mentions a case involving one called Maharash Ḥota who had shared an inheritance with his mother. Upon her demise the community wanted to claim the mother's portion. A letter was sent to the rabbis of Fez who judged that the mother had no authority over the object which she controlled while she was alive, which apparently was in the synagogue. The reason that the son, Maharash Ḥota granted it to his mother was because it was his duty to support her, but after her death it reverted back to the son. Therefore, no individual or community can claim authority over the item in question. This decision was never copied nor is it to be found in the possession of the writer, nor is he able to acquire a copy of it, yet, he does recall that such a decision was rendered.

Ms. 201
P. 270a

An emissary corresponds from Ṣefrou with Ham-Malakh R. Raphael

The writer of this letter, who is an emissary from the Holy Land, commences his letter with a flowery introduction. Then he invites R. Raphael to come to the Galilee to live (the writer is probably from Safed). He informs R. Raphael (Ibn Ẓur of Fez) that he is presently in Ṣefrou collecting funds and that in spite of a dispute in the town amongst the Jewish inhabitants, he was able to collect five Durham. He expects to visit R. Raphael on the writer's way to Meknès. He also states that while he is asking for money for his fundraising activities R. Raphael should not think that this was the main purpose of the letter. Rather, the letter was prompted by his friendly concern. Regards are then sent to R. Solomon, R. Ḥayyim Kohen, and to R. Abraham. In an addendum the writer inquires about a sum of money that was sent through the person of Jacob ibn Zimra, to Gibraltar (which is spelled in one word, not as in the Arabic) wondering whether it arrived safely. He asks for a response to his letter.

Ms. 202
P. 271a

A court decision concerning the erection of a structure that impedes the public right of way and commerce

In the past, vendors of fruit who had shops in the marketplace called Suq Al-Ksasin had wanted to construct a roof out of matted reeds to protect them from the sun. Owners of the adjoining courtyards complained that such a structure would block the view of their windows which faced the public thoroughfare. The undersigned rabbis responded that there was no substance to their claim and they could not impede the construction. Subsequently, the awning was constructed.

Some members of the community had tried to impede the construction on the grounds that damage might occur to passers-by on the public thoroughfare when rainfall accumulated on the awning and dripped on them, thereby preventing passers-by from access to the street. The rabbis rule that this claim has merit and even though construction has already taken place, that does not give those who are having it built the legal right to assert their claim (called Ḥazaka) that the awning shall remain as it was constructed. This document was signed on the twentieth day of Adar II, in the year 1851. It was signed by R. Reuben Serero, R. Judah Elbaz, and R. Yedidia Monsonyego.

Ms. 203
P. 272a

A court document (from Ṣefrou) to R. Raphael Ibn Ẓur of Fez to serve as an interim overseer of the estate of the late Raphael Ha-Kohen

This document is written to R. Raphael Ibn Ẓur at Fez, and signed by the rabbinic tribunal composed of R. Ḥayyim Elijah (Ģayni), R. Raphael Moses Elbaz, and R. YeKutiel ibn Elbaz. They ask R. Raphael to accept the appointment of overseer of the estate of the late R. Raphael Ha-Kohen, of blessed memory, for the benefit of the orphans, until such time when a trustee shall be appointed for the estate. In this capacity R. Raphael is requested to examine the financial accounts of the departed and to call the deceased's partners to settle the matter of the partnership, as well as to take care of the keys of the shop. He will arrange to hire an artisan to seal the doors of the house of the deceased and R. Raphael shall keep the keys with him, "for one does not know what a day will bring." The last sentence is written in Judaeo-Arabic in this document. The document was composed in Ṣefrou, although it is mentioned in the text.

Ms. 204
P. 273a

R. Raphael Ibn Ẓur (of Fez) is informed of the appointment of a trustee for the estate of Raphael Ha-Kohen o.b.m. (Cf. Ms.203)

This document [which is related to *Ms.203* and follows it chronologically and in the order in which it appeared in the Bension collection] informs R. Raphael Ibn Ẓur of the appointment of Isaac ibn Shitrit as the trustee of the estate of the late Raphael Ha-Kohen, o.b.m. He will serve the interests of the orphans, negotiate with the deceased's partners, and collect the debts incurred by non-Jews. If it is desirable that another trustee be appointed in addition to Isaac, this will be satisfactory provided that the delay will have no adverse effect upon the welfare of the orphans and the widow. Furthermore, the widow can seek someone who can act in her behalf if time is not of the essence. In that case, all that is contained in the apartment will not be opened until the widow secures one who will act on her behalf. R. Raphael is asked to send to the undersigned certain items that R. Raphael left with Isaac ibn Shitrit, as well as the account book, so that a proper evaluation of the estate can be arrived at. A copy of the account book can be sent so that the original may remain with Rabbi Raphael. The rabbis who signed the document (at Ṣefrou) are R. Ḥayyim Elijah (Ģayni), R. Raphael Moses Elbaz, and R. YeKutiel Elbaz.

Ms. 205
P. 274a

A letter of reconciliation written to R. Reuben Ibn Ẓur by Elijah Utmazgin

We are informed by the writer, Elijah Utmazgin, that R. Reuben Ibn Ẓur is not in good health, but that he has sons. The writer prays for R. Reuben's well being and implores him not to be angry with him. The writer wrote to R. Reuben on a previous occasion but has received no reply. The writer insists that there is no reason why R. Reuben should bear any ill-feeling towards him. If R. Reuben continues to act in this manner he will be guilty of afflicting the downtrodden. Instead he should renew his warm friendship of earlier days. R. Elijah adds a postscript after his signature wherein he prays for the welfare of R. Reuben. [Cf. *Ms.154* which gives additional information about the relationship between the correspondents.]

Ms. 206
Pp. 276a—275b

A correspondence from Ish Ẓair of Fez to the Alliance Israelite at Paris

The author, Ish Ẓair, commends the famous organization Alliance Israelite, based in Paris, for publishing the Responsa of R. Asher. Then he states his desire to write and his disappointment at not receiving a reply; therefore, he held back from writing further until he became possessed by the muse of the written word and he was obliged to correspond.

Increased taxes have caused friction between the Nagid and the community and, the writer says, he has had to mediate between them. It reached the stage where the community wanted to remove the Nagid. These events held back the appointment of the two delegates who were to go to Paris. A request is made for the appointment of a representative for Jewish matters to reside in Fez, as was done in Lebanon where it was successful. This would be an effective way of improving the condition of the Jews. The writer mentions having been in Gibraltar where money was raised for Jewish causes. Unfortunately, it is difficult to fulfill such a philanthropic goal in Fez because economic conditions, aggravated by the drought, have regressed considerably such that bread has increased in price three and fourfold.

Ms. 207
P. 277a

A plea to R. Jacob Ibn Ẓur to compel a husband who abandoned his wife to return to her and that the money taken from him under duress should be returned to him

This letter states that one who spoke on behalf of Masuda (daughter of Mîmun ibn Saluḥa) and the wife of Mordecai ibn Adhan, known as Ben Aiyna, related how Mordecai sent her a letter telling her that he had been delivered into the hands of the Nagid by Samuel ibn Saluḥa and Abraham ibn Saluḥa. Subsequently, he had been severely beaten and all his money had been taken from him by Samuel and Abraham so that they could send money to her and her children who were suffering from hunger. However, she has never received this money.

This letter, which was sent by R. Judah ibn Attar to R. Jacob Ibn Ẓur, refers to the aforementioned Mordecai who wandered away from his home to R. Jacob Ibn Ẓur's area and left his wife and her children without food or drink or means by which they could support themselves. R. Judah asks R. Jacob to aid the woman in her plight by asking Samuel and Abraham to return all the money to Mordecai and to compel him to return to his wife in Fez immediately.

Ms. 208
P. 278a

A letter of consolation and a poem

This letter and the poem were composed by Yeshua Abitbol of Ṣefrou. They were sent to R. Samuel Ibn Ẓur on the passing of his father. The writer expresses the hope that R. Samuel will ascend to his father's position. While R. Raphael Oḇed Ibn Ẓur is not mentioned as the departed, the letter was written to his son on his demise.

Ms. 209
P. 279a

A court document concerning the supervision of an estate

A scholar called Moharish has passed on. It is suggested that his wise son is the best one available to manage the estate. Even though the son does not want to get involved he is informed that he is obliged to do so since no one else is available. The son is considered to be entirely trustworthy and there is no legitimate fear that he would unjustly take anything of the smallest value. Whoever suspects otherwise is regarded as casting suspicion on the just.

Ms. 210
P. 280a

A correspondence to R. Abraham Parienté asking him to intercede on behalf of the writer in a judgement

This letter, which is partially written in the alliterative form, is sent to R. Abraham Parienté asking him to intercede for the writer in a judgement with a person identified as R. Reuben. The writer mentions having received a letter from the aforementioned R. Abraham who fulfilled all that he was asked to do. He again asks R. Abraham to try to persuade R. Reuben to do his bidding. A quick reply to this letter would be appreciated.

The alliterative form of literary expression appears in the flowery introduction when the Hebrew alphabetical letter "Mem" is prominently used from the beginning of line 3 through line 7. The writer pleads poverty in matters of poetic metre and he concludes with four more lines commencing each word with the letter Mem, from line 20 through line 23. He also expresses his suffering and tribulations and he looks forward to the coming of the Messiah, the son of David.

Ms. 211
P. 280b

A group of words commencing with the letter "Nun"

This group of words is compiled to be used as a thesaurus dealing with terms beginning with the Hebrew alphabetical letter "Nun," which for literary purposes refers to misfortune or calamitous events. [This text seems to be related to the literary device of alliteration used by the author in *Ms.210*, on page 280a, in his application of the letter "Mem," on the other side of this page.]

Ms. 212
P. 281a and b

Establishing trust in business contracts

The legal forms for establishing a basis of trust in various kinds of contracts are given on this page. The city of Tafilalet is mentioned on page 281a in one of the forms and one concludes that these forms were drawn up for use in commercial intercourse in that city. Also given is the legal form for granting gifts which are acquired by the same mechanism applying to other commercial acquisitions. This kind of gift excludes those granted by a person on his death bed. The forms that apply for pledges are given as well.

On page 281b a case is presented involving one called Reuben who is below the age of twenty and who desires to engage in a business transaction to sell property that he has inherited. According to the law, one who has not attained the age of twenty cannot engage in commercial acts involving legal transactions. In order to protect the purchaser of the property Reuben is required to take an oath that he will not demand the nullification of the purchase when he attains the legal age. It is also necessary to ascertain that Reuben understands all the ramifications of the transaction before the oath can be administered. This oath is unrelated to the act of acquisition itself.

Ms. 213
Pp. 282a and 283b

An extraordinary Bar Mitzva dissertation

This Bar Mitzvah address is delivered by one called Beẓalel. His mother passed away before he attained his majority. He devotes a portion of his text to his love for his deceased mother, thereby trying to console himself. He devotes some space to expounding on the role of righteous women in Israel. The rhythmic structure of the rabbinic texts cited and their exposition is characteristic of this genre of address in the Moroccan Jewish community until the present day.

Ms. 214
P. 284a

A document concerning part of an estate which must be evaluated

R. Jacob Ibn Ẓur directed Ḥayyim b. Mas'ūd who is called ben Magirz, to ask the rabbis Samuel Ḥasin and Mîmun Busidan to evaluate a property. This property is a courtyard. The small house located on the left as you enter the courtyard, however, was to be excluded from the evaluation. That house was given as a gift and there is a document to this effect. The house is presently owned by R. Yissakhar ben Saadon. The courtyard belongs to the inheritors of R. Amram ben Tata, may he repose in Paradise.

The undersigned state that they have evaluated the courtyard, excluding the aforementioned house. Since the market for real estate has depreciated recently, the courtyard is valued at only 240 uqiot. This document is placed in the possession of the aforementioned Ḥayyim. It was signed on Wednesday, the seventeenth of Tevet 1734, at Fez.

Ms. 215
P. 284a

A creditor's claim against the estate of the late Dinar B. Amram

[This document is related to *Ms.214*, which precedes it on page 284a. It informs us of some other transactions that took place with the same piece of real estate.] Testimony is given to the existence of a bill of indebtedness for a huge sum owed to R. Jacob Halevi of the town of Salé (son of R. Samuel Halevi, of blessed memory) and charged against Dinar (son of Amram) known as ben Tata. Dinar declares his trust in Jacob, and those acting for Jacob, with regard to the authenticity of the bill of debt and the payment thereof without any oath requiring to be taken. This admission is made on the twentieth of Tevet, in the year 77 (1717).

Another transaction is reported in this document wherein Jacob Halevi, of the aforementioned contract, made his holdings available to Ḥayyim bar Mas'ūd bar Ḥanun ben Magirz for one thousand uqiot, on the fifteenth of Ab, in the year 93 (1733). Therefore, Ḥayyim ben Maġirẓ investigated and found that half of the courtyard (mentioned in *Ms.24*), excluding the house, belonged to those acting for the estate of R. Mîmun ben Adhan, may his soul repose in Paradise. The other half belonged to Aaron ben Haroush. Miriam, the wife of Dinar ben Tata, sold part of her dowry and bought a half-interest in the courtyard that had belonged to R. Aaron ben Haroush. Dinar has now passed on, but the courtyard still belongs to his family by virtue of the sale of his wife's dowry. At this point the document breaks off.

Ms. 216
P. 285b

A Bar Mitzvah address

The name of the celebrant is Abraham, therefore he cites texts from the bible referring to Abraham. He prays for the gift of understanding to be endowed to him from on high. Then he follows with the usual opening for the traditional Bar Mitzvah address. [There is only one side of one page of this text. The rest of the address is not available.]

Ms. 217
P. 286a

A court document of Fez affirming a pledge

A woman called Tamar (see *Ms.218*), who held a previous claim valued at one thousand uqiot, now carries half of that amount in the form of a pledge. The rabbinic court in Fez which affirmed this document consists of the following who added their signatures: R. Jacob Ibn Ẓur, R. Shalom Edery, R. Abraham Alel, and R. Samuel Elbaz. The document was drawn in the year 1735. [The following document *Ms.218*, page 286b is related to this one.]

Ms. 218
P. 286b

The court in Fez affirms a monetary claim of a wife against her husband

Tamar, (daughter of R. Shem Toḇ Ha-Kohen) and the wife of R. Mîmun (son of the scholar R. Joshua Serero, of blessed memory) has made a claim against her husband to pay her the sum of one thousand uqiot. Without her knowledge, he had appropriated an estate that she had brought to the marriage, promising to pay her for this as soon as he has obtained the money. Tamar is now suing him for it. R. Samuel ibn Saadon and Judah b. Joseph here state that Mîmun must immediately pay his wife five hundred uqiot. The other five hundred uqiot still owing to her must be pledged in the form of a courtyard that he acquired as an inheritance from his father. He has agreed not to redeem this property for a stipulated time and his wife may use it for any commercial pursuit that she chooses. The wife will be protected from any claims that might be made against that property. This document was composed on Monday, the twenty-sixth day of Nisan 1735.

Ms. 219
P. 287a

A claim against one who has taken domicile in a house illegally

One known as Mordecai ibn Amozag took up residence for over six months in a dwelling and paid no rent whatsoever. Maḥlouf Boutboul was asked to act for the claimant against Mordecai, but was unsuccessful. Mordecai subsequently wrote a letter stating that he could not be sued since his brother Azriel had given him permission to live in the house and any claims should henceforth be brought against Azriel. Mordecai was warned to vacate the premises but he ignored these demands. Therefore, the claimant has turned to R. Jacob Ibn Ẓur to order Mordecai's removal.

The claimant says, too, that R. Moses ibn Maman lent money to Ḥayyim, the son of the aforementioned Mordecai, and he was not paid back. After pleas Ḥayyim finally agreed to have a bill of debt drawn, and his books were given to the claimant (the writer of this letter) as a pledge. After five or six years had passed, R. Shem Ṭob ibn Amozag asked to borrow one part of the scriptures with Ibn Ezra's commentary. Hayyim permitted the writer to lend that text to R. Shem Ṭob. The writer says that this was done with the creditor, R. Moses' permission also. R. Shem Ṭob passed away soon after and the text is now in the hands of his inheritors. It is not known whether Ḥayyim ever asked that his books should be returned. There was a copy of the work called Minḥot ha-Luḥot written only on paper and because of dampness the text was ruined. The writer states that he placed it in the Genizah. In the rest of the letter the writer informs R. Jacob Ibn Ẓur of many misfortunes that befell him both on his journey and at his home. The last few lines of this correspondence are difficult to decipher.

Ms. 220
P. 288b

R. Menaḥem Serero writes to R. Jacob Ibn Ẓur concerning some mystical works

This letter is written by R. Menaḥem Serero to R. Jacob Ibn Ẓur. The writer informs R. Jacob that he received a letter, just before the Sabbath, from R. Ḥabib Toledano, who stated that he was sending a mystical book to R. Jacob called Sefer Zerubbabel, which was composed by the author of Pirkei Haikhalôt, the talmudic master, R. Ishmael Kohen-Gadol. R. Menaḥem mentions that he has had the privilege of viewing the aforementioned work which is preceded by the mystical work Brit Menuḥa. R. Menaḥem hopes to receive R. Jacob's comments concerning that mystical work. Regards are sent to R. Reuben Ibn Ẓur, the father of R. Jacob.

Ms. 221
P. 289a

R. Isaac Palaggi writes to R. Ẓuf Devash, of Jerusalem, about a newly published work

R. Isaac Palaggi (of Turkey) writes to R. Ẓuf Devash, of Jerusalem, in the year 1876, to inform him that the former is sending him his most recent work called Yafeh Le-Layv, Part Two, as a gift. An additional copy is being sent to R. Ẓuf Devash who is asked to forward it to one of the cities in the Maghreb wherefrom money would be forthcoming to help the writer defray the considerable costs of publishing the work. The writer expresses the hope that at least the cost of shipping the books will be covered by a forthcoming grant. [The Devash family seems to have served the interests of the Palaggi family on other occasions, cf. *Ms.145*, page 203a.]

Ms. 222 P. 290b

A plea for charitable aid

Zikhri Meshash commences the first half of his letter to R. Ham-Malakh Raphael Ha-Ṣarfati (of Fez) with a flowery and poetic introduction. He then expresses his sorrow for not having followed R. Raphael's advice to him. Since Zikhri left R. Raphael's community he and his family have suffered much privation, especially during the past winter, when sufficient clothing was not available to them. Zikhri was apparently involved in a disputed transaction which left him without any monetary resources. He tried to reach a compromise on the matter but could not find the other party. As Passover is coming very soon he is in dire straits and he is depending on R. Raphael's merciful nature. Zikhri blames his adversity on having departed from his ancestral home, but he states that he cannot turn to the masses for charitable aid for, while they are gracious in the amount of ridicule that they offer to those who turn to them for aid, they offer little benevolence in return.

Ms. 223 P. 291a

Court action is taken in Fez and Meknès concerning the non-payment of a debt

The rabbis Saul ibn Danan and Raphael Oḇed Ibn Ẓur (of Fez) wrote to the rabbis Jacob Toledano and Mordecai Berdugo (of Meknès) in the year 1760, concerning the payment of a debt. The original transaction and bill of debt was dated the twenty-seventh of Tammuz 1754. It was to be paid in installments. The principals in the present state of affairs are Moses ben David-Ve-Joseph and Yedia ibn Laḥbari who brought this debt owed by Simeon b. Mordecai Wahnunu, to the attention of the rabbis, so that Joseph (son of R. Moses Amiel) who is the creditor, will receive the sum of two hundred uqiot. This is done because the appointed time of the installment payments was the twenty-second of Sivan 1755, and still no payments are forthcominq. Now Isaac b. Ḫayyim is delegated to act for the creditor, Joseph, to make Simeon pay his debt. The writer asks the rabbis to aid Isaac in his attempt to collect the debt.

R. Jacob Toledano (of Meknès) signs the second document, which is given as a response below the earlier document. He cites from Ḥoshen Mishpat 73:8, the following words of R. Joseph Caro, "If one took an oath to pay his debt at a stipulated time and when that time arrived the creditor didn't claim it, the debtor is not obliged to pay it until the creditor claims it." The Sema is also recorded as in accord with this opinion. The latter quotes R. Solomon ibn Adret, o.b.m., as saying that the debtor is not obliged to pay the wife or the children of the creditor until such time as the creditor demands his money.

Ms. 224 Pp. 292a—296a

Four poems with an introduction by Moses B. Aaron Attiya, of the nineteenth century

The author of the poems, Moses ben Aaron Attiya, commences with a three-page introduction which is followed by four pages of poetry. He moralizes about the fact that the power of speech can be utilized for negative purposes and that it should rather be ennobled through religious expression in poetry. He quotes scripture, from the Psalms, and a rabbinic text to this effect. He notes that there are numerous occasions for poetic expression such as on the Sabbaths, at festivals, Bar Mitzvot, and wedding celebrations.

The writer informs us that he composed and wrote many poems on individual pieces of paper and because he did not collect them into one volume they were lost and he could not recall them. He therefore composed, for posterity, this work called "Yashir Moshe" to record those poems that he still remembered. He also added explanations of terms in the text. All the texts contained in this work were approved by R. Abner Israel Ha-Ṣarfati. He mentions that he was asked to compose appropriate words of verse for a pleasant Arabic tune so as to elevate the melody from its secular state to the holy.

The first liturgical poem consisting of eight stanzas is composed in honor of the New Month—Rosh Ḥodesh. All the poems are composed in the acrostic form. The second poem is supplicatory in nature and is appropriately to be recited during periods of distress. The third prayer characterizes the yearning for restoration of the holy places in Zion. The fourth prayer is supplicatory in nature dealing with the plight of exile which Jews suffer. A call for their redemption is sounded and their oppressors are to be dealt with so that the Throne of God will be complete.

Ms. 225
P. 297a

Verse composed by Elijah Utmazgin in honor of a bride called Esther and her bridegroom called Saul

The six verses on this page are written in praise of a bride called Esther. Each verse concludes with the Hebrew word "Ḥen"—"Grace." The last paragraph mentions the name of the groom as Saul. The writer, who appears to be a rejected suitor of the bride, is Elijah Utmazgin. He offers his best wishes to the newlyweds.

Ms. 226
P. 298a

R. Ḥasdai Almosnino writes to the rabbis (at Fez) to aid a widow in receiving payment of a debt owed to her late husband. In a second case they are asked to help an Agunah (fettered wife) receive compensation and a divorce

[*The original manuscript was stolen but a photocopy exists.*]

R. Ḥasdai Almosnino writes, in the year 1715, to the scholars Judah ibn Attar and Jacob Ibn Ẓur (of Fez) asking them to intercede on behalf of the widow and orphans of R. Abraham Attiya, may he repose in paradise, by contacting R. Solomon ibn Yaîsh to aid her in her plight. After initial attempts nothing has yet been accomplished on her behalf. A young man, Moses (son of Isaac Ha-Kohen), had negotiated a loan from the late R. Abraham Attiya and he still has not made payment on it. Previously this young man lived in R. Ḥasdai's area (Tetuán), but now he has moved to Fez. The late R. Abraham's brother-in-law, Isaac Ṣarfati, came to Fez with the bill of debt and managed to collect part of it but forty-six-and-a-half uqiot are still outstanding. R. Ḥasdai now asks the rabbis (of Fez) to summon Moses to pay the outstanding amount.

In the second case, a fettered wife, an Agunah, Ḥaîta, the sister of the aforementioned late Abraham Attiya, and the wife of R. Aaron Azirad, is brought to the attention of the rabbis of Fez, since Aaron is in their area. Aaron, who had incurred debts, fled eleven years previously, and his wife was held captive by the non-Jews for a long time because of non-payment. Ḥaîta's brother and relatives had to pay the outstanding debts in order to free her. Her husband has even married another woman, thereby violating his marital oath to Ḥaîta. She now demands that he pay the value of her marriage contract and grant her a divorce immediately. Previous correspondence on the matter has not received a response, which is not the kind of treatment one would expect from a sizable Jewish community such as Fez, which has rabbinic courts. The writer closes with a remark that this is a classical case of a fettered wife which should be dealt with by the rabbis (at Fez).

Ms. 227
P. 299a

R. Judah Ibn Attar writes to R. Jacob Ibn Ẓur about the internal politics and personalities of the Jewish community of Fez, which has a bearing on the reason for R. Jacob Ibn Ẓur's departure for Meknès

[*The original manuscript was stolen but a photocopy exists.*]

R. Jacob Ibn Ẓur has left (Fez) for some reason that is, at best, hinted at in this letter from R. Judah ibn Attar. The latter takes pains to keep R. Jacob's confidence a private matter. R. Judah alludes to R. Jacob's present economic privation and to a disorganized state of affairs that affects the Jewish community as possible causes for R. Jacob's departure (to Meknès). R. Judah states that he was never in favor of R. Jacob's move (from Fez) because of his responsibilities to his many children and because it is not in the best interests of a scholar such as R. Jacob to wander from place to place. R. Judah writes that he would only take up the matter with local communal officials upon R. Jacob's return (to Fez).

R. Judah continues that one day R. Solomon ibn Danan, R. Solomon Cabaliero, and the latter's partner, Mas'ūd ibn Samuel, came to see him on a matter of litigation and while there brought up the subject as to whether R. Jacob Ibn Ẓur (referred to, by them, as Ploni-anon) had written anything to him about the move to Meknès. Then they showed him a signed letter sent to them by R. Jacob Aspag, Mas'ūd ibn Adhan, and Saadya Lahaboz in which they were asked to persuade the anonymous party (R. Jacob) to write to the Nagid so that he, in turn, would persuade anon to return home (to Fez). Many signatures of community members were attached to this letter. At this juncture in the conversation R. Judah could not restrain himself any longer so he blurted out, "must anon (R. Jacob) initiate the process of conciliation and appeasement with a note of good will when he suffers so much privation because of the situation?" He then writes that he showed R. Jacob's letter to the assembly, who then agreed to R. Judah's evaluation of who should initiate the conciliation. Then R. Judah hid the letter and did not discuss the matter with them until some further action could be taken.

The Nagid had sent a note to R. Judah concerning the appointment of R. Saadya Lahaboz as financial overseer of the community. R. Judah informs R. Jacob that he responded to the go-between of the Nagid by stating that the community did not want R. Saadya to fill that position. It prefers that two other people should be appointed as overseers of the community's finances, namely, R. Mordecai Dery and R. Saul Kohen. At this time R. Judah inquires whether a note was sent to the Nagid to appease Anon (R. Jacob)? R. Judah has been informed that R. Moses ibn Adhan was given oral instructions to serve as a go-between to reconcile the Nagid and Anon (R. Jacob). R. Judah expresses his opinion that because of the situation and the personalities involved there can be no realistic improvement in their relations unless R. Jacob confronts the Nagid face to face. Only then will the matter be restored and R. Jacob will not have to exist in exile, as it were. R. Judah concludes his correspondence with a prayer that God will give R. Jacob good counsel.

Ms. 228
P. 300a

Commentaries on two Aggadic texts

The first text discusses the distinction between the prophets of Israel and those of other nations. The second text discusses R. Hillel's statement in the Babylonian Talmud, Sanhedrin, folio 99a, "There is no Messiah for Israel for he was consumed in the days of Ḥezekiah." Merit that can cause the Messiah to come before the appointed time was appropriated in the days of Ḥezekiah, so that one should not expect an earlier redemption to take place. No copyists' names are mentioned in these texts.

Ms. 229
P. 300b

A correspondence concerning a group transporting merchandise who concluded their task prematurely because they were accorded safe passage by others

Shalom Abitboul sends this letter to R. Ḥayyim Yamin Ha-Kohen of Fez. He informs the latter that he met with a group of Jews from the town of Ouarzazat, which is located in the vicinity of Tafilalet, at the caves of the Saints which the Jews visited. The writer apparently made his wages as a guide at the caves of the Saints. This group of Jews gave the writer a letter to forward to R. Ḥayyim informing him that they had sold the merchandise, consisting of dates that they had brought with them, because they had encountered a caravan that could guarantee them a safe return journey to their town.

Ms. 230
P. 301a

A correspondence from David Meshash

This letter was written by David Meshash on the seventh of Tishri 1871. The first part of this unusual rhythmic letter is very cryptic. A portion of the second part of this letter is written in Judaeo-Arabic. The writer explains why his response to a previous letter is late in coming. The letter was first directed to another person by mistake since the present writer's name was not indicated on the envelope. Furthermore, the writer's duties prevented him from writing sooner. R. David Meshash asks that regards should be sent to Joseph Levi at Marrakesh, a tailor, to whom the former sent a letter a week before and from whom he would like to receive a reply. A request is made by the writer that a beautiful citron should be sent to him through the first available person. Any price should be paid for it, as he has been unable to acquire any. The writer asks that regards be sent to R. Raphael Agayni and he excuses himself to R. Raphael for not having had time to pen a couple of lines. The name of the person to whom this letter is written might be Habib and his father's name appears to be Jacob.

Ms. 231
P. 302a

A court document of Fez permitting an individual the use of public air rights belonging to communal property

Ayush ibn Asayaig needs to set certain beams from his property onto the wall of the public poor house, which is in the street of the peddlers, in Fez, in order to construct a ramp. He has an agreement with the communal leaders to pay a certain amount towards the needs of the poor of the city for appropriating the public property for his own use. The undersigned members of the rabbinic tribunal, upon ascertaining that the aforementioned Ayush paid to the treasurer of the poor fund a bolt of velvet for the needs of a poor bride, grant him permission to set in the beams onto the wall of the aforementioned structure for the erection of a ramp. However, he is instructed not to exceed the number of beams that have been assessed for the task lest he cause the courtyard entrance way to collapse because of excessive weight. This document is attested to by the rabbis Judah ibn Attar, Abraham ibn Danan, and Jacob b. Reuben Ibn Ẓur, at Fez, in the month of Ḥeshvan 1714.

Ms. 232
P. 303a and b

A letter from Joseph Sasson of Jerusalem to R. Raphael Ibn Ẓur concerning the acquisition of books

Joseph Sasson of Jerusalem writes to R. Raphael Ibn Ẓur of Fez asking him to reply concerning a list of books that he supplied at R. Raphael's request and upon which the latter has neglected to act. Joseph also asks for payment of some books that were ordered and delivered through the services of Moharam Susin on a previous occasion. He also asks that the present list of books and the money for them should be given to R. Jacob Ha-Kohen, who would deliver both on his return to the Holy Land. The writer sends regards to all the rabbis. A list of books is given on the lower half of page 303a. First, those books already sent through R. Susin are listed. They include the work Sha'ar Asher in two volumes and another set of the same two volumes for R. Abner Ha-Ṣarfati. Also the book Minḥat Ani was accessible but the Sha'ar ha-Melekh was unavailable. Two books are sent from Rabbi Rosen, one is for R. Raphael and the other book is for R. Abner. Among the new acquisitions are the work Ḥiqrei Lev, Part II, Neḥpaz ba-Kesef Parts I and II, and a volume of the Rashba. The price for these books is seven durham. The address is found on page 303b.

Ms. 233
P. 304a (top of page)

A letter from Raphael Arzi to R. Malakh Raphael

The writer is from the Holy Land. He lauds R. Raphael in this letter of friendship and he prays for the merit of R. Meir Ba'al Ha-Nes and Elijah to extend to R. Raphael. He states that his preoccupations prevented him from writing before.

Ms. 234
P. 304a (bottom of page)

A letter from Ḥayyim Toledano to Malakh Raphael

This letter by Ḥayyim Toledano which is dated 1821, conveys the writer's best wishes to R. Raphael. [It is conceivable that the letter which is *Ms.233*, on the top of page 304, was sent from Meknès by Raphael Arzi and that Ḥayyim Toledano utilized the opportunity to convey his best wishes to R. Raphael.]

Ms. 235
P. 304b

Two medicinal prescriptions

This document is entirely written in Judaeo-Arabic. The page begins with a prayerful hope for a speedy recovery. The contents of two prescriptions given below are comprised of various kinds of spices.

1. The ingredients are one half kilo of honey, one half kilo of peeled garlic, spices, and sesame, and fifteen grams of dried mint, all of which are pounded in a mortar and moistened in water. The garlic and honey are cooked together and then all the ingredients are compounded into a thick mixture. The concoction is taken twice daily, once in the morning before the meal and once before bedtime.

2. The second prescription contains dried rose petals, cinnamon, and myrtle which are pounded together. An inscribed amulet is then suspended in the mixture so that the inscription is washed off. The medicament is inserted in the womb with a piece of wool.

Ms. 236
P. 305a

A plea to R. Raphael Ha-Ṣarfati by an emissary to render a judgement against those in Meknès who would claim a portion of his collected contributions for the community's charitable needs.

Israel Jacob Ha-Levi is an emissary engaged in a fundraising campaign in Meknès. The Nagid of Meknès, R. Isaac Yitaḥ, has claimed that it was agreed that one-quarter of the funds raised should be earmarked for the poor in Meknès, but this had never been agreed to or discussed prior to the campaign. In fact, on the day of the fundraising effort, the assembled people stated that they had no claim on any portion of what was collected. The writer says that he lost seventeen mitkalim as a result of the perfidy of the group who later supported the Nagid's claim in the name of the community of Meknès. He lost, besides, other sums that were pledged but not paid to Israel. Other injustices were also perpetrated against the writer. He now asks R. Raphael Ha-Ṣarfati to take up his case since there is no higher authority to appeal to. The writer is unable to elaborate more since he is preoccupied with his fundraising activities. The writer prepared this letter when he was in Rabat after he had left Meknès.

Ms. 237
P. 306b

An appeal is made to the rabbis of Fez to help the rabbis (of Meknès) re-open a case by having one of the Monsano brothers appear (at Meknès)

R. Ḥayyim (son of the scholar R. Michael Ashkenazi, of blessed memory) came before R. Jacob (Toledano) and R. Mordecai Berdugo (of Meknès) with a complaint against the brothers R. Abraham and R. Immanuel Monsano concerning an item that R. Ḥayyim's late father had deposited with them. The rabbis of Meknès now write to the rabbis in Fez saying that since the matter had already been adjudicated by a rabbinic tribunal and a decision rendered they could do nothing further. Ḥayyim claims, however, that the previous judgement was rendered while he was under duress and that he was forced to agree to an unfair decision by threats. Immediately thereafter a copy of a document was produced which provided that the aforementioned object, which was now in the possession of the Monsano brothers, did, indeed, belong to himself. The undersigned rabbis, Jacob (Toledano) and Mordecai Berdugo, suggest that the rabbis (in Fez) should help to reopen the case. This letter is addressed to the following rabbis: Saul ibn Danan, Raphael Oḅed Ibn Ẓur, Elijah Ha-Ṣarfati, and Matitya Serero asking them to oblige one of the Monsano brothers to come (to Meknès) so that justice will finally be done and tranquility will again prevail.

Ms. 238
P. 307a

A transaction involving the purchase of books from Jerusalem by R. Ham-Malakh Raphael via Gibraltar

This letter was written to R. Ham-Malakh Raphael by Ha-Ẓevi Me'at Devash, of Jerusalem in 1872. The writer informs Ham-Malakh Raphael of a number of books that he has made available to him through the agency of Moses Ha-Levi of Gibraltar. The following books are enumerated: the two-part work of Ḥoshen Ha-Mishpat with all the commentaries, and the Netivôt ha-Mishpat, Sefer Kezôt ha-Ḥoshen, Sefer Even ha-Ezer with all the commentaries, and two books composed by R. Abraham Palaggi. Excluding the two works by R. Abraham, the other books cost the sum of ten durham and they come via Jaffa. The last edition of Ḥoshen Mishpat, volume 3, has just become available to the writer and it costs four durham. The total cost of the books is fourteen durham. The writer notes that he has incurred additional expenses and that he would like to be informed as soon as the books arrive. He concludes by stating that he is always at the service of R. Raphael. The seal of the writer is applied at the end of the letter.

Ms. 239
P. 308a

R. Ḥayyim Toledano extends an invitation to Ham-Malakh Raphael Ha-Ṣarfati to stay with him when he arrives at Meknès

R. Ḥayyim recalls the close relationship that prevailed between his father, of blessed memory, and R. Raphael Ha-Ṣarfati. R. Ḥayyim says it will give him honor if R. Raphael will accept his hospitality on his forthcoming journey (to Meknès). The writer also sends greetings to R. Raphael's son, Joseph.

Ms. 240
P. 309a

A letter from the rabbis of Fez introducing an emissary from Tiberias to the communities surrounding Tafilalet

This document, which was composed in Tammuz 1838, was sent by the following rabbis of Fez: Jacob Serero, Jacob (Ibn Ẓur), and Ḥayyim Abraham Ha-Ṣarfati to the communities in the region of Tafilalet, and as far away as Tidga (currently referred to as Taghaoust in the far south-western corner of the Anti-Atlas). They are asked to support the efforts of the emissary from Tiberias, in the Holy Land. In the introductory portion of the letter, which contains the acrostic Raphael Jacob (Simḥon), the calamities that have befallen the community of Tiberias such as famine and bandits are enumerated. The emissary had brought with him a letter from Tiberias. The rabbis of Fez proclaim a malediction and excommunication on those who would refuse to extend aid, and a blessing on those who will grant it. The rabbis ask that all amenities should be extended to the emissary, since his journey is quite dangerous and he can use all possible support.

Ms. 241
P. 309b

A supplicatory prayer with mystical elements

"For the sake of the merit of our patriarchs . . . Your prophets, seers, and saints, Tannaim and Amoraim . . . Gaonim and Poskim, commentators, righteous and reverent ones who sanctify and cherish Thy great and Holy Name, for the sake of Israel and the poor in their midst . . . Young and old, righteous women and children . . . Our matriarchs . . . Sarah, Rebekah, Rachel and Leah, whose station is elevated above men, for the sake of the Ofanim and Seraphim, Ḥashmalim and Tarshishim and the Holy Ḥayyot, may you separate from me, your servant the son of your maidservant, all those who would despise me and harm me."

Ms. 242
P. 310b

A plea for a divorce to be granted to the daughter of Abraham Ibn Danan, who was abandoned by her husband, who resides in Meknès

This letter was written by R. Judah ibn Attar to R. Jacob Ibn Ẓur, in Meknès, in the month of Kislev 1722. Esther (daughter of Abraham ibn Danan) of Fez has been abandoned by her husband, Saul Joseph b. R. Moses Ha-Kohen, who has recently taken up residence in Meknès. The tax collector continues to oppress her by constantly reminding her that she owes the payments that her husband has not met. Only by getting her husband to grant her a divorce, through the power of agency, will she no longer be subject to the threats of the tax collector for non-payment of taxes.

It is true that on an earlier occasion when the husband was willing to grant divorces to both his wives, R. Judah states that he was not of the opinion that a divorce would have been the proper course of action. However, since the tax collectors do not accept the fact that the husband is unable to pay and continue to treat the wife mercilessly, the need for a divorce is now urgently requested. The aggrieved father, Abraham ibn Danan, mentions in his addendum to this letter that R. Judah ibn Attar had written to R. Moses ibn Attar (of Meknès) to intercede. However, since the latter was apparently unsuccessful, R. Abraham appeals to R. Jacob Ibn Ẓur to do his best to facilitate the divorce. R. Abraham notes that while R. Judah states that the husband has no money, he does possess land from which payment should be made towards his daughter's marriage contract. R. Abraham will abide by whatever action R. Jacob takes. R. Abraham sends regards to Rabbi Jacob Ibn Ẓur's family and R. Jacob's wife's sister also sends her regards to them.

Ms. 243
P. 311a and b

The rabbis of Meknès write to the rabbis of Fez concerning one who is unfit to take a second wife since he does not possess the financial means and he is not mentally well

This document was sent by members of the rabbinic tribunal in Meknès to the rabbis of Fez, in the year 1867. The former relate that Joseph Niẓẓam, of their city, who desires to take a second wife (in addition to his first wife) is not mentally balanced nor is he even capable of supporting his first wife. He also mistreats his first wife in every way imaginable. (A similar case involving a decision by R. Raphael Berdugo, of blessed memory, contained testimony prohibiting one from taking a second wife when he could not support her.)

The rabbis of Meknès state that as they have already written, even if the first wife is pregnant the husband will still be permitted to take a second wife if the pregnancy is the only grounds on which to prevent the second marriage from taking place, since at present there is no living male offspring from this wife. What is, however, at issue in this case is the husband's inability to support a second wife. If he *does* have means of support, in accord with testimony given before the rabbis of Fez, then he should make available land or movable property in the value of his first wife's marriage contract and the second wife could live with him while the first wife would have the option of suing for divorce. This ruling is in accord with the author of Beit Yehuda (R. Judah Ayyash) in responsum no. 5, where he quotes the Ribash.

The first wife's brothers have brought forward two groups of witnesses who have testified that her husband is unable to support two wives. This testimony is in direct contradiction to that given on the husband's behalf in the court at Fez. The wife's witnesses are deemed superior by their number in a case where estimations, not facts, are being presented.

Support must include the provision of food, clothing, and furniture in accord with Maimonides' ruling in his code, Yad ha-Ḥazakah, in the section dealing with the Laws concerning Married Life, Hilkhort Ishut, chapter 14:3. This ruling is also in accord with R. Jacob in his Code, Tur, chapter 76. Thus, when this mentally unbalanced man comes to the rabbis in Fez they are asked to evaluate his real wealth and they should not permit him to marry a second woman until he appears in Meknès and reaches financial settlement according to the law, as R. Raphael Berdugo, o.b.m., decided. This document is signed in Meknès by the rabbis, Matityah Berdugo, Abraham Amar, and Jacob Berdugo.

Ms. 244
P. 312a and b

A response to Aaron Ibn Ẓur's request for a Ktav Yuḥasin—a family tree, on the occasion of his daughter's wedding, is reluctantly given

Aaron Ibn Ẓur desires to produce his family tree called Ktav Yuḥasin, on the occasion of his daughter's marriage. He receives a response to this request from his brother who apparently does not want his name divulged for reasons of security. The brother extends his best wishes and prays that the parents of the bride will lead their other sons and daughters to the wedding canopy. The writer does not particularly want to divulge the historical-biographical information and prefers the dead to be left in peace.

The writer associates his family's origins with the rabbis and scholars of Castile of whom he numbers five generations. He begins with R. Moses Ibn Ẓur, o.b.m., who was known as Abraham the Hebrew, his only son the luminary, R. Isaac, o.b.m., and then he mentions the second R. Moses o.b.m., the son of Jacob, o.b.m., who is the fifth generation. "We are the scion of the saintly Rabbi Reuben, o.b.m., the son of the aforementioned R. Jacob, who was a brother to R. Moses II. At that point in history the family branched out into six groups." The writer indicates a family tradition which maintains that the ancestors are buried (in Spain) in the place where the Edict of Expulsion of 1492 was declared. In any event he reiterates that his brother has good cause to be proud of his family tree. The writer implores that after the letter's contents are read to Mordecai ibn Ḍo it should be torn into a thousand pieces and then burned. Aaron is also exhorted not to divulge who is the source of his information. The letter was composed on Purim day, 1876.

Ms. 245
P. 313a

A husband alleges that his young wife is rebellious and he wants the matter to be adjudicated

Rabbi Raphael Moses Elbaz writes to R. Raphael Ibn Ẓur in the month of Tammuz 1877 about a husband, R. Meir ben R. Isaac called Asbag, also known as ibn Asaboni, who had asked that R. Raphael Ibn Ẓur be informed about Meir's wife, the daughter of R. Moses called Asayaig, who dwells in Fez. The husband presented a claim against his wife, in R. Elbaz' court, saying that she was rebellious and that she deserted him for a lengthy period. The party pleading the wife's case disclaimed the charge against her as unfounded. Furthermore, he argued, the husband probably had a prospect for another bride and so had trumped up a false claim against his present wife. It was decided that the matter should be judged on the testimony of witnesses to see which claim was correct.

The cross-examination of witnesses for both parties produced the same stalemate as before. The young wife was a minor and her alleged rebelliousness could not be ascertained. The case was recessed indefinitely. At about this time her mother was about to give birth in Fez, so she asked her daughter to come to Fez to help her. The husband, Meir, prevented his wife from going to her mother's aid. When she finally went to Fez her father would not give her leave to return to her husband. This action was improper, the writer says, for even if she refused to have sexual relations with him at night, she still could serve him in other capacities during the day. R. Raphael Elbaz asks R. Raphael Ibn Ẓur to try to arrange a compromise between them but if he is unsuccessful, the matter will have to be made subject to litigation.

Ms. 246
P. 314a

An enactment (in Ṣefrou) prohibited Jews from another place to marry women of their community. A situation arose which was complicated by this enactment

R. Raphael Moses Elbaz writes to R. Raphael Ibn Ẓur about R. David ben R. Elazar called Adhan, who has moved to Ṣefrou under the pressure of creditors. He has taken a second wife from a far off area and subsequently sent a bill of divorce to his first wife. After the divorce, she arrived in R. Elbaz's jurisdiction with their son and when the husband saw his son and his former wife he was moved to compassion for them. He divorced his new wife and now desires to remarry his former wife and this is where the problem begins. An enactment was promulgated in R. Elbaz's locality which said that a man who is a stranger, who comes from another land, cannot marry a woman in the community (of Ṣefrou), for well known reasons. Therefore, the writer was instructed by the man to correspond with R. Raphael Ibn Ẓur concerning the entire matter.

Ms. 247
P. 315a

A query concerning the custom (in Fez) governing one who acquires groves, fields, or gardens if he also acquires the right of domicile therein?

Rabbi Raphael Moses Elbaz inquires of R. Raphael Ibn Ẓur concerning the custom, in Fez, governing the acquisition of groves, fields, and gardens, as to whether the owner also acquires the right of domicile therein, particularly when they are outside the city limits. This question applies also to cases where the property is received as a pledge or is rented by Jews from non-Jewish owners. What prompts this question is that many Jews rent or take as a pledge gardens and groves, and then find that the non-Jewish owners also rent them to others and no one is able to do anything about this practice.

The writer also inquires about a particular case concerning a garden outside the city limits and the house belonging to it that adjoins the wall of the city. The garden was completely enclosed and given on pledge to a Jew by its non-Jewish owners. Presently the non-Jewish owners decided to build an inn in the garden. Now the writer asks whether the Jewish owners have rights of domicile in the garden, called Ḥezkat ha-Yishuv. Or, he says, do we say that since the Jews never thought about claiming rights of domicile until the present situation arose that they have no such claim? If the Jews try to change the terms of the agreement to establish their rights of domicile by the fact that the garden is pledged to them and they have sowed vegetables thereon for a number of years so that they can demonstrate a solid claim to the land, can they prevent the building of this inn? The need for a response to this query is pressing.

Ms. 248
P. 316a

An Halakhic enquiry is posed concerning the possibility of rendering a lenient decision in a case dealing with a levirate

The writer of this letter, Joseph Sasson, who is serving as an emissary from Jerusalem, informs R. Raphael Ibn Ẓur that in the course of his travels he arrived at the community called Klaya, amongst the towns of the Rif. A question was raised with regard to the practice of the law of the Levirate. Since few books are available here except for the Code Even ha-Ezer, wherein a minority opinion is mentioned on this particular subject, the writer refuses to render a lenient decision based on that citation. He asks R. Raphael to provide a basis for a lenient decision on the subject of the Levirate and to render a speedy reply. The writer refers to the strange customs that the people of this locale practice, especially with regard to Levirate procedures. Regards are sent to R. Abner Ha-Ṣarfati. This letter was written on the eighth day of Tammuz 1877.

Ms. 249
P. 317a

One who was in debt gave the creditor securities in excess of the value of the debt and he demands that an oath be taken if the creditor denies receiving the securities

R. Judah ibn Attar responds to the letters that had been previously sent to him by R. Ḥasdai Almosnunia concerning a bill of debt that Jacob Konsina held against Saadya Lahabusi. Jacob collected some of the debt, but claiming that there was still money owing, he gave his power of attorney to Solomon ibn Amara to collect the amount that was still outstanding. Subsequently, he gave Solomon half of a bolt of woolen material to deliver to Saadya but, wielding his power of attorney, Solomon confiscated it as payment for the remainder of the debt. All these details had been included in the letter sent by R. Ḥasdai.

R. Judah now writes that he summoned Saadya and read him the contents of the letter which R. Ḥasdai had sent him. Saadya replied that he had given securities to Jacob which were worth in excess of the sum that was supposed to be outstanding so how could Jacob claim that the debt was not fully paid? Saadya further suggested that Jacob and his friend Moses Marago should take an oath stating that they did not receive the whole sum of the debt in the form of securities, and that this oath should be recorded. Afterwards, Saadya said, he would challenge R. Solomon in the courts concerning the way he had exercised his power of attorney. R. Judah tells R. Ḥasdai he must now summon R. Jacob and R. Solomon to inform them of Saadya's reply and that affirmation of their oaths should be forwarded by the first available courier. Then Saadya can enter into litigation with Solomon. A speedy reply is awaited from R. Ḥasdai.

Ms. 250
P. 318a

An inquiry is made as to the availability of documents which can substantiate the claim of inheritors which has a bearing on the redemption of captives

R. Judah ibn Attar writes to R. Jacob Ibn Ẓur concerning deeds of the inheritors of Isaac and Ephraim ibn Amara that were deposited with the latter. He asks R. Jacob to send them to him because the courtyard containing a new ritual bath, which was built by Isaac ibn Amara, is presently held in the possession of R. Joseph Adhan as a pledge and the descendants of R. Levi ibn Amara, may his soul repose in paradise, are pressing their claim to it based on the existence of the aforementioned deeds. R. Judah's court tried to render a decision in the nature of a compromise so that the claimants, the descendants of R. Levi ibn Amara, should agree to monetary settlement and cease pressing any further claim. This decision will remain in force as long as deeds of ownership are not produced. If they are produced then a judgement can be rendered accordingly. Until such time judgement will be suspended. Thus, the court, having written to R. Jacob on two or three occasions, awaits the forwarding of those documents by R. Jacob.

Concerning other documents held by R. Jacob, R. Joseph Adhan needs to produce a pledge in order to redeem himself with its value because he and his two brothers are being held by a non-Jew who causes them grief and has placed them in confinement on his property for over two weeks. The non-Jew caught the young son with the intention of converting him to Islam. The non-Jew freed them on the condition that cash would be made available to him immediately. The adversity of the times makes it impossible for others to help so that the pledge must be redeemed. For this reason Joseph Adhan sends his eldest son, Mîmun, to R. Jacob to receive the documents from him directly since Joseph is in such an oppressed situation. The son will not leave R. Jacob until the documents are made available. If perchance the documents have been destroyed, R. Jacob should make this information available at once so as not to prolong any false hopes, since this case involves the religious act of redemption of captives. If the deeds are not available then R. Jacob might be able to offer testimony or produce witnesses concerning them in hopes that some benefit will arise from this kind of evidence in lieu of the missing deeds.

Ms. 251
P. 319a

A final exhortation of Isaac Ibn Amara to produce deeds in substantiation of his claim or the judgement will remain in Joseph Adhan's favor

R. Judah ibn Attar writes to R. Shalom ibn Lakhraif concerning a judgement which was discussed in *Ms.250*, on page 318a. A favorable decision concerning the redemption of the pledge was given to Joseph Adhan against the claims of Isaac ibn Amara, the son of Mîmun, who resides in the vicinity of R. Shalom. Thus, the descendants of R. Isaac ibn Amara have had to admit that the pledge held on the land in the yard of Zeraḥ ibn Pargin belongs to Joseph, since a thirty-day period and every opportunity was given for documentary evidence to be presented but it never was. R. Judah asks R. Shalom to send for Isaac and to read to him all that is contained in this letter as a final warning that he either shall immediately produce all pertinent documents or else Joseph Adhan can immediately begin to appropriate the pledge for his own needs.

Ms. 252
P. 320b

Abraham Ibn Amara is in trouble with the ruling authorities and he can only redeem himself by calling in all debts owed to him and by what he can realize from what is due to him from a partnership

The rabbis Judah ibn Attar and Jacob Ibn Ẓur, at Fez, signed this document which they wrote to the rabbis Isaac Nahôn and Isaac Halevi, the communal leaders, and also to R. Samuel Abudarham and Joseph Abudarham (at Tetuán). The case concerns R. Abraham ibn Amara who holds a bill of debt owed to him by Mordecai ibn Amozag in the amount of one thousand uqiot. The creditor, Abraham, received his claim through Jacob ibn Ramukh and his wife who received the money as part of her dowry. Jacob's wife was the daughter of Solomon ibn Danan, of blessed memory, who held a bill of debt against the aforementioned Mordecai, which became Jacob's wife's portion of the inheritance from her late father.

Abraham ibn Amara is now in dire straits with the ruling authorities and requires large sums of money to redeem himself from his poverty and his oppressors. The king's agents were about to descend on him to demand their money, but he managed to put off their arrival until a response should be forthcoming to this letter. Therefore, a reply should be sent on receipt of this letter as to whether the money will be readily paid, or, if the debtor is not able to pay the debt immediately, what other arrangements can be made. As soon as payment is received the bill of debt will be destroyed. The debtor is warned that if he does procrastinate then the money will be collected by force. Any additional expenses incurred as a result of the coercive measures will be added to the total amount of the loan.

Abraham ibn Amara also has a contract of partnership with Abraham Adrutiel in a meat concession, for one year, to be renewed every month. Both parties have agreed to divide the profits on the basis that R. Adrutiel will run the business's day-to-day transactions, while Abraham ibn Amara will keep the accounts, rendering exact reports to R. A. Adrutiel whenever he asks for them. R. Adrutiel has placed complete trust in R. Amara in all matters and no note can be drawn up to disturb the legal force of the contract for the duration of the time therein stipulated. The partnership shall extend from the seventeenth of Av 1727 until the month of Av 1728. The contract of partnership registers that R. Solomon Abudarham will pay for the hides. The undersigned ask their correspondents to compel R. Adrutiel to make payment to R. Amara of monies that he still owes him for this year's receipts.

Abraham ibn Amara also holds a bill of debt against R. Mas'ūd ibn Israel ibn Haroush. Under its terms payments should be forthcoming on demand and any expenses incurred should be paid. The writers state that R. Mas'ūd ibn Haroush should now be compelled to pay R. Abraham ibn Amara what he owes. If these debtors are not able to make payment then the order of law shall prevail, officers will be sent, and the debtors will be forced to pay the additional expenses. With regard to the sharing of profits that was agreed upon between R. Adrutiel and R. Amara, calculations will be worked out at a later meeting. Apparently, Abraham ibn Amara must accompany the King's couriers to Tangiers where he will make payment. Therefore, the undersigned ask that future correspondence on the matter should be forwarded to Tangiers.

Ms. 253
P. 321b

Jacob Ibn Malka writes a letter of reference for R. Suleiman Algaz to the rabbis Jacob Ibn Ẓur and Samuel Ibn Elbaz

R. Jacob ibn Malka of Tetuán writes a letter of reference for R. Suleiman Algaz to the rabbis Jacob Ibn Ẓur and to Samuel ibn Elbaz (at Fez), since R. Suleiman is travelling to their area. The subject was born in Tunis but he presently dwells in Algiers. The rabbis are asked to extend all possible forms of hospitality to R. Suleiman, who is not well, and to write letters of introduction for him to all the areas where he will travel. He is a humble scholar and he is not forward in spite of his need for financial aid. This letter was written in 1748.

Ms. 254
P. 322a

Elijah Ibn Dahan asks scholars and prominent personages to aid the medical doctor and scholar Ḥayyim Bonan who is in need

Elijah ibn Dahan of Meknès writes to the scholars R. Moses Azagouri, R. Shalom Legimi, R. Shalom Alenqari, R. Aaron Halevi, and to the philanthropists David Abirgil, Shalom ben Labaz, and Slieman Ouizigan asking them to extend financial aid to the physician and scholar Ḥayyim Bonan, who has suffered great economic misfortunes. Previously, he was economically independent but he is now forced to seek aid. He is ashamed to have to plead for aid as he is a man of humility. Every deference should be extended to him in his hour of trial.

Ms. 255
P. 323a and b

Agron—a collection of forms for correspondence copied from actual sources. The author is Immanuel Monsano

[Page 323b should have preceded page 323a. This collection of correspondences for various occasions is part of a larger collection.]

The first letter, on the top of page 323a, is a plea to aid a scholar, Moses Ha-Kohen (son of Aaron Ha-Kohen) who must finance his only son's wedding. Since he is poor he is obliged to raise funds by appealing to others. The importance of supporting such an undertaking is underscored by the statement "that even a Torah Scroll should be sold for the purpose of Torah study or for marriage." Not only should financial aid be made available to the bearer of this letter but he should be accorded hospitality that is fitting for his station. A prayer is inscribed at the end of the letter for the safety of his journey and his return to the Holy Land. This letter was originally composed in the month of Adar 1760, at the city of Fez.

The second letter, which commences at the bottom of page 323a, is incomplete. It is a letter of consolation that is written to Jacob b. Malka on the murder of his son Samuel, may the Lord avenge his blood. The letter was composed in the year 1760-61 by Immanuel Monsano whose name appears in acrostic form.

The third letter, which commences at the top of page 323b, is an epistle of consolation to the exalted scholar Moses ibn Maman on the untimely passing of his wife, on the tenth of the month of Tevet, in the year 1758-59. The poetic style borrows much from scripture, especially from the chapter on the Woman of Valor, in the book of Proverbs. This letter was composed by Immanuel

Abraham, at Fez. The author's name, Immanuel Monsano, appears as an acrostic.

The fourth letter, which appears at the bottom of page 323b, is the introductory form used by a scholar who is an emissary for charitable institutions and who wishes to correspond with scholars and leaders of communities to inform them of his campaign. The date of this letter is given as the month of Adar 1760. The name of the author, Immanuel Monsano, appears in the letter in the form of an acrostic.

It may very well be that all the letters in this collection were composed by Immanuel Monsano.

Ms. 256
P. 324a

R. Shalom B. Moses Ben Ẓur asks R. Jacob Ibn Ẓur to render a decision in a dispute between partners

Shalom ben Moses Ben Ẓur writes to R. Jacob Ibn Ẓur asking him to render a decision in a dispute between two partners that has been submitted to litigation. Apparently the litigants presented their arguments in the presence of the writer but since a decision was not reached the parties are willing to submit to the decision of another authority, which is R. Jacob. The particulars of the dispute were forwarded to R. Jacob but they are not stated in this correspondence. The writer asks for a comprehensive and speedy reply as he has received on several other occasions when he turned to R. Jacob to render a judgement.

Ms. 257
P. 325a

R. Judah Ibn Attar writes to R. Jacob Ibn Ẓur about two different cases in Jewish Law

R. Judah ibn Attar writes to R. Jacob Ibn Ẓur about two different cases. The first case deals with a woman who claims that a pledge given for a loan was redeemed on her behalf. The plaintiff, Solomon ibn Yaîsh is now claiming that the pledge is unredeemed and he is pressing his claim against her. The first part of this correspondence is written in Ladino. The woman has not been permitted to take an oath to support her statement since there is cause for questioning her testimony. R. Judah gives her fifteen days to defend her position which is that she has already redeemed the pledge from her son-in-law, Isaac, and that she has subsequently torn it up. The woman has agreed that if she cannot offer additional evidence in the allotted time, then Solomon ibn Yaîsh's claim will stand. The pledge is supposed to have been deposited with R. Samuel Arwaẓ.

The second case originates in Debdou. With the authorization of his community, Jacob Kohen of Debdou has brought a complaint, against Samuel Kohen stating that the latter has sworn falsely. But, from the reaction of R. Joseph Ha-Kohen, R. Judah ibn Attar deduces that Samuel is being unjustly charged, especially since the scholar who was reported to have signed the charge against Samuel, namely, R. Joseph has actually signed nothing. The claimants, led by Jacob Kohen, have made many attempts to oblige Samuel to pay a penalty for his huge debts that they claim are outstanding. Furthermore, R. Judah says, Jacob is acting presumptuously in that he refuses to obey his own authority in Fez and is demanding that the case be heard in Meknès. Once before R. Judah had washed his hands of the affair, because Jacob was so contemptible, but Samuel's pleadings oblige him once again to involve himself in the case. He will attempt to achieve a settlement of the dispute by a compromise, whereby Samuel would pay a certain sum for every book of recorded accounts that was at the base of the dispute. However, he fears that Jacob has taken an uncompromising position just to hurt Samuel and to cause bad reports to be spread about him. Samuel is known for his intelligence, and his charitable nature has gained him much renown, so he has become the victim of animosity because others are jealous of him.

Ms. 258

P. 326a and b and P. 330a and b

A chronicle

[Portions of this chronicle were recorded by Saadya ibn Danan and the final copyist was Immanuel, son of Joshua Serero. The major portion of page 326a is written in Judaeo-Arabic. What follows is a translation of the Hebrew portion of page 326a and the entire page 326b.]

"It is written in the hand of my grandfather R. Samuel ibn Danan o.b.m., that the Castilian expulsion transpired in the year 1497. Lest I forget the date I have recorded it here. Saadya ibn Danan. Also he (R. Samuel ibn Danan) records that the expulsion that transpired in Fez Albali (the old city of Fez) to the Toshavim took place in the year 1438. The expulsion that befell the Mellah occurred in the year 1465. (Recorded by) Saadya ibn Danan."

"In the year 1636, on the seventh of the month of Adar II, an earthquake was heard which caused a great panic in Fez. People grabbed weapons and they attacked one another in confusion. This was recorded by Saadya ibn Danan and it was copied by Immanuel Serero." A solar eclipse is also recorded and the amount of sunlight is measured. Stars were seen in the afternoon on the twenty-eighth of Nisan, circa 1630. A great quake was felt in an early morning of 1624, whereupon a great number of houses and towers were demolished in Fez Albali and about 3,500 people were killed. More people were injured after the quake because of the weakened condition of the houses. It was regarded as a miracle that not one Jew was killed although their houses were demolished, especially as their houses were not so well constructed as those of the non-Jews. The reason why this event was recorded is stated as follows, "to make known to future generations the magnitude of this miracle that occurred." The author is recorded as Saadya, the son of Abraham, the son of Samuel ibn Danan, o.b.m. All this transpired on the occasion of the reading of (the portion of the scroll) "and I remembered my covenant with Jacob."

"Another incident that is reported to have occurred on Wednesday, the eve of Shavuot (Pentecost), 1624, is that the sky darkened and small creatures fell from the sky. The upper portion of their bodies were like that of a locust and the bottom like a worm. At the same time a storm of large (hail) stones fell from the sky. One stone weighed four uqiot and in all probability the stones were larger before they reached the ground. People who were in the marketplace were hurt by the falling stones. One stone came through the window of R. Moses Almosni's house and it broke a vessel. It was also reported that a lion entered the Giza gate of Fez Albali and killed a donkey and he took another donkey with him. It is not known whether this is true but most of the non-Jews say that it transpired. In the courtyard of Maḥmoud ben Gidar two cats fought and one ate the other.

"All the foregoing were copied from Saadya ibn Danan's Ms., by Immanuel b. R. Joshua Serero in the month of Ḥeshvan 1724."

[Page 330a and b is part of *Ms.258* which is found on page 326a and b. At the bottom of page 330a historical information is recorded in Judaeo-Arabic and it continues on page 330b and page 326a, which are actually the same page.] The contents of page 330a are given below.

As well as Fez the communities of Marrakesh, Dera, Tafilalet, and their environs are mentioned. A prediction of events based on when the New Year will fall is offered for the cities of Morocco. Brigands will abound and wars will be fought. The end of the year will be appreciably better than the early part. Plentiful rain will reduce the price of wheat. The day on which the New Year will occur will affect weather conditions, health conditions, and also whether difficulties will be encountered with the crops. This type of forecasting reminds one of a kind of Almanac.

Ms. 259

P. 327a and b

Writing exercises. Calculations of the value of a marriage contract

The writing exercises appear on page 327a. On the right side of the page a verse from Canticles 7:9 is copied several times as a writing exercise, while on the left side of the page the alphabetical system of Atbash is copied as a writing exercise.

On page 327b calculations are made concerning the value of a marriage contract.

Ms. 260
P. 328a and b

A letter of consolation to the Serero family from Amor Abitboul and Amram Elbaz, of Ṣefrou, on the death of Jacob Serero, o.b.m.

This letter of consolation is written to members of the Serero family by Amor Abitboul and Amram Elbaz of Ṣefrou, on the passing of R. Jacob Serero, of blessed memory. The mourners to whom the letter is written are R. Reuben Serero, R. Matitya Serero, R. Shalom Serero, and R. Joshua Serero. The praises of the departed are formulated into four paragraphs, each one commencing with the word Ẓaddik and concluding with a popular saying culled from Talmudic literature. The letter was composed in the year 1855-56.

Ms. 261
P. 329a and b

Exposition of an Aggadic text from the Talmud

Various Aggadic interpretations are offered for a text found in the Babylonian Talmud, Tractate Gittin, folio 36b. The text is as follows: "Those who are insulted but do not return insults in kind to those who insulted them act out of love (of God) and they rejoice with the portion which the Almighty meted out to them." [For page 330a and b, see *Ms.258*.]

Ms. 262
P. 331a

R. Mordecai Birdugo asks R. Jacob Ibn Ẓur to set the record straight in a dispute concerning two widowed women

This letter deals with the case of the first widow of Jacob Pariente who is undergoing much anguish. R. Mordecai wants R. Jacob Ibn Ẓur to inform him whether the woman's suffering resulted from a decision and action taken by R. Jacob Ibn Ẓur or whether the second wife, who is a person of a bitter disposition, is the cause of the first wife's suffering? If the former is the case then why does R. Jacob not inform R. Mordecai about it? At least R. Jacob should respond to R. Mordecai's last correspondence wherein the latter proposed a settlement in favor of the first wife.

If R. Jacob Ibn Ẓur does not agree with R. Mordecai's viewpoint then "he should have sent her forth with nothing, as naked as the day that she was born." Furthermore, R. Mordecai would surely abide by R. Jacob's decision because of the esteem in which R. Jacob is held. R. Mordecai asks, "why was it necessary to introduce the non-Jewish ruling authority into the situation?" It is the writer's intention to attempt to arrange a settlement between the disputing parties. However, if the second wife took the action that she perpetrated without R. Jacob's permission then he should denounce her, since because of her actions the first wife was obliged to come before the authorities and she continues to incur a great loss. Therefore, a speedy reply is expected from R. Jacob wherein he should set the record straight.

Ms. 263
P. 332a and b

An exhortatory prayer, called Tokheha, composed by R. Baḥya Ibn Paquda and copied by R. Jacob Ibn Ẓur

R. Jacob Ibn Ẓur states, in his introduction to this liturgical poem, called Tokḥeha, that it was composed by the author of the Ḥovot ha-Levavôt, R. Baḥya ibn Paquda. The latter states in the aforementioned work that he composed this poem as an exhortation to the soul. R. Jacob further states that this composition subsequently appeared in Maḥzorim (High Holy Days prayer books) and it is also noted in the work Sha'arei ha-Teshuvah. He desired to possess a copy of this composition, until the day he happened to find it in an edition of the Maḥzor of Rome which was filled with a multitude of liturgical pieces referred to as Yôẓrôt, Krôṿôt, and Tôkheḥôt. R. Jacob copied this text for his friend, the scholar R. Neḥemiah Ha-Kohen, as a gift of remembrance.

Ms. 264
P. 333b

A letter from Ha-Ẓevi Me'at Devash to R. Raphael Ibn Ẓur concerning the availability of books for purchase

This letter was sent in response to R. Raphael Ibn Ẓur's request for a set of the Codes of Jewish Law. Ha-Ẓevi Me'at Devash, the writer of this letter, who resides in Jerusalem and is a book dealer, informs R. Raphael that, while recently there was an overabundance of this work, supply of this edition has now virtually been exhausted. However, no effort will be spared to fulfill R. Raphael's request. Once the books are located they will be sent to Gibraltar, to the Halevi family. R. Raphael is asked to wait until they are made available.

Ms. 265
P. 334a

Ẓevi Judah Birdugo asks that certain conditions stipulated for an estate be nullified so that he may utilize the estate for capital to enable him to settle in the Holy Land

[This letter was sent after a previous letter which is found in *Ms.11*, on page 22a.] R. Ẓevi Judah Birdugo, who resides in Jerusalem, requires funds which he can realize from his portion of an estate left by his grandfather. The latter stipulated certain conditions, namely, that the land should not be used in payment for a claim originating from a marriage contract nor should it be sold or given as a pledge. These conditions were set in order to maintain the estate in perpetuity so that the descendants would be able to benefit from the land's produce.

R. Ẓevi Judah's brother waived his family's rights to the land in favor of the former. R. Ẓevi Judah asks R. Solomon Ibn Ẓur and the young scholar R. Y. Monsonyego to render a favorable judgement which will render null and void the conditional element of the deed so that he can sell the land to acquire what he needs; especially since he is utilizing it for the religious duty of settlement in the Holy Land. This letter was sent from Meknès to Fez in the year 1862.

Ms. 266
P. 335a

A letter of consolation on the demise of R. Jacob Ibn Ẓur, o.b.m.

This letter of consolation is written by Joseph Israel on the death of the great Rabbi Jacob Ibn Ẓur. The writer appears to curse those aspects that are related to the decay of mortals rather than to death itself. In fact, he characterizes death itself as "good" for it liberates the soul and enables it to ascend to those celestial spheres where it will partake of eternal bliss. The writer extolls the wisdom of the author of Ecclesiastes who saw, according to this writer's interpretation, joy in the act of lament. Thus does he see the day of death as the day of Hilula—celebration.

The greatness of the deceased is extolled as his prospective spiritual rewards in the world of eternal bliss are recounted. The Almighty is absolved from any wrongdoing that might be related to the act of death.

Ms. 267
P. 336a

R. Elijah Solomon Ibn Ẓur is asked to make available a copy of a decision rendered by another scholar that he possesses, which may serve as a precedent in a case that must presently be adjudicated

R. Matityah ibn Zikhri asks R. Elijah Solomon Ibn Ẓur to provide a copy of a legal judgement that was rendered by Mahari Mas'ūd, of blessed memory, called Yitaḥ. R. Matityah is prepared to pay the expense involved in preparing the copy which is needed to resolve a pressing problem in Jewish law. The case involves the falling in of a roof which is mortgaged to others. Do the owners of the roof lose their rights to the roof or not? An answer to a similar problem was rendered by Mahari Mas'ūd and therefore a copy of his judgement is called for.

Ms. 268
P. 337a

A plea to the rabbis Yedidia Monsonyego and Solomon Elijah Ibn Ẓur to right an injustice perpetrated against a dead orphan

A woman called Rebecca, the wife of R. Isaac Afriat, was shattered by the death of her grandson, the youth Ayush ibn Joseph ben Haroush who was the son of her daughter, especially since she had no money with which to provide him with shrouds, burial needs, a candle for his soul, or the recital of memorial prayers on his behalf. The grandmother had to borrow money in order to get all the paraphernalia that was necessary for his burial. Two months later the creditor came to collect his due and the grandmother could no longer put him off. Therefore she came before the rabbis Matitya ibn Zikhri and Raphael Moses Elbaz asking them to write to the rabbis (of Fez) (Yedidia Monsonyego and Solomon Elijah Ibn Ẓur) to support her claim.

The deceased youth had been in partnership with Joseph Ṣaba and with Moses Yalu, and during this time, his father, Joseph, had been killed by non-Jews. The grandmother has heard from reliable sources that Moses Yalu took the money that was given in recompense for the murder of the father of the dead youth. The rabbis (of Fez) are asked to summon Moses Yalu to make payment with the money that was given on behalf of the murdered father to cover the loan for the burial expense of the dead son; for, indeed, the latter was the rightful heir. Were it not for her advanced age and her weakened condition the grandmother would travel (to Fez) to enter into litigation with Moses Yalu. The rabbis (at Fez) are asked to render judgement on the grandmother's behalf for the court is the proper caretaker of the orphan and the widow. The address directs this letter to Fez.

Ms. 269
P. 338a

A plea is written to R. Solomon Ibn Ẓur on behalf of Mordecai Elbaz who is destitute. A claim that a debtor should pay the additional penalty for a debt paid late

Rabbi Raphael Moses Elbaz asks R. Solomon Elijah Ibn Ẓur to extend aid to R. Mordecai Elbaz, who is a relative of the writer, and whose family has recently, become afflicted with poverty and hunger. R. Mordecai has never had to depend upon the help of others before and has always lived a frugal life. He still devotes himself to Torah study constantly and especially to the study of Zohar.

A second subject is dealt with in this letter. The case involves a debt that had to be paid in two installments by Reuben to Simeon. There was an agreement between both parties that if the payments were not made on time then Reuben would be obliged to pay an additional amount of money as a penalty. Reuben made the first payment on time but, just before the second payment was due Simeon left town. Reuben delivered the money that he owed, to the court stating that the creditor was not presently available. When the creditor returned he demanded that the penalty should be paid since he received the money after the deadline. R. Raphael Moses Elbaz presently inquires of R. Solomon what decision should the court render? The writer refers R. Solomon Elijah Ibn Ẓur to Ḥoshen Mishpat, chapter seventy-three, paragraph 8, and he cites the Sema on that text. He also mentions the responsa of the Rashba cited by the Beit Yosef, chapter seven; also the Kelalei Ha-Rôsh, Kelal No. 8, paragraph 6; and finally the work Avodat ha-Gershûnî, part I, chapter 7. A speedy reply is requested.

Ms. 270
P. 339a

R. Raphael Maman inquires about a daughter's share of her father's estate after his demise although he had previously granted her an inheritance as she was a child from a previous marriage

This query was sent to R. Elijah Solomon Ibn Ẓur at Fez, by R. Raphael Maman. A daughter from a first marriage who benefitted by receiving an inheritance from her father's estate is now entitled to receive an additional inheritance from her father's estate after his demise in accordance with the enactment referred to as 'Isur Nikhsei,' which means a tenth of the property. What amount is she entitled to receive if there is a second wife and sons who survive the deceased father? For example, if for argument's sake there are one hundred silver pieces to be divided, do we give this daughter ten pieces of silver and divide the remainder between the second wife and her sons? If that were done, then the wife would receive fifty percent of what remains, which is forty-five silver pieces, and the remaining forty-five pieces of silver would be divided amongst the sons. Or, does the second wife receive fifty percent of the total estate at the outset which gives her fifty silver pieces and the remainder divided as follows—ten silver pieces to the daughter and the remaining forty pieces to the sons? Perhaps the second wife's portion does not enter into the calculation of 'Isur Nikhsei' at all, in which case the daughter is only entitled to one tenth of what the male and female issue receive, which is a considerably smaller sum. The writer states that this is an actual case that is pending and he requires that a decision be rendered. A speedy reply is desired.

Ms. 271
P. 340a

A divorcée claims that she is the victim of an unjust decision concerning the financial settlement that she received for her marriage contract and she wants to press a claim against a third party

R. Elijah Solomon Ibn Ẓur had previously written to R. Matityah (ibn Zikhri) concerning a divorcée who is claiming that the financial settlement of her marriage contract was unfair and is now demanding a more just and equitable settlement. R. Elijah states that since the woman and her three daughters are in economic distress a more favorable settlement should be accorded to her. R. Raphael Maman, the writer of this letter, responds to R. Elijah Solomon, of Fez, to clarify for the latter why the original judgement should stand.

This woman deserves no special consideration in respect of her marriage contract for the following reasons. Firstly, she and her former husband were involved in collusion by trying to coerce others to divest themselves of property which was originally accorded to her in her marriage contract but was sold to others a long time ago. Her husband would remarry her once she had extracted the money from the third party under false pretense. Secondly, her marriage contract was mortgaged for a debt so that she has no rights to negotiate on the strength of her marriage contract. Furthermore, a compromise settlement could have been reached were she willing to waive any future claims on her marriage contract. R. Y. Adhan sought such a compromise and it was only out of respect for him that there was a willingness to entertain such an arrangement. Strictly according to the law, no compromise should have even been introduced.

When the woman saw that she could get no satisfaction she turned to the ruler to try to obtain a ruling in her favor. The divorcée charged that a bad judgement had been rendered against her. The ruler decreed that the case should be sent (from Meknès) to the rabbis of Fez for review. The charges that this woman made must be proven to be unfounded so as to clear the court of any false accusations in the way they had rendered their verdict. The writer himself is involved in this litigation with the divorcée as the third party that acquired the property which she claims belongs to her. That is why Raphael Maman responds to R. Elijah Solomon Ibn Ẓur instead of R. Matityah (Zikhri), to whom Ibn Ẓur wrote originally. The writer does not desire to elaborate any more to R. Ibn Zur except in a face to face confrontation. If R. Elijah Solomon stills wants to grant the divorcée and her children some funds as a result of the earlier compromise, the writer is not averse to her receiving some aid, especially since the orphans, the children of the divorcée, are cousins to the writer. However, the writer refuses to permit this grant to be given a guise of legality in the form of a compromise, since the cause of justice will not be served in that manner.

In the last paragraph of the letter, R. Raphael takes issue with R. Elijah Solomon who cited a ruling of R. Judah ibn Attar o.b.m., that witnesses should write their testimony that they saw a bill of pledge. He states that even R. Judah ibn Attar would have agreed that where the bill of pledge is still in force such written testimony is irrelevant. The writer states that he follows Maimonides' ruling in this case. The writer also notes that the Rema's view expressed in Ḥoshen Mishpat 115:5 is rejected by most authorities, especially since R. Caro is in disagreement with that view. [The address to Fez is on the other side of this letter.]

Ms. 272
P. 341a

A letter of introduction written on behalf of R. Jacob Oḥana who requires economic aid

This letter is written to R. Solomon Elijah Ibn Ẓur on behalf of a scholar, R. Jacob Oḥana, of Rabat, who requires financial assistance. The writer, Raphael ibn Arzi, asks R. Solomon Elijah to ensure that the community extends a helping hand to R. Jacob. He also requests that since the rainy season will soon commence the fundraising effort should be expedited as soon as possible, so that the scholar can return home. [The address to Fez is given on the other side of the page.]

Ms. 273
P. 342a

Raphael Maman writes a short note to R. Solomon Ibn Ẓur concerning two cases that were under litigation

Raphael Maman informs R. Solomon Ibn Ẓur that the author of a legal decision [unknown to us] has pleaded that the judgement should not be revealed to R. Joseph Halevi for reasons known only to that individual. The writer asks R. Solomon to affirm the decision so that the matter can be concluded. Raphael Maman mentions another case that was brought to litigation, and informs R. Solomon that he wrote to Raphael Agayni to make payment in accord with the decision rendered. [The address to Fez is given on the other side of the page.]

Ms. 274
Pp. 343a—347a

Two allegorical folk tales and a poetic composition of sixteen stanzas, by Raphael Arzi. Another poetic composition of six stanzas by Ḥayyim Toledano, and a metaphorical epistle by Raphael Arzi

The first of two allegories relates the tale of a maiden who was fooled by a Don Juan type lover. He wooed her, married her, and then he abandoned her. He returned to her after many years, only to abandon her again and leave her shattered and forlorn. A sage warns her against him and informs her of his philandering nature. The narrator breaks off before the end of the tale of woe is concluded. He states, in his puckish way, that it is better to save the paper.

The second tale relates the story of how a virtuous young man was able to succeed in the moral battle and how he avoided the clutches of wayward women who desired to ensnare him. One woman, however, succeeded with her wiles and the young man succumbed to her charms and wed her. However, she proved to be unfaithful to him and he reviled her. Yet he wanted her to receive her just desserts so he went to seek her out. On the way he encountered her but she did not appear at all familiar to him. The woman fabricated a story that her husband had been imprisoned for more than ten years. After this chance encounter she had twins and she justified her ways before her unknowing husband.

Sixteen verses follow which characterize

women. They are penned by Raphael Arzi, the author of the aforementioned allegories. Another six verses similar in style to the previous verses were composed by Ḥayyim Toledano.

The final text in this group of writings is by Raphael Arzi and is an epistle to R. Judah, the father of Samuel and Amram (Elbaz), in a metaphorical literary style. Raphael Arzi writes that he feels he has been unjustly treated by R. Judah and he affirms his love and friendship for him and his two sons. This is a unique letter of reconciliation wherein Raphael asks that their quarrels should cease. Even in this text the female figure is used to symbolize waywardness.

Ms. 275
Pp. 348a—355a

A chronicle recorded by Immanuel Monsano

The chronicler commences with a lament about the unfortunate times in which he lives. "In the year 1739 no rain fell in the month of Adar I until the seventeenth day of the month. On the eighteenth day prayers of thanksgiving were recited. In the month of Adar II no rain fell until the seventh day at which time a public fast was declared, although some people were fasting anyway because it was the anniversary of Moses' death. At the morning service supplicatory prayers and scriptural verses were read. At the afternoon service the Torah scroll was read and additional prayers were recited. On Thursday, the ninth day of Adar II, a public fast was again declared. At the morning service supplicatory prayers were offered, including 'Our Father Our King.'"

The head of the academy and leading rabbi of the community delivered a lecture after which the service was concluded. The lecture stressed that the denial of rain was directly related to the sin of neglecting Torah study, since Torah study leads to good behavior. The speaker also stated that gossip and other improper exercise of speech cause the rains to cease; this is based on interpretation. Public violation of Sabbath laws, especially by the vendors of liquor, is also a factor. Therefore, an enactment was made to the effect that even if only one witness saw a vendor sell liquor, whether to Jew or non-Jew, on the Sabbath, then he should pay a fine to be used on behalf of the poor. Another lapse recounted by the scholar was that Jewish women go to Fez to work for the non-Jews and remain there day and night and on the Sabbaths. They must behave in accordance with the code that Jewish women are accustomed to live by. It was decided that an emissary should make them return and if they refused then the ruler should be asked to intervene to oblige them to do so. R. Azriel ibn Amozag was appointed overseer in these matters.

In that same day good news arrived for the Jews concerning Ahdwan Al-Wadaya, one of the infamous bands during the days of King Mulay Mahmad ibn La-Ariba. There was an eclipse of the sun during the latter's reign. Many of the misfortunes of this period were recorded in the chronicles of R. Immanuel Monsano. The non-Jew Maḥmad ibn Abu ibn Sa'id suffered a terrible death at the hands of King Mulay Lamuztadi, at Meknès. There was tranquility in the land during the latter's reign. His accession was in Tammuz, 1738, and he was declared king, in Fez, on Friday, the eighth of Av.

"In the same day it became cloudy and very windy, so much so that we thought it appropriate to recite the 'Great Hallel' prayer at the afternoon service. The scriptural text of Vayeḥal was followed by supplicatory prayers at the afternoon service. We must praise the giver of life for He sent rain on Sunday, the twelfth of Adar. All day rain fell on and off, the sun shone and set, and much rain fell in the evening. Great thundering was followed by the appearance of the rainbow. It again became cloudy with much rain falling on the night of the thirteenth (of Adar)." A prayer follows that rain may be sent by God. On the fourteenth, which is the Festival of Purim, after the customary gifts were sent, the rabbi took a Torah scroll in his arms and Piyyutim (liturgical poems) were read. The price of wheat was still exorbitant. A prayer for economic sustenance and the coming of the Messiah is recorded, followed by the name of the chronicler, Immanuel Monsano. The chronicler continues on:

"On Sunday, the sixteenth of Shevat, 1740, while we were engaged in Torah study, a man informed us that King Mulay Lamuztadi had fled to Fez and the entire city was in an uproar because of the reign of terror that would follow, especially for the Jewish populace, which was the usual course of events during unsettled times. That same day R. Jacob Monsonyego was wounded in the arm and head and as a result lost much blood. The king left the city and fled eastward since he saw no relief in Fez. On Tuesday, the eighteenth of Shevat, Mulay Abdallah was declared king. This was his third term as ruler. The supporters of the king who had fled, known as LeBukhari, went after him to try to persuade him to return. In the month of Tishri 1740, the ruling king arrived at Meknès. When the Al-Wadaya heard of the king's arrival at Meknès they rebelled against him for two months, during Tishri and Ḥeshvan, and they still maintained the state of rebellion after that. On the twenty-fifth of Ḥeshvan, the king sent his representative to them with an offer of amnesty. They refused to trust the king." A prayer is added that the Messiah might come. The name of Immanuel Monsano concludes the statement.

"In the middle of the month of Kislev, 1740, the king's officers went to Argil to give warning to the Al-Wadaya. They accepted the king's authority because they received a stern warning. On Sunday, the twenty-first of Kislev, they went to meet the king who received them and a reconciliation was effected.

"In the year 1758-59 no rain fell from the fifteenth of Tevet until the beginning of Adar. Clouds began to appear on Tuesday, the thirtieth of Shevat followed by much rain. Consequently, the prayer of thanksgiving was recited. However, the rain ceased again and the gentiles asked the Jews to pray for rain; so the court decreed a public fast for Monday, the twentieth of the month, for old and young, men and women, alike. Penitential and supplicatory prayers were recited at the morning service. The people went to the cemetery and recited prayers at the graves of the saints. Psalms were recited at the grave of the Great Rabbi Judah ibn Attar. Rabbi Elijah Ha-Ṣarfati gave a lengthy discourse. Afterwards, penitential prayers were recited between the gates of the city, at the graves of those who were murdered there. Then the entourage proceeded to the adjoining burial grounds at Al-Karsalin to recite Psalms there. They returned, in great distress, to the Synagogue of the Toshavim where they recited Psalms. The entire congregation assembled there for the afternoon service at which time Rabbi Saul ibn Danan addressed the people.

"On Wednesday, the twenty-second, rain fell the first part of the day and then ceased. The rabbinic tribunal decreed a fast for Monday, the twenty-seventh, to be observed in similar fashion to the earlier fast. Rabbi Elijah Ha-Ṣarfati addressed the people in the morning while Rabbi Raphael Ibn Ẓur addressed the people at the afternoon service. After the Torah reading, seven circuits were made around the reader's stand. At each circuit the twenty-ninth Psalm was recited and a poem from the Hoshanah Rabbah liturgy was read. Penitential prayers were again recited but no relief came. On Wednesday, the twenty-ninth of the month, on the eve of the New Moon, a decree was issued by the court for a fast and each group prayed in its own synagogue. The afternoon service followed a fast day ritual. That same day it became cloudy. On Friday, the second of Nisan, towards evening, rain fell. On the Sabbath, after midday, great winds and thunder and lightning were followed by much rain and hail which affected the fields. Then, no rain fell from that day until Sunday night, the third eve of the intermediate days of Passover, at midnight, when much rain fell until the morning." A blessing for a prosperous year concludes this section.

"After the conquest of the city of Fez by the King Muḥammad ben Mulay-Abdallah, on Friday the twenty-sixth of Av 1760, he brought a cannon to the Mellah and placed it in the cemetery. He told the troops to fill it with gunpowder and to shoot it in order to see what distance the missile would attain. On Sunday, the New Month of Av, the ruler made an inspection of the cannon. When he returned home he was welcomed by cheering women and he received gifts from the populace. On the eve of the New Month of Elul, which was a Monday, a storm wind arose and one could almost feel the earth quaking. This was followed by thunder, lightning, and rain." The king's tent is described as being very big. Another tent of lesser size fell from the impact of the storm. More than two hundred Al-Wadaya who were imprisoned and who subsequently fled, were given amnesty, money, and seed for planting by the ruler. He sent them to dwell in the environs of Meknès where the children of the leader were living off brigandage.

The ruler finally went to Marrakesh and left Mulay Idris in charge. The Jews suffered much at the hands of Mulay Idris.

Additional documents

The following manuscripts, documents, and texts did not appear in the Yalkut Roĩĩm volume. Those desiring to use copies of the manuscripts in this section for their research should prefix the manuscript number for which they are asking with the classification B.C.Ms. followed by a number. B means Bension and C means Cohen. The names, places, literary works, and subject matter which appear in this section are also noted in the Indices. Again, printed texts will be prefixed by the designation "Pr." rather than "Ms."

Ms. 276 **A Ketubbah from Ṣefrou in the tradition of the Megorashim**

This handwritten Ketubbah (legal marriage contract), which is the only one appearing in the Bension Collection, was composed in the city of Ṣefrou, Morocco, on the fifth day of the month of Nisan, 5603 (1843). The groom's name is given as Abraham the son of Maḥlouf and the bride is called Esther the daughter of Mordecai. The witnesses whose signatures appear on the document are Amram Elbaz and Elijah Azulai. The total value of the Ketubbah is given as eight thousand and eight hundred uqiot. This contract stipulates that the groom will never oblige the bride to leave the city of Ṣefrou against her will and that he will not take an additional wife unless the bride is willing to give her assent. If he violates the last two stipulations then he will be obliged to pay her the aforementioned sums and he must immediately grant her a valid bill of divorce. This Ketubbah follows the practices of the community of Castilian exiles of the city of Fez.

This Ketubbah was originally pasted on the inside cover of the bound manuscript volume of The Kelalei ha-Rosh, the responsa collection of R. Asher b. Yeḥiel, which is found in the Bension collection [cf. *Ms.292.*]

The upper left hand corner of the Ketubbah was torn away from the inside corner of the Ms. volume Kelalei ha-Rosh; that portion of the Ketubbah still remains therein.

The upper third of the Ketubbah is artfully decorated by the process of rubrication. The main body of the text of the Ketubbah consists of nineteen lines including the signatures of the witnesses. The Ketubbah measures 33 x 18 cm. Portions of the written text have been affected by the depredations of time.

A package containing correspondences, novella, and Midrashic texts composed by the emissary of Tiberias, R. Ḥayyim David b. Abraham Gigi, and one letter written to him, are now presented in the following Mss.

Ms. 277 **A letter by an emissary asking for aid for the scholars of Tiberias**

This correspondence is sent by R. David b. Abraham Gigi, in the year 1776, to Yauda Franko asking him to extend support to the scholars of the community of Tiberias, in the Holy Land. The writer's distinctive signature is given at the conclusion of the epistle as David b. Abraham Gigi.

Ms. 278 **A letter by the emissary R. David Gigi to R. Joseph Ha-Kohen**

This letter is written by the emissary R. David b. Abraham Gigi to the rabbinic scholar and judge R. Joseph Ha-Kohen. The writer informs R. Joseph that he suffered a fall from which he is presently convalescing in the town of Slieman. [He probably fell from his mule which was of the male gender. That is why in subsequent letters he is insistent that only a mule of the female gender should be made available to him for his return journey to the Holy Land.] R. David describes the treatment he is receiving which consists of constantly being bled by a series of physicians and this has weakened him considerably. Another form of treatment involves the barbecuing of meat which is placed on R. David's shoulder. During the past fifteen days, R. David states, he has been staying in the home of R. Judah Balish in Slieman, where he is convalescing.

R. Judah's father stayed at R. David's home on one occasion for several months and the son, R. Judah, is now repaying the kindness.

R. David states that were it not for his present misfortune he would have spent some time at the home of R. Solomon Alfasi. The writer asks R. Joseph Ha-Kohen to extend himself in behalf of R. David and the mission which he serves, by collecting some monies that are due. R. David would not trouble R. Joseph if he was well. As it is, he only relates a small part of the tribulations that he suffers.

Ms. 279

A list of expenses and calculations composed by R. Ḥayyim David Gigi

This recorded expense account by R. Ḥayyim David Gigi is very revealing since it includes the notation that he paid for the expenses incurred for treating his injured hand over a period of three months. The wages he had to pay to one who assisted him, are also recorded. Incidental expenses for religious articles, food, clothing, and other items are noted as well.

This list is also revealing in that an emissary was held accountable for any sum that was spent. Therefore exact records had to be kept.

Ms. 280

An emissary requests that a mule should be purchased for him

This letter is written in Judaeo-Arabic to R. Abraham ibn Paroz by R. Ḥayyim David Gigi. The latter who serves as an emissary for the community of Tiberias informs R. Abraham that he lacks nothing. R. Ḥayyim asks R. Abraham, however, to request of Moses ibn Ḥayon that he sell him his mule since R. Hayyim is accustomed to that particular animal, having used it on a previous occasion. It would be a favor to R. Ḥayyim because he is going to be obliged to purchase another animal in any event. The writer states that he had acquired two horses but they did not satisfy his needs. If Moses refuses to part with the animal then the writer asks Abraham to acquire another animal from someone else. R. Ḥayyim states that he will arrive on Thursday since the campaign (for charity) has gone well in his present location. R. Ḥayyim prefers that a female mule should be bought, and figures the price to be twelve or thirteen mitkalin. R. Ḥayyim inquires about the well-being of Abraham's son, Samuel. On previous occasions R. Ḥayyim signed his name David, but now he has added the name Ḥayyim to his signature.

Ms. 281

R. Ḥayyim David Gigi inquires of R. Moses Ḥayon whether he will sell him his mule

R. Ḥayyim David Gigi is preparing to return to the Holy Land after having completed his mission as an emissary and he requires a mule. He asks the prosperous R. Moses Ḥayon if he will perform an act of kindness by selling a female mule to him for this purpose. R. Ḥayyim is preparing to embark on Thursday, therefore, he would like the animal to be delivered to him before that day. Upon delivery of the animal R. Moses will be paid. If R. Moses cannot himself bring that animal, or another female mule that would be suitable, then he should give the animal to R. Abraham ibn Paroz who will deliver it. In his introduction to the letter R. Ḥayyim sends greetings to the distinguished R. Aaron Arwaẓ and to the members of his household, as well as to R. Moses Ḥayon. This letter is written in Judaeo-Arabic.

Ms. 282

Receipts that the emissary David Gigi composed for charitable donations given by the community of Kanaya

R. David Gigi, the emissary of Tiberias, declares that the fixed sum of money that was pledged by the holy community of Kanaya was paid in full by their prosperous members. The members of the community have further pledged to give a sum of money over the next four years which will amount to five gerush a year per householder may they be doubly rewarded from heaven. The author concludes this receipt with a multitude of blessings. [This document was composed and signed by the writer David b. Abraham Gigi in Kanaya, at the end of the month of Elul 1776.]

Another receipt states that the emissary of Tiberias, R. David Gigi, attests that he received from the chosen citizens of the holy community of Kanaya and from the hand of the prosperous scholar R. Ḥayyim Kustantin, the sum of one hundred gerush. This sum made up the thirty-five gerush that was owed according to the previous pledge and twenty gerush towards the new pledge, while the remainder is given as a new contribution and to pay for the travelling expenses incurred by the emissary. The new pledge, which commences in the year 1781, is given as five gerush per householder. This is followed by blessings.

Ms. 283 R. Ḥayyim David Gigi is asked to support the claims of a contract that was disputed

This letter is sent to the emissary R. Ḥayyim David Gigi who is located, on this occasion, at Ṣefrou. The writer, Maḥmoud Zikhri ibn Yaḥya refers to him as the 'Avrekh' David Gigi. [The term "Avrekh" is usually bestowed on one who is a young scholar.] The writer, who has rendered a decision concerning a betrothal contract that is being disputed, maintains that it should be adjudged in agreement with his view which is in accord with Jewish law. If the contract is invalidated according to the premise of the other party then it will not be in accord with Jewish law. Mordecai b. Moses is mentioned as in support of the writer's contention. The rumor that declares the documents to be faulty and says that the writer took a bribe to support its validity, is regarded as too much to bear and the violators should be separated from the community (excommunicated).

Therefore R. Ḥayyim David is asked to support the claim of Reuben b. Mas'ūd for the Ketubbah of his daughter which obliges that she shall receive sustenance for three years. Isaac b. Judah had attempted to claim wheat on this basis and was turned away empty-handed. The writer pleads with R. Ḥayyim David to support a just claim.

Ms. 284 The written credentials of the emissary David B. Abraham Gigi

This document contains the official credentials of the emissary R. David b. Abraham Gigi who serves the interests of the Kollel in Tiberias to the several communities and territories of the Western Mediterranean mentioned in the text, namely Gibraltar, Portugal, the North West African coast, and the cities of Crete, Candia, (the largest community of the Island of Crete), and Canea. Blessings are pronounced for the leaders of the communities and Messianic hopes are expressed. The needs of the Jewish community of Tiberias are related. This document is fragmented with the lower half missing.

Ms. 285 An Halakhic dissertation entitled "Derush"

This Halakhic dissertation commences with a text from Maharam Galante which poses the question: "Why, in The Sh'ma prayer does Talmud Torah (Torah study) precede the duties of Tefillin and finally Mezuzah while in the second chapter of the Sh'ma, "Ve-haya im Shamoa," Tefillin precedes Talmud Torah and the law of Mezuzah follows?"

This text prepared by R. David Gigi follows for about six pages, many of which are fragmented.

Ms. 286 Halakhic dissertations on two different Talmudic texts

These texts composed by R. David Gigi take up two pages. The first topic which comes from the tractate Gittin states that if a slave flees to the Holy Land his master is obliged to free him according to the Biblical law of the runaway slave. The Ran 576 folio b is cited. A second text from the tractate Ketubbot is the basis for the second exposition.

Ms. 287 An Halakhic exposition by R. David Gigi

R. David Gigi writes a four page exposition on a statement of Maimonides on the laws pertaining to the writing of a Torah scroll.

Ms. 288

A legal document affirming the claims and business relationship between two litigants

The emissary R. Ḥayyim David Gigi and Israel Sharbit, who are the undersigned on this document, attest to the veracity and the righteousness of the settlement that has been arrived at between the creditor R. Judah ibn Ḥayyim and the debtor Joseph ibn Ẓahakon. The latter owed R. Judah four measures of barley and a sum of money. The profits that have accrued from an enterprise they previously held in partnership shall be shared.

There was a sum of seven uqiot which Joseph owed to Judah. If Joseph will take an oath that he received this sum from Judah and give that amount in payment to the elementary school teacher in lieu of tuition fees, then the matter will be concluded. If, however, Joseph refuses to do this, then he will be obliged to pay it as one who received a loan. All other matters outstanding. between the parties will then be null and void. This document is signed in the town of Oujda, Morocco, on the eve of the first day of the month Kislev 1778.

Ms. 289

A document concerning the charitable pledges of the community of Candia, Crete, which is suffering economic privation

This document, composed by R. Ḥayyim David Gigi, although his name does not appear in it, deals with his efforts to secure funds from the community of Candia, Crete. The members of the community have stated that they have no set pledge levied on them and they have shown him a note from the scholar R. Nehemiah Kalil indicating that this is indeed so. R. Ḥayyim David Gigi approached them, with a plea for funds to redeem captives and on behalf of R. Meir Ba'al Ha-Nes, but the people responded that because of their destitute state they did not even possess the wherewithal to contribute to R. Ḥayyim David for his travelling expenses.

R. Ḥayyim David states that since he could himself attest to their poverty he settled with them for the sum of twenty gerush so that they could still participate with adjacent communities in these important charitable undertakings. The members of the community have also agreed to fulfil an annual pledge of three gerush per annum which they will pay to the emissary of Tiberias who will come to collect it. The emissary's travelling expenses will be settled with them according to the conditions of the times. This document is composed on Thursday, the eve of Hoshana Rabba, in the year 1777.

Ms. 290

A letter written by R. David Gigi, also containing novellae, (in a damaged condition)

This letter is written by R. David b. Abraham Gigi, from Acco. It is difficult to ascertain to whom this letter is written because much of the letter is torn away. R. David states that he is again going on a mission as an emissary and he prays for divine guidance on his journey. He states that in the months that have passed there has been no tranquility in matters pertaining to the government. The writer requests that the person to whom he writes should be attentive to the scholarly needs of R. David's son, R. Abraham, and that his teacher should be concerned that Abraham should not be disturbed from his studies. R. David concludes the letter with his signature, which is given as David b. R. Abraham Gigi.

The first side of this page is devoted to the distinction that R. David draws between the view of the Talmudic Tractate Gittin concerning the subject of a servant that has fled from the diaspora to the land of Israel and the view of the Tractate Ketubbot on the same subject. The opinions of medieval commentators, namely the Ran, Rabbenu Tam, and the Rambam, are given on this subject.

Ms. 291 **A copy of the text of a Halakhic query sent by R. Abraham Laredo of Gibraltar and the response thereto**

One day, Reuben, who was ill and bedridden, sent for the wealthy Simeon and for some others and related to them that when he was financially well off many years ago, two Ashkenazi Jews stayed with him leaving money in the sum of four thousand darham for safekeeping. They stipulated that if they returned then the money should be given to them, but if not then the money should be utilized for some religious purpose. The Ashkenazi gentlemen never returned. In the course of time, Reuḅen said, he lost his wealth and the aforementioned money was mixed together with his own, now all of which was spent. Subsequently, however, he managed to put some money aside, and now he would like Simeon to administer a special fund of four thousand darham, which is to be invested, and any dividend income used to maintain Torah scholars and a house of study in the city of Rabat.

The writer, R. Abraham Laredo, states that he was concerned as to what form the act of possession should take when Simeon received the money from Reuḅen. The symbolic form of affirming possession by the handing over of an object from one to the other of the contracting parties, called ḥalifin, which is also referred to as 'Kinyan Sudar,' would not be applicable in this case, for this procedure involved the transference of actual money to which the procedure for acquiring objects did not apply. Furthermore, in order to ensure the acquisition by transference of ownership through the use of an object, the governmental authorites would have to record the sale and this would only lengthen the procedure and would require additional expense. The writer therefore decided that Reuḅen should transmit the money directly to Simeon and thereby obviate all the aforementioned procedures and difficulties. This had been agreed to by Reuḅen and Simeon.

A technical problem had arisen, since the money was hidden in the sides of a box and because it was not easy to remove the money it had been decided that Simeon should pick up the box. There was more money in the box than the four thousand darham and Reuḅen was asked if this money, as well should be used for the establishment of the academy, to which he replied in the affirmative. The aforementioned transaction was duly recorded. Reuḅen also stipulated that his other properties should be used to support his wife and his daughter and if these properties came to be exhausted then the wife and daughter should share in the dividends of the four thousand darham that was designated for the scholars. This transaction took place in the spring of the year 1841.

A few days after the aforementioned transaction took place, Reuḅen reneged. He demanded that Simeon return the box and the money to him, and maintained that he had previously promised to pay his father-in-law a sum of money that they had both agreed upon. However, since he did not have the money at that time, it was incorporated into the additional sum that was stipulated in his wife's marriage contract. Therefore, he was now obliged to make that money available to his wife. Simeon was not moved by Reuḅen's claim. Shortly thereafter the scribes of the non-Jewish governmental courts informed Simeon that if he did not return the box and the money to Reuḅen immediately then the authorities would seize all his household goods and he would be imprisoned for theft since the transaction (which was not affirmed by the non-Jewish authorities) was performed in an unofficial manner. Simeon, who was sufficiently frightened, returned the money and the box to Reuḅen, who died thereafter.

R. Abraham Laredo who supervised the aforementioned transaction and recorded all the details now composes several queries pertaining to this case for which he awaits a reply. One is: did Reuben have the right to renege on his original commitment and if so, did he also have the right to the additional amounts over the four thousand darham? Does the wife take precedence in collecting for her marriage contract or not?

R. Abraham Laredo adds the following before he concludes his query. He states that anything that he records relating to this case should not be regarded as testimony since he writes what he recollects and there is a measure of doubt in his report. He notes that he did not see the actual transmission of the money between the parties to the transaction, only the handing over of the box. R. Abraham regards himself as the student of the anonymous authority to whom he directs this query. This query is dated at Jebel Tor (Gibraltar) in the month of Sivan 1841.

The anonymous scholar notes at the outset of his response that this matter has not yet been brought to litigation by the descendants of Reuḇen, yet he feels obliged to deal with the controversy to satisfy the query of the scholar R. Abraham and the wealthy Simeon. [While we possess twelve pages of response there are indications that more pages were written.]

Ms. 292

A manuscript volume of R. Asher B. Yeḥiel's responsa known as Kelalei Ha-Rosh

The manuscript volume Kelalei Ha-Rosh, which was composed by R. Asher b. Yeḥiel, is a unique compilation since it bridges the cultures of the Franco-German Tosaphist schools of Ashkenazic Jewry and the Spanish halakhic system of the Sephardim at the beginning of the fourteenth century. R. Asher had enjoyed a distinguished career as a rabbinic leader in Germany before R. Solomon ibn Adret welcomed him to Barcelona. Subsequently, R. Asher served as rabbi in Toledo. He joined the anti-philosophic camp of the Talmudic traditionalists and supported R. Solomon ibn Adret's ban on the study of philosophy by anybody under the age of twenty-five.

The manuscript volume of the Kelalei ha-Rosh, which is written in Sephardic Mashait script, was probably located at one time in Ṣefrou, Morocco since a marriage contract from that city, dated 1843, was found pasted in the inside cover of this work [cf. *Ms.276*]. The text of this manuscript volume follows to a certain extent the text of the first printed Constantinople edition of 1522 which consists of one hundred and eight chapters, numbering one thousand responsa. The manuscript volume commences with chapter four in the middle of law twenty-one, as the first four chapters are missing. The text that is extant contains one hundred and sixty-seven pages, and is written on folios a and b. The text concludes with chapter ninety, the laws of Pledges, law number six. There is no colophon. The manuscript volume can be dated *c.* the fifteenth century. There are thirty-three lines to a page and the size of each page is 39 x 22 cm. The text is written on vellum. While no pagination is given the heading on each page notes the particular section and law that is being discussed on that page.

The copyist added texts in the margins of the manuscript. These notes were originally composed by R. Asher b. Yeḥiel and they provide additional material, some of which do not appear in the printed editions. The additional texts appear on pages 66; 86; 11a [is incorporated in the printed edition]; 13a [is incorporated in the printed edition at the end of Kelal "Yud"-"Aleph" p. 146, but in a truncated version while the Ms. contains a more complete text]; 72a [is incorporated in the published edition on p. 41a and b]; page 101a [is incorporated in page 54b and 55a of the published work, but in chapter 58 instead of chapter 57, see below]; and 133a. The arrangement of the Kelalim (chapters) differ in the Ms. version and the published edition. Thus, chapter 57 in the Ms. volume is chapter 58 in the published edition. The variants between the manuscript and the published edition, as well as the change in the order of chapter classification, including additional elements that appear in the Ms. volume, make it a valuable addition to the field of responsa literature.

Ms. 293

A manuscript volume of R. Solomon Ibn Adret's responsa known as Teshuvot Ha-Rashba

The appearance of two manuscript volumes of Responsa in the Bension collection, namely, the Kelalei Ha-Rosh (*Ms.292*) and the Teshuvot ha-Rashba (*Ms.293*), makes it characteristic of its time and place, since the early masters of Sephardic culture prepared many such collections for their own scholarly needs. This effort which began in Spain was perpetuated by North African scholars who copied earlier collections of Responsa while also making original contributions to the field.

R. Solomon ben Abraham ibn Adret (1235-*c.*1310) served as rabbi in Barcelona for more than four decades. His scholarly acumen gained him a reputation while he was still a young man and queries in matters of Jewish law were sent to him from all the countries of Europe, North Africa, and the Middle East. R. Solomon's correspondences exceeded ten thousand responsa. This well preserved corpus on Jewish law left its imprint on the Codes known as Shulhan Arukh.

This new collection of Adret's responsa (*Ms. 293*) is a welcome addition to other collections of his responsa that are presently extant. The text was written in Sephardic mashait script. In the absence of any colophon it could probably be dated as a product of pre-expulsion Spain *c.* the fifteenth century. There are sixty-seven pages and the writing appears on folios a and b, apart from the Index. There are thirty-four lines on each folio. The work commences with an Index of seventeen pages and thirty-four folios, which records the subject of each responsum. Although the first three sections, and a part of the fourth section of the Index are deleted, the major portion of the Index which originally contained twenty-five sections, referred to as "Batim," houses, is extant. The fact that the first chapters of the Index are missing is not a great loss since the contents of these sections are given in their entirety in the main body of the text. The main body of the text is given plenum only until Dinei Shkhiv-Me'ra, part of responsum number four. The main sections will now be presented, along with the numbers of those responsa which do not appear in the published editions of the Rashba's responsa.

On the first page of the main text the bold script declares this work to be "The second part of the Rashba."

1. "ha-Bayit ha-Alfed"—"Dinei Kiddushin Ve-Shiddukhin Ve-Sivlonot," containing thirty-nine responsa.

Unpublished Responsa:
Nos. 24, page 14;
32, page 19;
34, page 19;
35, page 20;
36, page 20.

2. "ha-Bayit ha-Bet"—"Dinei Ketubbah," containing eleven responsa.

Unpublished Responsa:
Nos. 4, page 23;
6, page 24;
10, page 25.

3. "ha-Bayit ha-Gimel"—"Hilkhot Gittin," containing sixty-eight responsa.

Unpublished Responsa:
Nos. 1, page 25;
2, page 26;
3, page 26;
44, page 46;
46, 47, 49, page 47;
56, page 51;
34, page 42;
38, 39, 40, 41, page 44;
42, 43, page 45;
58, 59, page 52;
61, page 53;
64, page 55.

4. "ha-Bayit ha-Dalet"—"Hilkhot Yibum, Ve-ḥalizah, Ū-Mi'ūn," containing nineteen responsa.

Unpublished Responsa:
Nos. 1, 2, 3, page 58;
9, 10, 11, page 60;
16, page 62;
18, page 63.

5. "ha-Bayit ha-Hay"—"Dinei Nashim Ve-Yiḥudan Ū-Mee Ra'uy Le-Hay'id Alayhem," containing fourteen responsa.

Unpublished Responsa:
No. 4, page 65;
Responsa:
Nos. 13 and 14, page 73.

6. "ha-Bayit ha-Vav"—"Dinei ha-Ish Im Ishto Ve-Im Banav ha-Ketanim Ve-ha-Gedolim," containing ninety-five responsa.

Unpublished Responsa:
Nos. 1, page 75;
6, page 77;
22, page 84;
24, page 85;
35, 36, page 95;
44, page 99;
45, page 100;
46, page 101;
57, 58, page 110;
60, page 111;

67, page 114;
68, 69, 70, 71, 72, 73, page 115.
75, page 117;
79, pages 118-119;
81, 82, page 119;
85, page 121;
87, 88, page 122;
89, page 123;
94, page 126.

7. "ha-Bayit ha-Zayin"—"Dinei Zava'at Shkhiv Me'ra," containing thirty-eight responsa.

Only the first four responsa are given and then the collection breaks off. The additional sections mentioned in the Index were probably originally part of the collection. The only unpublished responsa available in section seven is Responsum No. 1, page 126.

The additional sections will be outlined according to the way they are listed in the Index. While the subject of each individual responsum is given in the Index, those interested must apply to the University of Alberta to receive them; they are not given in this presentation.

8. "ha-Bayit ha-Ḥet," "Dinei Almanah ve-Yatom," containing one hundred and ten responsa.

9. "ha-Bayit ha-Tet," "Dinei Nahalot," containing thirty-five responsa.

10. "ha-Bayit ha-Yud," "Dinei Zekhiyah Ū-Matanah u-Meḥilah," containing twenty-nine responsa.

11. "ha-Bayit ha-Yud-Alef," "Dinei Halukat Karka'ot," containing one hundred and forty-five responsa.

12. "ha-Bayit ha-Yud-Bet," "Dinei Mekomot Beit Ha-Knesset," containing ten responsa.

13. "ha-Bayit ha-Yud-Gimel," "Dinei Heqdesh," containing thirty-four responsa.

14. "ha-Bayit ha-Yud-Daled," "Hilkhot Ribit," containing thirty-two responsa.

15. "ha-Bayit ha-Tet-Vav," "Dinei Mashkonah," containing sixteen responsa.

16. "ha-Bayit ha-Yud-Vav," Dinei She'elah, Ū-Sekhirut, Ū-Piqadon," containing twenty-two responsa.

17. "ha-Bayit ha-Yud-Zayin," "Dinei Sheluhin Ve-Shutafin," containing thirty-six responsa.

18. "ha-Bayit ha-Yud-Het," "Dinei Mekah Ū-Memkar," containing eighteen responsa.

19. "ha-Bayit ha-Yud-Tet," "Dinei Shetarot," containing fifty-five responsa.

20. "ha-Bayit ha-Kaf," "Hilkhot Loveh Ū-Malveh," containing ninety-seven responsa.

21. "ha-Bayit Kaf-Alef," "Dinei Shemitat Kesafim," containing ten responsa.

22. "ha-Bayit Kaf-Bet," "Dinei Dayanin Ve-ha-Dinin," containing twenty-four responsa.

23. "ha-Bayit ha-Kaf-Gimel," "Hilkhot Edut," containing seventeen responsa.

24. "ha-Bayit ha-Kaf-Daled," "Dinei Moser Ū-Malshin," containing twelve responsa.

25. "ha'Bayit ha-Kaf-Hay," "Dinei Misim," containing fifty-three responsa.

The Index which is written in double columns on each folio enumerates one thousand and thirty-nine responsa which originally comprised this collection. Two hundred and fifty responsa are given plenum with pagination. These extant responsa are valuable because their variant readings, when compared to the published responsa, are very illuminating in helping to establish a critical text.

It is probable that Ariel Bension, the compiler of this entire collection, penned the corresponding citations in the margins of the pages of this manuscript indicating where the particular responsum can be found in the published edition of the same work. A similar script appears at the beginning of the first page of the Yalkut Roĩĩm. It is important to note that the sequence of the responsa in the manuscript volume is entirely different from that of the published editions.

A copy of the first printed edition of Sefer Ha-Zikkaron, 1555

Pr. 294

R. Ishmael Ha-Kohen Tanuji served as a rabbi in Tunis, North Africa during the early decades of the sixteenth century. In 1543 R. Ishmael felt obliged to leave Tunis because of the difficult political situation that had developed there and made his way to Egypt where he served as chief rabbi. The synagogue which R. Ishmael frequented in Egypt subsequently became known as the Tanuji synagogue.

R. Ishmael completed his work, Sefer ha-Zikkaron in Egypt upon his arrival, in 1543. The author formulated this work as a Code of Law by classifying the halakhic rulings which he extrapolated from the text of the Talmud according to the order of the Tractates In his introduction to his work the author states "I desired to compose a concise digest of all the laws that pertain to our times [thereby excluding those laws which would pertain to the practices during the days when a Temple would be established] that are found in the Talmud according to the order of the Tractates. This digest should serve as an introduction to the Talmud and the legal decisions rendered by the Rif, [R. Isaac Alfasi of the eleventh century]." The author became aware of the legal digest of R. Jacob b. Asher, and he mentioned that work in his manuscript.

The text of the Sefer ha-Zikkaron which is found in the Bension collection is a copy of the first printed edition of this work. According to the colophon it was published in Ferrara, on a Tuesday, the twenty-sixth day of Av 1555 by the publisher Abraham ibn Usque, Sefardi. R. Judah Doron aided in the production of this work. The ruler of the duchy is noted to be Don Herculi Diasti. No pagination is given and the first part of the work is missing. The book commences with the laws which conclude the first chapter of the Tractate Megillah. The rest of the work is complete. The size of a page is 19.2 x 14 cm. The original cover and binding of the book appears to be intact.

Ms. 295 A manuscript collection of fragments of Maimonides' commentary on the Mishnah

R. Moses b. Maimon (1135-1204) composed his Commentary on the Mishnah, during the early years of his scholarly career. It was his intention to present the basic principles of the various halakhic topics discussed in the Talmudic Tractates and their rulings for those who might find the rambling discussions of the Talmud too difficult to follow. In his introductions to the various tractates he launched into theological formulations which could serve as a guide to the general reader in an age when polemic forced the various faith systems to present their beliefs in a concise and orderly fashion. Thus, the Jew would be able to respond to a wide range of questions such as the Judaic view on an afterlife, the concept of God, the psychological function of ethics, and the role of prophecy and revelation, among other topics which were discussed in the age of belief.

In his design of the Commentary on the Mishnah one could already discern the beginnings of the formulation of Maimonides' later works such as his halakhic code called "Mishneh Torah" and his philosophic magnum opus, "Guide of the Perplexed." Throughout his works concise definition of terms and classification of topics are his hallmark. In his introduction to the tractate on ethics called "Avot," Ethics of the Fathers, Maimonides attempts to harmonize Aristotelian ethical thought with Talmudic ethical teachings.

Maimonides completed his commentary to the Mishnah, called Siraj, in 1168, at the age of thirty-three.

The fragments that comprise the manuscript of Maimonides' Commentary on the Mishnah which are found in the Bension Collection [*Ms.295*] consist of twenty-eight pages, folios a and b, and they are written in Temanic Mashait script. Many of the pages are in a damaged condition. There is no colophon available and no pagination is given. There are generally about twenty-six lines to a folio. The script is large and clear and the average size of the letters of each word is one-half centimeter. The length of each page is twenty-three centimeters with a width of eighteen centimeters, except where the pages are truncated. On the whole the texts that are presented are legible except where the pages are torn or perforated. The Commentary which follows each Mishnah is written in Judaeo-Arabic. The fragments can be regarded as having been written in the fourteenth century. The following are the contents of the available texts. [Albeck's edition of the Mishnah was used as the basis for numbering the respective Mishnayot.]

Tractate Shabbat

Chapter one commences with the commentary to the first Mishnaic text, while the page containing the Mishnah text itself is missing. In chapter one, Mishnayot two to four inclusive are given. The concluding portion of the first chapter is also given. No introduction is available to the Order of Mo'ed in this collection. The fragments contain pointillation for the Mishnah text up to chapter seven.

Chapter two contains Mishnayot one, two, five, six, and seven, wlth the commentary given.

Chapter three contains only the text of Mishnah six and its commentary.

Chapter four appears to be given in its greater part. Mishnah one is given complete with commentary but the commentary on Mishnah two is truncated.

Chapter five is almost entirely deleted except for some concluding lines of the commentary to the last Mishnah text of that chapter.

Chapter six is given in full with the entire commentary.

Chapter seven is given almost in its entirety except for a few concluding lines of the commentary to the last Mishnah.

Chapter eight has the first four Mishnayot missing. The last portion of the commentary to the fourth Mishnah is available followed by Mishnayot five, six, and seven which conclude the chapter.

Chapter nine commences with the first Mishnah and its commentary, but Mishnayot two and three and their commentaries are missing. A few concluding lines of the Commentary to Mishnah three are available, followed by Mishnayot four to seven inclusive, with commentary. The lines of the commentary to the seventh Mishnah are badly blurred.

Chapter ten is given in full, except that Mishnah five appears as two Mishnayot in the manuscript.

Chapter eleven also appears in its entirety. Diagrams are provided in the commentary to the second Mishnah. The third and fourth Mishnayot are combined in the third Mishnah of the manuscript edition.

Chapter twelve is given in full, but the fifth Mishnah is very blurred except for the last line.

Chapter thirteen is also given in full except that part of the fourth Mishnah is partly missing and the writing is blurred. No more text is available on the Tractate Shabbat.

Tractate Yoma [Dealing with legislation pertaining to the Day of Atonement.]

Several pages of fragments on the Tractate Yoma are found in the collection. There are, however, no texts available of the first four chapters.

The first fragments on Yoma commence with chapter five where Mishnayot one and two appear as one Mishnah. Otherwise chapter five appears in its entirety; parts of the pages however, are torn, perforated, or blurred.

Chapter six is complete except that the final passages of the eighth Mishnah commenced with the words "Rabbi Ishmael" were deleted by the copyist and then restored in the left hand column in a different script.

Chapter seven is given in full. The fourth and fifth Mishnayot are combined in one text. Maimonides provides, in his commentary to the last Mishnah, a diagram of the sequence in which the names of the tribes appear on the stones of the Ephod.

Chapter eight has, as the only text available in the Tractate of Yoma, the concluding (ninth) Mishnah and commentary prefaced by some of the lines which conclude the commentary to the eighth Mishnah. The upper portion of this text is blurred and a portion of it is torn away; there are also perforations.

The Tractate Yoma is concluded with the benediction "Barukh Notain Laya-aif Ko'ah U-le-ain Onim Oẓmah Yarbeh."—"Blessed be He who gives strength to the weary and to the powerless He imparts much might." Excluding the first word (Barukh) the rest of the text is a passage from Isaiah 40:29. This blessing is also given in Judaeo-Arabic. Folio b of this page commences with the Tractate Sukkah.

Tractate Sukkah [Laws pertaining to the construction of booths for the festival of Tabernacles.]

The first Mishnah of the first chapter of the Tractate Sukkah is given with the commentary which contains diagrams pertaining to the construction of a Sukkah. The Mishnah is blurred and perforated, and a portion of the text is torn away.

Tractate Ta'anit
The available fragment from the Tractate Ta'anit contains the commentary to the first Mishnah of the fourth chapter followed by the second and third Mishnayot, including their commentary. The third Mishnah is divided into two Mishnayot in the manuscript fragment. The first part of the third Mishnah is almost entirely obliterated and the upper part of the text is torn away. No other texts from the Tractate Ta'anit are extant in this collection of Mishnaic fragments.

Variant readings are noted when the manuscript fragments of Maimonides' Commentary on the Mishnah are compared to the texts of the printed editions on the same work.

Pr. 296 **An early printed edition of the Tur Shulḥan Arukh, Yoreh De'ah. This is an incunable and a unicum.**

R. Jacob ben Asher, more popularly known by his major work "The Arba'ah Turim," or "The Ba'al ha-Turim," arrived in Spain from Germany [c.f. *Ms.292*] at the beginning of the fourteenth century with his scholarly father R. Asher ben Yeḥiel, R. Jacob was concerned that individual Jews and communities should be guided by the corpus of halakha, Jewish law, in all their activities. In order to facilitate his aim, because he found that the available works on Jewish law were unsatisfactory, he formulated the whole field of Jewish law into a code which contained four subdivisions.

Volume I, which he designated as Oraḥ Ḥayyim, in 697 chapters sets forth the laws dealing with daily duties of Jews and the legislation pertaining to blessings, prayers, holidays, fasts, and the Sabbath day.

Volume II, Yoreh De'ah, contains 408 chapters which deal with legal decisions pertaining to ritual law. In the purview of ritual law are such subjects as the dietary laws, mourning for the dead and their preparation for burial, organic deficiencies in animals which prohibit them for human consumption, laws on usury, the menstrual cycle, and many other topics.

Volume III, Even ha-Ezer, deals with laws involving the legal relationships between men and women, such as marriage and divorce, and contains 178 chapters.

Volume IV, Ḥoshen Mishpat, is a corpus on all matters pertaining to civil law.

The printed edition of the Tur, Yoreh De'ah, which is available in the Bension Collection is from the late fifteenth century. The first part of the work is missing and it commences in the midst of chapter fifteen. Chapter sixteen is designated by the letters "Yud" and "Vav." The volume concludes with chapter 298, the Law of Orlah. In some editions the Law of Orlah is recorded under chapter 294. This discrepancy can be explained by the fact that the Spanish editions of the Tur, Yoreh De'ah, follow one Ms. tradition while the Ashkenazi tradition follows a different Ms. text which was used by the Jewish printers in Italy, as may be noted when one examines the Soncino edition of 1490.

The size of a page is 30 x 21.5 cm. No pagination is given. There are thirty-six lines to a page with two columns to each folio. While the work is sewn together the book's covers are missing. No colophon is available and both the beginning pages and those at the end of the book are missing. The publisher used Sephardi Mashait type except at the beginning of new chapters and paragraphs when Sephardi Square type is used. This type differs from that in the Guadalajara edition of 1482 by the publisher Solomon ibn Al-Kabiz, and from that of Eliezer Atlantansi's Ixar edition of 1487. While the latter was produced in long lines rather than double columns, it conforms in all other respects with the layout of the text in the Bension Collection edition. The source of both works appears to be the same Ms. Unlike the Italian editions, which contain 403 chapters, the Sephardic Text contains 408 chapters.

A first edition of the Sefer Abudarham, Lisbon, 1489.

Pr. 297

R. David b. Joseph Abudarham was a Spanish rabbinic author of the early fourteenth century who was concerned about the lack of understanding, by his co-religionists, of prayer, it origins, and its structure. He therefore wrote his commentary on Jewish liturgy which traced the origin of prayer to its Talmudic and Gaonic sources. He explained ritual procedures and elaborated on the meaning of various prayers. His works cited the following authorities who wrote on the subject of prayer, such as the author of the Manhig, R. Abraham ben Nathan ha-Yarḥi of Lunel, R. Asher ben Yeḥiel, and the latter's son R. Jacob, author of the Ṭurim, who was contemporaneous to R. David, among other authorities.

R. David was also perceptive in his discernment of the various traditions that were perpetuated by different communities. The Sefer Abudarham was completed in Seville in 1340. Appended to the work were a section explaining the various benedictions, calendrical tables, and a commentary on the Passover Haggadah. The first edition was published in Lisbon in 1489. The edition in the Bension Collection is a copy of the first edition, and an incunable. Another copy was recently acquired for the Jacob M. Lowy Collection in the National Library, Ottawa. The work is preserved almost in its entirety. Each page measures 29.5 cm in length and 19.5 cm in width. No pagination is given. The author's Introduction and the first two sections designated as ha-Sha'ar ha-Rishon and ha-Sha'ar ha-Sheni are missing. These sections discuss the time of the performance of the Sh'ma and the institution of prayer, respectively.

The first few pages of the Sha'ar ha-Shlishi, which deals with the laws concerning blessings recited upon the performance of commandments, are also deleted. At the conclusion of the book, Tables of Calculations are given.

This is the second book printed in Lisbon; an edition of Nahmanides' Biblical Commentary preceded it by a few months.

A manuscript volume of Samuel Ibn Tibbon's Hebrew translation of Maimonides' "Guide of the Perplexed," known as Moreh Nevukhim

Ms. 298

Maimonides, the luminary of Jewish scholarship during the twelfth century, is represented in the Bension Collection by two of his works. His halakhic work is represented by fragments of his Commentary to the Mishnah [cf. *Ms.295*]. Moses b. Maimon as philosopher is represented by his magnum opus which was originally written in Arabic as Dalalat al-Ha'rin, "Guide of the Perplexed." It appears in the Bension Collection in the Hebrew translation of Samuel Ibn Tibbon entitled "Moreh Nevukhim." The fact that Maimonides prepared most of his major works in Arabic is indicative of the familiarity that Jews had with that language in the twelfth century, apart from the fact that Maimonides' literary activity was produced in Islamic lands, namely, Spain, North Africa, and Egypt.

Moses ben Maimon, after studying Aristotelian philosophy, felt his Jewish faith, which is based on God's revelation of Himself to man, confronted by the challenge of knowledge, which is based on human reasoning. Moses Maimonides tried to meet the challenge by seeking ways of achieving a reconciliation between the systems of faith and reason. Similar efforts at reconciliation were attempted by Muslim theologian-philosophers and by Christian scholastics who followed Maimonides, such as Thomas Aquinas, who is known to have been influenced by him.

Maimonides devoted portions of the "Guide" to presenting a philosophic interpretation of scripture, defining terms related to God in scripture, and discussing the problems of God's unity and Divine attributes, the proof of God's existence, unity and incorporeality; theories on creation, the nature of prophecy, evil, and Divine Providence; and finally a substantial section discussing the reasons for the biblical commandments. While Maimonides made a valiant effort to achieve the sought-after reconciliation between religion and philosophy he paid a price for engaging in that pursuit. He was seduced by the Aristotelian view of ethics which placed the subject in a subordinate role. For Maimonides, as for Aristotle, morality is only the third perfection, while the dianoetic virtues are for them the fourth and highest perfection. Thus does Maimonides state in the concluding chapter of the "Guide," III:54, "The third type of perfection is more closely connected with man himself . . . It includes moral perfection, the highest degree of excellency in man's character. Most of the precepts aim at producing this perfection; but even this kind is only a preparation for another perfection . . . The fourth kind of perfection is the true perfection of man; the possession of the highest intellectual faculties; the possession of such notions which lead to true metaphysical opinions as regards God."

Fortunately, among the post-Maimonidean philosophers of the thirteenth century, Shem Tob ibn Palqera refused to accept Maimonides' view on ethics even though he defended the latter's approach, which sought to achieve a reconciliation of revelation with reason. After all, the God of biblical tradition revealed Himself as the activator of mercy and grace, and not as the detached Mind thinking thoughts. Thus Palqera, who was primarily an ethical and a pedagogic philosopher in the authentic Judaic tradition, would not permit himself to be seduced by Aristotelianism on this vital point. Even Maimonides felt the tension of the biblical ethical protest pitted against sterile intellectualism when he stated, (Mishneh Torah, hilkhot De'ot, 5:1), "The scholar must be recognizable by his activities."

The manuscript volume of the Moreh contains one hundred and fifty pages and three hundred folios, two columns to a page and thirty lines to each column, which are written on vellum in Provençal-Sephardic Mashait script, of pre-expulsion Spain. The largest complete page measures 29.8 x 23.5 cm. However, since the work was written on vellum even the measurements of complete pages vary. Where the pages are not torn as a result of wear or decay, they have been cut away to be utilized as writing material. Many pages were cut almost to the bottom line or margin of the text. No pagination is given. The work commences with Samuel ibn Tibbon's Thesaurus of Philosophic Terms which consists of twenty pages. The first four introductory pages to ibn Tibbon's Thesaurus are missing, as well as the following sections of the alphabetical terms: from the term "Kamut" at the end of letter "Khaf" to the term "Kotev" in the section of the letter "Koof." The remaining terms classified under the letters "Raish," "Shin," and "Tof" are complete.

The aforementioned text concludes with a new paragraph consisting of four lines which are written in Maaravic Cursive script wherein the following is stated:

"I composed this section [The Thesaurus] on a ship which was located four miles from the coast of Al-Akliba and a distance of one and one-half day's travel from Tunis, on my journey from Alexandria [Egypt], in the month of Tammuz, in the year 4973 from creation [1213], may the Almighty return our group in peace to our city and our homes."

We often dismiss the translator as merely the secondhand instrument of the author of the original text. This attitude towards translators, especially one of the caliber of Samuel ibn Tibbon, must be dispelled. After Maimonides had composed the "Moreh" in Arabic, R. Jonathan ha-Kohen of Lunel approached Samuel ibn Tibbon asking him to render a service to the scholars of the Provence by translating the "Moreh" into Hebrew. Although Samuel possessed excellent credentials as a translator (he was the son and student of the master translator Judah ibn Tibbon) he still approached the task of translating Maimonides' "Moreh" with trepidation. The Hebrew language had to be recast to express philosophical terms which were the products of a culture that was foreign to medieval Judaism until that time. Not only the translator but the Hebrew language was put to a severe test.

Samuel ibn Tibbon maintained personal communication with Maimonides so that the author could clarify his intended meaning for the benefit of the translator. Finally, Samuel journeyed to Egypt to receive Maimonides personal confirmation of his work. Fourteen days before the demise of Maimonides, on November 30, 1204, the translation was completed at Arles. A cataclysmic revolution commenced as ibn Tibbon's translated work was rapidly disseminated. It

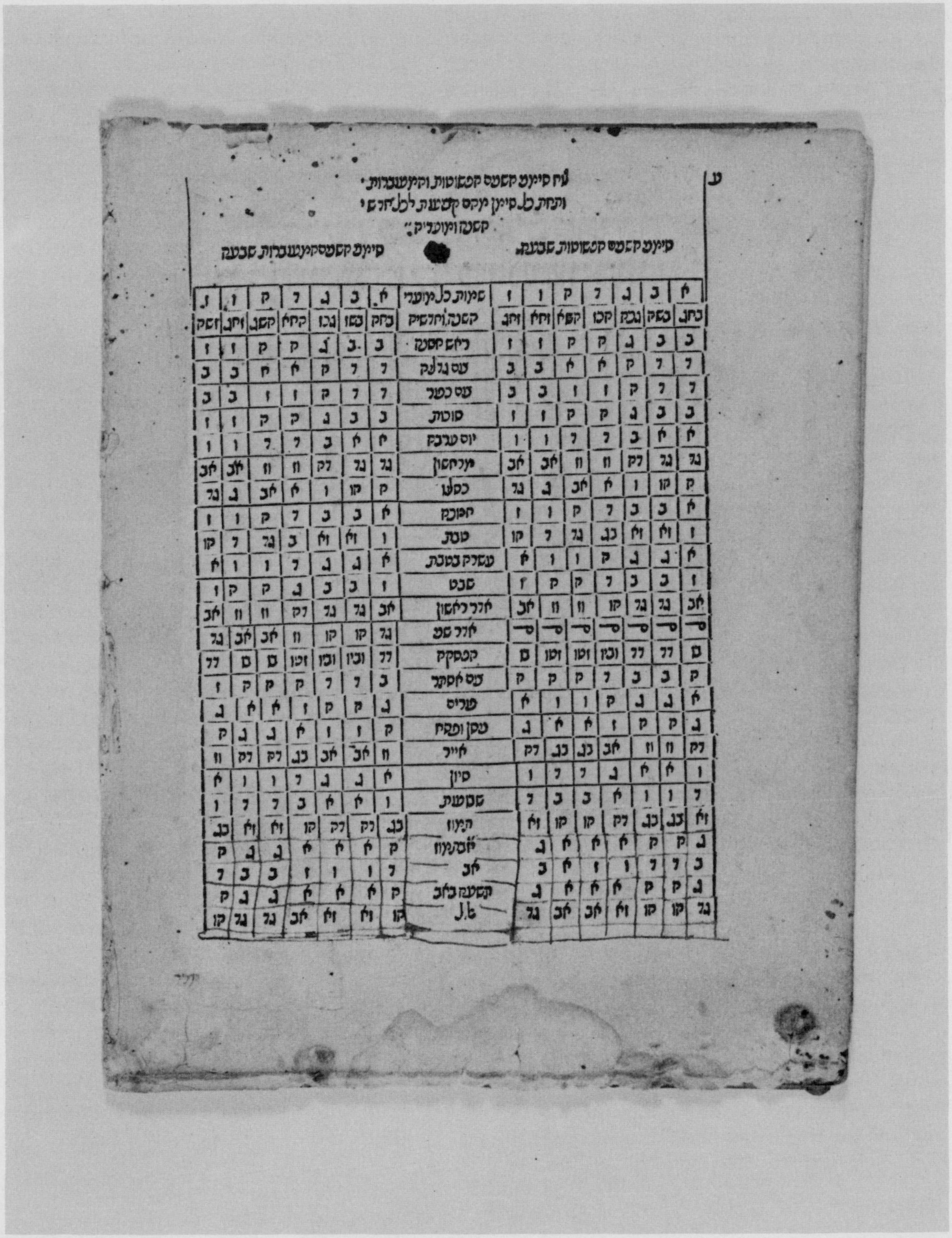

Pr. 297
From the second book ever printed in Lisbon, in 1489, the Sefer Abudarham

became an instant best-seller as it served as fuel for the conflagration which burst out between traditional conservatives and those who were adherents of a liberal intellectualist tradition in the Jewish and, subsequently, the Christian faith systems. The Dominicans officially consigned the "Moreh" to the flames at Paris. Thereafter, the Dominican Thomas Aquinas enhanced the value of the "Moreh" in scholastic circles. While Samuel ibn Tibbon was engaged in his meticulous effort to produce a precise translation, Judah Al-Harizi was urged to offer *his* Hebrew translation of the "Moreh." The latter's work was not as technical an effort as was that of ibn Tibbon.

It may be that Samuel ibn Tibbon realized that his more technical language might be an obstacle to the serious student who was unfamiliar with the nuances of philosophical Hebrew terminology that he had devised, so he attempted to remedy the situation by offering a Thesaurus of Philosophical terms as an aid to the reader. Thus, we are informed in his concluding paragraph, after the Thesaurus, that he completed it in the year 1213.

We noted above that the script of the concluding paragraph to the Thesaurus was written in Maaravic Cursive script while the main body of the text before and after this paragraph, which serves as a colophon to the Thesaurus, was written in Provençal-Sephardic Mashait script. This oddity can be explained in the following manner. We often use a cursive script and suddenly we switch to a square script. This same technique was practiced by the copyist. Before the expulsion from Spain there was no clear distinction in the writing style between those Sephardic Jews who lived on either side of the Strait of Gibraltar and Provençal Jewry. When subsequently the cultural connection was severed the Jews indigenous to each geographic location developed their own peculiar writing styles. One could be tempted to speculate that since ibn Tibbon was from the Provence, he might have been the copyist of the manuscript, especially since he states in the concluding paragraph to the Thesaurus, "I composed this section," instead of the usual "Samuel ibn Tibbon said." Furthermore, why would the copyist change the nature of the script unless he was, indeed, Samuel ibn Tibbon, who desired to personalize the text? If we accept this theory then this manuscript would have to be dated as early as 1213. However, since this is improbable, we must at least conclude that this manuscript dates from the period of pre-expulsion Spain. However, the mystery concerning the change of script remains.

Samuel ibn Tibbon's preface to the work which follows the problematic four lines is now written by the copyist in the same script with which he began the Thesaurus of Philosophical Terms. This preface is given almost in its entirety with only the last few lines missing. The last part of Maimonides' Introduction to the Moreh, in Hebrew translation, is also available on two pages. The next section commences with almost the entire first part of the Moreh, chapters 1 to 76. Chapters 14, 15, 16 of Part One are missing in their entirety, and half of chapter 46. While most of the pages are intact and they are sewn together, some pages have been severely torn. At the end of chapter thirty of the First Part, a note is given by the copyist which does not appear in printed editions of the Moreh. It consists of twelve lines which were written in a similar but smaller size script than that which is available in the main body of the text. This note appears in the main body of the text, not in the margin. The following chapters are missing in Part Two of the Moreh—chapters 8, 9, and 10; otherwise Part Two is complete. Sections of chapters 21, 24, and 50, and chapters 52, 53, and 54 in their entirety, are missing from Part Three. Variants are noted throughout the text when it is compared with the printed edition. No colophon other than the paragraph after the Thesaurus is available. While many of the pages are bound together, other pages are severed from the text.

An early printed edition of the homiletic work called Menorat ha-Ma'or

Pr. 299

R. Isaac Aboab was a noted rabbinic author and preacher who lived towards the end of the fourteenth century. His major literary achievement was the Menorat ha-Ma'ôr, which is to this day among the most popular ethico-Aggadic works of Judaism. This work has undergone more than seventy editions, with the first edition published in Constantinople in 1514 and the latest Hebrew edition published in Jerusalem in 1961. The Menorat ha-Ma'or was subsequently translated into Spanish, Ladino, Yiddish, and German. Preachers and study groups in synagogues found this work to be an indispensable source of aggadic material and a basic text for ethical instruction.

The author sought to restore Aggada to its rightful place as an essential part of rabbinic tradition. Until his own time only the legal material of the Talmudic tradition, known as Halakha, was deemed a necessary object of study for Jewish survival. Thus, it was his desire to compose the kind of structured work for Aggada which would oblige scholars to notice its intrinsic value. R. Isaac utilized the symbol of the seven-branched candlestick of the biblical Tabernacle as the central image of his work, which in English translation means "Candlestick of Light."

R. Isaac Aboab provided a special service to scholars by making available to them passages from aggadic works which are no longer extant and by citing from variants of Talmudic and Midrashic texts which were utilized in the Spanish-North African schools and which differed from those texts used by scholars of the Franco-German tradition. R. Isaac Aboab was eclectic in his use of sources. He utilized texts from the rational philosophic tradition as well as from the halakhic and mystical traditions. Among the authors from whose works he quoted we have Alfasi, Rashi, the Tosafists, Abraham ibn Ezra, Maimonides, Abraham ibn David, Jacob Anatoli, Nahmanides, Solomon ibn Adret, Abudarham Baḥya's Ḥovot ha-Levavot, Joseph Gikatilla's Sha'arei Orah, Asher b. Yeḥiel, and Jacob b. Asher's Tur. Aboab's use of sources belies his own world view which appears to have been syncretic, since he co-mingles Kabbalistic views with philosophic notions. Religious practices were also explained in his moralistic work.

The Menorat ha-Ma'or in the Bension Collection is a complete printed volume of the 1623 Venice edition.

A volume of the printed edition of the biblical commentary Ẓuf Devash

Pr. 300

The volume known as Ẓuf Devash is a compilation of four works of biblical commentary by R. Vidal II Ha-Ṣarfati (1631-1703) of Fez, the son of R. Isaac Ha-Ṣarfati and the grandson of Vidal I Ha-Ṣarfati. [The Encyclopaedia Judaica, 14:879, Jerusalem 1973, is in error when it ascribes the authorship of Ẓuf Devash to Vidal I.] The first work, Ẓuf Devash, is a commentary on the Pentateuch. It appears on pages 1 to 19. The second work which appears on pages 19 to 32 is entitled Megilat Setarim, a commentary on the Scroll of Esther. The third work is Ha-Ẓa'at Rut, a commentary on the Scroll of Ruth, which is found on pages 32 to 42. A fourth work by R. Vidal II Ha-Ṣarfati, called Ozar Neḥmad, a commentary on the Psalms, is found on pages 42 to 60.

Another work which appears at the end of this volume was composed by R. Aaron Ṣarfati, a grandson of the author R. Vidal II Ha-Ṣarfati. The title of the work is Misgav ha-Imahot, a commentary on Eshet Ḥa'Yil, the Woman of Valor, which is found on pages 60 to 65. Another grandson of R. Vidal II, who was a noted scholar, was R. Samuel Ha-Ṣarfati, author of the work Sefer Nimukei Shmuel.

The manuscript of the work Ẓuf Devash which was published in Amsterdam in the year 1718, was brought to that city by R. Isaac b. R. Joseph Bueno De Mosquita. He came to Amsterdam which was a center of scholarship to pursue his studies. This information is made available in the colophon to the work. The publisher was R. Solomon b. Joseph Kohen-Ẓedek Proops. The work was published two columns to a folio and contains sixty-five pages.

Ms. 301 A manuscript fragment of Naḥmanides' biblical commentary on the Decalogue

R. Moses b. Maḥman (1194-1270), who was also known as the Ramban, was born in Gerona in the province of Catalonia, Spain where he maintained an academy. R. Moses was proficient in many scholarly fields but his special renown was established in the fields of Kabbala, biblical exegesis, and in Jewish law. R. Moses was acknowledged as the leading halakhic authority of his age, and one of his most outstanding students was R. Solomon ibn Adret of Barcelona [cf. *Ms.293*].

Naḥmanides is the latinized form of R. Moses' name. He composed his biblical commentary when he was advanced in years. While most of the work was completed in Spain, the finishing touches were applied after R. Moses b. Naḥman arrived in the Holy Land, in 1263. The author fled to the Holy Land as the result of a disputation he had with the apostate Pablo Christiani, over whom he was victorious. The Dominicans, who initiated the disputation, were disappointed with the outcome especially since the victor's views were subsequently recorded at the request of the Bishop of Gerona. The Dominicans requested that Pope Clement IV should intervene and request that Naḥmanides be punished for his calumny against the Church. It was at this point that Naḥmanides fled from Spain.

The manuscript fragment was written in Sephardic Mashait script in pre-expulsion Spain. It is considerably damaged and worm-eaten. The commentary that is extant gives an exposition on the last words of Deuteronomy 4:25—5:5. The fragment, which bears writing on both sides, measures 25.5 x 17.3 cm.

Ms. 302 A Ms. fragment of a philosophic text

This one-page fragment appears to be a copy of a philosophic text by Ḥasdai Crescas from his "Or Adonai." Each folio contains twenty-four lines and the size of the fragment is 27 x 15 cm. The copyist wrote in Sephardic Mashait script of the fifteenth century. In this fragment the author dwells upon the nature of the leader and the effects that he has upon those whom he governs. The Hebrew term "Munhagim" which appears to be peculiar to Crescas' style is noted in the text.

Ms. 303 Manuscript fragments of a Talmudic text

Two manuscript fragments of a Talmudic text which were composed in a beautiful Sephardic Mashait script, *c.* late fourteenth century, are available in the Bension Collection. The pages measure 35.9 x 12 cm with thirty-five lines to a page. The text appears on two pages, folios a and b and it is quite worm-eaten. The subject that is recorded in these texts corresponds to the material that is under discussion in the Babylonian Tractate, Yeḇamot, pages 36b to 38a. However, these fragments do not just contain Talmudic texts. The author intersperses the views of medieval commentators such as R. Zeraḥiah Halevi, Rabbenu Tam, Rashi, and Rav Alfasi, on parallel texts to the topics that are under discussion.

Among the topics discussed in these fragments is the case of a woman awaiting levirate marriage who inherited property; both the schools of Shammai and Hillel agree that she may sell it or give it away and the action will be regarded as valid. However, if she passes away, what will be done with her marriage contract [Ketubbah] and other properties that come and go with her [designated Nikhsei Melog]? In this case the School of Shammai maintains that the heirs of the deceased's husband share in her estate together with her father's heirs. The School of Hillel maintains that her property designated as "Ẓon barzel," the wife's property which upon her death or divorce the husband must restore entirely, falls equally to the first husband's heirs and the father's heirs; while the Ketubbah falls to the first husband's heirs, and the property that comes in and goes out with her belongs to the father's heirs. The views of Amoraic authorities

Ms. 301
A manuscript fragment of Nahmanides' Biblical Commentary on the Decalogue

such as Bar Kappara and R. Yoḥanan are noted as they are recorded in parallel texts in the Tractate Bava Batra. Finally, the decisions of medieval authors called Rîshônim are given.

Ms. 304 **Manuscript collections of liturgical poems and a maḥzor from Morocco**

It can be stated that the field of liturgical poetry is a preoccupation of Moroccan Jews of all ages. Unlike the Ashkenazi Jew who has little occasion to innovate or to alter the program of the daily, Sabbath, or Holiday services, the Sephardi, who draws from a vast storehouse of liturgy, did not give up his creativity in this field in the early sixteenth century. Rather, Moroccan Jewish masters of liturgical poetry continued to compose new poems for sad and joyous occasions as well as for the prayer services throughout the synagogue calendar. On the occasion of my marriage in 1969, in the town of Tivon, in Israel, the leader of the Sephardi congregation of Moroccan Jews signalled a halt to the routine of the regular Sabbath service as he sang songs of joy for the wedding occasion. These beautiful religious compositions lasted for more than a half-hour before the regular service routine was resumed.

Among the most celebrated authors of liturgical literature noted in the several collections of the first section of this manuscript, the following are mentioned; Solomon Ḥaluah, David b. Aaron b. Ḥasin, Shalom Ẓur, Solomon ibn Gabirol, Israel Najara, Jacob Ibn Ẓur, Isaac ibn Ḥaluah, Moses b. Ezra, Abraham ibn Ezra, Mîmun b. Solomon, Jacob Adhan, and Moses b. Jacob Adhan. Several poems in these collections are unpublished and have not heretofore been mentioned in liturgical reference works. The complete manuscript text, which is bound together with a prayer book, consists of two sections. The first section contains ninety-seven pages of collections of liturgical poems and it appears before the text of the printed edition of the prayer book. The poems are written on sides a and b and the size of the pages in this section vary. Some pages were measured at 14.5 x 10.5 cm while others measured 15.8 x 10 cm. The second section, which appears after the conclusion of the printed edition of the prayer book, consists of forty-seven pages and contains Penitential prayers known as Seliḥot, which are recited before the High Holy Days, and a Maḥzor for Rosh Hashanah. The writing appears on folios a and b of each page which measures 16.1 x 11 cm. The manuscript dates from the late eighteenth century. This work originated in Morocco and the signature of Abraham ibn Adhan is written on the inside cover of the book. Most of the prayers are written in Maaravic Mashait script. One collection is written in Maaravic Square script.

The types of liturgical compositions are Piyyutim, Pizmonim, and Bakashot. Piyyut is the name applied to liturgical poetry which is usually composed for recital at the synagogue service. Pizmon is a hymnal poem which concludes with a refrain after each verse. It is sung by the reader and repeated by the congregants. Bakashah is a prayerful petition representing the relationship between God and the people of Israel. The Angel of Mercy, Throne of Glory, and Torah are called upon to intercede for Israel. A detailed analysis of the contents of this manuscript follows.

The first page of the manuscript is part of an incomplete liturgical piece but what is available in the acrostic indicates that the author was R. Solomon Ḥaluah. The letters of the acrostic are given twice; part of the page is torn away. The Piyyut on the other side of the page (1b) was also composed by R. Solomon Ḥaluah according to the acrostic. The first stanza is as follows:

> "Ashir Shirah Ne'emanah, Le-Ẓur; dar Me'onah, Yom Zeh Al Siyyum Mishnah, Ba-Kol Shemurah Mefo'arah Tehorah Barah, Ev'en Yekarah."

In the preface to a poem given on this page it is reported by the author, R. Solomon Ḥaluah, that he composed this piece in honor of the scholars R. Yekutiel Berdugo, his sons and sons-in-law, and in honor of R. Solomon Toledano. The work commences with the words, "Or ha-Ne'erav, Mizraḥ Ma'arav. . . ." A poem on the exalted nature of the Almighty, which follows on pages 3a to 4a was also composed by R. Solomon Ḥaluah.

R. Solomon Haluah composed a poem on the occasion of his completion of the study of the

Tractate Ketubbot, which appears on page 5a. He also composed a poem (page 5b) which was based on the following text from the first chapter of the Tractate Eruvin, "Kol Davar Dibbur Al Ofano Ta'amo Ve-Nimuko Emo."

On page 6a a new series of supplicatory prayers are introduced under the title Bakashah. The first part of the first prayer is missing. The second prayer under this title was composed by David b. Aaron b. Ḥasin according to the acrostic. [See Davidson, Thesaurus of Medieval Hebrew Poetry, Vol. I, 1970, P. 115, No. 2435.] This prayer concludes on the bottom of page 7a. It may be that the copyist did not know that the authorship of this text was by Ḥasin, since he made no effort to reveal the acrostic. The Bakashah at the top of page 7b, "Shima Tefilatee ha-Shem Ve-Shavati ha-Azayna..." was attributed by scholars to one called Isaac. The final prayer, called Bakashah in this section, which commences at the bottom of page 7b–8b, is "Ereh Yomi U-Mitraḥek Ve-Hapoalim Aẓaylim..."

The next section, commencing in the middle of page 8b, begins a series of prayers introduced by the word Piyyut. They are given below.

Page	*Prayer*	*Author*
8b	Piyyut—"Sha'ar Asher Nisgar..."	Solomon ibn Gabirol
8b–9a	Piyyut—"Ya'alat Ohavim Simḥi Va-roni..."	
9a	Piyyut—"Shulamit be-shir be-shir yasfah..."	
9a–9b	Piyyut—"Ahuvai Ke-Ẓevi U-Mesanai Ke-Aryeh..."	
	This text is not noted in Davidson's Thesaurus.	
9b	Piyyut—"El Melekh Ne'eman be-Mo'adekha..."	
9b–10a	Piyyut—"Man Ve-Nofet Tee-Tof Sefat Kallah..."	
10a	Piyyut—"Ya'alem She-b'hee Ne'elam Zemani..."	Israel Najara
10a–10b	Piyyut—"Yi-hee-yu Ka-moẓ Ovday Chemosh..."	Israel Najara
10b–11a	Piyyut—"Esa Ainai El he-Harim May-Ayin Yavo Ezri May-Adir Adirim..."	
11a–11b	Piyyut—"Le-Akarah Lo Yalada El Elyon Go'el Tavi..."	
11b–12a	Piyyut—"Ya'uf Ḥalomi Ve-Yoded Ḥezyoni..."	Israel Najara
12a	Piyyut—"Le-Kha Ẓur Geoni Kaltah Ruḥi..."	Israel Najara
12a–12b	Piyyut—"Yonati Mah La-Kh Nodedet Me-Ken..."	Israel Najara
	At this point in the text some pages are missing. What we will call page 13a commences in the middle of a prayer. The next prayer will now be described.	
13a	Piyyut—"Yafu Dodai'ikh Ne'imah Ayuma Ke-Nidgalot..."	Israel Najara
13a–13b	Piyyut—"Eshkol ha-Kofer Dodi, Sharbit ha-Zahav..."	
	This poem which is not noted in Davidson's Thesaurus, it would seem, concludes this section of liturgical poetry. However, pages 14a and b appear to be reversed. What in fact did occur was that page 14a which commences the new section with an artfully framed design surrounding the first prayer was to be treated as a title page and the second side was left blank. Subsequently, a copyist took advantage of	

Page	Prayer	Author
	this space and wrote a prayer on it. This new section will now be described.	
14a, 15a & 15b	Piyyut—"Kol Aḥainu b'nei Britainu ha'azinu . . ."	Jacob [Ibn Ẓur]
14b	Piyyut—"Yoẓri Ḥalati ha-El Meitim Meḥayah . . ." This poem is not noted in Davidson's Thesaurus.	Isaac ibn Ḥaluah
15b	Piyyut—"Dirshu Shmee Hamonai, Tamid Ve-Lee Ḥeeku . . ."	Moses b. Ezra
16a	Piyyut—"Segulati Ve-Or Ainai Ve-ḥai Olam Asher Heḥeyeh . . ." This prayer is treated in two separate texts while Davidson describes them as stanzas which are part of the same text in some editions.	
Thus 16a & b	Piyyut—"Elohim Ekra'ah Elyon Shmekha Ki Kakh Teshukati . . ." is part of the previous composition in some editions.	
16b	Piyyut—"Yehidah he-Ḥokhmah, Yefeh Nava Mah Lakh Homeeyah . . ." This text, which is attributed to one called Judah, appears with variants from that which is noted in the Thesaurus, "Yud," No. 2625.	
16b–17a	Piyyut—"Eshalah Ge'ulah May-Elohay Avi, Ani Lo Oḥilah . . .	Aaron is given as the author.
17a	Piyyut—"Sha'ar Petaḥ Dodi Kumah, Petaḥ Sha'ar Ki Nivhalah . . .	Solomon ibn Gabirol
17a	Piyyut—"Yah Lakha Nafshi, Kalta Laḥazot Yekarkha . . ." This prayer is incomplete because the next page appears to be missing. Page 17b is a Tabula rasa.	
18a	Piyyut—"Shiru be-Shirah Alai Torah, ha-Durah Ve-Yekarah . . ." This text is not noted in Davidson's Thesaurus.	
18a	Piyyut—"Hag Ve-Shabbat Ke-Ofarim Teumi Raya Ẓiviiya . . ." This text is not noted in Davidson's Thesaurus.	
18b	Piyyut—"be-peh Azamrah Zimrai Araivim . . ." This text varies little from Davidson's Thesaurus, "Beit," No. 1235.	Jacob Ibn Ẓur
18b	Piyyut—"Ve-hayshiv Kohanaynu Le-Dvir Ve-Ulam, U-Ven Levi Al Dukhano . . ." This text does not appear in the Thesaurus.	
19a–20a	Piyyut—"Im Amarti Asaprah be-Leshani Ve-Nifleotekha . . ." The acrostic spells out David Ḥazak.	
20a	Piyyut—"El Ḥai Bera'ani Ve-Amar Ḥai Ani Ki Lo Yirani . . ."	Abraham ibn Ezra
20a	Piyyut—"Ḥai Ani Go'el Avi Lakham, Aaleh Etkhem, Me-Kur Galut . . ." This text does not appear in Davidson's Thesaurus.	
20b	Piyyut—"Dai Lemayvin Ki Zeh Helko Be'elohav . . ." This text is not noted in the Thesaurus.	

Page	Prayer	Author
20b–21a	Piyyut—"Yonah Domi Umlalekhem, Rashim Kolam ha-Shay . . ." This text does not appear in the Thesaurus.	
21a	Piyyut—"Yedidi Mivḥar Hamonai Amod Tokh Kehal Emunai . . ."	Jacob [Ibn Ẓur]
21a–21b	Piyyut—"Amru be-Mora B'nai El Ḥai Nora Barukh ha-Makom . . ."	
21b	Piyyut—"Torat Emet Nattan Lanu Barukh Asher Baḥar Banu . . ."	
22a	The copyist commences this page stating, "I will begin to write Pizmonim of Rosh Hashanah with the help of God."	
22a–23b	Pizmon—"Barukh Asher Yaẓar Sheḥakim Va-Arakim B'asarah Ma'amarot . . ." This Pizmon was composed for the preliminary prayers called Pesukei d'Zimra.	
23b–24a	Pizmon—"Yom be-Dinekha Eh-Ehmod Elohay Olam Rom Ba-Mishpat . . ." This text is a variation of Thesaurus, "Yud," No. 1634 which was composed by David ibn Bakudah as a Selihaḥ for Rosh Hashanah.	
24a–24b	Pizmon—"Yah Zuri Or Nayri ha-Nisa Ve-Hane'elam . . ." This was composed by one called Isaac as a Pizmon for the prayer "Barukh She'amar."	
24b	Piyyut, for the prayer "Yiru Ainaynu." "El Kadosh be-Ẓedakah Nikdash be-Kehal Am Arome-menu . . ." composed by "Ani David Ḥazak."	
25a	Piyyut—"Oz Ga'avati, Ha'er et Panekha U-Phedei Et Amkha Meyad ben ha-Amah . . ." This text is not noted in the Thesaurus.	
25a–25b	Piyyut—"Be-Shir Aniya Golah, El Ram Al Kol Na'alah . . ." This text is not noted in the Thesaurus.	
25b–26a	Piyyut—"Ahuvi Ẓur Misgabi, Amod Yakar Ahuvi Maḥmad . . ." This text is not recorded in the Thesaurus.	
26a–27a	Piyyut—"Kumah Dodi El Haikhalei Shen . . ."	Israel Najara
27a–27b	Bakashah—"El beit El Henay Kamti Lo Aiḥarti, Eshmerah Mishmarti . . ." This supplicatory prayer was composed by Mîṃun b. Solomon.	
27b	Bakashah—"Yedid Nafshi Gam Ahuvi, Ainekha Me'meni Al Ta'alim . . ." While this text is not noted in the Thesaurus, a variation on the opening theme was composed by Jacob Adhan.	
28a	Bakashah—"Kum Yeḥidati Le-hallel El Be-yom Shabbat Menuḥah Fiẓḥi Shirim Temallel . . ." Only one stanza is presented.	
28a	Piyyut—"Yishtabaḥ Shimkha Malkeinu,	

Page	Prayer	Author
	ha-El ha-Gadol ha-Nora, Ki Atah hu Elo-haynu, Melekh Nezar be-Gevurah . . ." This is not noted in the Thesaurus.	

This section of liturgical poems concludes on page 28a. A new series containing four Piyyutim and two Bakashot are contained on pages 29a–32b.

Page	Prayer	Author
29a	Piyyut—"Im Kami le-ḥaradati Alai Nosdu Yahad henai El Yeshuati . . ." The name Jacob appears in the acrostic.	
29b	Contains a list of the following names: Mîmun ibn Harous, Jacob ibn Aluj, David Amsili, Mardukh Asudri, Yaḥya ibn Khalfon, and Joseph ibn Abu. Below is a second longer list with the following names: Mîmun ibn Harous, Jacob ibn Aluz, David Amsili, Mardukh Asudri, Yaḥya ibn Khalfon, Joseph ibn Abu, Jacob Alfasi, Makhlouf ibn Yinaḥ, Aaron ibn Abu, David ibn Azidi, Abraham Alfasi, Abraham Waknin, Makhlouf ibn Abu, Joseph Benno, Mas'ūd Adhan, Isaac ibn Harous, and Judah ibn Harous.	
30a–b	"Meshiah ben David Malkenu, Bimhayrah Yavo Be-Yamaynu." The acrostic spells "Ani David ben Aaron Ḥazak," who is the composer of	David Hasin

Page	Prayer	Author
	these verses.	
31b	Bakashah—"Yad Ẓor ha-Tam Yoshev Kedem Ramah Ateret Tiferet." The acrostic is Israel [Najara].	
31b–32a	Bakashah—"Yonah Mini Kol me-Bekhi Ani Oshia Banekha." The author is Jacob Ibn Ẓur.	
32a	Piyyut—"Anah Yah Hodi Braḥ Memehni El Ram." Isaac is noted to be the author.	
32a–32b	Piyyut—"Im Kami Alu Alai, Adon-Al Maygin Ba'adi." This Piyyut was composed by David ibn Ḥasin whose name appears in the acrostic as "Ani David ben Ḥasin."	
33a–34a	"Ḥasdei Adon-ai Azkir Tehilot Adon-ai Ke-Al Kol Asher Gemalanu." No authorship is noted.	
34b	Piyyut—"Meedat Yamai U-Ẓeva Shanai Oḥil Som Avim rekhuvo." Composed by one who is known as Moses, which also agrees with the acrostic.	
35a–35b	Piyyut—"Borkhu Le-El be-Shirah, Borkhu Al ha-Sefirah." This text was composed by one called Shemayah, whose name also appears in the acrostic.	
35b–36a	Piyyut—"Yom La-yabashah Nehefkhu Mezulim Shirah Ḥadashah Shibḥu Ge-ulim." This text was	

Page	Prayer
	composed by Judah Halevi.
36b–37a	Piyyut—This particular text appears to be unpublished and not mentioned in reference works. The author's name appears in the acrostic and is noted at the beginning of the text as Judah.
37a–37b	Piyyut—"Anokhi Asiah be-lev Sas Ve-Sameah." This text was composed by David Ḥasin and "Ani David Ḥazak" appears in the acrostic.
37b–38a	Piyyut—"Avarekh Et Shem ha-El ha-Godol Ve-ha-Nora." This poem was recited at the commencement of the Havdalah ceremony. It was composed by one called Joseph, whose name appears in the acrostic.
38a–38b	Piyyut—"Yekabeẓ El Eder Ẓono Ke-Me'az Be'ereẓ Ẓevi." This poem is recited after Havdalah and it was composed by Jacob Ibn Ẓur. The name Jacob appears in the acrostic.
38b–39a	Piyyut—"Eftaḥ pee be-Shir Ve-Mizmor U-reshut Me-El Eshalah Le-Khevod Dodi Ẓror ha-Mor." This poem was composed by Moses b. Jacob [Adhan]. The last part of the text is missing but the name Moses does appear in the acrostic.

More collections of Piyyutim follow and some of them which are repeated were noted in the two aforementioned collections that were analyzed.

The next collection is written in a beautiful and clear Maaravic Square script. These poems appear from pages 40a to 47a. The Piyyutim were composed by Solomon Ḥaluah and David b. Ḥasin. David b. Aaron [Ḥasin]'s poem Mashiaḥ, mentioned in the previous collection, appears again; also a poem by Shalom [Ẓur], a Piyyut for evening, and a Piyyut by David b. Aaron Ḥasin. The last Piyyut in this collection was composed by Solomon Ḥaluah on the occasion of the performance of the Mitzvah of Milah.

47b–48b	A Piyyut is offered which belongs to a new collection but it is incomplete and written in Maaravic Mashait script. Several pages are missing thereafter.
49a–60a	This section, designated Tikkun Ḥaẓot, commences with elegies called Kinot.
60a–79b	Midrash Ha-Ne'elam on Aikha [Lamentations] and followed on pages 70b to 79b by Parshat Lekh Lekha. This material is Zoharistic.
80a–97b	Bakashot are commenced at this point. R. Jacob Ibn Ẓur is mentioned as the author of the Bakashah on page 93a.

At this point the printed Siddur commences. After the conclusion of the printed Prayerbook text the penitential prayers preceding the Holy Days of Rosh Hashanah, the Jewish New Year, are presented in manuscript form. The printed 1968 edition of the Maḥzor "Zekhor Le-Avraham," in accordance with the Sephardic ritual, was used as a basis of comparison with the text of the manuscript.

The Penitential prayers commence on page 98a [this pagination is used as a continuation of the first manuscript which preceded the printed edition of the prayer book], and conclude on page 113b. The order of Hatarat Nedarim, Release from Vows, commences on pages 114a to 115a. The order of the evening service for Rosh Hashanah follows, from pages 115a to 121a. The Pizmonim of the morning services for both days of Rosh Hashanah begin on page 121a while the morning services conclude on page 134b. The Musaf service commences on page 134b and concludes on page 144b, which is also the conclusion of this manuscript.

Ms. 305

An unbound manuscript volume of a High Holy Days Maḥzor with penitential prayers and fragments of Hoshanôt

This manuscript volume was found unbound and in fragmented sections. It was written in Sephardic Square script on vellum with lineation called "Shirtut," and pointillation. The size of each page is 23 x 17.8 cm except where the pages are truncated. The text is given on sides a and b of each page. No pagination is given but the special Piyyutim were numbered in sequence by the scribe. There are ninety-five pages and introductory sections to the Rosh Hashanah, Yom Kippur, and Hoshanôt services are written in Judaeo-Arabic in a script which is indigenous to the Eastern Mediterranean. While no colophon is given, this manuscript appears to be a product of the late sixteenth or early seventeenth century. Several of the liturgical poems are not noted in Davidson's Thesaurus nor do they seem ever to have been published. It can be ascertained by a review of this volume that a number of the pages are missing.

A perusal of the authors of the Piyyutim found in this Maḥzor reveals that they span a period of over one thousand years. A composition by the celebrated and the earliest of the known liturgical poets of *c.* the fifth century, who is given the appellation Yose b. Yose Kohen Gadol, of the Holy Land, appears at one end of the spectrum and a composition by R. David ibn Abi Zimra (1479–1573) appears at the other end of this time span. R. David was born in Spain and it is surmised that his family left via Fez for the Holy Land and he arrived in Safed when he was still a teenager. Finally, he made his way to Egypt where he ascended to the rabbinic leadership of that community. The time period in which R. David lived enables us to ascertain that the Maḥzor could not be earlier than from the end of the sixteenth century.

Other authors whose compositions appear in this Mahzor are representatives of the classical schools of French, Provençal, and Spanish liturgical poetry of the tenth to the thirteenth centuries. Among them are the following authors; Joseph ibn Abitur, *c.* tenth century, who was the first Sephardi to compose a Ma'amad prayer; Levi b. Jacob Altabban; David b. Elazar ibn Bakuda; Abraham ibn Ezra; Moses ben Ezra; Solomon ibn Gabirol; Isaac b. Judah Gerondi; Isaac ibn Ghayyat; Judah Halevi; Joseph Ḥazan; Benvenist ha-Katan bar Ḥiya; Isaac Halevi bar Zeraḥiah Yarondi (Gerondi); Joseph b. Isaac of Orleans; Joseph Kimḥi; Judah b. Samuel; Moses Katan b. Jacob of Grenoble; Rabbenu Nissim; and Joseph b. David ibn Suli.

The terms Pizmon, Piyyut, and Bakashah, which are different types of poems that appear in this volume, I have already defined in *Ms. 304*. In addition to those types of poems, there appear also the Tokheḥah, a type of poem which contains self-chastisement in the form of prayerful expression, and Seliḥah, a penitential prayer wherein one seeks Divine forgiveness. This last type is usually recited on occasions for fasting, on the nights before the High Holy Days, and also on the Day of Atonement. The poems of this manuscript volume were checked against Davidson's Thesaurus of Mediaeval Hebrew Poetry for variants, as well as to see if they were extant in other collections. Most of the poems in this manuscript are in accord with Spanish and North African rites. The first section commences in the middle of the Ma'amad for the seventh night. The term Ma'amad hearkens back to temple times when representatives of the Jewish people stood by as the offerings were made and they recited scriptural passages. This term eventually was

Ms. 305
From an unbound manuscript volume of a High Holy Days Mahzor with penitential prayers and fragments of Hoshanôt

applied to an assemblage that met for penitential exercises, especially before the High Holy Days. The following is a description of the entire content of this manuscript volume. The first fifty-seven poems are missing. The last part of poem No. 58 is given.

"Ū-Vekhen Adon-ai Mah Adir Shimkha Be-Khol Ha'areẓ . . ."

Poem No. 59 "Adir Noteh Sheḥakim Ve-Yosed Me'Maday Arakim . . ." Author: David bar Elazar Bakudah Ḥazak.

Poem No. 60 Bakashah. "Be-Hasdekḥa Yah Avon Avdekha Selaḥah . . ." Author: Benvenist ha-Katan bar Ḥiya.

Poem No. 61 Pizmon. "El Dimati Yah Ẓapeh Ū-Vinah Ḥemlatkha Karev . . ." Ma'amad Lail Shevii.

Poem No. 62 Pizmon. "Yinam Mahalal Shavat Ma'amadot Heẓavta . . ." Author: Isaac [Ghayyat].

Poem No. 63 Pizmon. "Yeminkha Nosay Avonai Peshutah Le-Kabel Teshuvah . . ." Author: Judah [Halevi].

Poem No. 64 Pizmon. "Haḥairshim Shimu Me-pee Nara'ôt . . ." Author: Moses Ha-Katan. This poem was popular in the North African communities of Argil and Tunis. Pages are missing which included poems Nos. 65–68. The last portion of Poem No. 69 is given. Ma'amad Lail Shemini.

Poem No. 70 Pizmon. "Yom Ẓadu Ẓa'adai Ve-Natta Lamot Raglal . . ." Author: Isaac.

Poem No. 71 Pizmon. "Yaḥid Mo'ed Sho'khen Ve-Lo Melukha Kadmonit . . ." Author: Isaac [Ghayyat]. This text contains variants.

Poem No. 72 Pizmon. "Yom Lehaitiv Tikreh Me Zeh Yikhleh Toovekha . . ." Author: Judah [Halevi]. Popularized among Yemenites.

Poem No. 73 Pizmon. "Sh'ma Elyon Kol Evyon, Ū-Meḥeh Ka'av Pisho . . ." Author: Solomon [Ibn Gabirol].

Poem No. 74 Pizmon. "Yeẓav ha-El Le-Dal Sho'el Ve-Yi-He-Yoo Delatav Petuḥôt . . ." Author: Judah [Halevi].

Poem No. 75 Selihah. "Kol Ma'aseh Adon-ai Me'od Nora Hoo . . ." This text is in accord with North African traditions. "Ẓedek Ū-Mishpat Makhon Kisakha Ḥesed Ve-Emet Ye'Kadmu Fanekha"

Poem No. 76 "Ye'erav Siaḥ Nidaḥ Me-Meonav Ve-Tisheh Ke-Korban Merkaḥ . . ." Author: Joseph. This text contains variants.

Poem No. 77 Tokheḥah. "Be-Hafak ha-Zeman Zemamakh, Enosh Al Ta'amen Be-Aẓmakh . . ." This text is not noted in the Thesaurus. Ū-Vekhen Malkhutkha Malkhut Kol Olamim.

Poem No. 78 "Shokhen Ad Me'az Ve-Nisgav Shem Malkhuto Me'yuḥad . . ." Author: Solomon ha-Katan bar Judah [ibn Gabirol].

Poem No. 79 Bakashah. "Be-Raḥamekha Elohai Raḥamayni Ve-hot Ozen Le-Shavi . . ." Author: Benasht ha-Katan bar Ḥiya, Fez. Ma'amad Lail Te'She'ii.

Poem No. 80 Pizmon. "Yom Lariv Ta'amod, Ū-Ledin Amim Lee-bee be Yeḥerad . . ." Author: Levi Ḥazak [Al-Tabban]. This text is in accord with the Spanish and North African traditions of Barcelona, Aragon, Tunis, Tlemçen, and Argil. This text is incomplete because some pages are missing, as are poem No. 81 and the first part of poem No. 82.

Poem No. 83 Pizmon. "El Elyon She'ay Elyon, ha-Ba'im Adekha Aizon Lahsham . . ." This text is not noted in Davidson's Thesaurus.

Poem No. 84 Pizmon. "Yom be'ad Yoẓri Ve-ro'ee, Leḥapais Esa Day'ee . . ." Author: Isaac [Ghayyat].

Poem No. 85 Seliḥah. "Le-Makdim Le-Makkah refuah, ha-yom Ainai Teluyah . . ." This text is not noted in Davidson's Thesaurus.

Poem No. 86 Seliḥah. "Ye'eruni Rayonai, Ve-Sod Libi Ū-Mishalo ha-Gut Divray Hegyonai . . ." Author: Judah [Halevi]. This text offers variants. Zedek U-Mishpat Me-Khon Kisekha.

Poem No. 87 "Yaḥid Le-Vakesh rezonkha Amaditi, Ū-Veẓel Ke-Na-Feh-Kha . . ." Author: Joseph b. Suli [b. David Ḥazan]. The upper right corner of the page is torn.

Poem No. 88 Tokheḥah. "Aikh Tamu Ma'ava-Yai Yom Yom Yirbu Ḥolyai . . ." Author: Abraham ibn Ezra Ḥazak. Some variants are noted. Ū-Vekhen Atah Moshel be-Gay'oot ha-Yam.

Poem No. 89 "Atah Adon Le-Khol ha-Nimẓa'ôt, Atah Eloha Kol Beri'ôt . . ." Author: Ani Moses Katan bar Jacob Ḥazak. Variants are noted.

Poem No. 90 Bakashah. "Aḥaleh Na Penei ha-El Kedoshi, Ve-Etvadeh Alei Ḥet-ee Ve-Khaḥshi . . ." This text is not noted in Davidson's Thesaurus. Ma'amad Lail Asiri.

Poem No. 91 Pizmon. "Yom be-Dinkha Eh-Emod, Elohay Olam Yom be-Mishpat Tifkod . . ." Author: David [ibn Bakuda]. Variants are noted.

Poem No. 92 Pizmon. "Asher Lo ha-Yam Va-ḥaravah Ve-Khol Moshav Ū-Meẓavah . . ." This poem is noted in Seliḥôt Temanim.

Poem No. 93 "Yom Gashti Le-halelakh be-Tokh Am Dal Ve-ḥay-Lakh raḥem . . ." Author: Joseph ibn Abitur. Variants are noted. The entire text is written in the margin.

Poem No. 94 Seliḥah. "Ait Sha'arei raẓon Le-he-patay-aḥ Lail Eheyeh Kapai . . ." This text contains variants. Author: Judah b. Samuel. The term Oked appears at the end of this text. This prayer which is designated as Akedah stresses the element of martyrdom which is exercised to sanctify God and thereby ask for atonement.

Poem No. 95 Seliḥah. "Mee Yasad Shmee Gevohim, Mee Natah Galgal Negohim . . ." This prayer is recited on Rosh Hashanah in some traditions.

Poem No. 96 Pizmon. "El Ḥai be-Khol Oẓar, Ū-Vekhol Ainav Me-Shot-Tetôt . . ." Author: Abraham [Ibn Ezra]. Ū-Ve-Khen Ve-hoo Raḥum Ye-Kha-per Avon.

Poem No. 97 "Evilim Me-Derekh Pish'am Zikhru May-raḥok . . ." Author: Ani Levi ha-Katan Ḥazak [b. Jacob Altabban]. This text was widespread in North Africa.

Poem No. 98 Bakashah. "Aromem El Asher Lo ha-Gedulah Ve-Lo Ta'avat She-vaḥah Ū-Tehilah . . ." Author: David [ben Bakudah]. Poem No. 99 is missing, as is the beginning of poem No. 100.

Poem No. 101 Seliḥah. "Shnei ḥayai U-Ma'avayai Larik Safu be-Ḥovotai . . ." Author: Solomon b. Gabirol. This text was known in Tlemçen.

Poem No. 102 Seliḥah. "A-Erah Shenat Ainai Leḥaber Et Zemirotai . . ." Author: Moses b. Ezra.

Poem No. 103 Selihah. "Be-Lev Ḥaraid Me'od Ro'ed, Seliḥat El Sha'alti . . ." Author: Moses b. Ezra. Mee-Ma'amakim Keratikha Adon-ai.

Poem No. 104 "Adir Noteh Aliyôt Ve-roka Me-mah-dei Neshiyôt . . ." Author: Ani David bar Elazar

Bakudah Ḥazak.
Poem No. 105 Tokheḥah. "Me'od ḥalti Ve-Zaḥalti, Le-Tokha-ḥat Lakaḥti Mah Ashiv Al Tokhaḥti . . ."
Poem No. 106 Bakashah. "She'arekha be-Dafki Yah Petaḥah, Ve-Yom Eh-Etof Be-Dal . . ."
This text has variants.
Poems Nos. 107–111 are missing but the last part of No. 112 is available.
Poem No. 113 Seliḥah. "Yizrei Raishit Zarai, Hitani Kashikor Ū-Mah Yitron Le-Devarai . . ."
Author: Judah.
Ū-Vekhen Shuvu Banim Shovavim.
Poem No. 114 "Shuvu El Avikhem She-ba-Shamayim ha-Omer Shuvu Shuvu Pa'amayim"
Author: Ani David ben Judah.
Poem. No. 115 and the first part of poem No. 116 are missing.
Ma'amad Lail Shelosh Asar.
Poem No. 117 Pizmon. "Yah Ayom Zekhor ha-Yom Brit Shivah Temimekha . . ."
This prayer was used on different occasions based on local customs. Variants are noted. Six stanzas are given.
Poem No. 118 Seliḥah. "Amku Maḥshevotekha Ve-Aẓmu Nifleotekha . . ."
Author: Isaac Ghayyat. Generally this text is read at the Yom Kippur morning service.
Poem No. 119 Seliḥah. "Ailekha Ailekha Ve-Ainee Le-Me'onekha be-Lev Nishan Alekha . . ."
Author: Judah Halevi. This poem is part of Yemenite liturgy.
Poem No. 120 Seliḥah. "Bat Ayuma Ka-hama Ū-Khe-Shaḥar Nishkefah . . ."
Author: Moses ben Ezra.
Poem No. 121 Seliḥah. "Zeman Hevli Yemei Sikhli, Yefeh Le-Libi Shekarav . . ."
Author: Moses b. Ezra. This text was recited in Tlemçen.
Be-Shem Ha-Shem El Olam.
Poem No. 122 Seliḥah. "Adamôt Ū-Tehomot Nikraoo, Orot Ū-Mezarot Al Piv Yazaoo . . ."
This text is not noted in Davidson's Thesaurus.
Poem No. 123 Tokhehah. "Yehidah Akevakh Kerukh ba-Keẓ Ū-Zeman Lo Arokh . . ."
Author: Isaac Halevi bar Zerahiah Yarondi Zikhro Le-Verakhah Amen.
Poem No. 124 Bakashah. "Yehidah Shahri Bet-El Ve-Safav Ve-Khiktoret Teni Shirekh . . ."
Author: Judah [Halevi]. Variants are noted.
Ma'amad Lail Arba'ah Asar.
Poem No. 125 Pizmon. "Yah Sh'ma Me-Shamekha Ba'im El kevod Sh'mekha . . ."
While this text does not appear in the Thesaurus, the poem follows another Piyyut stylistically.
Poems Nos. 126 to the beginning of 130 are missing.
Zekhor Adatekha Kanita Kedem.
Poem No. 131 "Asurah be-Galut Medukeh, Me-Ūreh Ve-Dema . . ."
Author: Ani Isaac Meshakran Ḥazak.
Poem No. 132 Tokhehah. "Shikh-ḥee Yegonekh Nefesh Homiyah Lamah Tifḥadi . . ."
Author: Solomon [ibn Gabirol].
This text was known in Tlemçen.
Poem No. 133 Bakashah. "Terem Heyoti Ḥasdekha ba-ani ha-Som Le-Yesh Ayin . . ."
Author: Solomon ibn Gabirol.
Poem No. 134 Bakashah. "Sho'ef Ke'mo Eved Yish'af Le-Yad Rabo Ḥasdekha . . ."
Author: Solomon [ibn Gabirol].
Popularized in Barcelona and Tunis.
Ma'amad Lail Ḥamishah Asar.
Poem No. 135 Pizmon. "Yoẓer Merômôt Ve-Nagham Yasher Lev he-Akov . . ."
Author: Isaac [Halevi ben Zeraḥiah Yarondi]. Usually recited

on Rosh Hashanah.

Poem No. 136 Pizmon. "Yegaleh Ẓur Yeshuato Le-Am Mepaḥdo Nidham Ve-Yaḥish Et Ezrato . . ."
Author: Isaac [Gerondi ben Judah]. This poem was known in North Africa.

Poem No. 137 Seliḥah. "Yosed ha-Adamah U-Maziv Kol Gevuleha Ve-Som Zohar Ka-Hamah . . ."
Author: Judah [Halevi].

Poem No. 138 Seliḥah. "Malakh Shimkha be-kirbo Le-Temokh Yemini Ve-Limod Boshesh . . ."
Author: Judah Halevi. Variants are noted.

Poem No. 139 Selihah. "Be-Lei-Li Al-Mishkavi Aiẓot Be-Nafshi Samti . . ."
Author: Moses ben Ezra.
Ū-vekhen Maẓil Ani Mai-Ḥazak Me-Men-u.

Poem No. 140 "El Elohai Nafshi Ayahel Ū-Lai Or Seliḥati Yahel . . ."
This text is not noted in Davidson's Thesaurus.

At this point in the manuscript volume, the next nine liturgical poems are missing and the Seliḥot section for the days preceding Rosh Hashanah concludes. An introduction to the Rosh Hashanah services follows in a Judaeo-Arabic script of the Eastern Mediterranean area. The concluding prayer of the Shaḥarit Amida for Rosh Hashanah is followed by the service for the blowing of the Shofar. The Musaf Amida follows without any special piyyutim noted. The usual sections of Malkhiyôt Zikhrônôt and Shofarôt are given. Direction for the conclusion of the Musaf service is given in Judaeo-Arabic as well as directions for the Minḥah service of Rosh Hashanah and the Fast of Gedaliah. The aforementioned introduction and prayers appear on fourteen pages.

The next section is introduced with directions for the recital of the Minḥah service before the eve of Yom Kippur, and the Confessional that is added to this service is given. Additional directions are given in Judaeo-Arabic pertaining to the conclusion of the Minḥah service and the introduction of the Ma'ariv service which commences with the text of Kol Nidrei which is given. The text of the evening service follows. Three liturgical pieces in fragmented form, are presented at the end of the Ma'ariv service, but only the following Seliḥah is identified.

"Ya'aseh Tevuah Ū-Feri, Taḥanun Tiknu Emunai . . ."
Author: Isaac [Ghayya]. This text was known in Spain.

The last part of liturgical composition No. 151 follows.

Poem No. 152 Bakashah. "Selaḥ Bor-ee Avon Ish Zed Ve-Ḥata . . ."

The next poem follows under the heading "Pesukei De-rahmei."

Poem No. 153 "Lekha Ha-Shem ha-Ẓedakah Ve-Lanu Voshet ha-Panim . . ."

The balance of the evening Seliḥôt follows with the last liturgical piece which is now noted.

Poem No. 157 Pizmon. "Ha-Melekh Adon-ai Rom Ve-Taḥat Koneh Hegdilu Emunim be-Noam Shir Ū-Ma'aneh . . ."
It is interesting to note that this text is generally recited as a Piyyut for blowing the Shofar and here it appears as the concluding portion of the Seliḥôt for the evening service of Yom Kippur.

It is customary in many communities to recite additional prayers after the regular evening service on Yom Kippur. These are given next.

Ma'amad Le-Arvit Lail Ha-Kippurim.

Poem No. 158 "Shelaḥ Malakh Meiliẓ, Ve-Haflei Ot Ve-Siba, Le-Tahareinu be-Lail Zeh Me-Shemeẓ Ve-Diba . . ."
Author: The acrostic spells the name Solomon [ibn Gabirol]. This text was popular in Fez.

Poem No. 159 Pizmon. "Delatekha ha-Lailah Le-Shavei Ḥet Hutaru . . ."
This text was also known in Fez.

Poem No. 160 Pizmon. "Avinu El Erekh Le-Shavaina Ha-Teh Na Ozna'im . . ."

This poem appears in a collection of The Jews of Fez.

Poem No. 161 Pizmon. "El Ḥasdekha Yiḥalnu El rav ha-Aliliyah . . ."
Ū-Vekhen Kaper Le-Amekha Yisrael.

Poem No. 162 "Ariid be-Siḥi Ve-A'hemah, Ve-Nafshi be-Khapi Asimah . . ."
Author: Ani Joseph ibn Sol [ibn David Ḥazak] is noted in the acrostic.

Poem No. 163 Pizmon. "Ana Ve-Korainu Le-Kol Shavainu Adon-ai Shema'ah Ana be-Raḥamekha Avon Beẓainu Adon-ai Selaḥah . . ."
Author: Ana David Ḥazak [Ben Bakudah] is given in the acrostic. This text was disseminated in Sephardic and North African traditions.

Ma'amad Yom Ha-Kippurim Kodem Shaḥarit. Prior to the morning service on the Day of Atonement supplementary prayers were to be recited. The poems that follow belong to this category.

Poem No. 164 "Be-Asor La-Ḥodesh Yom Kippur Avonai Ke-ḥu Imakhem . . ."
This poem is a variation on a theme which was a popular composition not only in Western Sephardic circles but also in Yemen.

Poem No. 165 Pizmon. "Yom Zeh Lamarom, be-lev Nakhon Se-Ū Ain Khem . . ."
This poem was widely disseminated in liturgical literature.

Poem No. 166 Pizmon. "Mee-Kol TuM'otakhem Yom Ẓam-Tam Ve-Sartam . . ."
This text is not noted in Davidson's Thesaurus.

Poem No. 167 Pizmon. "Be-Lail Asor Le-Hitkapare, Yah Raẓti Aḥarekha . . ."
Author: Moses [ben Ezra]. This poem was popular in the Western Mediterranean.

Poem No. 168 Seliḥah. "Mishtaḥavim Le-Hadrat Kodesh har Ariel . . ."
Author: Judah [Halevi]. There are variants here. This text was popular in Spain and North Africa.

Poem No. 169 Seliḥah. "Yom La'amod Lefanekha Le-Hitkhapar Ho-Ḥalti be-Ma'amadot Arbaiim . . ." This text is not noted in Davidson's Thesaurus.

Poem No. 170 Seliḥah. "Yah Shavat Mitanah Me-Yaḥel Kippurekha . . ."
Author: Isaac [Halevi ben Zeraḥiah Yarondi]. This text contains variants.

Poem No. 171 Seliḥah. "Zekhut Avotai Le-Ẓivotai, Anot Bom Layom . . ."
This poem is not noted in Davidson's Thesaurus.
Poems Nos. 172 and 173 are missing.

Poem No. 174 "Be-Terem Sheḥakim Va'arakim Nimtaḥu . . ."
This text was known in all sections of the Jewish Afro-Asian world.

Poem No. 175 "Adirei Ayumah Yadiru be-Kol . . ."
The style of this text was taken from R. Eleazar Kallir *c.* the eighth century.
Hodu La-Adon-ai Kirū Vee-Shmo.

Poem No. 176 "Alay-Khem Ekra Zera Emunav Dirshu Adon-ai Ve-Oozo . . ."
Author: The acrostic has Ani Shem Tob̤ Ḥazak.

All the poems from Nos. 177 to 189 are missing. An introduction in Judaeo-Arabic is given before the next section, which is designated as Ma'amad Le-Shaḥarit. The Nos. 190 to 192 are contained in this section, while the poems 193 to 200 have been deleted. Additional liturgical poems, Nos. 201 to 208, are given. Number 208 commences a section designated as Ma'amad Le-Minḥah, special poems for the afternoon service of Yom Kippur Day. Poems Nos. 209 to 211 are missing while Nos. 212 to 218 are given.

Poem No. 218 Bakashah. On the "Yud-Gimel Yesôdôt," the thirteen principles of faith, "Ve-Eser Sephirôt," and the ten spheres.
"Adon-ai Hoo Menat Ḥelki Ve-Khosi, Ū-Ma'oozi Ū-Mivtaḥi Menusi . . ."
Author: David ibn Abi Zimra. This

poem is available in other North African collections.

Poem No. 219 "Tephilah U-Bakashah Le-R. Abraham ben Ezrah."
"Yehee razon Meel-fanekha Adon-ai, Adon-ai, Zevaot Asher Asher Eheyeh Elohay Yisrael Yoshev ha-Keruvim Ram Ve-Nisa Shokhen Aad Ve-Kadôsh Shemo."
This text is at variance with other texts of this prayer and the text of the prayer is lengthy.

Poem No. 220 "Viddui Le-Rabbenū Nissim Z.T.L."
"Ribono Shel Olam Kodem Kol Ain Lee Peh Le-Hashiv . . ."
This text contains many variants of this prayer which was disseminated in Italy, Spain, North Africa, and the Middle East.

Some poems have the section containing their numbers cut away. They are given below.

The following two texts pertain to the description of the Yom Kippur service during Temple days which is read in the part of the Musaf service known as Seder Avodah.

"Reshut Le-Seder Avodah Le-R. Solomon ibn Gabirol Z."L.
"Aromimkha Ḥezki Ve-Ḥelki be-Voee Ve-Rov Davki Ve-Dafki..."
This text was known to the Jewish communities of the Mediterranean.

On the other side of this page is contained the "Seder Avodah Le-R. Yose ben Yose Kohen Gadôl." "Atah Konanta Olam Me-Kedem Yisadeta ha-Kol ve-ha-Kol Pa'alta Ū-Viryot Yaẓarta . . ." Many variants are noted in this text. Davidson writes in his Thesaurus, Volume I, the letter "Aleph," No. 8816, that the author of this famous text is unknown. Yet, in our text, Yose ben Yose Kohen Gadôl is declared to be the author.

Eight pages contain the text of the aforementioned Seder Avodah.
An unnumbered Pizmon is recorded on another page.
"Pizmon Le-R. Solomon ibn Gabirol N[ishmato] "E[den].
"Ashrei Ayin Ra'atah Kol Aileh, ha-lo Le-Mishma Ozen Da'avah Nafshaynu . . ."
Davidson notes that Solomon ibn Gabirol's Pizmon commences from the second line of our text "Ashrei Ayin Ra'atah Shoshanat ha-Sharon Ve-ha-Kavod Meḥofef," rather than from the aforementioned first line. This poem is an addition to the Seder Avodah.

Additional psalms and poems follow the Musaf Service and some of them are numbered, from 234 to 253. Among these poems are supplementary piyyutim and seliḥôt for Rosh Hashanah. The last numbered poem is No. 253, "Barukh She'amar Le-Yom Ẓom Kippur." "Barukh El Adir ba-Meromim Ve-Lo Ye-Khalkeluhu . . ." This poem is recorded as a Pizmon in other collections.

Two liturgical poems which are not numbered are very significant since the copyist also gave the names of their authors; something which we find but rarely in this manuscript volume. They are given below. The first is, "Nishmat Le-R. Joseph B. R. Isaac Z.Z.L." "Ashkimah Shaḥar Yom Yee-ḥadetow Le-Ẓom Heh-Asor..." The author of this work is Joseph Kimḥi.

The next text is titled, "Ve-Ailu Finu Malei Le. R. Abraham ben Ezra, Z.Z.L." The opening line is now given; "Ve-Ailu Finu Malei, Ve-Ailu Finu Malei, Shir Ẓur Lo Ye-Suleh..." This poem is not noted in Davidson's Thesaurus. Thus, we have discovered a poem by the celebrated poet of the twelfth century, Abraham ibn Ezra, which has heretofore been unknown.

The last section, which contains several pages, is in a poorly fragmented condition. It contains supplementary prayers called Hoshanôt which are read in the synagogue on the festival of Tabernacles. While most of these prayers are available in other collections they have variants which will be of scholarly interest. Some of the texts are not referred to in liturgical reference works. Unlike most of the prayers contained in the Maḥzor no numeration of these prayers is available.

Ms. 306 A manuscript volume of the kabbalistic work Eẓ Ḥayyim

R. Ḥayyim b. Joseph Vital Calabrese (1542-1620) was one of the great Kabbalists and a principal disciple of the founder of Ari Kabbalism, R. Isaac Luria. R. Ḥayyim devoted his literary activities to elaborating on the teachings of Isaac Luria in a compulsive manner. He hoped to be the sole transmitter of what he comprehended to be the authentic ideas of Lurianic Kabbala, to the exclusion of all other interpreters of the master. A group of disciples followed R. Ḥayyim even though he demanded a certain amount of secrecy from them. When R. Ḥayyim left the inner circle at Safed, for Jerusalem, where he served as rabbi and head of an academy from 1577 to 1585, the group dissolved. During this period R. Ḥayyim composed his final version of the Lurianic system.

R. Ḥayyim returned to Safed and remained there for several years. During this period it is reported that he became ill, and while he was unconscious, some scholars of Safed bribed his younger brother Moses to allow them to copy six hundred pages of Ḥayyim Vital's writings which were subsequently circulated. Ḥayyim's youngest son, Samuel, inherited all the manuscripts containing his literary output. The two major works Eẓ Ḥayyim and Eẓ ha-Da'at were disseminated in several versions. The various treatises were divided into "Gates," "She'arim." Even during R. Ḥayyim's lifetime many of the copies of his works in circulation were poorly arranged.

Vital's last version, which he prepared during his stay in Jerusalem, was discovered there in a Genizah by Abraham Azulai. During the early decades of the seventeenth century Jacob b. Ḥayyim Ẓemaḥ, who studied Kabbala in Safed, arrived in Damascus where he studied Kabbala under the direction of Samuel, the son of Ḥayyim Vital. Jacob Ẓemaḥ began to draw on Ḥayyim's rediscovered Jerusalem manuscript for his own literary efforts. Meir Poppers, a disciple of Ẓemaḥ, produced his final edition of Vital's works in 1653. A colleague of Poppers, Nathan Shapira, edited a Kabbalistic work called Me'ôrôt Natan.

Shalom Sharabi (1720–1777), of Yemen, arrived in the Holy Land via Damascus. He studied at the celebrated Kabbalistic academy Beth-El, which was founded in 1737 by the Kabbalist Gedaliah Ḥayon, where prayers were recited according to the directives of Isaac Luria. Sharabi studied Lurianic Kabbala according to R. Ḥayyim Vital's tradition as was the practice of other Kabbalists of Jerusalem. He succeeded Ḥayon as head of the academy after 1751. Sharabi wrote comments and glosses which elucidated much that was obscure in the works of R. Ḥayyim Vital.

The aforementioned scholars, namely, Jacob Ẓemaḥ, Nathan Shapira, and R. Shalom Sharabi, have their glosses contained in the manuscript volume of Eẓ Ḥayyim, Ms. 306. This work, which is written in Maaravic Mashait script, might have been copied from a late eighteenth or early nineteenth century published edition of the Eẓ Ḥayyim. The text is written on two hundred and two pages, and on sides a and b. It contains the following sections:

pp. 1a–4a	Sha'ar 26—Sha'ar ha-Ẓelem, 4 chapters
pp. 4a–7a	Sha'ar 27—Sha'ar Peratei Ibbur Ū-Moḥin, 4 chapters
pp. 7a–11a	Sha'ar 28—Sha'ar ha-Ibburim, 4 chapters
pp. 11b–21a	Sha'ar 29—Sha'ar ha-Nesirah, 9 chapters
pp. 21b–28b	Sha'ar 30—Sha'ar Parẓufei Zakhar Ū-Nekevah, 6 lectures
pp. 28b–33b	Sha'ar 31—Sha'ar Parẓufei Zakhar Ū-Nekevah, 5 chapters
pp. 33b–45b	Sha'ar 32—Sha'ar Ha'arot Zakhar Ū-Nekevah, 8 chapters
pp. 45b–51a	Sha'ar 33—Sha'ar ha-Ona'ah, 5 chapters
pp. 51a–61b	Sha'ar 34—Sha'ar Tikkun ha-Nukva, 7 chapters

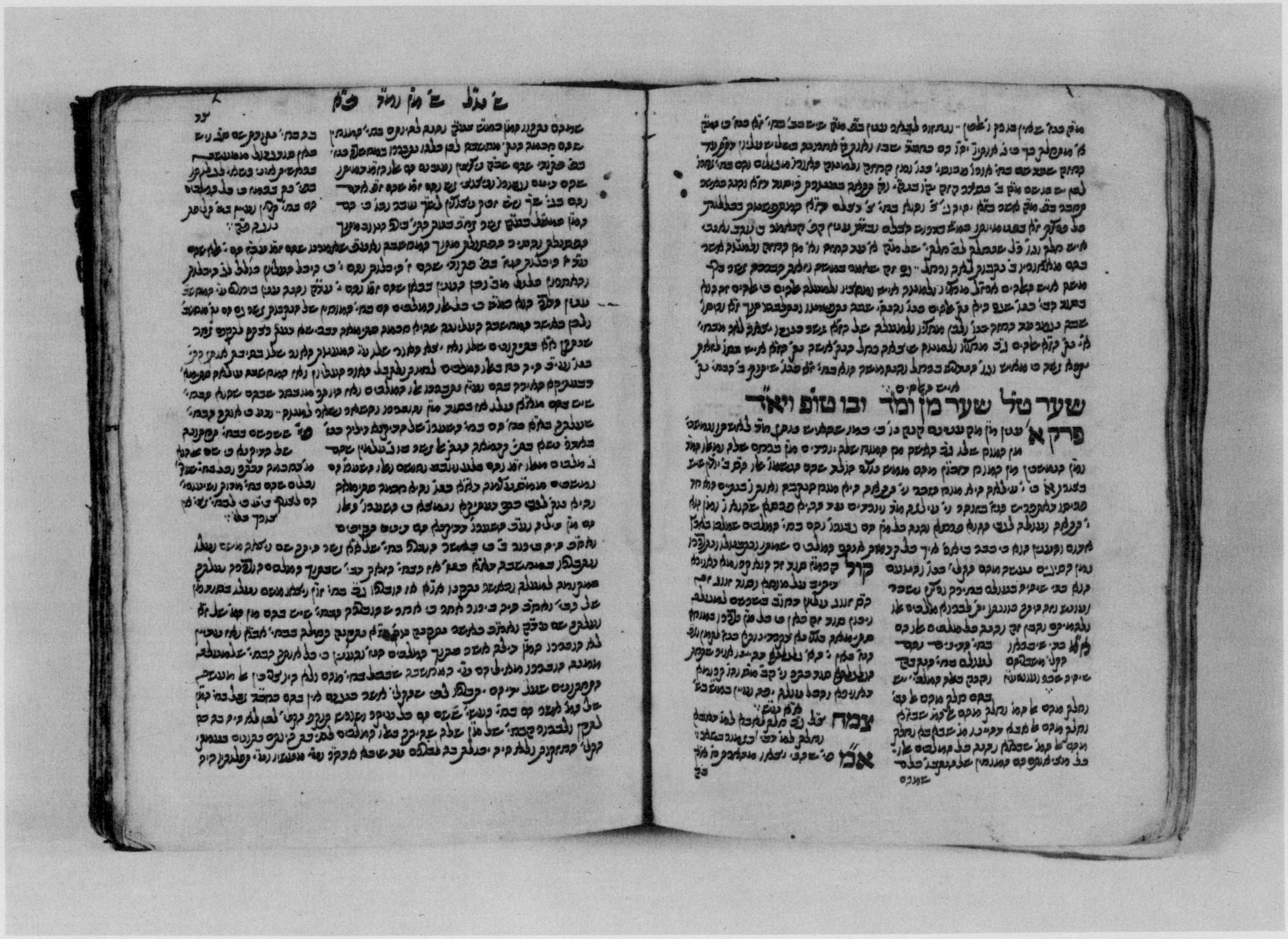

Ms. 306
From a manuscript volume of the Kabbalistic work Eẓ Ḥayyim

pp. 61b–71b	Sha'ar 35—Sha'ar ha-Yarai'ah, 5 chapters
pp. 71b–77b	Sha'ar 36—Sha'ar Mee'ūt ha-Yarai'ah, 4 chapters
pp. 77b–82b	Sha'ar 37—Sha'ar Ya'akov Ve-Leah, 5 chapters
pp. 82b–93b	Sha'ar 38—Sha'ar Raḥel Ve-Leah, 9 chapters
pp. 93b–117a	Sha'ar 39—Sha'ar M"N" Ve M"D", 15 chapters
pp. 117a–122a	Sha'ar 40—Sha'ar Penimiyôt ve-Ḥiẓôniyôt, 6 chapters
pp. 122b–133b	Sha'ar 40—Derush Peratei ha-Ôlamôt Kulam, (Sha'ar ha-Ḥiẓoniyôt Ū-Penimiyôt Batra'ah), chapters 7–9
pp. 133b–137a	Sha'ar 41—Sha'ar ha-Ḥashmal, 3 chapters
pp. 137a–148b	Sha'ar 42—Sha'ar Derushei A"B"I"A", (The text indicates that 5 chapters are missing) 13 chapters
pp. 148b–153a	Sha'ar 43—Sha'ar Ẓiyyur ha-Ôlamôt, 3 chapters
pp. 153a–163b	Sha'ar 44—Sha'ar ha-Shay'môt, 7 chapters
pp. 163b–166a	Sha'ar 45—Sha'ar ha-Makifim, 4 chapters
pp. 166a–170a	Sha'ar 46—Sha'ar Kisei ha-Kavôd ve-Ha-haykhalôt, 4 chapters
pp. 170a–178a	Sha'ar 47—Sha'ar Seder A"B"I"A", 7 chapters
pp. 178b–183b	Sha'ar 48—Sha'ar Derushei ha-Kelipôt, 9 chapters
pp. 183b–192a	Sha'ar 49—Sha'ar ha-Kelipôt, 9 chapters
pp. 192a–202b	Sha'ar 50—Sha'ar Kelipat Nogah, 11 chapters

Although the manuscript is complete, no colophon is given. The bibliophile Ariel Bension, the originator of this Collection, would have developed an avid interest in this manuscript because his family was quite involved in the movement of the Beth-El mystical community of Jerusalem where this type of literature was intensively studied. Bension also composed a published work on Sar Shalom Sharabi. The influence that Ari Kabbalism had in the past and its echoes that still reverberate in theosophical literature and in Ḥasidic movements, is ample testimony to the important role that R. Ḥayyim Vital played as the penman of Kabbalism.

Ms. 307 Four manuscript volumes of the work Torat Emet Tikkun Soferim

The work Torat Emet Tikkun Soferim was intended to serve as a model text by which a scribe could be guided to write a scroll containing the text of the Pentateuch which could then be used for the ritual of the Torah reading at synagogue services. The scribe added the prophetic reading which is introduced at the conclusion of each Sabbath text. Occasional readings from the prophets for the festivals and the new month were also included. Only four of the bound Pentateuchal volumes, Exodus, Leviticus, Numbers, and Deuteronomy are available. Genesis is missing. According to the title pages to the books of Numbers and Leviticus, these four volumes were written by a scribe in the city of Meknès.

The text, which is probably from the eighteenth century, is given in Sephardic Square script throughout. No pagination is available. Scribal lines called "Shirtut" are given. All four volumes are written on vellum and they follow the Sephardic ritual. Sentence endings are also designated. Each volume will be described separately.

The Exodus volume The title page is torn away almost entirely. The size of each page is 13 x 10 cm. After the text of the first Haftorah (prophetic reading) for the section of Exodus, the scribe introduces a second prophetic reading from the sixteenth chapter of Ezekiel. He prefaces that text with the remark that it is in accord with the view of the Rif and the Rosh, and that is why he included this reading. The work concludes with the prophetic readings for the Arba Parshiyot and the blessings which are recited before and after the prophetic section. Notes for the cantillation are given on side a of the last page. On side b the names of Daniel Toledano and Raphael Legimi appear. The scriptural passage from Ecclesiastes 7:23 is quoted. No pointillation is given in this volume.

The Leviticus volume The work commences with a title page. The names Raphael Legimi and Mîmin Legimi appear on the first page. In addition, a list of names with numbers in the form of alphabetical letters are given. Some of the names that are distinguishable are Mas'ūd ibn Sharbit, Menasseh Kohen, Levi, Isaac ibn David Oḥayūn, Shalom Edery, Musa ibn Shitrit, Mordecai ibn Shitrit, ibn Biri, Jonah, Isaac ibn Shalilo (Baleiro), Abraham, and Aaron. Calculations are given on the opposite page.

The Pentateuchal and prophetic readings for Sabbath which falls on the New Month is given as well as those readings which pertain to the Passover festival. The Haftorah reading is given with the Targum (Aramaic translation) of Jonathan ben Uziel. A special prayer is added after the Haftorah reading for the first day of Passover. The last page, side a, gives the notes of cantillation with pointillation.

The Numbers volume The title page of this volume is the only one that is rubricated. The page prior to the title page contains two beautiful signatures by Raphael Legimi. A faded name is given in Square script and the name Elijah ibn Maman also appears. Four lines of verse appear on side b of the page which contains the signatures. One page containing the conclusion to the Haftorah of the last section of the Numbers reading is missing.

The Deuteronomy volume The title page is missing in this volume. Side a of the first page is given with pointillation. At the end of this volume the text of the scroll of Esther is given in full with the blessings which are recited both before and after the ritual reading of Esther. The prophetic readings and blessings for the High Holy Days and the feast of Tabernacles conclude this volume.

There is some slight variation in the size of the pages of the four volumes. Some pages measure 14.3 x 10 cm while others measure 13 x 10 cm.

An introduction is given to the section on Biblical texts and fragments which appear in the Bension Collection *Ms. 308* to *Ms. 322*.

The above enumerated manuscripts are all part of a collection of Biblical texts which were written in Sephardic Square script, on vellum, *c.* the fourteenth century. The manuscript texts follow the Masoretic text; however variants abound. Pointillation is given, the conclusion of sentences are marked, and to a certain extent the Petuḥôt and Stumôt are adhered to. There is no pagination or other demarcation of the Biblical chapters. The size of each page is 16 x 16 cm, except where the pages have been truncated. It appears that originally all these texts were bound together as part of one work and they were composed by one scribal hand. Two columns of text appear on each side and there are twenty-one lines to a page. There are one hundred and three separate texts available in this collection.

The classification of the manuscripts is ordered according to the traditional sequence of the prophetic texts. Thus, all fragments of Isaiah are enumerated under the same classification number, followed by Jeremiah, Ezekiel, and the twelve minor prophets in sequence. The only exception is the fragment from the Second Book of Kings. Originally, this collection of Biblical texts was larger. Additional fragments from the books of Isaiah, Jeremiah, Jonah, and Habbakuk, once part of this collection, are known to be extant.

Mss. fragments of scriptural verses from Isaiah **Ms. 308**

34:5 - 36:4 44:5 - 45:1 60:16 - 62:6 37:24 - 38:8 51:13 - 53:1 64:2 - 65:16 40:5 - 41:2 53:1 - 54:15

Ms. 309 **Mss. fragments of scriptural verses from Jeremiah**

2:17 - 3:3	21:12 - 22:22	42:19 - 43:6-12
3:3 - 3:25	22:22 - 23:14	43:12 - 44:3
3:25 - 4:27	23:15 - 23:38	44:3 - 44:8
4:28 - 5:19	23:40 - 25:7	44:8 - 44:12
7:11 - 7:32	25:9 - 25:30	44:16 - 44:20
7:32 - 8:21	25:31 - 26:15	44:21 - 44:27
8:21 - 9:23	26:15 - 27:10	44:28 - 45:1

9:23 - 11:2	27:10 - 28:7	45:1 - 46:2
11:2 - 11:22	29:11 - 29:31	46:2 - 46:8
11:22 - 13:7	30:20 - 31:18	46:8 - 46:13
13:7 - 14:6	31:30 - 32:20	46:13 - 46:19
14:6 - 15:4	32:20 - 32:41	48:8 - 48:39
15:4 - 16:7	32:41 - 33:15	49:17 - 50:1
17:7 - 18:4	33:25 - 33:30	50:2 - 50:25
18:4 - 19:4	34:14 - 34:22	51:29 - 51:57
20:8 - 21:2	42:1 - 42:11	51:57 - 52:13
21:2 - 21:12	42:16 - 42:19	

Ms. 310 **Mss. fragments of scriptural verses from Ezekiel**

1:24 - 2:2	21:11 - 21:12	34:25 - 34:27
3:4 - 3:10	21:17 - 21:19	35:1 - 35:4
10:11 - 11:15	21:20 - 21:27	35:9 - 35:11
11:15 - 12:13	22:1 - 22:8	36:4 - 36:5
12:13 - 13:11	23:6 - 23:32	36:21 - 36:23
13:11 - 14:7	23:33 - 24:8	36:23 - 36:25
15:16 - 16:25	24:9 - 25:7	36:25 - 36:28
16:25 - 16:52	25:7 - 26:16	36:29 - 37:2
16:52 - 17:15	26:16 - 27:22	37:2 - 37:5

17:15 - 18:16	27:22 - 28:16	37:5 - 37:8
18:16 - 18:21	28:16 - 29:12	38:2 - 38:8
19:2 - 19:10	29:12 - 30:15	38:8 - 38:13
19:10 - 19:12	30:15 - 31:14	38:13 - 38:18
20:3 - 20:13	32:18 - 32:24	38:18 - 38:23
20:13 - 20:14	33:2 - 33:8	39:25 - 40:17
20:19 - 20:24	33:8 - 33:12	41:14 - 42:1
20:26 - 20:28	33:25 - 33:30	41:15 - 42:11
20:30 - 20:32	33:30 - 34:3	42:11 - 42:16
20:34 - 20:40	34:3 - 34:13	44:9 - 44:31
20:41 - 20:43	34:13 - 34:18	45:1 - 48:35
21:3 - 21:7	34:18 - 34:21	

Ms. 311 **Manuscript fragments of scriptural verses from Hosea**

The commencement of the scriptural text of Hosea is connected to the concluding portion of Ezekiel.

1:1 - 2:17	4:16 - 7:4
2:18 - 4:16	9:7 - 11:13

Ms. 312 **Manuscript fragments of scriptural verses from Joel**

The fragment 1:17 – 2:23 of the prophetic text of Joel is connected to Hosea 9:7 – 11:3.

1:17 - 2:23
4:18 - 4:21

Ms. 313 **Manuscript fragments of scriptural verses from Amos**

The commencement of Amos is connected to the concluding portion of Joel.

1:1 - 2:7	7:17 - 8:12
2:7 - 4:3	8:12 - 9:8
7:4 - 7:17	9:8 - 9:15

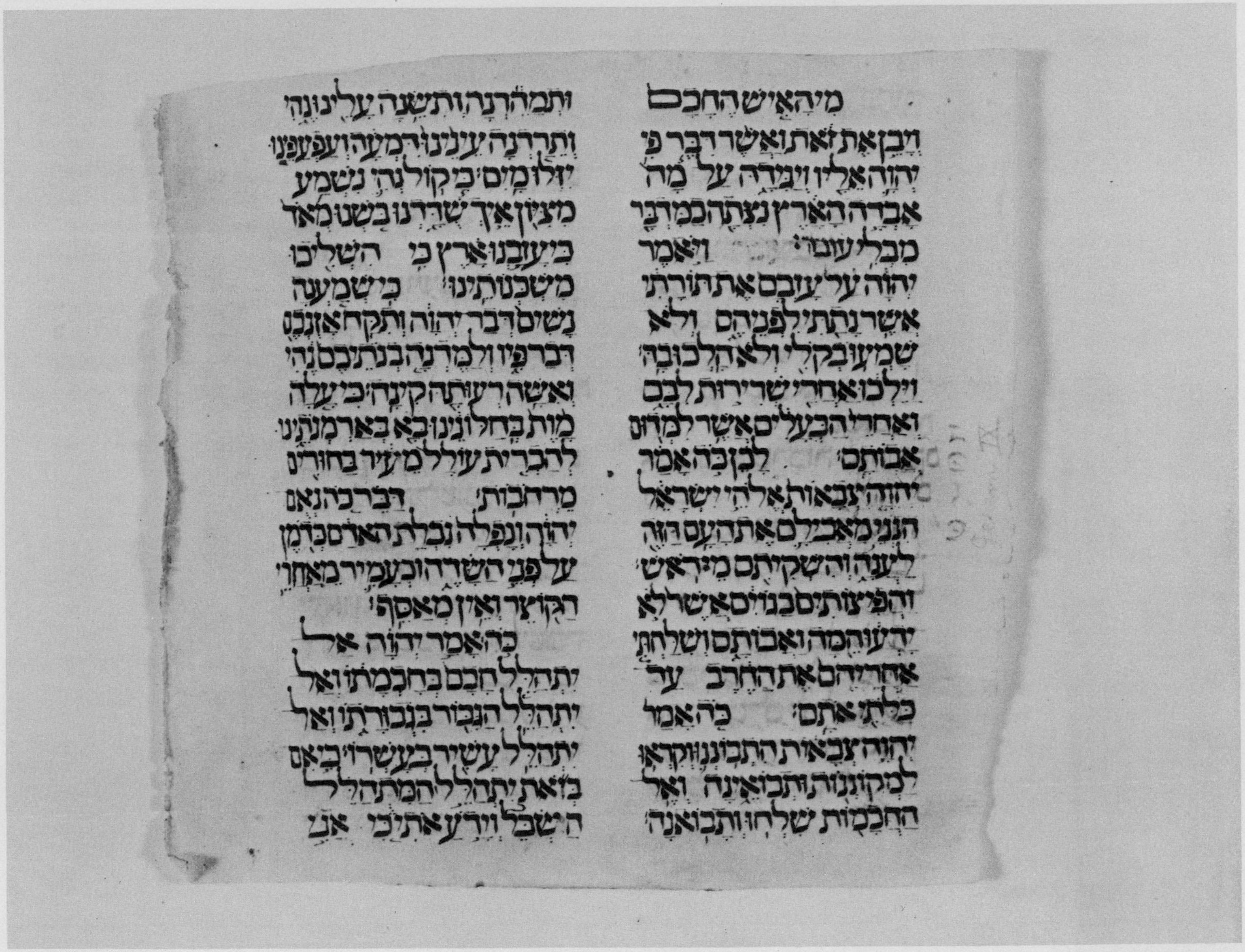
מי האיש החכם
ויבן את זאת ואשר דבר פי
יהוה אליו ויגדה על מה
אבדה הארץ נצתה כמדבר
מבלי עובר: ויאמר
יהוה על עזבם את תורתי
אשר נתתי לפניהם ולא
שמעו בקולי ולא הלכו בה:
וילכו אחרי שרירות לבם
ואחרי הבעלים אשר למדום
אבותם: לכן כה אמר
יהוה צבאות אלהי ישראל
הנני מאכילם את העם הזה
לענה והשקיתים מי ראש:
והפיצותים בגוים אשר לא
ידעו המה ואבותם ושלחתי
אחריהם את החרב עד
כלותי אתם: כה אמר
יהוה צבאות התבוננו וקראו
למקוננות ותבואינה ואל
החכמות שלחו ותבואנה:

ותמהרנה ותשנה עלינו נהי
ותרדנה עינינו דמעה ועפעפינו
יזלו מים: כי קול נהי נשמע
מציון איך שדדנו בשנו מאד
כי עזבנו ארץ כי השליכו
משכנותינו: כי שמענה
נשים דבר יהוה ותקח אזנכם
דבר פיו ולמדנה בנתיכם נהי
ואשה רעותה קינה: כי עלה
מות בחלונינו בא בארמנותינו
להכרית עולל מחוץ בחורים
מרחבות: דבר כה נאם
יהוה ונפלה נבלת האדם כדמן
על פני השדה וכעמיר מאחרי
הקוצר ואין מאסף:
כה אמר יהוה אל
יתהלל חכם בחכמתו ואל
יתהלל הגבור בגבורתו ואל
יתהלל עשיר בעשרו: כי אם
בזאת יתהלל המתהלל
השכל וידע אתי כי אני

Ms. 309
Verses from Jeremiah 9:11, middle of verse 23

Ms. 314 **A manuscript fragment of scriptural verses from Obadiah**

The commencement of the Book of Obadiah is connected to the concluding section of Amos Obadiah 1:1 - 1:5.

Ms. 315 **A manuscript fragment of scriptural verses from Jonah**

Jonah 4:1 - 4:11.

Ms. 316 **Manuscript fragments of scriptural verses from Micah**

The commencement of the book of Micah is connected to the concluding portion of Jonah.

1:1 - 1:13
1:14 - 3:11
3:11 - 5:6
7:5 - 7:20.

Ms. 317 **A manuscript fragment of scriptural verses from Naḥum**

The commencement of the book of Naḥum is connected to the concluding portion of the prophet Micah.
Naḥum 1:1 - 3:17.

Ms. 318 **Manuscript fragments of scriptural verses from Ḥabbakuk**

Ḥabbakuk 2:18 - 3:18
3:18 - 3:19.

Ms. 319 **A manuscript text of the complete scriptural work of Zephaniah**

The commencement of the book of Zephaniah is connected to the concluding portion of the prophet Ḥabbakuk. The complete text of Zephania is given.
1:1 - 2:5
2:5 - 3:15
3:15 - 3:20

Ms. 320 **Manuscript fragments of scriptural verses from Haggai**

The commencement of the book of Ḥaggai is connected to the concluding portion of the prophet Zephaniah.
Haggai 1:1 - 2:2
2:23

Manuscript fragments of scriptural verses from Zechariah

Ms. 321

1:1	- 1:8
1:9	- 2:17
4:2	- 5:3
6:3	- 7:13
7:14	- 8:21

The commencement of the book of Zechariah is connected to the concluding portion of the prophet Ḥaggai.

A manuscript fragment of scriptural verses from the Second Book of Kings

Ms. 322

II Kings 19:2 - 19:23.

Appendix

The nature of the Hebrew script in the Bension collection.

Three types of script are prominent in the Bension Collection. The first is used in ritual works such as prayerbooks, facsimiles of Torah Scrolls, and Biblical texts, and is designated as Sephardic Square script. It is noted in the descriptions of *Ms. 304*; *Ms. 305*; *Ms. 307*; *Mss. 308* to *322*. The second type most commonly found in the collection is known as Cursive script. This least formal of all scripts was most widely used in correspondences, court documents, and personal records and notes. Most of the documents and correspondences in the Yalkut Roîîm Manuscripts *Ms. 1* to *Ms. 275* are characteristic in their use of this script. The third type is usually used in the more formal works not generally utilized for ritual purposes and this is designated as Mashait script. Examples of this third class of script can be found in major halakhic, philosophic, mystical, and liturgical works which were principally written in book form for study purposes. This script can be found in *Ms. 292*; *Ms. 293*; *Ms. 295*; *Ms. 298*; *Ms. 301*; *Ms. 302*; *Ms. 303*; *Ms. 304*; and *Ms. 306*.

At the very outset of this book we characterized this collection as Sephardic. The movements of Sephardic Jews, after the Spanish expulsion of 1492, brought them to the shores of the Eastern and Western Mediterranean. There were also historical periods when Jews, whom we regard today as distinct from one another, were drawn together culturally. As they shared similar traditions so did their script manifest similarities. External influences also had an effect upon Jewish life. Those diverse communities who lived under the Moorish influence, such as the Jews of North West Africa, the Iberian Peninsula, and the Provence, manifested a similarity of script as long as they were able to share the same cultural contacts. Thus, we find in *Ms. 298* two different scripts, by the same scribe, adjacent to one another. In the post-expulsion period these scripts were classified as Provençal-Sephardic and as Maaravic. In the pre-expulsion period they could be regarded as Sephardic scripts shared by three major literary contributors, namely: Spanish Jewry, Provençal Jewry, and the Jews of North West Africa.

The scribal tradition of the Eastern Mediterranean is represented in the collection by the Maḥzor, *Ms. 305*. When Jews from the Maghreb migrated to the Holy Land, their descendants developed an affectation in their script which developed its own characteristics. This script can be regarded as a Holy Land or a modern Western Palestinian Cursive script. Examples of it are manifested by Holy Land emissaries and book dealers whose correspondences appear in *Ms. 30*; *Ms. 31*; *Ms. 44*; *Ms. 45*; *Ms. 54*; *Ms. 95*; *Ms. 99*; *Ms. 101*; *Ms. 103*; *Ms. 120*; and *Ms. 125*. This type of script must be distinguished from the Temanic or Parsic types which, although contemporaneous, developed their own peculiarities apart from the Western Palestinian types but these are not available in this collection. A script which seems to conform to the scribal tradition of Egypt does appear in the Cursive script which introduces the different sections of the Maḥzor in *Ms. 305*.

The Cursive script was utilized by copyists in an ornamentalized fashion which we call Mashait when they sought to give their work the quality of a book script. An example of this can be seen in Jacob Ibn Ẓur's poetic compositions which appear in Maaravic Mashait script in *Ms. 84*. A peculiar development took place in modern Holy Land Mashait script of the nineteenth century when the writer tried to achieve an ornamental effect similar to printed works, even in his correspondences such as shown in *Ms. 56*. The ornamentalized form can also be detected when formal documents for certifications of officials such as ritual slaughterers were composed, as may be noted in *Ms. 16*. Authors and copyists of Chronicles also wrote those texts in a more ornate Mashait script as may be noted in *Ms. 87*.

Signatures were developed into a special art form especially in the North African communities. Note the listings of signatures in the Index of Subjects. One of the many examples of signatures can be noted in *Ms. 43*, a product of the mid-seventeenth century. Few examples of the signatures indigenous to writers of the Holy Land communities are available in this collection (*cf. Ms. 100*). However, these writers did develop a distinctive signature type, though it was less elaborate than those of the Moroccans.

In the past the tendency was to designate what we call Mashait script as rabbinic script. This developed because most of the scholarly tomes that were read by Jews were halakhic works whose authors wrote in a specialized scribal style which had to be less painstakingly produced than the traditional square script if voluminous works were ever to reach completion. This "rabbinic" script was even adopted by the nascent printing industry in the late fifteenth century.

One halakhic work in the collection which dates from the fourteenth century and is written in a Temanic Mashait script is *Ms. 295*, Maimonides' Commentary on the Mishnah. Each text of the Mishnah is translated into Judaeo-Arabic. Several documents of this collection are written wholly or partially in Judaeo-Arabic, which is the Arabic language in Hebrew characters. Different Arabic dialects can be detected and the script in which they are written usually indicates whether the Arabic is a North Western African dialect or an Egyptian dialect.

Occasionally, liturgical poems known as Piyyutim are written in square script, but most Piyyutim, especially of Morocco, are written in Cursive or Mashait script. This genre of literature was used extensively at prayer services; since many of the collections of Piyyutim were not published they were recorded by many individuals who had neither the time nor the inclination to render them in an ornate script.

It sometimes occurs that a copyist will render a text, that originally was written in another locale and in a different script, into his own script. Therefore the reader must consider whether the text before him is an original text or correspondence, or a copy of the original. An example of this can be noted in *Ms. 4*, where letters from the Holy Land were copied by a Moroccan scribe into Maaravic script. When a colophon is offered by the writer or copyist it gives valuable information concerning the provenance of the text and other details. However, sometimes a colophon might be copied as well; as may be the case in *Ms. 298*.

Certain types of script seem to endure through the centuries. This is particularly true with regard to those used by scribes who write texts which are used as ritual items such as Torah Scrolls. However, when Jewish migrants come under new influences, scripts are inclined to change. The first generation might retain the script of their previous land, but new or syncretic forms of writing usually evolve among their descendants, and often come to dominate. When political conditions are relatively static, the uniformity of a script can endure for a few centuries. The trained eye can detect a certain uniformity of style in *Ms. 292*; *Ms. 293*; *Ms. 298*; *Ms. 301*; and *Ms. 303*. They were all produced before the end of the fifteenth century and under the influence of the Sephardic Mashait script. While there are divergences among the texts, there are certain features in the writing which places them together in a group. The trained eye can recognize the work of certain copyists even though no clear indicators are available other than the script. In collections of correspondences such as appear in the Yalkut Roîîm one can notice the evolution of a particular individual's script or signature when a series of documents or epistles by the same author are offered spanning decades. Such is the case with the signature of R. Raphael Moses Elbaz (cf. Introduction). One can study the evolution of R. Jacob ibn Ẓur's signature over half a century. The effects of age on handwriting can be noted in one document and one letter by Ḥayyim Joseph Ḉayni in *Ms. 158* and *Ms. 159*.

Index of persons

Moses, Mordecai b., Ms. 283
Muḫammad ben Mulay-Abdallah, Ms. 275
Mulay Abdallah, Ms. 87; 275
Mulay, Idris, Ms. 275
Mulay, La-Muz Tadi, Ms. 275
Mulay, Maḫmad, Ms. 55; 87
Mulay, Maḫmūd ibn La-Ariba, Ms. 275
Mulay, Rashid, Ms. 17
Mulay, Slieman, Ms. 111
Mulayl, see Ben Mulayl
(Murçiano, Murẓiano)
Murçiano, David, Ms. 97
Murçiano, family, Ms. 41
Murçiano, Isaac, Ms. 97
Murṣiano, Joseph, Ms. 97
Murçiano, Solomon ibn David, Ms. 97
Musa, Ali ibn, Ms. 187
Musi, see also Zerah
Musi, Abraham b. Zerah, Ms. 71
Musi, Donna, Ms. 71
Musi, Solomon, Ms. 71

Naḫmanides (Moses b. Naḫman), Ms. 301
Naḫmias, Judah ibn, Ms. 105
Nahon, Isaac, Ms. 128; 252
Nahon, Isaac, Ms. 42
(Benaim, Na'im, Ben Naim, ibn Na'im)
Na'im, Jacob ibn, Ms. 48
Na'im, Moses ibn, Ms. 45
Najara, Y., Ms. 166; 304
Navot, Miriam (daughter of Joseph), Ms. 134
Neḫunya b. Hakana, Ms. 85
(A) (Niẓẓam, Niẓẓam)
Niẓẓam, Abraham ibn, Ms. 108
Niẓẓam, Joseph, Ms. 156; 243

Oḫana, Jacob, Ms. 156; 272
Oḫana, Joseph, Ms. 90
Oḫana, Yaira, Ms. 103
Oḫayūn, Abraham b. David, Ms. 31
Oḫayūn, Isaac ibn David, Ms. 307
Ouizigan, Slieman, Ms. 254
Ozen, Abraham, Ms. 186

(Palaggi, Palache)
Palaggi, Abraham, Ms. 145; 238
Palaggi, Hayyim, Ms. 61; 145
Paaggi, Isaac, Ms. 221
(Pardosh, De Paridise, De Pardosh)
Pardosh, Ezra De, Ms. 141; 144; 160
Pargon, David, Ms. 105
Pargon, Zeraḫ ibn, Ms. 251
Pariente, Abraham, Ms. 2; 72; 210
Pariente, Eli, Ms. 98
Pariente, Jacob, Ms. 262
Paroz, Abraham ibn, Ms. 280; 281
Paroz, Samuel, Ms. 280
Pinto, Abraham Ḥayyim, Ms. 9
Pinto, Barukh, Ms. 9; 39
Pinto, Isaac, Ms. 95
Pinto, Jacob, Ms. 4; 9
Pinto, Moses, Ms. 95
Parot, Isaac, Ms. 34

Qanizal, Jacob, Ms. 174

Rabuḫ, Abraham, Ms. 170
Rabuḫ, Shalom, Ms. 170
Ramaz, see Zacut, Moses
(Ramukh, ibn Ramukh, Ben Remokh)
Ramukh, Jacob ibn, Ms. 252
Ramukh, Saul b. Saadys ben, Ms. 58
Ramukh, Shem Tob ibn, Ms. 43
Romano, Ḥayyim, Ms. 150; 152
Rosilio, Y., Ms. 116
Rotî, Isaac, Ms. 171
Rotî, Jacob, Ms. 87
Rotî, Joseph, Ms. 171

(Saadon, Bensaadon, ibn Saadon)
Saadon, Aaron ibn, Ms. 133
Saadon, Ephraim ibn, Ms. 68
Saadon, Ḥayyim b. Mas'ūd b. Moses ibn, Ms. 109
Saadon, Yissakhar b., Ms. 214
Saadon, Menaḫem ibn, Ms. 143
Saadon, Samuel, Ms. 217
Saadon, Solomon, Yom Toḇ, Ms. 58
Saadon, Yom Toḇ ibn S., b. Yissakhar, Ms. 143
Saadya Gaon, see Gaon Saadya
Ṣaba, Joseph b. Mordecai, Ms. 161
Ṣaba, Joseph, Ms. 175; 189
Ṣaba, Joseph, Ms. 268
Ṣaba, Judah ibn Jacob, Ms. 164
Ṣaba, Judah, Ms. 195
Ṣaba, Menaḫem, Ms. 44; 45; 48
Sabag, Isaac, Ms. 64; see also Asbag
Ṣaban, Aṣaban
(A)Ṣaban, Mordecai, Ms. 187
Ṣaḫiq Tamia Galul
Sai'id, Benjamin b. Solomon, Ms. 58
Saiivar, Samuel ibn, Ms. 40
Saluḫa, Abraham, Ms. 207
Saluḫa, Mas'uda (daughter of Mîmun) ibn, Ms. 207
Saluḫa, Samuel, Ms. 207
(Samuel, ibn Samuel)
Samuel, Hillel ibn, Ms. 146
Samuel, Moses b. Judah ibn, Ms. 146
Samuel, Simḫa (the daughter of Hillel ibn), Ms. 146
Samuel, Solomon b., Ms. 68
Ṣarfati, see Ha-Ṣarfati
Sas, Isaac b. Daniel, Ms. 134
Sasportas, David, Ms. 137
Sasson, Joseph, Ms. 54; 232; 248
(Aṣayaig, Ṣayaig, Aṣaig)
(A)Ṣayaig, Abraham ibn Joseph ibn, Ms. 62
(A)Ṣayaig, Ayush ibn, Ms. 231
(A)Ṣayaig, Moses, Ms. 116
(A)Ṣayaig, daughter of Moses, Ms. 245
(A)Ṣayaig, (anon), Ms. 35
Serero, David, Ms. 87
Serero, Ḥayyim David, Ms. 2; 184
Serero, Immanuel b. Joshua, Ms. 258
Serero, Immanuel b. Menahem, Ms. 199
Serero, Jacob, Ms. 3; 108; 240; 260
Serero, Jonathan, Ms. 186
Serero, Joshua, Ms. 258
Serero, Joshua, Ms. 32; 44; 48; 260
Serero, Matitya, Ms. 48; 78; 114; 237; 260
Serero, Menaḫem, Ms. 35; 105; 197; 220
Serero, Mîmun b. Joshua, Ms. 218
Serero, Reuben, Ms. 108; 202; 260
Serero, Saul b. David (I), Ms. 87
Serero, Saul (II), Ms. 72
Serero, Saul (III), Ms. 48; 111
Serero, Shalom, Ms. 260
Shalilo, Isaac ibn, Ms. 307
Shamama, Nissim, Pr. 73.5
Shaprut, see ibn Shaprut
Sharabi, Shalom, Ms. 306

Sharbit, Donna (daughter of Abraham b. Solomon ibn), Ms. 108
Sharbit, Israel ibn, Ms. 288
Sharbit, Mas'ūd ibn, Ms. 307
Shazbona, Ms. 118; 119
Shemaya, Ms. 40
Shitrit, Hayyim b., Ms. 67
Shitrit, Isaac ibn, Ms. 204
Shitrit, Jacob ibn, Ms. 170
Shitrit, Joseph, Ms. 67
Shitrit, Joseph b. Abraham b., Ms. 143
Shitrit, Mahlouf, Ms. 170
Shitrit, Mas'ūd (son of Ḥayyim), Ms. 67
Shitrit, Mordecai ibn, Ms. 307
Shitrit, Moses, ibn, Ms. 133
Shitrit, Musa ibn, Ms. 307
Simeon, Bar Yohai, Ms. 125
Simḥon, ibn Samhūn
Simḥon, Abraham ibn, Ms. 54; 176; 178
Simhon, Jacob, Ms. 90; 146; 183
Simḥon, Mahari, Ms. 120
Simḥon, Mahlouf ibn, Ms. 143
Simḥon, Mas'ūd, Ms. 178
Simḥon, Moses, Ms. 143
Simḥon, Raphael Jacob, Ms. 3; 5; 240
Simḥon, Simeon, Ms. 90
Simḥon, Solomon (Abraham's brother), Ms. 178
Siqron, David b., Ms. 105; 257
Siqron, family ibn, Ms. 116
Siqron, Joseph ibn, Ms. 133
Siso, Abraham ibn, Ms. 184
Siso, Maḥlouf (Moses' brother), Ms. 158
Siso, Moses b. Abraham, Ms. 158
Siso, Reuben ibn, Ms. 170
Siso, Shalom ibn, Ms. 170
(Scali, Skali, Kohen-Skali, Ha-Kohen Skali)
Skali, Aaron Ha-Kohen, Ms. 111
Skali, Abraham ibn Jacob Ha-Kohen, Ms. 97
Skali, Esther (daughter of Masuda and Solomon), Ms. 161
Skali, Masuda (wife of Solomon Kohen and daughter of Salim Ha-Kohen), Ms. 161
Skali, Solomon Kohen b. Jacob, Ms. 161
Suli, Joseph b. David ibn, Ms. 305
(Bensusan, Susan ibn Sussan) see also Ben Susan
Susan, ibn, Ms. 168
Susan, Solomon, Ms. 157
Susi, Epharaim, b. Solomon, Ms. 58
Susi, Moses Solomon, Ms. 58
Susin, MOHARAM ibn, Ms. 232
Suzin, Maharam, Ms. 54

Tamakh, Reuben, Ms. 130
Tanuji, Ishmael Ha-Kohen, Ms. 194
Tapiero, Solomon, Ms. 78
(Ibn Tata, Ben Tata, Tata)
Tata, Amram b., Ms. 181; 214
Tata, Dinar b. Amram ben, Ms. 215
Tata, Joseph ibn Amram, Ms. 96
Tata, Miriam (wife of Dinar ibn T.), Ms. 215
Tata, wife of David b. T., Ms. 17
Tibbon, Samuel ibn, Ms. 298
Toledano, Daniel b. Phineas, Ms. 196
Toledano, Daniel, Ms. 307
Toledano, Ḥabib, Ms. 73; 220
Toledano, Ḥayyim, Ms. 19; 132; 234; 239; 274
Toledano, Jacob (a/k/a MAHARIT), Ms. 19; 35; 78; 96; 98; 117; 118; 119; 223; 237
Toledano, Moses, Ms. 78; 128
Toledano, Solomon, Ms. 78; 126; 127; 155; 304
(ATurgeman, Turgeman)
(A)Turgeman, Isaac Slieman b., Ms. 143
Turgeman, Jacob, Ms. 55
Turgeman, Maḥmoud, Ms. 55
Turgeman, Moses, Ms. 55

Utmazgin, Elijah, Ms. 154; 205; 225
(Uçeda, Uẓeda)
Uẓeda, Samuel, Ms. 66
(Uziel, Ouziel)
Uziel, Bilyada (daughter of Isaac b. Judah b. Joseph b. Judah b. Joseph b. Abraham), Ms. 58
Uziel, Judah, Ms. 160

Vital, Ḥayyim, Ms. 306

Waḥnish, David b. Jacob, Ms. 158
Wahnunu, Simeon b. Mordecai, Ms. 223
(Waîsh, Benwaîsh)
Waîsh, Abraham b. Samuel, Ms. 184
Waknin, Abraham, Ms. 304
Walid, Abraham ibn, Ms. 100
Walid, Shem Ṭob ibn, Ms. 128
Walidun, Isaac ibn, Ms. 42
Walila, Mîmun ibn, Ms. 180
Waqil, Moses, Ms. 112

(Yaabeẓ, R. Jacob Ibn Zur)
Yaabeẓ, Ms. 19; 20; 27; 36; 71; (his widow Donna), Ms. 116; 160; 166
(Yaḥya, ibn Yahya)
Yahya, Isaac ibn, Ms. 137
Yahya, Maḥmoud Zikhri ibn, Ms. 283
(Yaîsh, Ben Yaîsh, Abenaes)
Yaîsh, Solomon ibn, Ms. 226; 257
Yalu, Moses, Ms. 268
Yehonatan, see Jonathan
Yeshurun, family, Ms. 47
Yinaḥ, Makhlouf ibn, Ms. 304
(Yitaḥ, Ben Yitah)
Yitah, Abraham b. Maḥlouf b., Ms. 34
Yitah, Isaac (Nagid of Meknès), Ms. 236
Yitah, Mahari Mas'ud, Ms. 267
Yoḥanan, R., Ms. 303
(ibn Yulee, Yuly, Aben-Yuly, Levy-Yuly)
Yulee, Samuel Halevi ibn, Ms. 90; 133; 152

Zabara, MAHARAM, Ms. 90
Zacut, Judah b. Moses, Ms. 147
(Zacut, MAHARAM, Ramaz)
Zacut, MAHARAM (Moses), Ms. 151
(Ẓadoq, Ẓadok)
Ẓadok, Elazar, Ms. 116
Ẓadok, Jacob, Ms. 105
Ẓaḥakon, Joseph ibn, Ms. 288
Zaqen, see also Ben Zaqen, ibn Zaken
Zaqen, Abraham, Ms. 3
Zarmon, Judah, Ms. 52
Zazun, Judah b., Ms. 35
Zazun, Mordecai ibn Abraham b., Ms. 123
Ẓemaḥ, Jacob, Ms. 306
Zeraḥ, Abraham ibn, Ms. 71; see Musi
Zikhri, David ibn, Ms. 293
Zikhri, Ḥananiah ibn, Ms. 113

Index of places

(*Note*: Numbers without parentheses indicate that the document was despatched from or received in that city, or that the city is definitely indicated in the text. Numbers in parenthesis mean that it is not certain that the city was involved, but that it most probably was so. For example, in *Ms. 162*, R. Judah ibn Attar wrote to R. Jacob Ibn Ẓur in the year 1720. Even though no cities are mentioned it is known that R. Jacob established his residence in Meknès during that period while R. Judah lived in Fez. Therefore we classify the document under Fez [162] and Meknès [162].)

Index of subjects

279; 280; 281; 282; 284; 288; 289; 290
Enactments, Ms. 13; 14; 47; 74; 88; 119; 122; 198; 246; 270; 275; see also Edicts, Takkanot
Epistolary art, see Agron, Correspondences
Estates, claims to, Ms. 31; 33; 41; 42; 47; 55; 57; 63; 68; 69; 71; 88; 90; 97; 161; 173; 175; 194; 199; 203; 204; 209; 214; 215; 218; 236; 250; 265; 270; 291; 303
Ethical proverbs, see Aphorisms
Ethics of the Fathers, Ms. 66
Eulogy, Ms. 37; see also Letters of consolation
Evaluation, of estate, Ms. 142; 204; 214;
of property, Ms. 294
Evidence, new, Ms. 117
Examination of lungs, see Kashrut
Excommunication, see Ban
Exhortation, Ms. 98; 226
Exile, Ms. 224; 227
Expulsion, Castilian, Ms. 52; 244; 258
Fez Albali (Old City), Ms. 258
Mellah (of Fez), Ms. 258
Faith, principles of, Ms. 84
Falsehood, see Truth and Falsehood
Family tree, see Yuḥasin
Famine, Ms. 87; 130; 174; 206; 240; 275
Fast of Gedaliah, Ms. 305
Fasts, Ms. 65; 87; 174; 275; see also Famine
Fees for legal services, Ms. 23
Fiancé, Ms. 198
Financial support for widow, Ms. 70
Fines, see Penalties
Flogging, Ms. 134; 146; 156; 198; 207
Folk tales, Ms. 274
Forfeiture of rights, Ms. 96; 173
Fundraising, Ms. 30; 39; 41; see also Emissaries

Garments, Ms. 90; 105
Genealogical tables, Ms. 58; 163; 244; see also Yihus
Genizah, Ms. 219
Geonim, Ms. 104; 241
Gifts, Ms. 117; 142
Form for granting, Ms. 212; 214; 263; 275
Glue, Ms. 44
God, Ms. 46; 166; 174; 190; 227; B.C. Ms. 304; 305
Love of, Ms. 261
and Death, Ms. 266; 275 see also Names of God
Gog and Magog, Ms. 51
Gossip, Ms. 275
Government authority, Ms. 98
Exhortation against introducing non-Jewish officials into legal action, in Holy Land, Ms. 150
Interference with Jewish communal authority, Ms. 156
Makhzan, Ms. 252; 262; 271
Non-Jewish authority, Ms. 262; 271
Non-Jewish court, Ms. 171; 172
Recording of sale, 291
Graves, see Tombs
Guarantor, document of, Ms. 121; 168; 188; 198
Gunpowder, Ms. 275

Hailstones, Ms. 258; 275
Hakhnasat Kallah, Ms. 153; 255
Halakha, citations, Ms. 74; 86; 271
Exposition, Ms. 285; 286; 287; 290
Laws, on collection of debts
Laws on property modification affecting others, Ms. 38; 104
Queries, Ms. 10; 11; 12; 13; 50; 63; 105; 110; 116; 130; 131; 133; 157; 184; 191; 247; 248; 270
Rabbinic succession, Ms. 15
Riddles, Ms. 191
Works, 292; 293; 294; 295; 296; 297; see also Novellae, Responsa
Ḥalifin, Ms. 291
Ḥalizah, Ms. 189
Ḥalukah, see Emissaries
Ḥanukah, Ms. 174
Ḥashmalim, Ms. 241
Havdalah ceremony, Ms. 51; 304
see Piyyut
Ḥayyôt, Ms. 241
Ḥazaka, Ms. 15; 202
Heiress, Ms. 31
Ḥezekiah, Ms. 228
Ḥezkat ha-Yishuv, Ms. 247
Hilula (celebration), Ms. 266
Historical material, Ms. 14; 40; 43; 52; 58; 72; 85; 87; 111; 130; Pr. 133.5; Ms. 150; 156; 171; 174; 178; 190; 192; 197; 219; 227; 240; 244; 250; 258; 275
Holidays (festivals), Ms. 59; Pr. 133.5; Ms. 222; 224; 258; 275; see also Intermediate Days
Holy, Ms. 224
Holy Land, Ms. 4; 8; 9; 11; 30; 32; 39; 41; 54; 55; 56; 60; 67; 72; Pr. 73.5; Ms. 95; 99; 100; 101; 112; 125; Pr. 133.5; Ms. 135; 145; 147; 150; 153; 163; 176; 178; 183; 192; 201; 221; 232; 233; 236; 238; 240; 248; 255; 264; 265; 277; 278
Migrations to, Ms. 8; 11; 55; Pr. 73.5; Ms. 100
Homiletical work, Pr. 299
Hoshana Rabbah, Ms. 275
Hoshanot (prayers), Ms. 305
Hospitality, Ms. 48; 64; 99; 163; 178; 239; 253; 255
Criticism of hospitality, Ms. 186
Hostages, Ms. 188; see also Imprisonment, Redemption of captives
House of Prayer, see Synagogues
House of Study, Ms. 107; 190; see also Academy
Hunger, Ms. 207

Illness, Ms. 28; 48; 54; 55; 64; 65; 84; 87; 97; 105; 116; 120; 152; 154; 177; 197; 198; 212
Eyes, Ms. 120
Mental, Ms. 243; 277; 279
Immoral acts, Ms. 130; 143
Imprisonment, Ms. 40; 156; 275
Infidelity, Ms. 191
Informer, Ms. 143; 156
Inheritance, Ms. 10; 11; 20; 31; 33; 42; 47; 55; 57; 63; 69; 97; 98; 111; 116; 117; 118; 119; 155; 161; 162; 167; 172; 173; 194; 199; 200; 203; 204; 209; 212; 214; 218; 219; 250; 252; 265; 268; 270
Widow's inheritance, Ms. 88; see also Estates
Installments, paying by, Ms. 89; 182; 223; 269
Insult, Ms. 261
Inter-Communal, Ban, Ms. 26; 72; 261

268
Paternity suit, Ms. 146
Patriarchs, Ms. 241
Payment of debts, Ms. 223; see also Debts
Payytan, Ms. 105
Peace, Ms. 200
Penalties, Ms. 108; 133; 142 143; 146; 198; 269; 275; see also Flogging
Periodicals, Pr. 73.5; Pr. 133.5
Perjury, Ms. 137; 143; 156
Perpetuity, Ms. 31; 265
Personality clashes, Ms. 3; 20; 35; 119; 133; 205; 227; 257
Petuḥôt and Stumôt, Mss. 308–322
Philanthropists, Ms. 254
Philosophical work, Ms. 298
Physician, Ms. 254; 283
Pilgrimage to tombs, Ms. 229
Pillage, Ms. 43; 87
Pirates, Ms. 70; see also Bandits
Pledges, Ms. 29; 57; 96; 111; 121; 194; 199; 212; 217; 218; 219; 247; 250; 257; 265; 271; 292
Poetry, Ms. 3; 7; 18; 84; 93; 102; 105; 149; 151; 162; 166; 208; 210; 211; 224; 225; 255; 274; 275 (piyyut); see also Prayers
Pogrom, Ms. 41; 43; 87
Political situation, Ms. 87; 227; 275
Pollution, Ms. 50; 53; 109
Polygamy, Ms. 193; 226; 242; 243; 246; 276
Poor, Ms. 79; 108; 241
Poor Fund, Ms. 231
Poorhouse, Ms. 231; 268
Poskim, Ms. 241
Poverty, Ms. 23; 35; 36; 55; 56; 64; 69; 79; 82; 95; 108; 113; 114; 129; Pr. 133.5; Ms. 134; 138; 147; 159; 178; 189; 190; 193; 194; 195; 207; 222; 227; 231; 236; 241; 253; 254; 255; 269; 272; 275
Power of agency, Ms. 115; 168; 242; 249
Power of attorney, Ms. 199; 249
Power of speech, Ms. 224
Prayers, Prayer services, Ms. 13; 27; 51; 59; 65; 84; 93; 105; 112; 115; 133; 154; 166; 177
  Mystical Prayers, Ms. 177; 179; 185; 200; 224; 241; 263; 275; 304; 305; 307
Pregnancy, Ms. 177; 193; 243
Premature birth, Ms. 63
Prenuptial agreement, violation of, Ms. 198
Prescriptions, medical, Ms. 177; 235
Principles of faith, Ms. 84
Prison, Ms. 143; 156
Promissory notes, Ms. 35
Property, alterations which infringe on property rights, Ms. 38; 202; 231
  Claims, Ms. 17; 25; 28; 47; 71; 271
  Communal property rights, Ms. 43
  Confiscated, Ms. 49
  Minor exercises rights over, Ms. 212
  Movable and immovable, Ms. 161; 199
  Pledged property, Ms. 29; 218
  Pollution of, Ms. 38; 50; 109
  Right of access, Ms. 169
  Transference of, Ms. 29 see also Land and Real estate
Prophets, Ms. 228; 241
Prose, Metaphorical, Ms. 274
Protection, Ms. 148; 177
Proverbs, Ms. 255
Psalms, Ms. 80; 92; 174; 224; 275
Public right of way, Ms. 202
Publishing, Pr. 133.5; Ms. 206; 221; see also Books
Purim, Ms. 275

Query, see Halakha

Rabbinic authority, Ms. 76
Rabbinic succession, Ms. 15; 35; 132; 208
Rabbinic tribunal, Ms. 79; 123; 226; see also Courts
Rain, Ms. 65; 87; 174; 202; 258; 272; 275
Raisins, see Commodities
Ransom, Ms. 43; see also Redemption of captives
Rape, Ms. 87, 143
Rashi commentary, Ms. 173
Rashi script, Ms. 52
Real estate, Ms. 17; 35; 49; 155; 169; 214; 215; see also Property
Rebellion, Ms. 275
Rebellious wife, Ms. 245
Reconciliation between husband and wife, Ms. 175; see also Marriage
Redemption of captives, Ms. 84; 163; 226; 250; 289
Redemption of pledge, Ms. 251
Refuge, Ms. 146
Reign of terror, Ms. 275
Remission of debts in the sabbatical year, Ms. 172
Rent, Ms. 219; 247
Reproof, Ms. 72; 98; 114
Responsa, Ms. 11; 38; 50; 74; 105; 109; 111; 115; 133; 191; 206; 243; 260; 291; 292; 293; see also Halakha
Restitution, Ms. 198
Restoration in Zion, Ms. 224
Retail merchants, Ms. 14
Revelation of Elijah, Ms. 85; 198; see also Elijah
Revenge, Ms. 143
Riddles, Ms. 36; 162; 191
Right of access, Ms. 169; 202
Right of domicile, Ms. 247
Righteous women, Ms. 213
Ritual bath, Ms. 250
Ritual slaughter, Ms. 13; 16; 178
Robbery, Ms. 180
Rosh Hashanah, Ms. 174; 258
Rosh Hodesh, Ms. 224
Runaway husband, see Abandonment and Women

Sabbath, Ms. 197; 224
Sabbath violation, Ms. 275
Sabbatical year, see Remission of debts
Saints, Ms. 32; 229; 241; 275
Sandalphon, Ms. 177
Scholars, Ms. 3; 23; 39; 72; 98; 99; 107; 114; 117; 122; 133; 159; 178; 186; 190; 192; 198; 227; 255; 291
Scholarship, Ms. 15; 178; 190; 197; 198; 206
Scribal ink, Ms. 86
Scribal profession, Ms. 22; 52; 86; 120; 133; Pr. 133.5; Ms. 259; 307
Scriptural verses, Ms. 179
Scriptural texts, Ms. 307
Scrolls of the law, see Torah scrolls
Seals, Ms. 41; 145; 238; 264
Secular, Ms. 224
Security, see Collateral
Seduction, Ms. 146; 191
Sefirôt, Ms. 84; 241; 305
Seraphim, Ms. 241
Serbian Jewry, Pr. 73.5
Settlement by compromise, Ms. 119; 123; 158; 162; 188;

206; 222; 245; 250; 257; 262; 271; see also Compromise
Sewage disposal system, Ms. 53
Sexual acts, Immoral, Ms. 87; 143; 146
Sexual relations, Ms. 245
Shekhinah, Ms. 107
Sh'ma, Ms. 285
Sh'ma, blessings of, Ms. 115
Siege, Ms. 87; 17
Signatures, Ms. 7; 8; 10; 11; 12; 13; 14; 17; 19; 21; 22; 23; 24; 25; 26; 28; 29; 30; 32; 33; 34; 35; 36; 39; 40; 41; 42; 43; 44; 45; 48; 49; 52; 54; 55; 56; 57; 60; 62; 64; 65; 66; 67; 68; 69; 70; 71; 72; 73; 75; 76; 77; 78; 79; 84
in Acrostic form, Ms. 85; 88; 89; 90; 95; 96; 97; 98; 99; 100; 101; 103; 105; 107; 108; 111; 112; 113; 116; 117; 118; 119; 120; 121; 122; 123; 125; 126; 127; 128; 129; 130; 132; 133; 134; 135; 136; 137; 138; 139; 141; 144; 145; 146; 147; 150; 152; 154; 155; 157; 158; 159; 160; 162; 164; 165; 167; 171; 172; 175; 176; 178; 180; 181; 182; 183; 184; 185; 186; 187; 188; 189; 190; 192; 193; 194; 195; 196; 197; 198; 199; 200; 201; 202; 203; 204; 205; 206; 207; 208; 214; 217; 218; 220; 221; 222; 223; 225; 226; 227; 229; 230; 231; 232; 233; 234; 236; 237; 238; 239; 242; 243; 245; 246; 247; 248; 249; 250; 251; 252; 253; 254; 256; 257; 260; 262; 264; 265; 266; 267; 268; 269; 270; 271; 272; 273
Sin, Ms. 80; 275; see also Moralizing
Slavery, Ms. 87
Soul, Ms. 263; 266; 268
Spices, Ms. 235
Stars, Ms. 258
Starvation, Ms. 87; 130
Sterility, Ms. 177
Stipends, Ms. 133; 190
Stolen articles, Ms. 171
Stripes, Ms. 207; see also Flogging
Students, Ms. 22; 133; 197
Subsidy, for scholars, Ms. 133; 190; 291
Succession, see Rabbinic succession
Suicides, Ms. 87
Summons to court, Ms. 62; 197; 237
Sunlight, is measured, Ms. 258
Supplication, see Prayers
Synagogues, Ms. 20; 28; 35; 38; 43; 84; 87; 101; 107; 116; 133; 162; 174; 200; 275
Property of, Ms. 28
Tabernacles, Ms. 59; Pr. 133.5; 305
Takkanot, Ms. 13; 47; 74, 88; 108; 119; 122; 197; 246; 276; see also Edicts, Enactments
Tales, Ms. 36; see also Folk tales
Talmudic commentary, Ms. 173; 303
Talmudic literature, Ms. 104; 260; 261; 303; see also Agada
Tannaim, Ms. 241; 303
Tarshishim, Ms. 241
Taxation, Ms. 70; 72; 114; 193; 195; 206; 242
Tax collector, Ms. 242
Teacher, Ms. 22; 133
Tefillin, Ms. 105; 285
Tenancy, Ms. 49; 50; 121
Expiration of, Ms. 25
Testimony, Ms. 19; 26; 53; 76; 143; 181; 192; 197; 215; 243; 257
Written testimony, Ms. 271; see also Witness
Theft, Ms. 39; 76; 108
Thesaurus of philosophical terms, Ms. 298
Thief, Ms. 137; 143
Thieves, Ms. 87; 108; see also Bandits, Pirates
Throne of God, Ms. 224
Tikkun Ḥaẓot, Ms. 304
Tobacco, Ms. 183
Tombs, Ms. 3; 32; 50; 79; 170; 174; 229; 275
Torah crowns, Ms. 20; 43; 47
Torah scroll, Ms. 20; 35; 47; 72; 86; 87; 116; 174; 255; 275; 287; 308; 309; 310; 311
Torah study, Ms. 269; 275; see also Scholarship
Toshavim, Ms. 43; 139; 140; 141; 144; 161; 175; 197; 198; 246; 247; 258; 270
Transference, document of, Ms. 29
Travel, dangers of, Ms. 39; 41; 60; 64; 84; 87; 148; 177; 178; 180; 198; 219; 229; 240; 272; 298
Tribulation, Ms. 87; 179; 275
Tribulation of the grave, Ms. 51; 85
Tribute, Ms. 43; 87
Troops, Ms. 275
Trust, establishing in business, Ms. 212
Trusteeship, Ms. 203; 204; 209
Truth and falsehood, Ms. 36

Ulterior motive, Ms. 198
Under age for legal-commercial transactions, Ms. 212; see also Minor
Unfair pricing, Ms. 108
Unfaithful husband, Ms. 134
Unfaithful wife, Ms. 191
Upheavals, Ms. 111

Variants, Ms. 292; 293; 295; 298; 304; 305; 308–322
Verse, for bride, Ms. 225
On women, Ms. 274
Poetic, Ms. 149
Violation of enactment, Ms. 198
Violation of marital oath, Ms. 226
Violence, Ms. 87
Vows, Ms. 123; 183
Release from vows, Ms. 304

War, Ms. 258; 275
Waywardness, Ms. 146; 274
Weapons, Ms. 258
Weather reports, Ms. 65; 174; 202; 258; 275
Weddings, Ms. 30; 105; 244
Weights and measures, Ms. 108
Widow, see Women
Wills, Ms. 31; 63; 71; 90; 97; see also Documents, Estates, Inheritance
Witness, Ms. 20; 47; 58; 97; 98; 116; 121; 143; 156; 165; 175; 182; 243; 244; 245; 271; 275; see also Testimony
Womb, Ms. 235
Women, abandoned wife, Ms. 134; 193; 198; 207; 226; 242
Agunah (fettered wife), Ms. 128; 134; 165; 187; 226; 242
Bride, see Bride
Claim against Women, Ms. 17; 257
Claim by Women, Ms. 218; 271
Community Enactment, Women Cannot Marry Outside, Ms. 246

Index of Scholarly Works

Bibliography

Aboab, Isaac. *Menorat ha-Maor, Mossad Harar Kook.* Jerusalem: 1961.

Abrahams, I. *Jewish Life in the Middle Ages.* New York: Macmillan, 1927.

Abudarham, D. *Sefer Abudarham.* New York: Saphograph Co. (M.A. Kempler)

Albeck, Hanokh. *Shishah Sidrei Mishnah, Mo'ed Volume.* Jerusalem: Bialik Institute, 1958. Tel Aviv, D'Vir: 1958.

Amram, D. W. *Makers of Hebrew Books in Italy.* Philadelphia: Greenstone, 1909. (Reprinted 1963).

Arberry, A. J. *Sufism, An Account of the Mystics of Islam.* New York and Evanston: Harper & Row, 1970.

Attal, Robert. *Les Juifs D'Afrique Du Nord, Bibliographic.* Leiden: E. J. Brill, 1973.

Attar, J. *Minhat Yehudah.* 1940.

Azulai, H. J. D. *Shem ha-Gedolim.* Jerusalem: 1954.

Baer, Fritz. *A History of the Jews in Christian Spain.* 2 Vols., Philadelphia: Fritz B. Yitzhak, 1961–1966.

Baron, Salo W. *A Social and Religious History of the Jews.* Vols. XI, XII, XIII and XIV, New York: Columbia University Press, 1969.

The Benaim Collection of Hebrew and Judaeo-Arabic Mss., Library of the Jewish Theological Seminary of America, University Microfilms. Ann Arbor.

Benaim, Joseph. *Malkhei Rabbanan.* Jerusalem: 1931.

Benayahu, M., *Rabbi H. Y. D. Azulai*: 1959.

Bension, Ariel. *The Zohar in Moslem and Christian Spain.* London: 1932. (Reprinted by Sepher-Hermon Press Inc., New York, 1974.)

Berliner, A. *Ueber den Einfluss des ersten hebraeischen Buchdrucks auf den Cultus und die Cultur der Juden.* Frankfurt: Kauffman, 1896.

Bernheimer, C. Codices hebraici bibliothecae Ambrosianae. Florence: Olschki, 1933.

Birnbaum, Solomon A. *The Hebrew Scripts.* 2 Vols., London: Paleographica, 1956 and 1971.

Braithwaite, J. *History of the Revolutions in the Empire of Morocco*, London: Darby and Browne, 1729.

Brody, H. and Wiener, M. *Anthologia Hebraica, Poemata Selecta A Libris Divinis Confectis Usgne Ad Iudaeorum Ex Hispania Expulsionem*, Insel-Verlag. Leipzig: 1922.

Brody and Albrecht. *The New-Hebrew School of Poets of the Spanish-Arabian Epoch.* London: Williams and Norgate, 1906.

Chavel, H. *Pirushei ha-Torah Le Ramban* (*Nahmanides*). Vol. 2, Jerusalem: Mossad Harav Kook, 1963.

de Chenier, L. *Present State of the Empire of Morocco.* 2 Vols., London: Robinson, 1788.

Chones, S. *Toledot ha-Poskim.* Warsaw: 1929.

Chouraqui, Andre N. *Between East and West.* Philadelphia: Jewish Publications Society, 1968.

Chouraqui, Andre N. *L'Alliance Israelite Universelle et la renaissance juive contemporaine* (*1860–1969*). Paris: 1965.

Cokcas, D. *Les Juifs de Maroc et leur Mellahs.* 1970.

Cokcas, A. *Etablissement des dynasitcs des Cherifs on Maroc.* Paris: Leroux, 1904.

Davidson, Israel. *Ozar ha-Meshalim ve-ha-Pirgamim.* Jerusalem: Bialik Institute, 1957

Davidson, Israel. *Thesaurus of Medieval Hebrew Poetry.* 4 Vols., New York: Ktav Publishing House Inc., 1970.

Davidson, J. *Notes Taken During Travels in Africa.* London: Cox and Sons, 1839.

Delitzsch, F. *Zur Geschichte der jüdischen Poesie seit dem Abschluss der Schriften des Alten Bundes.* Leipzig: 1836.

Efros, I. *Ancient Jewish Philosophy.* Detroit: Wayne State University Press, 1964.

Efros, I. *Medieval Jewish Philosophy. Systems and Problems.* Tel Aviv: Dvir Co., Ltd., 1965.

Efros, I. *Mediaeval Jewish Philosophy, Terms and Concepts.* Tel Aviv: Dvir Co., Ltd., 1969.

Eisenbeth, M. *Les Juifs au Maroc.* Alger: Charnas, 1948.

Elbogen, I. *Studien zur Geschichte des judischen Gottesdienstes.* Berlin: Mayer and Müller, 1907.

Encyclopaedia Le-Haluzei ha-Yishuv U-Bonav. ed. Tidhar, Vol. 4, Tel Aviv: 1950.

Encyclopaedia Judaica. Jerusalem: Keter Publishing House Ltd., 1971.

de Foucauld, *Ch., Reconnaissance au Maroc.* Paris: Challamel, 1888.

Friedlaender, M. *Essays on the Writings of Abraham ibn Ezra.* London: 1877.

Gaon, M. D. *Yehudei ha-Mizrach be-Erex Yisrael.* 2 Vols., Jerusalem: 1938.

Geiger, A. *Salamo Gabirol und Seine Dichtungen.* Leipzig, 1867.

Goldziher, Ignaz. *Mohammed and Islam.* New Haven: Yale University, 1917.

Goltein, S. D. *Jews and Arabs.* New York: Shocken, 1964.

Gottlieb, E. *Ha-Kabbalah be-Sof ha-Me'ah ha-Yud Gimel, Akadamon*. Jerusalem: 1969.

Goulven, J. *Les Mellahs de Rabat-Sale*. Paris: Geuthner, 1927.

Grayzel, Solomon. *A History of the Jews*. New York and Toronto: New American Library and the Jewish Publication Society of America, 1968.

Guttmann, Julius. *Philosophies of Judaism*. (Eng. Trans., by D.W. Silverman), New York: 1964.

Halper, B. *Descriptive Catalogue of the Genizah Fragments in Philadelphia*. Philadelphia: Dropsie College for Hebrew and Cognate Learning, 1924.

Hershman, Abraham. *Rabbi Isaac bar Sheshet Perfet and His Times*. Jerusalem: Mossud Harav Kook, 1957.

Hirschberg, H.Z. *A History of the Jews in North Africa*. Two Vols., Jerusalem: Bialik Institute, 1965.

Hirschberg, H.Z. *Me-Erez Mevo ha-Shemesh*. 1957.

Hirschfeld, H. *Descriptive Catalogue of the Hebrew Mss. of the Montefiore Library*. London: 1904.

Husik, Isaac. *A History of Mediaeval Jewish Philosophy*. New York and Philadelphia: Meridian Books and the Jewish Publication Society, 1960.

Hyamson, A. *Sephardim of England*. London: Methuen, 1951.

Ibn Danan, S. *Sefer Asher li-Shlomo*. 1906.

Ibn Zur, J. *Mishpat U-Zedakah be-Ya'akov*. 2 Vols., 1894, 1903.

Ibn Zur, J. *Kerem Hemed (1869–71)*.

Katsh, A. I. *Catalogue of Hebrew Mss. Preserved in the USSR*. New York: University Library of Judaica and Hebraica, 1957.

Kaufmann, David. *Mehkarim be-Sifrut ha-Ivrit Shel Yulmei ha-baynai'im*. Jerusalem: Mossad Harav Kook, 1962.

Kaufmann, David. *Studien über Salomon ibn Gabirol*. Budapest: 1899.

Klatzkin, J. *Thesaurus Philosophicus, Linguae Hebraicae et Veteris et Recentioris*. 2 Vols. New York: Feldheim Inc., 1968.

Klausner, Joseph. *The Messianic Idea in Israel*. New York: The Macmillan Co., 1955.

Loewe, J.H. *A Descriptive Catalogue of a portion of the Library of Louis Loewe*. London: printed by Mayence, 1895.

Löwinger, D.S. and Weinryb, B.D. *Catalogue of the Hebrew Manuscripts in the Library of the Jüdisch-Theologisches Seminar in Breslau*. Wiesbaden: 1965.

Luzzatto, S.D. *Mabo le-Mahzor bene Roma*. Printed with the Italian Mahazor, Leghorn: 1856 (Reprinted, Tel Aviv: 1966.)

Maimonides, Moses. *Mishneh Torah*. 5 Vols., Vilna: 1900.

Maimonides, Moses. *Moreh Nebukhim* (Samuel ibn Tibbon, translator). Jerusalem: 1960.

Mahzor. *Z'khor Le-Avraham*. 2 Vols., Jerusalem: 1968.

Margoliouth, G., *Catalogue of the Hebrew and Samaritan Manuscripts in the British Museum*. 4 Vols., London: 1899–1935 (Reprinted, 1965).

Massignon, L. *Le Maroc*. Alger: A. Jourdan, 1906.

Nahon, M. *Les Israelites au Maroc*. Paris: Geuthner, 1909.

Netanyahu, B. *Dan Isaac Abravaner*. Philadelphia: The Jewish Publication Society of America, 1968.

Neubauer, A. *Catalogue of the Hebrew Manuscripts in the Bodleian Library, I*. Oxford: 1886.

Neuman, Abraham A. *The Jews in Spain*. Philadelphia: Jewish Publication Society of America, 1942.

Nicholson, R. *The Mystics of Islam*. London: Routledge and Kegan Paul Ltd., 1970

Noy, D. *Moroccan Folk-Tales*. 1966.

Palqera, Shem Tob. *Moreh ha-Moreh*. Jerusalem: 1961. *Shelemut ham-Ma'asim*. Ms. on Microfilm.

Perush Ha-Mishnayot Le-ha-Rambam, Talmud, Vols. 2 and 5. New York: Otzar Ha-Sefarim Inc., 1961.

Responsa of R. Asher b. Yehiel. Jerusalem: 1971.

Responsa of R. Solomon ibn Adret. Vols. I and II, B'nei B'rak, 1958, 1971.

Responsa of R. Solomon ibn Adret. Vol. III, B'nei B'rak.

Responsa of R. Solomon ibn Adret. Vol. IV, Jerusalem: 1960.

Responsa of R. Solomon ibn Adret. Vol. V, Warsaw: 1883.

Rosin, D. *Reime und Gedichte des Abraham Ibn Esra*. Breslau: Schottlaender, 1885–1894.

Roth, Cecil. *The Jews in the Renaissance*. Jerusalem: Bialik Institute, 1962.

Sachs, M. *Die Religiöse Poesie der Juden in Spanien*, ed. by S. Bernfeld, Berlin: 1901.

Sarachek, Joseph. *Faith and Reason, The Conflict Over the Rationalism of Maimonides*. Williamsport: Bayard Press, 1935.

Sassoon, D.S. *Ohel David, Descriptive Catalogue of the Hebrew and Samaritan Mss.*, 2 Vols., Oxford: 1932.

Schiller-Szinessi, S.M. *Catalogue of Hebrew Mss. in the University Library of Cambridge*. Cambridge: 1876.

Scholem, Gershom. *Major Trends in Jewish Mysticism*. New York: Schockem Books, 1954.

Scholem, Gershom. *Ha-Kabbalah be-Provence* (Lecture Notes arranged by R. Schatz). Akadamon, Jerusalem, 1966.

Scholem, Gershom. *Ha-Kabbalah be-Gerona.* (arranged by Dr. Y. Ben-Shlomo). Jerusalem: Akadamon, 1969.

Schwarz, A. Z. Die hebräischen Handschriften d.K.K. Hoffbibliothek zu Wien, Wien: 1914.

Slouschz, N. *Etude sur l'Histoire des Juifs et du Judaisme au Maroc.* Paris: Archives Marocaines, 1905–06.

Slouschz, N. *Hebraes-Pheniciens et Judes-Berberes.* Paris: Leroux, 1908.

Slouschz, N. *Travels in North Africa.* Philadelphia: Jewish Publication Society of America, 1927.

Steinschneider, M. *Catalogue Librorum Hebraeorum in Bibliotheca.* Bodleiana, Berlin: 1931.

Steinschneider, M. *Die Arabische Literatur der Juden.* Frankfurt: Kauffmann, 1902.

Steinschneider, M. *Catalogue der heb. Handschr. in der Stadtbibliothek zu Hamburg.* Hamburg: Meissner, 1878.

Steinschneider, M. *Die Hebraischen Ueber Setzungen des Mittelalters.* Berlin: 1893.

Steinschneider, M. *Verzeichnis der Hebraeischen Handschriften.* 2 Vols., Berlin: Vogt, 1878.

Strauss. *Toledot ha-Yehudim be-Msrayim Ve-Suria Tahat Shilton ha-Mamelukim.* Vol. 2, Jerusalem: 1951.

Terrasse, H. *Histoire du Maroc.* 2 Vols., Casablanca: Atlantides, 1949–50.

Toledano, Jacob Moses. *Ner ha-Mama'arav.* Jerusalem: 1911.

Tur. *Yoreh De'ah, Otzar ha-Sefarim.* New York: 1967.

Urbach, E. E. *The Tosaphists: Their History, Writings and Methods.* Jerusalem: The Bialik Institute, 1955.

Vajda, G. *Un Recueil de Textes Historiques Judeo-Marocains.* Paris: 1951.

Yaari, A. *Hebrew Printers' Marks from the Beginnings of Hebrew Printing to the End of the Nineteenth Century.* 1943.

Zotenberg, H. *Catalogues des manuscrits hébreux et samaritains de Bibliothèque Impériale.* Paris: 1866.

Zunz, L. *Literaturgeschichte der synagogalen Poesie.* Berlin: 1865. (Reprinted, Hildesheim, 1969).

Zunz, L. *Die synagogale Poesie des Mittelalters.* Berlin: Springer, 1855.